PERFORMANCE S

The field of performance studies analyzes the   .. and impact of
on-stage performance, such as in a theatre or circus, and *off-stage* performance, such as cultural rituals and political protests. Because of its inclusive
approach, combined with its dedication to researching and communicating across fields, arts disciplines and cultures, performance studies is one
of the most *transdisciplinary* and fast-growing fields in universities today.
In effect of its extensive scope of subject matter, which includes the various theories and methodologies it uses to explore performance, students
learn to better comprehend performance as an operative concept and lived
factor in everyday life. With 34 essays by internationally distinguished
scholars on topics paramount to the future of performance studies, *Performance Studies: Key Words, Concepts and Theories* introduces students to that
future while also contributing to the field's wide-ranging, adventurous and
conscientious nature that continues to make performance studies so innovative, valuable and exciting.

Bryan Reynolds is Chancellor's Professor of Drama at the University of
California, Irvine, USA. Raised in Scarsdale, New York, he received his BA
at the University of California, Berkeley and his PhD at Harvard Univer-
sity, both in English and American Literature. He has held visiting profes-
sorships at Queen Mary, University of London, University of Amsterdam,
Utrecht University, University of Cologne, University College Utrecht,
Goethe University Frankfurt, the University of California, San Diego, and the
American University of Beirut; and he has taught seminars and workshops at
Deleuze Camp, The Grotowski Institute, Beirut's Laban Theatre, the Gdańsk
Shakespeare Festival, The Jenin Freedom Theatre, among other academic
and arts institutions. He is the Artistic Director of the Amsterdam-based
Transversal Theater Company, a director of theatre, a performer and a play-
wright, whose plays have been produced in the US, Europe and Asia.

Authored books:

Transversal Subjects: From Montaigne to Deleuze after Derrida (Basingstoke: Palgrave Macmillan, 2009).

Transversal Enterprises in the Drama of Shakespeare and his Contemporaries: Fugitive Explorations (Basingstoke: Palgrave Macmillan, 2006).

Performing Transversally: Reimagining Shakespeare and the Critical Future (Basingstoke: Palgrave Macmillan, 2003).

Becoming Criminal: Transversal Performance and Cultural Dissidence in Early Modern England (Baltimore: Johns Hopkins University Press, 2002).

Edited books:

The Return of Theory in Early Modern English Studies, vol. 2, co-editor, with Paul Cefalu and Gary Kuchar (Basingstoke: Palgrave Macmillan, 2014).

The Return of Theory in Early Modern English Studies: Tarrying with the Subjunctive, co-editor, with Paul Cefalu (Basingstoke: Palgrave Macmillan, 2011).

Critical Responses to Kiran Desai, co-editor, with Sunita Sinha (New Delhi: Atlantic Publishers, 2009).

Rematerializing Shakespeare: Authority and Representation on the Early Modern English Stage, co-editor, with William West (Basingstoke: Palgrave Macmillan, 2005).

Shakespeare Without Class: Misappropriations of Cultural Capital, co-editor, with Donald Hedrick (Basingstoke: Palgrave Macmillan, 2000).

Performance Studies

Key Words, Concepts and Theories

Edited by

Bryan Reynolds

First published 2014 by
PALGRAVE

Palgrave in the UK is an imprint of Macmillan Publishers Limited, registered
in England, company number 785998, of 4 Crinan Street, London N1 9XW.

Palgrave Macmillan in the US is a division of St Martin's Press LLC,
175 Fifth Avenue, New York, NY 10010.

Palgrave is a global imprint of the above companies and is represented
throughout the world.

Palgrave® and Macmillan® are registered trademarks in the United States,
the United Kingdom, Europe and other countries.

ISBN: 978-0–230–24729–1 hardback
ISBN: 978-0–230–24730–7 paperback

This book is printed on paper suitable for recycling and made from fully
managed and sustained forest sources. Logging, pulping and manufacturing
processes are expected to conform to the environmental regulations of the
country of origin.

A catalogue record for this book is available from the British Library.

Library of Congress Cataloging-in-Publication Data
Performance studies : key words, concepts and theories / edited by Bryan
Reynolds, UCI Chancellor's Professor, University of California, USA.
     pages cm
   ISBN 978-0-230-24729-1 (hardback)
   1. Theater--Philosophy. 2. Performing arts--Philosophy. I. Reynolds, Bryan,
1977- editor.
   PN2039P3955 2014
   792.01--dc23
                           2014028983

Typeset by Aardvark Editorial Limited, Metfield, Suffolk.
Printed and bound in the UK by The Lavenham Press Ltd, Suffolk

Contents

Contents

List of Figures

Notes on Contributors

Elaine Aston is Professor of Contemporary Performance at Lancaster University, UK. Her monographs include *Caryl Churchill* (3rd edn, 2010), *Feminist Theatre Practice* (1999) and *Feminist Views on the English Stage* (2003). She is co-editor of *The Cambridge Companion to Modern British Women Playwrights* (with Janelle Reinelt, 2000), *Feminist Futures: Theatre, Performance, Theory* (with Geraldine Harris, 2006), *Staging International Feminisms* (with Sue-Ellen Case, 2007) and *The Cambridge Companion to Caryl Churchill* (with Elin Diamond, 2009). She served as senior editor of *Theatre Research International* (2010–12).

Christopher Balme holds the Chair in Theatre Studies at the University of Munich. He has published widely on German theatre, intercultural theatre and theatre and other media. Recent publications include *Decolonizing the Stage: Theatrical Syncretism and Postcolonial Drama* (1999), *Pacific Performances: Theatricality and Cross-Cultural Encounter in the South Seas* (2007), *The Cambridge Introduction to Theatre Studies* (2008) and *The Theatrical Public Sphere* (2014). His current research interests focus on the globalization of the arts and theatre and the public sphere. He is director of the Global Theatre Histories project at Ludwig Maximilian University of Munich.

Stephen Barker, former Chair of Drama, Chair of Art, and Head of Doctoral Studies, is the Associate Dean in the Claire Trevor School of the Arts, University of California, Irvine. He has written books and articles on numerous artists and philosophers, such as Nietzsche, Derrida, Freud and Beckett, including *Autoaesthetics: Strategies of the Self after Nietzsche* (1992) and *Signs of Change: Premodern, Modern, Postmodern* (1996). He is a founder of the journal *Derrida Today* and is on the faculty of the London Graduate School. He has recently translated volumes by French philosophers Bernard Stiegler and François-David Sebbah.

Sarah Bay-Cheng is Professor of Theatre and Director of the MA/PhD in Theatre & Performance at the University at Buffalo, US, where she also serves as the founding director of the Technē Institute for Arts and Emerging Technologies. Her publications include *Mapping Intermediality in Performance* (2010), *Poets at Play: An Anthology of Modernist Drama* (2010) and

Mama Dada: Gertrude Stein's Avant-Garde Theater (2005), as well as essays on contemporary performance, digital historiography and avant-garde theatre and film. She co-edits the Palgrave Macmillan series Avant-Gardes in Performance with Martin Harries, and is working on a book and website focused on the intersection of performance and digital technologies.

Marin Blažević is Associate Professor of Dramaturgy and Performance Studies at the University of Zagreb, Croatia. His most recent publications include MIS-performance issue for *Performance Research* (co-edited with Lada Čale Feldman, 2010), *No* (2010), a collection of essays on Slovenian performance theatre company Via Negativa and *Izboren poraz* (*A Defeat Won*, 2012), on the theory of new theatre and its peculiar history in Croatia. Current projects include a monograph on the shifting concept and practice of dramaturgy and curating the PSi 2015 *Fluid States: Performances of Unknowing* project in 15 locations around the world.

Dylan Bolles makes performances with people and environments. He designs and constructs new musical instruments, cultivating co-creative relationships based in listening practice. His sound compositions, installations, physical scores and works on paper are rooted in a shared temporal experience. Dylan holds degrees in music composition from Middlebury College and Mills College. He is the co-founder of thingamajigs, a California non-profit arts organization, and received his doctorate in performance studies from the University of California, Davis. Dylan's ongoing research project, *Myth of Ten Thousand Things*, engages practices and theories of collaboration in performance.

Susan Broadhurst is a writer and performance practitioner and Professor of Performance and Technology, Brunel University, London. Susan's research entails an interrogation of technologies and the notion of the embodied performer, expressed in her publications, practice and interdisciplinary collaborations. Her publications include *Digital Practices: Aesthetic and Neuroesthetic Approaches to Performance and Technology* (2007), *Sensualities/Textualities and Technologies: Writings of the Body in 21st Century Performance* (2010) and *Identity, Performance and Technology: Practices of Empowerment, Embodiment and Technicity* (2012, Palgrave Macmillan). She is co-editor of the journal *Body, Space & Technology* and co-editor (with Josephine Machon) of the Palgrave Macmillan series Palgrave Studies in Performance and Technology.

Johan Callens teaches at the Vrije Universiteit Brussel, Belgium and has published widely on American drama and performance, with contributions ranging from Eugene O'Neill, T.S. Eliot to Gertrude Stein, from The Builders Association and The Wooster Group to Big Art Group and Joji Inc. His essays have appeared in, among others, *American Studies/Amerikastudien*, *Theatre Research International*, *The Journal for Dramatic Theory and Criticism*, *Modern Drama*, *The Drama Review*, *Theatre Journal* and *PAJ: A Journal of Performance & Art*. His most recent books are *Dis/Figuring Sam Shepard* (2007) and *Crossings: David Mamet's Work in Different Genres and Media* (2009).

Marvin Carlson is the Sidney E. Cohn Distinguished Professor of Theatre, Comparative Literature and Middle Eastern Studies at the Graduate Center of the City University of New York. He is the author of over 300 articles and many books on the history and theory of the theatre; most recently, *The Theatres of Morocco, Tunisia, and Algeria* (with Khalid Amine, 2011, Palgrave Macmillan). He is the founding editor of the journal *Western European Stages*, now *European Stages*. He is the recipient of many major theatre awards and has been awarded an honorary doctorate from the University of Athens.

Laura Cull is Senior Lecturer in Theatre Studies and Director of Postgraduate Research for the School of Arts at the University of Surrey, UK. She is author of *Theatres of Immanence: Deleuze and the Ethics of Performance* (2012, Palgrave Macmillan), editor of *Deleuze and Performance* (2009) and co-editor of *Manifesto Now! Instructions for Performance, Philosophy, Politics* (with Will Daddario, 2013). Laura is a founding core convener of the professional association Performance Philosophy and a co-editor (with Alice Lagaay and Freddie Rokem) of the Palgrave Macmillan series Performance Philosophy.

Maria M. Delgado is Professor of Theatre and Screen Arts at Queen Mary, University of London and co-editor of the journal *Contemporary Theatre Review*. She has published widely in the areas of modern Catalan and Spanish theatre and film, with a particular interest in the work of performers and directors, and the intersections between stage and screen cultures. Her publications include *Federico García Lorca* (2008), *'Other' Spanish Theatres* (2003), and nine co-edited volumes, including *Contemporary European Theatre Directors* (with Dan Rebellato, 2010) and *A History of Theatre in Spain* (with David Gies, 2012).

Rick Dolphijn is Assistant Professor of Media and Culture Studies and Senior Fellow at the Centre for the Humanities, Utrecht University, the Netherlands. His work has been published in *Angelaki*, *Deleuze Studies*, *Collapse* and *Women: A Cultural Review* and *Continental Philosophy Review* (with Iris van der Tuin). His latest book is *New Materialism: Interviews & Cartographies* (co-authored with Iris van der Tuin, 2012).

Lada Čale Feldman is a Professor in the Department of Comparative Literature, Faculty of Humanities and Social Sciences, University of Zagreb, Croatia, where she teaches drama, theatre and performance studies. Her publications include *Teatar u teatru u hrvatskom teatru* (*Play-within-the-Play in Croatian Theatre*, 1997), *Euridikini osvrti* (*Eurydice's Turns*, 2001, Petar Brecic Award, 2005), *Femina ludens* (2005) and *Uvod u feminističku književnu kritiku* (*Introduction to Feminist Criticism*) (with A. Tomljenović, 2012). She also co-edited *Fear, Death and Resistance: An Ethnography of War* (with I. Prica and R. Senjković, 1993) and *Etnografija domaceg socijalizma* (*An Ethnography of Indigenous Socialism*, with I. Prica, 2006).

Milija Gluhovic is Associate Professor of Theatre and Performance at the University of Warwick, UK. His research interests include contemporary European theatre and performance, memory studies, and discourses of European identity, migrations and human rights. His monograph *Performing European Memories: Trauma, Ethics, Politics* and *Performing the 'New' Europe: Identities, Feelings, and Politics in the Eurovision Song Contest* (co-edited with Karen Fricker) were published by Palgrave Macmillan in 2013. He is currently working with Jisha Menon on *Rethinking the Secular: Performance, Religion, and the Public Sphere*, which explores the itineraries of 'the secular' within the modern world and considers the ways 'the secular' has translated into the theatre and performance studies perspectives.

Lynette Goddard is a Senior Lecturer in Drama and Theatre at Royal Holloway, University of London. Her previous career as a stage manager with black theatre companies (including Black Mime Theatre and Nitro) continues to inform her research interests in the political impact of contemporary black British playwriting. Her publications on black women's theatre include *Staging Black Feminisms: Identity, Politics, Performance* (2007, Palgrave Macmillan) and she is currently completing *Contemporary Black British Playwrights: Margins to Mainstream* (Palgrave Macmillan) and co-editing, with Mary F. Brewer and Deirdre Osborne, *Modern and Contemporary Black British Drama* (Palgrave Macmillan).

Nadine Holdsworth is Professor of Theatre and Performance Studies at the University of Warwick, UK. She has published *Joan Littlewood's Theatre* (2011), *Theatre & Nation* (2010) and edited John McGrath's collected writings, *Naked Thoughts That Roam About* (2002), as well as *John McGrath: Plays for England* (2005). She has recently completed an edited collection *Theatre and National Identity: Reimagining Conceptions of Nation* (2014) and is currently researching amateur theatre in the Royal Navy.

Lynette Hunter is Distinguished Professor of the History of Rhetoric and Performance at the University of California, Davis. The writer and editor of over 20 books, she is interested in the rhetoric of Western democratic politics in written genres and performance modes and their constraints on different communities in the modern era, and diversity and the creation of value through performance including practice as research. Her *Disunified Aesthetics* (2014) explores the aesthetics of making art and criticism. Research areas range from feminism, ethics and aesthetics, to the history of science and medicine, situated knowledge and Daoist movement and philosophy.

Silvija Jestrovic is Associate Professor at Warwick University, UK. She studied dramaturgy and playwriting at the University of Belgrade and received her doctorate from the University of Toronto. Her publications include *Theatre of Estrangement: Theory Practice Ideology* (2006), *Performance, Space, Utopia: Cities of War, Cities of Exile* (2012, Palgrave Macmillan) and *Performance, Exile, 'America'* (co-edited with Yana Meerzon, 2009, Palgrave Macmillan). She is also the author of several stage and radio plays.

Adrian Kear is Professor of Theatre and Performance at Aberystwyth University, Wales, UK. He is the author of numerous publications investigating the relationship between performance, politics and ethics. His books include *Theatre and Event: Staging the European Century* (2013, Palgrave Macmillan), *International Politics and Performance: Critical Aesthetics and Creative Practice* (with Jenny Edkins, 2013), *Psychoanalysis and Performance* (with Patrick Campbell, 2001) and *Mourning Diana: Nation, Culture and the Performance of Grief* (with Deborah Lynn Steinberg, 1999). He is the co-director of Aberystwyth University's Performance and Politics international research centre, and course leader for the MA Politics, Media, Performance.

Suk-Young Kim is Professor of Theatre and Asian Studies at the University of California, Santa Barbara. She is author of *Illusive Utopia* (2010) and *DMZ Crossing: Performing Emotional Citizenship along the Korean Border* (2014). She also co-authored *Long Road Home* (with Kim Yong, 2009). She is a past recipient of the American Society for Theater Research Fellowship (2006), the Library of Congress Kluge Fellowship (2006–7), the Academy of Korean Studies Research Grant (2008, 2010) and the American Council of Learned Societies Fellowship (2014–15), among others.

Anthony Kubiak is Professor of Drama at the University of California, Irvine. He is the author of *Agitated States: Performance in the American*

Theater of Cruelty (2002) and *Stages of Terror: Terrorism, Ideology, and Coercion as Theatre History* (1991). His more recent work appears in *MLQ, Performance Research* and *PAJ*.

Petra Kuppers is a disability culture activist, a community performance artist, and Professor of English, Women's Studies, Art and Design and Theatre at the University of Michigan. Her books include *Disability and Contemporary Performance: Bodies on Edge* (2003), *The Scar of Visibility: Medical Performance and Contemporary Art* (2007), *Community Performance: An Introduction* (2007) and *Disability Culture and Community Performance: Find a Strange and Twisted Shape* (2011, Palgrave Macmillan). She leads The Olimpias, a performance research collective (www.olimpias.org). Her latest book, *Studying Disability Arts and Culture: An Introduction* (2014, Palgrave Macmillan), looks at arts-based classroom pedagogies.

Carl Lavery is Professor of Theatre and Performance at the University of Glasgow. His most recent publications include *The Politics of Jean Genet's Late Theatre* (2010), *Contemporary French Theatre and Performance* (with Clare Finburgh, 2011), *Good Luck Everybody. Lone Twin: Journeys, Performances and Conversations* (with David Williams, 2011) and On Foot, an edited volume of the journal *Performance Research* (with Nicolas Whybrow, 17(2) 2012). He is currently writing *Practising Location/Performing Ecology*.

Mark LeVine is Professor of Middle Eastern History at the University of California, Irvine, Distinguished Visiting Professor at the Center for Middle Eastern Studies at Lund University, and a professional musician. He is the author and editor of 12 books, including *Heavy Metal Islam* (2008), *Struggle and Survival in Palestine/Israel* (2012), and *One Land, Two States: Israel and Palestine as Parallel States* (2014). He is the producer of the album 'Flowers in the Desert' (2009) and the documentary *Before the Spring, After the Fall* (2014). He is a senior columnist at Al Jazeera English.

Peter Lichtenfels is a professional theatre director and educator who writes on Shakespeare and contemporary performance. He is currently researching postdramatic interactive strategies between performer and viewer. His directing links to conceptual work on the use of space primarily in European theatre staging. In countries that acknowledge there is no 'unoccupied' space, strategies for coexistence with ghosts, with history, with memory, with objects and the detritus of the past and present, become central to sustainability and theatre exploring these transformations is vital to an environmentally sensitive community. He co-edited *Performance,*

Politics and Activism (with John Rouse, 2013) in the Palgrave Macmillan series Studies in International Performance.

Jerzy Limon is a Professor of English and Theatre at the University of Gdańsk, Poland. His main area of research is the history and theory of English Renaissance drama and theatre. He has published four academic books in English; *Gentlemen of a Company* (1985), *Dangerous Matter* (1986), *The Masque of Stuart Culture* (1990), and *The Chemistry of the Theatre* (2010, Palgrave Macmillan), and six books in Polish. Limon's literary output includes four published novels and translations of plays by William Shakespeare and Tom Stoppard. He also runs a theatre in Gdańsk, and organizes an annual Shakespeare Festival.

Bruce McConachie is Professor and Chair of Theatre Arts, University of Pittsburgh. He has published extensively in theatre history, historiography and performance theory. His recent publications in the area of evolution, cognition and performance include *Performance and Cognition* (co-edited with F. Elizabeth Hart, 2006) and *Engaging Audiences* (2008). He co-edits (with Blakey Vermeule) the Palgrave Macmillan series Cognitive Studies in Literature and Performance.

Christina S. McMahon is Assistant Professor of Theater at the University of California, Santa Barbara. She is the author of *Recasting Transnationalism through Performance: Theatre Festivals in Cape Verde, Mozambique and Brazil* (2014, Palgrave Macmillan). She is a past recipient of the IFTR New Scholar's Prize and a Fulbright-Hays grant. Her articles have appeared in *Theatre Research International*, *Theatre Survey*, *Theatre History Studies* and the *Latin American Theatre Review*.

Mihai Maniutiu is the Artistic and Executive Director of the National Theatre in Cluj, Romania, and Distinguished Professor in the Drama Department of the Claire Trevor School of the Arts, University of California, Irvine. He has directed over 90 productions, which have won numerous national and international awards. He has published several books of theatre theory, including *The Golden Round* (1989), a study of power in Shakespeare's plays. In 2014, Maniutiu received the Lifetime Achievement Award at the UNITER Gala Awards.

Jennifer Parker-Starbuck is a Reader in the Department of Drama, Theatre and Performance at Roehampton University, London. She is author of *Cyborg Theatre: Corporeal/Technological Intersections in Multimedia*

Performance (2011, Palgrave Macmillan), as well as multiple book chapters and articles. Her work focuses on historical and theoretical implications of new media/multimedia and its relationship to the body in performance and has expanded to include work on animality and the non-human in performance. She is assistant editor of *PAJ: A Journal of Performance and Art* and associate editor of the *International Journal of Performance Arts and Digital Media*.

Patrice Pavis was Professor of Theatre Studies at the University of Paris (1976–2007) and is currently Professor in the School of Arts at the University of Kent at Canterbury. He has published a *Dictionary of Theatre* (1999, translated into 30 languages) and books on semiology, performance analysis, contemporary French dramatists and mise-en-scène. His most recent books are *Contemporary Mise en Scène: Staging Theatre Today* (2013) and *Dictionnaire de la Performance et du Théâtre Contemporain* (2014).

Mark Pizzato, Professor of Theatre at University of North Carolina, Charlotte, has published *Edges of Loss* (1998), *Theatres of Human Sacrifice: From Ancient Ritual to Screen Violence* (2005), *Ghosts of Theatre and Cinema in the Brain* (2006) and *Inner Theatres of Good and Evil: The Mind's Staging of Gods, Angels and Devils* (2011). He co-edited *Death in American Texts and Performances* (with Lisa Perdigao, 2010). He teaches theatre history, drama, performance theory, playwriting, screenwriting, and various topics in film. Short films, produced from his screenplays, have won New York Film Festival and Minnesota Community Television awards. He blogs at http://mpizzato.wordpress.com/.

Janelle Reinelt, Professor of Theatre and Performance at University of Warwick, UK, was president of the International Federation for Theatre Research (2004–07). She was awarded the Distinguished Scholar Award for lifetime achievement by the American Society for Theatre Research (2010). Her most recent book is *The Political Theatre of David Edgar: Negotiation and Retrieval* with Gerald Hewitt (2011). In 2012, she, together with Brian Singleton, was awarded the Excellence in Editing prize for their Palgrave Macmillan series, Studies in International Performance. Her current project is *The Grammar of Politics and Performance* (with Shirin Rai, forthcoming).

Bryan Reynolds is Chancellor's Professor of Drama at the University of California, Irvine. His books include, as author, *Transversal Subjects: From Montaigne to Deleuze after Derrida* (2009), *Transversal Enterprises in the Drama of Shakespeare and his Contemporaries: Fugitive Explorations* (2006), *Perform-*

ing Transversally: Reimagining Shakespeare and the Critical Future (2003) and *Becoming Criminal: Transversal Performance and Cultural Dissidence in Early Modern England* (2002); and, as co-editor, *The Return of Theory in Early Modern English Studies:* vols I & II (with Paul Cefalu and Gary Kuchar, 2014, and with Paul Cefalu, 2011), *Critical Responses to Kiran Desai* (with Sunita Sinha, 2009), *Rematerializing Shakespeare: Authority and Representation on the Early Modern English Stage* (with William West, 2005) and *Shakespeare Without Class: Misappropriations of Cultural Capital* (with Donald Hedrick, 2000). He co-edited, with Elaine Aston, the Palgrave Macmillan series Performance Interventions. He is also an internationally produced playwright, performer and director of theatre.

Jon D. Rossini is Associate Professor and Chair in the Department of Theatre and Dance at University of California, Davis, where he teaches courses in performance studies, theatre studies and playwriting. He is the author of *Contemporary Latina/o Theater: Wrighting Ethnicity* (2008), as well as 20 articles and book chapters on Latino theatre and ethnicity; in journals such as *Radical History Review, American Drama, Latin American Theatre Review*, and *Gestos*, and in collections such as *Performance, Politics and Activism, Neoliberalism and Global Theatres* and *The Oxford Handbook of American Drama*.

Maria Shevtsova is Chair Professor of Drama and Theatre Arts at Goldsmiths, University of London. She is the author of many books, notably *Dodin and the Maly Drama Theatre: Process to Performance* (2004), *Robert Wilson* (2007) and *Sociology of Theatre and Performance* (2009); and co-author of *Directors/Directing: Conversations on Theatre* (with Christopher Innes, 2009) and *The Cambridge Introduction to Theatre Directing* (with Christopher Innes, 2013). Her books and other publications, including 120 articles and chapters of collected volumes, have been translated into 10 languages. She is co-editor of *New Theatre Quarterly* and a member of the editorial teams and boards of various other international journals.

Nicolas Whybrow is Associate Professor (Reader) in the School of Theatre, Performance and Cultural Policy Studies at the University of Warwick, UK. His most recent books are *Art and the City* (2011) and, as editor, *Performance and the Contemporary City: An Interdisciplinary Reader* (2010). He also recently co-edited the On Foot issue of *Performance Research* (April 2012). *Performing Cities* (2014), his edited volume, presents 12 instances of writing the performing city by a range of internationally renowned scholars and performance practitioners.

Acknowledgements

This book grew out of work undertaken over five years (2005–10) by the University of California Multi-campus Research Group (MRG) in International Performance and Culture, which was initiated by Janelle Reinelt when at UC Irvine and subsequently directed by Lynette Hunter at UC Davis from 2006. Many of the ideas discussed by the contributors were first fielded in discussions among the members of the MRG, and several of them number within this volume. We would like to thank those who officially supported this work. Principal among these is Dante Noto at the Research Support unit of the University of California's Office of the President and now at the UC Humanities Research Institute; and at UC Davis, Barry Klein, then at the Office of Research, and Patricia Turner (interim Dean) and Jessie Ann Owens, the Dean of Humanities, Arts, and Cultural Studies. Beyond the MRG, I am grateful to all the authors for their excellent contributions and patience during the time it took to bring this book to press. Jenna Steventon, my editor at Palgrave Macmillan, and Felicity Noble, her assistant, helped to keep focus. I am especially grateful to Lauren McCue, my research assistant, for her relentless upbeat verve and steadfast commitment to moving the book forward and getting all the details in order. My family – wife Kris and kids Sky and Zephyr – enjoyed our discussions of the essays. This goes to show that the value of the book extends well beyond academia. It can be great fodder for conversations at the beach, dinner table, long car rides, and when talking about the importance of performance studies to all our lives.

Introduction: The Ethical Drive

Bryan Reynolds

This book is both long overdue and ahead of its time. It fills gaps as it opens gateways. It investigates as it expands. With 34 chapters by an international lineup of distinguished scholars, each on topics their authors consider paramount to the future of performance studies, the aim of *Performance Studies: Key Words, Concepts and Theories* is to introduce and welcome students to that future while contributing productively to the field's wide-ranging, adventurous, diverse and conscientious nature that has worked to make performance studies so innovative, valuable and exciting. As an academic field of research and teaching, performance studies is about 50 years old.[1] Although analysis of *on-stage* performance, such as in a theatre or circus, and *off-stage* performance, such as context-specific social interactions or political protests, has been common to academic study since antiquity, it was not until the later 20th century that scholars began to recognize performance studies as its own field, and not as a subfield of theatre, cultural, music, or visual studies, anthropology, psychology or sociology, among others. This led to the establishment of bachelor and doctoral degrees in performance studies as well as performance studies departments, organizations, journals and conferences. Thus, performance studies is not beholden to any one academic discipline or method in particular and is enthusiastically committed to interdisciplinary analysis of multiple variables to any performance, variables potentially related to everything from authorial intention to means of artistic production and dissemination to audience experience and political impact. Performance studies began as an interdisciplinary field, and because of its inclusive approach, combined with its dedication to researching and communicating across fields, arts disciplines and cultures, performance studies is now one of the most *transdisciplinary* and fast-growing fields in universities today. Because of performance studies' extensive scope of subject matter, which includes the various theories and methodologies it uses to explore performance, students learn to better comprehend performance – whether in a theatre, workplace, or the street – as an operative concept and lived factor in everyday life. Working along these lines, the primary purpose of this book is to introduce students to the directions in which the field of performance studies is moving through the key words, concepts and theories that are shaping its future.

My intention here is to highlight the methodology that the diverse chapters collectively embody. In other words, it is not my intention to introduce the individual chapters, but to introduce and discuss a mode of critical inquiry that is proposed by the contributions to performance studies that the chapters in this book jointly comprise. In doing this, I want to draw attention to what I term 'the ethical drive' that I believe has significantly fueled the field of performance studies since its inception, over the past 20 years especially, and that directly informs its future, as can be seen in the chapters assembled here. The ethical drive refers to the field's commitment, expressed by scholars working within the field, to critically and constructively address, through analysis of on- and off-stage performance, issues related to sexual, gender, class, race, cultural, aesthetic, ethnic and national differences, in the interest of fostering shared understanding and respect, social equality and the betterment of life for all people. The idea to edit a volume of new and forward-looking chapters on key words, concepts and theories in performance studies was inspired, first, by the longstanding need for such a book for introductory courses in performance, theatre and cultural studies. Second, the benefits to the publication of a volume with the originality, breadth and rigor demonstrated by the chapters are deep and far-reaching. This is not just for the fields of performance, theatre and cultural studies to which the chapters specifically contribute but also, as models in methodology and objective, for all fields aspiring to transdisciplinarity: researching, communicating and collaborating within and across traditional disciplinary boundaries. Hence, the volume contributes inwardly and outwardly at the same time. It performs the field's importance well beyond audiences – scholars and students – directly invested in performance studies while it reinforces, for the academy at large, the discipline's distinctiveness, constitution and authority as a site for the exploration and transfer of specific knowledge. As a necessary component to the structure of their investigations and statements, the chapters purposefully connect performance studies to a number of disciplines and subdisciplines, the aims of which it often shares. These include critical theory, political science, ethnography, social geography, cognitive neuroscience, philosophy, translation studies and visual arts.

The key words, concepts and theories posited by the chapters do not stem from a drive for the new, the trendy, or the marketable. Although there is considerable pressure within performance studies, as within most academic fields, to come up with a new concept or approach, such motivation is not the feeling one gets from reading the chapters. This indifference to such opportunism was a goal of mine when determining which chapters to include, but it was also an aspiration easily achieved within the field. The ethical drive at the core of performance studies makes the field serious, benevolent and activist. However idealist and utopian this might sound, I believe that the field is occupied predominantly by people hoping to contribute positively to the world through their scholarship and teaching. The ethical drive of performance studies is the field's common denominator, its most impressive attribute and its greatest source of inspiration. It does not take as its primary objective the determining of right and wrong either generally or within a given context. Instead, it is about revealing the stakes, contingencies, perspectives and other factors that come into play any time humans interact with each other, and in the cases discussed in this volume, when a modality of performance is involved – performance defined here as intentional expression for an audience. The ethical drive to performance studies is beneficent, affirming and generative rather than judgmental, divisive and policing.

In their identifications, formulations and delineations of key words, concepts and theories, the contributors have conducted what I would call, using the terminology of transversal poetics, 'fugitive explorations'.[2] Transversal poetics is a combined sociocognitive theory, performance aesthetics and critical methodology for which process, mobility, adaptability, inclusion and affirmation are vital. Simply put, transversal poetics is the name of an approach to conducting research, like psychoanalysis or structuralism, except that it is not restrictive or absolute, and thus could draw from psychoanalysis and structuralism if determined to be in the best interest of a particular analysis.[3] As a *praxis* (theory/method/practice) of transversal poetics, fugitive explorations reveal elusive, marginal or hidden objects – narrative, structural, performative, thematic, semiotic, institutional, etc. – in other words, the 'fugitive elements' of the subject matter under investigation. This could reveal, for instance, how the fugitive elements have been and can be overlooked, masked or contextualized to generate, undermine or uphold meanings and realities. Fugitive explorations do this by moving 'investigative-expansively': they call for analyzing relationships between variables immediate to the chosen subject matter as well as relationships of the variables to other variables, such as those at the margins or outside the subject matter's vicinity (whether structural, disciplinary, thematic or geographical). In turn, analytical reframing occurs processually in adaptive response to new information so that perspective on the subject matter, or the subject matter itself, changes and, consequently, the exploration reconfigures. This approach avoids myopism, reductionism and totalization. It does not define through negation or exclusionary logic. It allows multi-perspectivalism, relationality and transformation to remain possible throughout and beyond research, analytical and interpretive processes. To be sure, consistent with transversal poetics, an underlying premise and common ground to the chapters is the acknowledgement and acceptance of difference; that *positive differentiation* is doable and advantageous.

Examples throughout the chapters of fugitive elements investigative-expansively discussed are numerous, so I will underscore only some here. The following examples also reflect a primary way in which I intend students to use this book. The key word, concept or theory that is the focus of each chapter enables access into particular streams of discourse within performance studies that relate to modes of performance and how we might interpret and relate to them. In so doing, all the chapters contain themes, if not overlapping or straightforwardly relatable topics, which flow with, intersect, or pass through the discourses to which other chapters contribute. Identifying the connections between the chapters, then, however fugitive to one another, becomes one of the book's most valuable exercises.

Marin Blažević and Lada Čale Feldman identify 'misperformance', which refers to a performance inconsistent with the performer's intentions, with its inversions, shifting of parameters, and failings, as differential opportunities for positive creation. Blažević and Feldman bring the often discriminated against category of failure, for instance, into positive light and productive play. Misperformance is affirmed both as performance practice, such as on the stage, and as a measure for evaluation and interpretation. Blažević and Feldman's understanding of misperformance resonates with Dylan Bolles and Peter Lichtenfels' concept of 'intervallic play'. For Bolles and Lichtenfels, 'intervallic play' refers to innovative space of opportunity and unpredictability achieved through disjunction, such as when a performance is contradictory or apparently, as Blažević and Feldman would put it, 'misperformed'. Bolles and Lichtenfels demonstrate how trained control of dissonances in the vocal delivery of lines in a stage play, especially when the audience is expecting consonance, can generate intervallic play through which the actor can achieve creative agency not accessible, for instance, when constrained by traditional rules for the pronunciation of Shakespeare's poetry. Such dissonance allows the actor to realize affective presence as well as a performance free of restrictive coordinates that remains fugitive to performances without the equivocal and negotiable play space of interval. For Johan Callens, following the Deleuzian idea that difference precipitates new *becomings* (physical, aesthetic, subjective, conceptual, etc., changes into something else), 'recursion' refers to the creative possibilities as well as the limitations located within the differences (potentially 'misperformances' and 'intervallic play') that occur necessarily as result of attempts to repeat/reproduce performances, as is typically the case in theatre. This idea points to Marvin Carlson's essay on 'living history' (performances of historical events), in which he emphasizes the positive value of misrepresentation in the re-enactments, that it is the irreproducibility of the past that makes efforts to reproduce them so challenging for theatre makers and thrilling for audiences. What remains inaccessible or non-representable serves to make the represented all the more precious despite or in turn because of the actual history fugitive to the performance (that moment in space/time is forever in the past).[4] In her essay on 'translation' and 'cultural ownership', Maria Delgado shows how translation always involves migration, the movement of differences across domains, and maintains that it is ethically imperative that we remain aware of the migrancy involved. This is crucial as we determine the meaning of a text in a different language and cultural context from which it emerged and for which it was intended, for we must not permit its original meanings and values to become fugitive elements in the process of translation or interpretation. In her essay on 'social somatics', which refers to our embodiment or embodied experiences of the social systems of which we are a product and in which we live and operate, Petra Kuppers explains that the commonly used term in performance studies, 'somatic knowledge', which usually refers to knowledge inherent to or grounded in the body, is misleading. Instead, according to Kuppers, such 'knowledge' is influenced by multiple and fluctuating interactions, images, media, textures, intensities and practices. She proposes social somatics as an alternative mode of inquiry, logic and performance practice, for it produces new spaces as it insists on our political and ethical responsibility to imagine and embody ourselves otherwise – to occupy bodies and therefore subject positions radically different from our own. This makes empathy and understanding possible.

In these examples, the authors identify elements in certain discourses and practices that have been 'fugitive' to established or previous understandings of the phenomena in question. They locate these in, or in the interstices or results of, what Michel Foucault calls 'points of diffraction', 'points of incompatibility' and 'points of equivalence'.[5] As a result, by bringing the fugitive to the forefront, they produce opportunities by which to better comprehend the means by which elision, cover-up, marginalization and repression often occur. Insofar as they emphasize interconnectivity and inclusion, they also avoid negation, reductionism and totalization. In doing so, they elucidate mechanisms and operations of representation and presentation, repetition and difference, and rehearsal and performance. According to Gilles Deleuze, who, unsurprisingly, is cited in more than a quarter of the chapters in regard to questions of inclusion, connectedness and multiplicity, repetition always involves difference and discovery, and the process of differentiation generates variation more than resemblance and identification. Hence, differentiation is always positive and creative, comprising heterogeneous series always open to new connections, flows and becomings. As Deleuze eloquently puts it:

> We refuse the general alternative proposed by infinite representation: the indeterminate, the indifferent, the undifferentiated or a difference already determined as negation, implying and enveloping the negative (by the same token, we also refuse the particular alternative: negative of limitation or negative of opposition). In its essence, difference is the object of affirmation or affirmation itself. In its essence, affirmation is itself difference.[6]

For the contributors to this volume, and insofar as they represent performance studies, affirming difference and understanding affirmation as a positively differentiating and open-ended process is the ghost in the machine of performance studies' ethical drive. In his essay, 'Theatrum Philosophicum', Foucault writes: 'Difference can only be liberated through the invention of an acategorical thought.'[7] As a collective of freethinkers, or at least thinkers actively aspiring to such freedom, the contributors implicitly invite readers to engage their chapters with the conscientiousness, critical wherewithal and ethical drive with which they have engaged their subject matter.

Notes

1   For a concise and insightful history of the field of performance studies, see Marvin Carlson, *Performance: A Critical Introduction* (New York: Routledge, 2003).
2   For more on 'transversal poetics', 'fugitive explorations', 'fugitive elements' and the 'investigative-expansive mode of analysis', as well as related discussions on methodology and ethics, see, among other works, Bryan Reynolds, *Transversal Subjects: From Montaigne to Deleuze after Derrida* (Basingstoke: Palgrave Macmillan, 2009) and *Transversal Enterprises in the Drama of Shakespeare and his Contemporaries: Fugitive Explorations* (Basingstoke: Palgrave Macmillan, 2006).
3   For detailed discussion of psychoanalysis and structuralism as approaches to critical inquiry, see M.H. Abrams and Geoffrey Harpham, *A Glossary of Literary Terms*, 10th edn (Belmont, CA: Wadsworth, 2014).
4   Deleuze captures this idea, albeit somewhat inversely, when he writes of Marx's critique of the Hegalians who mediate with regard to history: 'to the extent that history is theatre, then repetition, along with the tragic and comic within repetition, forms a condition of movement under which the "actors" or the "heroes"

produce something effectively new in history'. In *Difference and Repetition*, trans. Paul Patton (New York: Columbia University Press, 1994), 10.

5   See Michel Foucault, *The Archaeology of Knowledge and Discourse on Language*, trans. A.M. Sheridan Smith (New York: Pantheon Books, 1977).

6   Deleuze, *Difference and Repetition*, 52.

7   Michel Foucault, *Language, Counter-memory, Practice: Selected Essays and Interviews*, ed. Donald F. Bouchard (Ithaca: Cornell University Press, 1977), 186.

I   The 'F' Word, Feminism's Critical Futures

Elaine Aston

That feminism has made significant interventions into theatre and performance scholarship is without question. However, at this moment in time, what is far less certain are the futures of feminism and feminist theatre scholarship. Co-editing *Feminist Futures?: Theatre, Performance, Theory*, Gerry Harris and I explain how the question mark in our title is crucial: 'this question mark poses the future of feminism and the relation between feminism and theatre and performance as a question and as being *in* question' (Aston and Harris 2006: 1). The purpose of these brief reflections on the 'f' word is to consider the current, uncertain state of feminism and to think of the possible ways in which feminism, given its state of uncertainty, may continue to have an impact on the scholarship and practice of theatre. In order to reflect on these future feminist-theatre uncertainties, I need to take a contextualizing step back into the feminist-theatre traditions of the past.

Feminism and theatre: beginnings

If feminism 'begins' anywhere, it begins with feelings of gender-based exclusion: with the growing awareness that women's lives have been marginalized and trivialized by male-dominated social systems and cultural values. For women theatre academics such as myself who, in the 1980s, were part of the 'first wave' feminist-theatre generation in the UK, it was this sense of exclusion that fuelled our desire to see women's theatre included, rather than excluded, from the syllabus. To achieve this inclusivity required feminist interventions into all three key areas of traditional theatre studies – history, theory and practice.

At first, feminist attentions concentrated largely on theatre history, mainly because the idea of recovery generally was important to feminism as women recognized that they had been hidden from history and culture, and so were keen to uncover a silenced past to ensure that they would be written into future histories. Recovering women from theatre history, recovering or finding plays by women that offered more roles for women and a greater attention to the representation of women's experiences, challenged the male-dominated theatre canon in terms of both the study and practice of theatre (see Aston 1995: Ch. 2). In terms of theatre practice, this began to suggest ways out of the difficulties created by the gender imbalance between the overwhelmingly large numbers of female to male students taking theatre courses, versus the relatively few decent roles for women in the male-dominated theatre canon. Previously this had meant adopting various canny gender strategies to adapt 'classical', 'canonical' texts to meet the gender demands of production contexts: the cross-casting of women in male roles or multiple shared castings for women so that you might have a show, for example, that featured Chekhov's thirty sisters, or one that had ever so many Juliets and one 'lucky' Romeo.

Alongside this challenge to canonical texts and the emergence of gender-aware practices came the theory explosion of the 1980s as theatre studies, along with many other disciplines, began to transform its modes of thinking through theoretical frameworks; was open to and opened up by new ways of seeing as it connected and intersected with a diverse body of critical theory. Semiotics, understanding the languages of theatre as a complex sign system, shifted critical attention away from what to *how* meaning is created and produced, while feminism had its own political and theoretical concerns regarding the cultural production of 'Woman' as sign and its own post-Lacanian objections to the 'lack' of a female subject. In this context, the critical turn towards French feminist theory proved highly influential. Ideas from this particular 'body' of feminist theory, such as Hélène Cixous' concept of an écriture feminine, were taken up, explored, adapted and translated into practices that aspired to challenge the objectifying male gaze of mainstream theatre texts and production contexts. In brief, the idea of 'writing' the body as a means of giving 'voice' to the experiences of women repressed and marginalized by patriarchal language and culture constituted an important 'stage' in the evolution of feminist ideas and practice. Indeed, for a moment in the late 1980s, it very much appeared as though feminist-theatre futures would lie with the possibilities of staging a 'feminine' language that would 'speak' differently to us as women.

Enter gender

However, in the 1990s, things were to take a rather different critical turn, by turning away from the idea of embodying language through an idea of writing the feminine towards the idea of the Butlerian 'beyond gender'

9

project that instead offered the critical promise of a subject deregulated by the governance of gender norms. Important though the 'beyond gender' project has been, at the same time it has had the effect of confining 'gender troubles' to an overarching grand narrative of anti-essentialism. As Sue-Ellen Case (1996: 12) cautions in respect to feminist and queer politics, poststructuralist, anti-essentialist theorizing risks 'operat[ing] in the refined atmosphere of "pure" theory and writing', thereby 'abandoning earlier materialist discourses that signalled to active, grassroots coalitions while claiming a less essentialist base'. In brief, as a critical manoeuvre, she warns that it constitutes a 'race into theory' that moves 'away from the site of material interventions' (37).

The 'race into theory' has also proved problematic for the relationship between theory and practice in the field of feminism and theatre studies. In the past, as previously explained, thinking feminism evolved through the *interplay* of feminist theorizing and gender-aware practice. The theatre of Caryl Churchill, arguably the most influential of women playwrights in the 'first wave' of feminism and theatre scholarship, helped to *create* ideas about what constituted feminist-theatre practice as her plays variously showed what could be *done* to demonstrate and alienate oppressive regimes of class, ethnicities, sexualities and gender. But this since has tended to give way to a hierarchical, dualistic frame where practice is relegated to a colonized 'other' serving a theoretical end in which the specificity of the performance, the practice, is lost to modes and models of interdisciplinary enquiry (see Aston and Harris 2008: Ch. 1).

In retrospect, it is perhaps not surprising to find this race into 'pure' (gender) theory coinciding with the decline of feminism as a political movement. Without the grassroots activism, the feminism of the streets and the protests that took place *outside* the academy and the groundswell of women practising theatre professionally, forming their own companies and collectives as they had done in the 1970s and 80s, then the world of academic ideas became increasingly divorced from social realities, and in theatre, theory was more inclined to split off from practice.

The decline in feminism generally is, in part, consequent upon feminism's own fragmentation – specifically, the rise of identity politics and the need to acknowledge differences that, as a result, made it hard to identify with 'women anything'. While feminism struggled with the divides of its own making, it also had to contend with the climate of a backlash against feminism and the generational divide between feminists of the 1970s generation and younger generations of women. Younger women have tended to distance themselves from the 'f word', not least – albeit not exclusively – on account of deeming the battle for women's liberation as having been fought and won. All of which has, in sum, contributed to the idea that now is the time of post-feminism.

With the climate of post-feminism, the absence of feminism as a movement, and the added complications of the anti-essentialist theory drive and the hierarchical theatre-theory-practice relations – what can I argue as a more progressive future for the project of feminism and theatre? In response, I want to propose the following strategies that have more hopeful futures in mind. Specifically, my proposals are for:

- A relaxation of the 'beyond gender' theory project
- A revisiting and re-evaluating of theory and practice relation
- A reconsideration and contestation of *Western* feminism and theatre
- A proposal for communiTIES of feminism and theatre, locally and globally.

No hierarchy is intended here, no either/or, but an interdependent mixing of these various strategies to weave a more progressive fabric of feminism and feminist-theatre futures.

'Beside' the 'beyond gender' project

Following through on the cautionary note sounded in Case's concerns about the 'race into theory' and the anti-essentialist drive, I want to advocate not a race away from theory, but rather a relaxation of the theoretical grip on anti-essentialism. My thinking here has been influenced largely by the late Eve Sedgwick's *Touching Feeling: Affect, Pedagogy, Performativity*. Introduced as 'a project to explore promising tools and techniques for nondualistic thought and pedagogy' (2003: 1), Sedgwick proposes 'the art of *loosing*' (3) as she orients her thinking outside the essentialist/anti-essentialist binary, by offering a non-dualistic paradigm of her own, one based on the notion of 'beside'. As a strategy, it gestures to the importance of thinking not in terms of what is already known, but of coming to think 'otherwise' – stepping to the side of a well-trodden theoretical path in the expectation of seeing and coming to know differently.

I am attracted to Sedgwick's proposition of 'beside' for thinking feminism. For me, the attraction of 'beside' lies in the possibilities of thinking outside the dualistic framework of essentialism/anti-essentialism and its encouragement of more heterogeneous modes of theorizing, which allow for embodied, situated knowledge to lie beside the discursive, textual modes that seek to trouble or deconstruct the governance of gender. The feminist shift from things to words that concerned sociologist Michèle

Barrett (1992: 201), that is, from 'things' like 'low pay, rape or female foet-icide' to a focus on 'the discursive construction of marginality in a text or document', might be revisited or undone through a critical practice that textures text and context, words and things in the same critical feminist writing space. Of course, in the practice of writing, all 'things' are textual, just as, in other ways, the embodied knowledge of 'things' are also discur-sively marked by the social and cultural spheres that script them. But in a textured critical practice, the writing of 'things', a materialist discourse, might be allowed to speak 'beside' other formulations or expressions of feminism without necessarily being returned to an earlier essentialist para-digm or being silenced by an anti-essentialist drive. This might then resist what sociologist Angela McRobbie (1999: 91) describes as making anti-essentialism the 'new point of faith, a new kind of thing'.

While Sedgwick's idea of 'beside' interests me as a feminist scholar, it also appeals to me as a feminist-theatre scholar, where I am attracted to the idea of undoing the hierarchical play between theory and prac-tice and of situating theory 'beside' practice, giving it a voice on its own terms and in its own right. In general, whatever the field of enquiry, the languages of theatre practice offer up their own strategies for relaxing the grip on theory, given that practice, the doing of 'things', does not obey any strict intellectual or political agenda, but rather mixes up ideas through its own creative process or labour. (For detailed reflections on a feminist resistance to non-hierarchical theory/practice relations, see Aston and Harris 2008.)

Towards feminisms and theatre

As I think my 'impure' theory thoughts and posit the possibility of opening up theory–practice relations, I also need to reflect on the term that haunts the fragments of the feminism and theatre story as I am telling it here: Western. And this is where I move towards the third of my four more hope-ful strategies to advocate a reconsideration and contestation of Western feminism and theatre.

Thinking feminism in the future tense must necessarily mean contesting the binary of Western feminism and any 'other', or all other kinds of femi-nism. Objections to the hierarchical (colonialist) arrangement of First and Third World feminisms have already made and are making a difference to feminism in an important and influential body of work by feminist post-colonial theorists such as Gayatri Spivak, M. Jacqui Alexander, Chandra Talpade Mohanty and Sarah Ahmed, among many others. Broadly, this critical terrain argues that there is every need for feminism to think outside its site of white Western privilege; every need to contest ways in which Western feminism has established its own apartheid of First and Third World feminisms.

The state of Western post-feminism, as described earlier, is especially unhelpful, dangerous even, to cross-cultural, cross-border feminist thinking because it declares a state of independence and in that declaration cuts itself off not only from the 'things' that still urgently need to be addressed in Western women's lives, but from attachments to different geopolitical feminist states, which it can only 'see' in its own false image. Writing the grand narrative of independence, Western feminism refuses to speak in any language other than its own. For feminism not to appear exclusively in its Western form or image, it needs to be an open rather than a closed 'text' of differently located feminisms. Rather than feminist 'independence', there is a need for feminisms to be in dialogue with each other, in ways that are mindful of differences but that allow for cultures of *interdependent* collaboration in the interest of future feminisms and feminist futures (for further discussion, see Aston 2010).

In the field of feminism and theatre, to be in touch with and touched by different stages in feminism and feminist stages is to offer some sort of redress to the dominant trend in the colonial trafficking of ideas, theories and theatre practices of a Western kind. For instance, presenting the work of the Feminist Research Working Group in the International Federation for Theatre Research (IFTR), the essay collection *Staging International Feminisms* endeavours 'to bring differently located feminisms and theatre cultures together – beside, alongside and in critical dialogue with each other, but not at the expense of each other' (Aston and Case 2007: 4). While the collection evidences some international trafficking of Western ideas, critical practices, strategies or performance practices signalling 'the continuing primacy of UK/US feminist movements', nonetheless, 'situating that primacy alongside feminist cultures from Nigeria, India or Korea' in turn serves as a means 'of opening up more familiar forms of Western feminism and theatre to contestation and debate' (ibid.).

CommuniTIES

To work in IFTR's Feminist Research Working Group, 'beside' feminist-theatre scholars from differing world theatre and feminist contexts, is to be reminded of the creative and political value of working towards women's theatre and performance networks, locally and globally.

This suggests a different strategy to that which has gained some feminist currency of late: to put the emphasis of community-building on the theatrical event. For instance, Jill Dolan (2005: 37) eloquently makes the case for the utopian possibilities that theatre itself may be able to offer of a 'better [socially progressive] future'; of theatre's potential to create 'temporary communities' by affective – spectators moved to feel together – means (40). Although I am drawn to this idea and agree with it in one way, at the same time this places a huge burden or emphasis on a particular show to fulfil the community-making, desire to imagine ourselves differently, tasks. Therefore, instead of charging theatre with the task of feminist community-making or relying on feminism as a movement (which is difficult in the prevailing climate of Western post-feminism), it might be possible to conceive of a feminism and theatre movement or network that builds through meeting grounds, in which it is possible to be in touch with the work of others and to engage in the critical labour of working towards understandings of different feminist cultures and sites of feminist-theatre activism. This is because, as Sara Ahmed (2000) warns, a community of feminist interests cannot be taken as a given, but rather is something that has to be worked through and for together. Indeed, one of the early and valuable lessons of 1970s feminism was not to assume the commonality of women's experience but to recognize the need to negotiate a complex array of differences in terms of class, ethnicities, sexualities and gender. In short, there can be no question of presuming to know others but, as Ahmed (2000: 180) argues, of needing to get to know others:

> In the very 'painstaking labour' of getting closer, of speaking *to* each other, and of working *for* each other, we also get closer to 'other others'. In such acts of alignment (rather than merger), we can reshape the very bodily form of the community, as a community that is yet to come.

Ahmed's point is crucial to minimizing the risk that 'we' build a new community of strangers: one in which the hierarchies of Western feminism which positions some women as stranger than others are kept in place.

Hence, rather than think in terms of a feminism and theatre community in a monolithic sense, I have come to think of this as working towards communiTIES, the latter a term I have stolen and adapted from Patrice Pavis. 'A few single communiTIES (political, geographical, ethnical, sexual, etc.)' are what Pavis (1998: 82–3) laments as all that is left to us in the absence of 'THE community'. But I want to revise or adjust this view more positively to advocate differently located communiTIES as the means to community-making, to creating attachments that are mindful of the different and diverse conditions of local feminist and theatre communities, that might provide the means by which theatre women, as artists and scholars, can find political and creative 'ties' to each other, locally and globally.

Labouring towards feminism and theatre communiTIES is arguably more empowering than working in feminist isolation; advocates a mode of interdependent feminisms and theatre connections, rather than a style of independent feminism confined to Western ways of 'seeing'. In the final analysis, it is a far more hopeful response to the question mark that hangs over the future of the 'f word' and the relations between feminism and theatre.

Works cited

Ahmed, S. *Strange Encounters: Embodied Others in Post-Coloniality*, London: Routledge, 2000.

Aston, E. *An Introduction to Feminism and Theatre*, London: Routledge, 1995.

– 'Swimming in Histories of Gender Oppression: Grupo XIX de Teatro's *Hysteria*', *New Theatre Quarterly*, 26:1 (2010): 38–48.

Aston, E. and Case, S.E. eds. *Staging International Feminisms,* Basingstoke: Palgrave Macmillan, 2007.

Aston, E. and Harris, G. eds. *Feminist Futures?: Theatre, Performance, Theory*, Basingstoke: Palgrave Macmillan, 2006.

– *Performance Practice and Process: Contemporary [Women] Practitioners,* Basingstoke: Palgrave Macmillan, 2008.

Barrett, M. 'Words and Things; Materialism and Method in Contemporary Feminist Analysis', in M. Barrett and A. Phillips, eds, *Destabilizing Theory: Contemporary Feminist Debates*, Cambridge: Polity Press, 1992, 201–19.

Case, S.E. *The Domain-Matrix: Performing Lesbian at the End of Print Culture*, Bloomington: Indiana University Press, 1996.

Dolan, J. *Utopia in Performance: Finding Hope at the Theater*, Ann Arbor: University of Michigan Press, 2005.

McRobbie, A. *In the Culture Society: Art, Fashion and Popular Music*, London: Routledge, 1999.

Pavis, P. 'Do We Have to Know Who We do Theatre For?', *Performance Research*, 3:1 (1998): 82–6.

Sedgwick, E.K. *Touching Feeling: Affect, Pedagogy, Performativity*, Durham: Duke University Press, 2003.

2   Public Sphere

Christopher Balme

The resurgence of interest in the public sphere across the social sciences and the humanities is a clear indication that this sometimes ill-defined realm has become a focal point of attention. Academic and artistic interest in something is usually a sure sign that matters are unclear, conceptual boundaries are blurred and old certainties are anything but that. There is also little doubt that the major challenges we face – the media revolution, globalization and migration, climate change, the erosion of public finances and services (to name just a few) – all have, in some way, a bearing on the public sphere, the realm where issues are debated and citizens are free to enter and engage in discourse. As this incomplete list suggests, any discussion of the public sphere within the context of theatre and performance immediately locates us in the field of politics in a fairly narrow and conventional sense of the word. As the public sphere is primarily a discursive arena located outside and between state bureaucracy, on the one hand, and economics and business on the other, it occupies a crucial role in the functioning of so-called 'free societies'. The question to be explored here is what role theatre and performance in practice play in this realm and how performance and theatre theory can contribute to the debates.

But what public sphere are we talking about? Any academic discussion of the term must begin with the seminal book by Jürgen Habermas *The Structural Transformation of the Public Sphere*, first published in German in 1962, but not translated into English until 1989. Habermas divides the public sphere into two historical iterations: a *representative* form typical of feudal and absolutist political regimes, where most political action is ruled by the dictates of secrecy, *arcana imperii*, on the one hand, and carefully staged forms of publicness in the context of absolutistic rule on the other. The second form that comes to replace the representative one he terms *bourgeois*. Its main characteristics are almost universal access, autonomy (participants are free of coercion) and equality of status (social rank is subordinated to quality of argument). The bourgeois public sphere emerges within feudal society, initially in the 'nonpolitical' arenas of the theatre, literature and the arts, where the discursive patterns and practices are trained as it were before entering the political arena proper. The defining feature of the bourgeois public sphere is reasoned discourse by private persons on questions of public interest with the aim of achieving rational consensus.

Since its original definition by Habermas, the semantic field of the term 'public sphere' has been extended considerably, especially in the wake of the English translation of Habermas's book in 1989. The English translation of the German term *Öffentlichkeit* as 'public sphere' is somewhat problematic because it does not adequately cover the semantic flexibility of the original. In the first instance, *Öffentlichkeit* connotes, depending on the context, persons, not a space, albeit in a collectivized and abstract sense. In this rendering, it is closer to the term 'public' or in a conceptual sense 'publicness'. *Öffentlichkeit* does not have a clear spatial orientation suggested by the word 'sphere'.[1] The spatiality of the term is not, however, just a chance residue of translation. In Habermas's definition of the concept and particularly in the context of its historical emergence, it can be thought of concretely in terms of a particular space. Central to the concept is the distinction between public and private spheres. As bourgeois society placed ever more emphasis and value on privacy and the private realm, particularly on the conjugal family in contrast to the theatrical openness of aristocratic intercourse, so too did it define and emphasize the importance of public discourse. This took place either through media, such as journals, newspapers, books, or, as Habermas famously argues, in new socially sanctioned spaces of communication, such as salons and coffee houses. Here, meanings were made, opinions formed and debated, and the seeds of democratic processes sown. In a recent, autobiographical note, Habermas emphasizes two types of *Öffentlichkeit*. The first kind refers to the public exposure demanded by a media society linked to staging practices of celebrities with a concomitant erasure of the borders between private and public spheres. The second type, more narrowly the public sphere in the theoretical sense, refers to participation in political, scientific, or literary debates where communication and understanding about a topic replace self-fashioning. In this case, Habermas (2005: 15) writes: 'the audience does not constitute a space for spectators and listeners but a space for speakers and addresses who engage in debate'.

Beyond its spatial connotations, the public sphere has become a sui generis concept. The public sphere does not just exist as a specific place of communication, it is also a conceptual entity with a history and discrete semantic dimensions. Since this identity has a diachronic dimension, it changes over time. It is also subject to social differentiation on the synchronic plane. An important part of Habermas's argument focuses on the multiple semantic dimensions of the term 'public'. It must be seen not just in contradistinction to the idea of the 'private' but also in the terms and sense of public service – that is, the emergence of bureaucratic institutions developed as a counterbalance to the 'representative' publicness of feudal rule.[2] While the diachronic dimension lies at the heart of Habermas's argument – the structural transformation and ultimately degeneration of the public sphere in its ideal-typical form – its social and functional differentiation is less apparent in the original formulation. A focus on differentiation is, however, one of the major contributions of recent studies of the idea of the public sphere. Today, it is more usual to speak of public spheres in the plural rather than as one single entity. Recent research has identified the formation of public spheres along class, racial and gender lines, to name only some of the possibilities.[3]

For a theatre historical perspective, it is important to understand the public sphere as a *relational object*. Certainly, the public, and perhaps also the public sphere in its spatial sense, come to be regarded as something that can be acted on, appealed to, influenced and even manipulated. This conception of a somewhat passive entity ultimately provides the precondition for the emergence of the practices of publicity, public opinion and public relations. All institutions highly dependent on public participation (e.g. museums, concert houses or theatres) expend considerable energy in assessing the nature of the public and the public sphere. What are their spatial and quantitative limits? How can the public be reached, exploited, or nurtured?

In summary, we can say that the theatrical public sphere must be understood as the interaction of these three mutually dependent categories. The spatial concept of a realm of theatrical interaction primarily outside the building merges into a conceptual entity that ultimately becomes so palpable that it functions as an extension of the institution.

A key component of any discussion of the public sphere in the context of theatre must take cognizance of institutional and medial questions. The adjective 'theatrical' implies an institutional component. If we take the classical formulation of the public sphere as a point of departure, then it immediately becomes clear that the creation and existence of a public sphere is predicated on the emergence of particular institutions. To cite just one of countless definitions of the Habermasian model:

The term modern or 'bourgeois' public sphere refers generally to those *institutions* open to the public and to those practices, which any member of the public may engage in, that are characteristic of modern societies – it refers, thus, to museums, theaters, libraries, galleries, schools, and universities; cafés, stores, stock exchanges (and, in general, markets); courts, legislatures, town halls; the print and, more recently, electronic media. The distinctive feature of the public sphere is that any member of the public enters, in principle, on equal terms and that communication and deliberation take place. (Reddy 1992: 136)

Theatre features as just one institution in the long list of domains where individuals may enter 'on equal terms'. As usual, the term 'institution' is used rather loosely and as a closer examination of institutional theory would show, one must differentiate when a theatre is an institution and when it is probably not. There are, of course, many forms of theatre of a programmatically subversive and oppositional nature for which the term institution is not appropriate. Nevertheless, there are some forms of theatre that do meet such criteria and these forms usually enjoy considerable cultural prestige, are often the beneficiaries of relatively large sums of public funds, and, in some cases, the employees enjoy the legal status of being quasi-civil servants.

In terms of the public sphere, we can state that theatrical institutions sustain a public sphere of debate, interest and attendance, although the latter is not necessary for all participants. Because some theatres are institutionalized, they engender a strong public sphere; in other words, their very institutional status is predicated on the existence of a public sphere.

A second feature of the public sphere is its imbrication with the media. This holds true in the 17th or 18th centuries as well as today. In his argument, Habermas places special emphasis on the rise of the press as a precondition for the emergence of a bourgeois public sphere. The increasing commercialization of the press in the 19th century and the dominating role of mass media in the 20th century contribute to the attrition of the classical public sphere that his book charts. More important for the discussion of the public sphere in relation to theatre and performance is the observation that participation in the public sphere requires mediation in the literal sense of the term. Although premodernist theatre could itself be regarded as a potential arena of and participant in the public sphere – and the history of theatrical censorship would certainly suggest that state authorities have regarded theatre in this way – theatre today is most potent when it links into other, mainly mass media. This may be in the form of debates surrounding controversial productions – theatre scandals – but it may just be the new forms of public discourse that are now emerging in the context of the internet. Even the smallest and most informally organized theatres and performance groups have an internet presence and an increasing number provide blogs and other forms of interactive interfaces for the public. In this sense, performance is becoming more pluralized and democratic in comparison to a former reliance on institutionalized theatre criticism as a benchmark for explicitly articulated public response.

The third form of the public sphere I would like to discuss in conclusion concerns the new trend towards performative intervention. If theatre risks becoming, in Dennis Kennedy's words, 'a cul-de-sac off the Infobahn' (2009: 154), a problem that not just scholars have noticed, then it is not surprising that performance artists and activists have sought new ways to engage with the public sphere. These activities almost invariably lead out of specialized performance spaces and into public spaces, both real and virtual. Two examples must suffice to delineate how the relationship between performance and the public is being redefined and re-energized. The first concerns the activist group, the Critical Art Ensemble, who understand performance quite literally in terms of a Habermasian public sphere where issues are articulated and debated. The second briefly discusses a recent performance by Marina Abramović – *The Artist is Present* (2010), where the traditional form of co-present performance is extended outside the here and now of performative encounter into a public sphere on the internet.

The Critical Art Ensemble (CAE) is a group of five political activists or 'tactical media practitioners', as they term themselves, who have been operating since 1987. Their aims and modus operandi have been extremely influential and can be seen as representative of the work of many interventionist groups active since the 1990s. That their activities are not just restricted to the virtual of theatre and performance can be adduced from the much publicized court case of one of the members, Steve Kurtz, who was accused of and ultimately cleared of charges relating to bioterrorism.

From the outset, they have engaged with and utilized electronic media. In their book *Electronic Civil Disobedience* (1996), which they freely invite to be plagiarized and distributed, they argue that conventional forms of political activism 'based solely on present-body embodied actions' (Schneider 2000: 125) such as sit-ins, marches, occupations etc. have become obsolete because such actions assume that power can be addressed in situ, at places and spaces where power is deemed to be actually present. Since global capitalist power has become 'nomadic', such forms of protest are futile because, so their argument runs, power has given the people the streets as a form of pseudo public space in which to perform. They term their own form of theatre, 'recombinant theatre', which involves, among other things, a variation of street theatre. The latter does not refer to performances literally enacted on the streets à la Bread and Puppet Theatre but rather interventions into everyday life in the tradition of the situationists:

What CAE does consider street theatre are those performances that invent ephemeral, autonomous situations from which *temporary public relationships* emerge whereby the participants can engage in *critical dialogue on a given issue*. (Critical Art Ensemble 2000: 157, emphasis added)

This definition makes clear that the onus and emphasis of performance is not on any kind of corporeal encounter in the here and now but on intervention in and generation of public debate on 'a given issue'. This amounts to an unequivocal commitment to performance in the public sphere in almost explicit Habermasian terminology.

Their central device, tactical media, refers to any kind of short-term action where media are employed to 'engage a particular socio-political context in order to create molecular interventions and semiotic shocks that collectively could diminish the rising intensity of authoritarian culture' (www.critical-art.net/TacticalMedia.html). Their activities are international and range from drawing attention to bad water quality in Hamburg to ensuring the dual naming (European and indigenous) of public places in Australia (to cite just two examples). In all cases, however, the aim is to generate public awareness and debate.

If CAE's understanding of the relationship between performance and the public sphere could be considered in some sense classical, Marina Abramović is better known as a pioneer of performance art performed more often than not in the confines of galleries for small groups. Here, we would speak of an audience rather than a public sphere. For this reason, it is not surprising that CAE has criticized this kind of performance art enacted before a 'passive audience' in hushed silence as having become 'defanged' in order 'to better serve the culture market' (Critical Art Ensemble 2000: 158). While Abramović's most recent performance *The Artist is Present*, staged in New York's Museum of Modern Art (MoMA) in 2010, took place largely in hushed silence and certainly served the culture market, it also challenged some of the older tenets of performance art and extended the range of response beyond the audience in a conventional sense to include a realm that could be interpreted in terms of a public sphere.

From March 2010, Abramović sat in silence at a table in MoMA's Marron Atrium, passively inviting visitors to take the seat across from her for as long as they chose within the time frame of the MoMA's hours of operation. The only contact permitted was eye contact, which visitors could maintain for however long they wished. The performance lasted a total of 77 days and over 700 hours. Abramović permitted herself no breaks, not even to visit the toilet while she was 'present'. What appears at first glance to be a durational performance of the kind she herself pioneered and which is predicated on an intense one-on-one corporeal encounter in a confined, usually gallery space – albeit of a very large kind – was in fact framed in much more complex ways. Although Abramović sat alone at a table opposite individual participants, the performance was video-taped live and this footage was streamed on the internet. In addition, the facial expressions of the participants were photographed and placed as 'portraits' on the internet, so that by the end of the 77 days a large archive of faces had been assembled. These were posted on a special site on the social networking site flickr.com as a fotostream. In turn, both video- and fotostreams generated a commentary in the form of short remarks and extended disquisitions. Some of the commentators had evidently been to the MoMA, others had not.

The performance created new kinds of spatial and discursive framing. If we look at the spatial arrangement, we can see that a kind of concentric framing was constructed. In the centre of the concentric circles was located the table at which the artist sat opposite the individual visitor staring at her. Around the table stood groups of visitors to the museum who observed the performance for as long as they wished, while opposite the table were also located video cameras, lighting and a photographer. The atrium also permitted spectators to observe proceedings from above. The whole setting resembled a film or photographic studio as much as it did a museum auditorium. For this reason, we can observe that the immediate corporeal encounter of performance art was mediatized at all stages. Because the performance was streamed over the internet as both video and digital photography, and because this information generated public comment, some of it of a highly complex nature, we can say that a discursive public sphere was created and sustained over the 77 days of the performance.

When we consider the spatial and discursive aspects of the performance, the title becomes itself complex and almost self-reflexive. While the artist was certainly present in a spatial and temporal sense – and in this respect she obeyed the laws of performance aesthetics – she was also present outside the coordinates of the here and now. The performance demonstrated that the concept of presence, as enumerated in the work of performance theorists from Peggy Phelan to Erika Fischer-Lichte, must now be revised to take into account new media configurations. In the age of the internet, the performance is both here and there, now and then. Such performances demonstrate that the public sphere will become a much more important and dynamic arena in the future.

Notes

1   In the original German, Habermas refers continually to *Öffentlichkeit* as a *Sphäre*, so that the English rendering of the term as 'public sphere', while emphasizing spatiality more than the German, is very close to Habermas's elaboration in some respects.
2   Habermas's historical argument hinges on two transformations: from a feudal 'representative' public sphere to a bourgeois rational-critical one during the 18th century, and then to the degeneration of the latter in the late 19th and 20th centuries under the influence of mass media and the commodification of culture.
3   The reception of Habermas's book in the English-speaking world only really begins in the 1990s in the wake of its translation in 1989. The first critical stocktaking can be found in Craig Calhoun (ed.) *Habermas and the Public Sphere*, Cambridge, MA: MIT Press, 1992, see especially his 'Introduction'. A review of post-1992 research and criticism of the concept within historical studies is provided by Andreas Gestrich (2006) 'The Public Sphere and the Habermas Debate'. *German History* 24(3): 413–30.

Works cited

Critical Art Ensemble (2000) 'Recombinant Theatre and Digital Resistance.' *TDR: The Drama Review* 44(4): 151–66.

Habermas, J. (1989) *The Structural Transformation of the Public Sphere: An Inquiry into a Category of Bourgeois Society*. Cambridge, MA, MIT Press.

Habermas, J. (2005) *Zwischen Naturalismus und Religion: philosophische Aufsätze*. Frankfurt am Main, Suhrkamp.

Kennedy, D. (2009) *The Spectator and the Spectacle: Audiences in Modernity and Postmodernity*. Cambridge, CUP.

Reddy, W.M. (1992) 'Postmodernism and the Public Sphere: Implications for an Historical Ethnography.' *Cultural Anthropology* 7(2): 135–68.

Schneider, R. (2000) 'Nomadmedia: On Critical Art Ensemble.' *TDR: The Drama Review* 44(4): 120–31.

3   Paramodern

Stephen Barker

'Paramodern' is a term directly applicable to performance *theory* in the broad sense, and indirectly to performance in the narrow sense. Though it has many connections to performance as practice, it is a term put to best use as a *frame* for performance practices, for a performance, within a conceptual structure. Since an exploration of the paramodern would be absurd without some sense of the deeply problematic 'modern', let alone the familiar but chimerical 'postmodern', the initial sections below offer a cursory map of that territory as preparation for confronting the paramodern.

Even a cursory look at the history of 'epochs' through which performance – art in general – has come will result in the realization that these designations can assist us in obtaining some sense of the trajectory, the narrative flow, of performance history. Some of this terminology is readily familiar: Classical, Neoclassical, Romantic, etc. Styles of performance, like styles of clothing, reading, music and much else, can be usefully identified through their relationships with such epistemological terms, which the historian or theorist of performance tends to turn into a genre with an initial capital letter. The most problematic of these terms, however, is 'Modern', since every age (rightly) considers itself to be modern, in the sense of 'in the current mode'. Did 'modern' performance begin with Shakespeare? With Romanticism or 'Realism' in the 18th century? With the various revolutions in art and culture at the beginning of the 20th century, with figures such as Ibsen, Chekhov, and Strindberg (and by extension Stanislavsky, Mayakovsky, or Gordon Craig)? With the Dadaism and Surrealism of the 1920s? The Social Realism of the 1930s? Each of these options provides a different sense of the 'modern', and its relationship with us in the 21st century. If this is true, how much more difficult is it to come to terms with the Postmodern, which seems to present itself as another of those historical designations: a period, and a style, following in the wake of the Modern. But even the theorists of the Postmodern do not treat it in that way: in *The Postmodern Turn*, Ihab Hassan addresses what he sees as the deeply problematic nature of the postmodern (to which he does not apply a capital P):

The word postmodernism sounds not only awkward, uncouth; it evokes what it wishes to surpass or suppress, modernism itself. The term thus contains its enemy within, as the terms romanticism and classicism, baroque and rococo, do not. (87)

Hassan asks whether the so-called 'postmodern' is the assassin of the modern, attempting to 'surpass or suppress' the paradigm from which it has seemingly evolved (as Romanticism 'suppresses' Neoclassicist and Enlightenment archetypes). Hassan sees the postmodern as the 'enemy within' of the modern in ways that none of its predecessors claim. And he goes further: 'Moreover, it denotes temporal linearity and connotes belatedness, even decadence' (87). The dilemma results from the fact that in the 20th century, first following the horrors of the mechanization of slaughter in World War I, then in the post-World War II atomic world – and then in the televisual epoch, then the digito-virtual, then ... – clearly something has happened to whatever we thought we meant by 'the modern' that demands some kind of adequate designation, at least a metaphorizing mnemonic by which what we consider descriptive of at least some significant aspect of our current circumstance can be classified.

Hassan calls attention to the inner contradictions, to what he calls the 'semantic instability' of the designation 'postmodern', and thus to the historical and theoretical fact that any consensus regarding the meaning, indeed of its existence, of the postmodern is chimerical. In both historical and theoretical terms, the so-called 'postmodern', somehow emerging from something equally tenuous called the 'modern', gives only illusionary satisfaction, since its very designation, as Hassan points out, undermines it. But Hassan clearly says that this phenomenon, usually designated as *after-modernism*, but which according to him could equally be seen as *within-modernism*, should be addressed seriously. He initiates this discussion in *The Postmodern Turn*, which attempts diligently to map it out.[1]

'Modern' = Unity

The 'awkwardness' of Hassan's dilemma results from the complexity of 'modern' performance, and the ways in which the modern itself is performed, both on the stage and off. If we think of an 'epoch' as a cohesive period in which a generally consistent sense of the world pertains, then 'the modern', specifically in performance and generally in Western culture, must be understood as the descendant of the 'Early Modern' epoch originating in the 16th century, catalyzed by the rediscovery of Greek (Aristotle) and Roman (Ovid, Cicero) texts concealed during the medieval period. Their re-emergence led to the enhanced development of an entirely new 'Renaissance' social consciousness (in works such as Thomas More's *Utopia* of 1516) and an explosive new aesthetics of art, poetry, science, and philosophy, as well as the revival of Protagoras's 'man is the measure of all things' notion, now adapted by a burgeoning humanism's elevation of the human as a primary value.[2] This anthropocentric modernity, despite the fact that it is by no means modern*ism*, displays all the seeds of the later obsession with the invention and empowerment of that new idea – the individual – and with the concomitant hegemonic relationship between the human and the world, the human and 'nature' (including human nature), the human and the universe (both physical and metaphysical).

This humanist paradigm crystallized in the latter 18th century, in the great shift from the Enlightenment values of *external forms* to the Romantic values of *inner dynamics*. This great shift is readily visible in many aspects of the performative between the mid-18th century and the first third of the 19th. The poetry of Thomas Gray or Thomas Chatterton are impossible in the 19th century, just as the poetry of Byron, Keats or Shelley are impossible in the 18th. The Rococo, Neoclassical and Academic art works of the 18th century are unmistakably *not* from the same epoch as those of William Blake, Francisco Goya, or early photography (invented in 1826). All these poets and artists are *per-forming*, producing works as *per* the *forms* of their times. In theatrical art, the worlds of Sheridan's *School for Scandal* and Goethe's *Urfaust*, both being written simultaneously in the 1770s, are radically different, the former remembering the Restoration comedy on which it is based, the latter foreshadowing the psychodramas of the 19th and 20th centuries. These disparate pieces and the theatre they crystallize require radically different performance techniques; indeed, the ways in which they can be staged at all indicate their divergent nature. No one would call *The School for Scandal* 'modern' in the sense in which we use it today, which informs contemporary performance techniques and theories.

The 'modern' can thus be framed as the time of the birth of the primacy of inner dynamics, the portrayal of the tensions, drives, and desires of all-too-human characters.[3]

In the 'modern', value is focused on inner processes and the forces at work within them; the modern introduces a new focus not only on the self but on the *inner* self, as a site of contradictory energies. This obsessive focus can be seen all the way from the scatological writings of the Marquis de Sade to the poetry and drama of Friedrich Hölderlin to the theatre (and theatricality) of Georg Büchner. In this regard, the 'modern' is the site of a growing fascination with subjectivity – with one's subjective existence as opposed to one's objective place in the cosmos. This amounts to a subject-obsession in art and literature, an explosively revolutionary renaissance presenting itself as a supernova of the Western humanistic zeal whose origins can be found in the aftermath of the Crusades, in the 'first' renaissance of the early 13th century (as in the humanized figures of Giotto in art and the human comedy of Boccaccio in letters), evolving into the 'high' Renaissance deification of human ascendency, process, and potential in a work like Sir Philip Sidney's *Apology for Poetry*.

But it is only within the more limited context of what we generally call the 'modern' that this complex tendency – the exaltation of subjective, individual experience *and* its energizing dynamic – reaches its contemporary formulation as a recognizable 'cultural performative', an identifiable behavior of the culture itself and recognizable as such. When interior states transcend exterior ones in value, 'behavior' must be seen as a performance *of* those inner states. Thus, the great German modernist Georg Hegel, in his *Lectures on Aesthetics*, notes compiled from presentations Hegel delivered in the 1820s, distinguishes among what he refers to as the three epochs of humanity's self-performance: the 'symbolic' epoch, the 'classical', and the 'romantic' (Hegel's 'romantic' being the 'modern' of our current designation).[4] In these lectures, Hegel, who saw performance as the very core of any culture, historicizes the relationship between *idea* and *spirit* (in German 'spirit' is *Geist*, a word that also means 'mind'). In the Romantic (i.e. modern) epoch, 'spirit', as human creativity, cannot be 'fully realized in the forms of the external world' but 'descends into the depths of its own inmost nature' (527). Hegel is clear about the interior nature of the modern and its unity: 'it is only in the interior world of consciousness that it finds, as spirit [*Geist*], its true unity'. This 'absolute internality, the adequate and appropriate form of which is spiritual subjectivity', transcends all exterior form in a 'simple unity with self' that Hegel calls 'the flame of subjectivity', thus setting the terms for the modern epoch. Hegel thus articulates the idea of the modern conceptualized as 'The Modern' and as 'Modernism' of Ezra Pound, T.S. Eliot and Virginia Woolf as the art of self-consciousness, formal experimentalism, aesthetic introspection, and the affirmation of human powers to create and manipulate the environment. We can see this Hegelian sense of the modern as a consistent through-line of the 20th and the early 21st centuries. In fact, it is somewhat surprising to discover that it was only in the 1960s that the term 'modernist' was applied *retrospectively* to what was a still recent generation of writers and artists whose aesthetic strategy was seen as having been supplanted by something else (thus producing, by default, the 'post' modern). But Hegel's simple designation for the contemporary revealed itself not as simple but as simplistic, given what Friedrich Nietzsche in the 1880s, critiquing Hegel, called the 'perspectivism' inherent within the modern, a perspectivism diametrically opposed to Hegelian unity. If 'descending into the depths of ... inmost nature' is 'the modern', small wonder that Hassan and others discover the *post*-modern to be the most floating of floating signifiers for which any stable meaning tends to float away, to remain perpetually unfixed.

But we would be committing Hegel's oversimplification to confine oneself to the received sense of 'the modern' or of 'modernity', let alone of 'modernism'. In fact, 'modern' and 'modernism' are many things, seen in many ways, from the outset. The modern has simply never been a settled issue; in fact, it has been fundamentally problematic since its inception: 'the modern' is always a hypothesis, not a fact, and never remotely a truth. An important late 20th-century view of modernity diverging from Hegel's is that of German sociologist, philosopher and aesthetic critic Theodor Adorno, who claims that

> modernity is a qualitative, not a chronological, category. Just as it cannot be reduced to abstract form, with equal necessity it must turn its back on conventional surface coherence, the appearance of harmony, the order corroborated merely by replication.[5]

For Adorno, the modern is *rejection* of the unity, certainty, harmony and coherence of Enlightenment art and thought. Adorno's interrogation of a fictional coherence and harmony, echoed by Peter Childs in his *Modernism*, temporalizes but complicates the modern:

> There were paradoxical if not opposed trends towards revolutionary and reactionary positions, fear of the new and delight at the disappearance of the old, nihilism and fanatical enthusiasm, creativity and despair.[6]

In Adorno's modernism, then, the problematic nature of (any version of) the 'modern', what Sigmund Freud will call its uncanny nature, is not its Hegelian unity but its disunity, as a disparate phenomenon either alien to modernism or, more interestingly and more disruptively, as an aspect of its unknowability: in this alternative version (and there are many of them), 'truth' or 'spirit' or 'mind' or 'self' are endlessly problematic, particularly in a world in which 'idea' and 'form', the rational and the emotional (let alone the great discovery of the 19th century, the unconscious) must be accounted for. It becomes clear, then, that apparently simple or straightforward designations for modernity, let alone modernism – modernism as unified, reasonable and emotional – are radically unreliable. The Hegelian view of the romantic/modern, constructed on the unified development, perhaps even perfectibility, of the human 'spirit', is not just naive for its own time but, fundamentally, in its very idea of itself, wholly inadequate for our time, not only wrong but unhelpful in an attempt to understand our epoch in general, and more specifically the relationship between the human, human agency and art production (i.e. performance).

Post ... what?

The dilemma of post ... what? attracted much attention in the 20th century. The received solution to it has been and remains what is referred to as the 'postmodern'. But given that the modern is so complex, so elusive, the so-called 'postmodern' is nothing less than an impossibility, an awkward receptacle for aspects of modern/ism that only serves to complicate our use of it as a comfortable historical tool 'solving' the problem of the modern. Descriptions of the postmodern generally begin with an apology for missing it: the *Stanford Encyclopedia of Philosophy* begins its substantial entry on postmodernism with the disclaimer: 'that postmodernism is indefinable is a truism'.[7]

Where did this curious term come from? The word 'postmodern' was first used in the 1870s: art critic John Watkins Chapman invented the word in order to provide an alternative to French Impressionism; he called it 'a Postmodern style of painting', by which he meant a return to classicism. By the early 20th century, in a completely different context but continuing to respond to the impossibility to accept a unified modernism, an article assessing changes in attitudes toward religion in the philosophical review *The Hibbert Journal* asserted that

> the raison d'etre of Post-Modernism is to escape from the double-mind-edness of Modernism by being thorough in its criticism, by extending it to religion as well as theology, to Catholic feeling as well as to Catholic tradition.[8]

Rudolf Pannwitz used the 'post-modern' – now not a name for a unique phenomenon but a description of a condition – in 1917 to designate a culture increasingly oriented toward concepts rather than practices; Pannwitz's 'post-modern' echoes Nietzsche's 1880s withering condemnation of modernity as terminally nihilistic; this condition would, Pannwitz claims, require a 'post-human' to overcome the dilemma.[9] By the 1920s, the term was being used to describe new forms of art and music, and by the 1940s it had spread to literature and architecture.

But the idea that *any* epoch is no longer 'modern', according to its own self-assessment, is oxymoronic: all epochs are 'modern' to themselves. Thus, the (and potentially any) 'postmodern' is clearly not 'post', since the modern, and modernism, flow on inexorably. Nonetheless, whether the Modern is defined as following the Industrial Revolution in the early 19th century, or the rise of the capitalist nation state and its art in the latter 19th century, or the artistic revolutions of the beginning of the 20th century,[10] there is a general consensus that a useful distinction can and should be drawn between a work that is modern and one that defies or undermines the apparent unity of modernism. Though it is the usual panacea, clearly the term 'postmodern' is simply not adequate nor accurate. In order for modernism to face that 'enemy within' that Hassan addresses – what he calls its 'indetermanence' – we need to search *inside* the complexity of the modern in order to find its *döppelganger*, its darker Other.

Para-site

If we can call the modern a 'site', however inadequately defined, then the paramodern is its para-site, immanent in and reliant on, but terminally and interminably dangerous to, its 'host'. The immanence of the paramodern *within* the modern separates it from any possible sense of 'post', dislodging chronology in favor of simultaneity, sequence in favor of coincident. The paramodern is an aspect *of* the modern, what Gilles Deleuze in *Pure Imma- nence* refers to as a phenomenon that

> can be distinguished from experience in that it doesn't refer to an object or belong to a subject. It appears therefore as a pure stream of a-subjective consciousness, a pre-reflexive impersonal consciousness, a qualitative duration of consciousness without a self. (25)[11]

For Deleuze, immanence, as the paramodern, is a connective force of universal and perpetual difference; echoing Nietzsche's eternal return, Deleuze's immanence continuously returns *as* difference. This elusive connectivity operates among relations, never identities; Deleuze's sense of difference echoes Jacques Derrida's *différance*, (mis)spelled to indicate that *this* difference operates in space *and* time, as difference and deferral. Thus, Deleuze, like Derrida, distinguishes (modern) Hegelian dialectics, relying on a transcendental principle of negation-in-unification, from (paramodern) Nietzschean perspectivity, which embraces negation but interrogates it affirmatively. The paramodern, as immanence, is multiplicity-at-the-origin, 'unity'-*as*-difference.

The *site* of the 'modern' is chimerical, and if the paramodern is its parasite, an aesthetio-narrative strategy functioning as the *différance* of modernity itself, then it emerges at the very moment[12] the Modernist (capital 'M', the formal designation of the category 'Modernist') strategies of form, genre, determinacy, grafting, and originality emerge as an *accompaniment*,[13] in a larger textual and musical sense, to the 'modern'. This sense of accompaniment, of going with, is what Heraclitus calls 'flow', a 'graphting' or splicing suspended between the semiotic and the organic, between writing and 'art' (Barker 214ff.).

It is Nietzsche who best orchestrates the paradoxes of the paramodern, which he refers to as the 'overabundant development of intermediary forms; atrophy of types' in which 'traditions break off, schools'.[14] Nietzsche treats the paramodern aspect of language, and indeed of thought itself, as performative; for Nietzsche, philosophy is performance theory. He formulates his play with and in the ironic form of a quasi-equation:

$$\text{non-dialectical hyperbolic 'intermediary'} + \text{hypobolic 'atrophy'} = \text{'}\textit{modernity}\text{'}$$

In this equation, the 'strategic' paramodern occupies the place of the +.

In an article in *Open Letter,* I approached the paramodern in these terms:

> While Kant and Hegel might declare that the world has been seduced by the gross error of radical subjectivity, the free fall of the unconscious, producing the videated image, undermines and disorients the logocentricity of Modernist metaphysics and its inherent cogitocentricity. The paradoxical juxtaposition of hegemonic codes we generally call Modernism and Postmodernism prompts yet another assault on the chronology inherent in that 'Post' of the Postmodern.[15]

'Para' is not and, in fact, obviates the problematics of 'post'; it is the interrogative *shadow* of the enemy poised within the modern, born not *of* but *with* modernity's *angst*, its indeterminacy, its inherent chimerical anomie. The paramodern calls attention to paradoxical juxtapositions and parallel strategies of textual construction, *textus ex machina* – a constructed, ghostly work presenting itself as a rhetorical tool and simulacrum. This kind of presentation is clearly adumbrated in the construction and 'contents' of Nietzsche's *Thus Spake Zarathustra*; Samuel Beckett's postwar prose and drama; Maurice Blanchot's many texts, whose genres remain disparate and whose meanings remain undecidable; the novels of Dave Eggars or Douglas Coupland; and numerous other works of art in a variety of genres. Their chief characteristics: the paramodern is *parodic*, interrogating textual strategies, par-odic in precisely the Greek sense of the *paros odos*, a turning-aside-from or running-parallel-to (in fact, parody is always para-sitic, whether paramodern or not). Like all parasites, the paramodern requires a host in order to exist. Identifying the paramodern strategy requires the reader/viewer to *stand aside* in order to view the strategy at work. When Nietzsche begins his short, revolutionarily philosophical 1872 essay 'On Truth and Lie in an Extra-Moral Sense' with 'once upon a time' – in the form of a fairy tale or fable – he is engaging the *form* 'fable' as laminated onto a fundamental philosophical insight (the claim is that 'knowing' is a myth perpetrated by humans and on ourselves, enabling us to occupy our 'rightful,' though utterly specious, place in the cosmos), then onto a brief children's story about 'clever beasts'.[16] Nietzsche's paradigm-changing strategy is an exemplar of the paramodern strategy of lamination concealed in plain sight. As Alphonso Lingis, in his commentary on Nietzsche, indicates, this strategy of the paramodern is, in fact, what he calls 'the force behind all forms':

> It is not an essence; it is neither structure, telos, nor meaning, but continual sublation of all telos, transgression of all ends, production of all concordant and contradictory meanings, interpretations, valuations. It is the chaos, the primal fund of the unformed … which precedes the forms and makes them possible as well as transitory.[17]

In fact, what is being described in 'On Truth and Lie' only clarifies itself *as Nietzsche writes it and we read it*: the forces (*treiben*) Nietzsche initially designates as 'Dionysian' and 'Apollinian', presented as a dialectical opposition, increasingly 'collapse' upon themselves and each other, forming a *unified set* of oppositions, folded (now) within what Nietzsche then simply calls the Dionysian. Here, Nietzsche is referring to what Heraclitus calls 'the counter-thrust' that para-doxically brings un-likes together such that 'from tones at variance comes perfect attunement', as an interrogation *in difference* and *as conflict*. For Heraclitus, as for Nietzsche, '"perfect attunement" is possible only in … art's *étrangeté*' (*Autoaesthetics* 223), what Nietzsche calls *entsagung*, resignation to the existential reality of the paramodern *within* language. This claim regarding truth and language (i.e. idea and form) is consistent throughout Nietzsche's thinking; no aspect of humanity is exempt from its reach, since 'humanity' as such is a product and a function of (*différant*) language, constructed within the terminological framework and on the textual stage we build for ourselves. In the world of paramodern play, 'we' even (perhaps especially) regard all metaphysical qualities, such as morality, as constructions:

> Moral judgment is never to be taken literally: as such it never contains anything but nonsense. But as semiotics it remains of incalculable value: it reveals, to the informed man at least, the most precious realities of cultures and inner worlds which did not know enough to 'understand' themselves. Morality is merely sign-language, merely symptomatology: one must already know what it is about to derive profit from it.[18]

Only as a sign system – as difference – is language finally to be 'understood': as the ineluctable gateway to the paramodern. When Nietzsche declares that 'those Greeks were superficial – out of profundity!', that they 'stop courageously at the surface', he is indicating precisely the fundamental lamination through which language relates to the paramodern.[19]

In this context, the paramodern, in myriad forms, avoids the baggage of the postmodern, solving the problem Hassan laid out for us, since unlike the postmodern it is predicated not on unities but on what Nietzsche calls 'abysses'. These atomic tensions open among and traverse 'layers' of language and experience that, as laminations, are cross-vectoral, perpetually *playing* in the field of meaning-making and, given that, as Derrida says, 'every process of signification is a formal play of differences; that is, of traces',[20] this play consists of 'syntheses and referrals ... constituted on the basis of the trace within it of the other elements of the chain or system', interwoven as a 'textile produced only in the transformation of another text', 'traces of traces'. Like the previous sentence, the paramodern manifests itself as complex, layered, anxious and ironic.

Para-doxa

Paramodern textuality is an effect of traces and transformations. As a strategy without (*hors de*) a system, it is chimerical.[21] Nietzsche's quasi-messianic, poetic prose in *Thus Spake Zarathustra* and his play with cross-vectoral fragmentation in *Human, All-too-Human* and numerous other texts lay the groundwork for Derrida's 'economy of traces', and his incursions into *différance*. Derrida's texts themselves, most notably *Glas* and *The Post Card*, are quintessential linguistic and visual performances, as is the multiply ironic *Jacques Derrida*, in which the philosopher/poet and his colleague Geoff Bennington write (non-)parallel texts across a 315-page dotted horizontal line that transforms Derrida's 'own' autobiographical[22] (sub)text into a book-length footnote entitled

> Circumfession, Fifty-nine periods and periphrases *written in a sort of internal margin, between Geoffrey Bennington's book and work in preparation (January 1989 – April 1990)*

A text consisting of fifty-nine numbered sections, each of which is a multi-page sentence (remember that a 'sentence,' as the basic building block of meaning in linear languages, ends in a 'period', the grammatical mark indicating the 'period' of the sentence). Thus, fifty-nine periods. The text performs itself as a *paraphrase*, in that the two narratives run side by side, literally parallel to each other on the page, and each consists of phrases (*phrase* is 'sentence' in French; the text consists of parallel sentences). 'Para-phrase' in English means 'to say in other, different words'; what is being performed in the ironically titled *Jacques Derrida* is paraphrase as a writing 'around', as in 'around a corner', detouring or deviating.

Samuel Beckett's fiction and poetry from the beginning of his writing in the late 1930s interrogate the relationship between visibility, as the practice and the idea of image-making, and its framing, in the form of actual image construction. Beckett's paramodern construction, his *poiesis*, shows us the problematics of making or *producing* laminated narrative. Beckett's central paramodern trope, 'I can't go on, I'll go on', the figure at the crossroads of what has been referred to as 'Beckettian time', is the oxymoronic '*both A and B*', insofar as '*both A and B*' is itself yet another oxymoron, since its 'and' is both 'and' and 'but'. Beckett's paramodern is a function of the sublime excess at the oxymoronic heart of language. His are stories about the (im)possibility of telling stories, as in the 'texts for nothing' on which Beckett was working when, to take a short break from their aridity, he wrote *Waiting for Godot*. At the heart of the final 'text for nothing' (number 13) we find

> Whose voice, no one's, there is no one, there's a voice without a mouth … there is nothing but a voice murmuring a trace. A trace, it wants to leave a trace, yes, like air leaves among the leaves, among the grass, among the sand, it's with that it would make a life, but soon it will be the end, it won't be long now … there will be silence.[23]

Beckett's ubiquitous oxymorons, messageless messianisms, voiceless voices, bottomless ditches, unfinished finishes, like Nietzsche's fable of the clever beast who invented knowing, are echoed in Derrida's para-auto-biographical text whose title is his 'own name', the book performing 'in the role of' Jacques Derrida, as all autobiographies (literally 'the self-written life') purport to do, even though in this case the 'circumfession' is in many ways a circumlocution. Derrida talks about the fact that he writes 'around' Beckett, not able to address Beckett's work directly, as one of those writers 'whose texts make the limits of our language tremble':

> He writes … texts which are both too close to me and too distant for me even to be able to 'respond' to them … A certain nihilism is both interior to metaphysics (the final fulfillment of metaphysics, Heidegger would say) and then, already, beyond. With Beckett in particular, the two possibilities are in the greatest possible proximity and competition. He is a nihilist and he is not a nihilist.[24]

And yet … The paramodern nihilist is always what Derrida calls a 'revenant', a spectral figure returning but never returned, afloat on the brink of un-inscription. At the opening of Beckett's *Endgame*, following Clov's pantomime (which is itself a voiceless voice), Clov begins to speak, and begins the play, with:

> CLOV (*fixed gaze, tonelessly*):
> Finished, it's finished, nearly finished, it must be nearly finished.
> (*Pause.*)
> Grain upon grain, one by one, and one day, suddenly, there's a heap,
> a little heap, the impossible heap.
> (*Pause.*)

Clov, the nail (*clou* in French) in the coffin of meaning in *Endgame*, split (cloven) between silent gesture and empty speech, begins the play like a revenant returning from another dimension in and through the heaped, incantatory repetition of his ironic *opening* word, 'finished', which then detours from its simple quasi-certitude to absolute conditionality: 'finished' to 'it's finished' to 'nearly finished' to 'it must be nearly finished', as though the figure (both on stage and as figure of speech), which Beckett's stage direction describes as 'toneless' (which is, of course, for spoken language, impossible) in his/its intonation of his (non-) characterological presence; Clov, as the paramodern *döppelganger* of a theatrical character, enacts the abyss between silence and speech. The 'I can't go on. I'll go on' of *The Unnamable* discovers its visual parallel in the non-conclusion of *Waiting for Godot*:

> VLADIMIR: Let's go.
> (They do not move.)
> CURTAIN

The play does not *end*, it *stops*, if a suspension of action without any sense of finality, can be called a 'stop', let alone an 'end'.

Beyond even Beckett, however, in no text is the paramodern more in evidence than in those of the little-known French writer and theorist Maurice Blanchot. Whereas Beckett buries the nature of storytelling 'beneath' the arid surface of the text and the play-text, in Blanchot's *The Writing of the Disaster* and *Le pas au-delà*, translated as *The Step (Not) Beyond*, but whose title is untranslatable, Blanchot works (or 'unworks', through what he calls *désœuvrement*) across the surface of the page from fragment to fragment, such that the 'disappointment at work' in each fragment of his writing

> is their airless drift, the indication [being] that, neither unifiable nor consistent, they accommodate a certain array of marks ... destined partly to the blank that separates them.[25]

The paramodern, as para-site and parasite, mirrors Blanchot's declaration that although 'reading is anguish', since 'any text, however important, or amusing, or interesting it may be (and the more engaging it seems to be), is empty – at bottom it doesn't exist; you have to cross an abyss, and if you do not jump, you do not comprehend' (*Disaster* 10). But it is not only reading that produces anguish. The paramodern strategies of Beckett, Blanchot and others have 'entered the culture' as a particular kind of irony.[26]

The paramodern, to return to Hassan's problem with which we began, is perhaps the 'better name' we might apply to the 'decadence' embedded within and endemic to language, indeed in semiosis in general. The traps of the so-called 'postmodern', let alone of 'postmodern*ism*', which retroactively entrap the modern in time and history, can be escaped if we see *différance* in its formative state of construction, produced as language in the broadest sense (including gesture, sound, signs in general) is produced. The most interesting conundrum lurking in Hassan's question is that if the paramodern were to become or to be seen and regarded as an 'independent' *strategy* within a text, theatre piece, film, etc., as a parasite no longer having access to a host (i.e. to a 'modern' or a 'modernism'), could – and *how* could – it survive? Perhaps the greatest paradox of the paramodern is its dependency on the energy of a host characterologically incapable of knowing of the parasite's existence. That is, in an epoch of ubiquitous irony, can the seemingly supreme paramodern continue to exist? And does the existence of the paramodern indicate that the modern remains robust? Such paradoxes will continue to take new forms as 21st-century performance, textual and paratextual, continues to evolve.

Notes

1 In *Paracriticisms* (Champaign: University of Illinois Press, 1975), Hassan confesses uncertainty about what he will later refer to as the postmodern turn (*The Postmodern Turn*, Columbus: Ohio State University Press, 1987):

> I am not certain what genre these seven pieces make. I call them paracriticism: essays in language, traces of the times, fictions of the heart. Literature is part of their substance, but their critical edge is only one of many edges in the mind. I would not protest if they were denied the name of criticism. Perhaps I should simply say: in these essays I write neither as critic nor scholar – nor yet impersonate the poet ... but try to find my voice in the singular forms that speculation sometimes requires. (Hassan 1975: ix)

He thus comes close to the designation I am ascribing to a phenomenon similar to Hassan's problematic 'postmodern'; 'mine' is also a 'paracriticism'. It could also be called a 'para-performance', in that the performance style, like the theatre, of any epoch both mirrors and foreshadows the general culture of which it is a part.

2 In all likelihood, this is not what Protagoras meant by his famous declaration.

3 Indeed, the contemporary idea of 'character', and certainly of 'a character' as we use it today, emerges from this new sense of inner dynamics we see most clearly in the Romantic poets and artists of the early 19th century.

4 Georg Wilhelm Friedrich Hegel, 'Symbolic Classic, and Romantic,' in *Dramatic Theory and Criticism: Greeks to Grotowski*, ed. Bernard F. Dukore, New York: Holt, Reinhart & Winston, 1974, 526–32.

5 Theodor Adorno, *Minima Moralia: Reflections from Damaged Life*, trans. Dennis Redmond, Creative Commons: Prism Key Press, 2005, 218.

6 Peter Childs, *Modernism*, New York: Routledge, 2008, 17. A useful, and more thorough, introduction to the modern and Modernism can be found at www.saylor.org/site/wp-content/uploads/2011/05/Modernism.pdf.

7 Gary Aylesworth, 'Postmodernism,' *The Stanford Encyclopedia of Philosophy* (summer 2013 edn), ed. Edward N. Zalta, http://plato.stanford.edu/archives/sum2013/entries/postmodernism/. It wasn't until 1939 that Arnold Toynbee used the term 'post-modern' in its current sense, as a defining signifier for a particular set of aspects of our epoch; in Toynbee's view, 'our own Post-Modern Age has been inaugurated by the general war of 1914–1918'.

8 J.M. Thompson, 'Post-Modernism,' *The Hibbert Journal*, 12.4, July 1914, 733.

9 Rudolf Pannwitz, *Die Krisis der europäischen Kultur*, Nürnberg 1917. The advent of the 'post-human', what is now popularly referred to as marking the end of the 'anthropocene', would also entail returning the earth to microbes or other creatures – or to machines. Either way, distinctions such as 'modern', 'postmodern' and 'paramodern' would cease to exist.

10 Many claim that Shakespeare is modern, and Arthur Kroker in *The Postmodern Scene* makes the case that St Augustine is the first modern.

11 Gilles Deleuze, *Pure Immanence*, trans. Anne Boyman, New York: Zone Books, 2001, 24.

12 See Kant's *Third Critique* for the sense of 'moment' intended here.

13 See Stephen Barker, *Autoaesthetics: Strategies of the Self after Nietzsche*, Atlantic Highlands, NJ: Humanities Press International, 1992, 214.

14 Friedrich Nietzsche, *The Will to Power*, trans. and ed. Walter Kaufmann, New York: Random House, 1967, 78.

15 Stephen Barker, 'Free Fall?: The Vertigo of the Videated Image,' *Open Letter*, Eighth Series, No. 1. Fall 1991, 19–36.

16 Friedrich Nietzsche, 'On Truth and Lie in an Extra-Moral Sense,', in *Philosophy and Truth: Selections from Nietzsche's Notebooks of the Early 1870s*, trans. and ed. Daniel Breazeale, Atlantic Heights, NJ: Humanities Press International, 1979, 79–100, 79.

17 Alphonso Lingis, 'The Will to Power,' in *Nietzsche: The World as Will to Power*, ed. Daniel Conway, New York: Routledge, 1998, 149–74, 150.

18 Friedrich Nietzsche, *Twilight of the Idols*, trans. Thomas Common, Mineola, NY: Dover Philosophical Classics, 2004, 25.

19 Friedrich Nietzsche, *The Gay Science*, trans. Walter Kaufmann, New York: Vintage Books, 1974, 38.

20 Jacques Derrida, *Positions*, trans. Alan Bass, Chicago: University of Chicago Press, 1981, 26.

21 The doubled idea of 'without' as *not-having* and 'without' as *outside* of is fertile paramodern soil. To be without a system is not to have one and to have one but be outside – parallel to – it.

22 Since we are still addressing Hassan's problem, note that Chapter 7 of *The Postmodern Turn*, a 'defense against the peril of autobiography', is entitled 'Parabiography', and confronts Nietzsche's self-referential texts thus:

> The Nietzschean self may be a 'fiction,' an empty space where various personages come to mingle, squabble, and depart; yet it remains a 'fiction' more dense than its desires – including self-annihilation – than any neutron star … Whatever the self may be, its earthly form reveals a fierce intricacy of asseveration. (149)

23 Samuel Beckett, *Stories and Texts for Nothing*, New York: Grove Press, 1967, 137.

24 Jacques Derrida, 'This Strange Institution Called Literature: An Interview with Jacques Derrida,' in *Jacques Derrida: Acts of Literature*, trans. Derrick Attridge, New York: Routledge, 1992, 33–75, 60–1.

25 Maurice Blanchot, *The Writing of the Disaster*, trans. Ann Smock, Lincoln, NB: University of Nebraska Press, 1995, 58.

26 An unexpected recent example of yet another kind of paramodern can be found in Jonathan Franzen's recent novel *Freedom*, in which, constraining himself both directly and ironically to echo *War and Peace*, of which Franzen's book is a paramodern descendent, he para-constrains himself to end the book with a wholly ironic 'happy ending'.

4   Digital Culture[1]

Sarah Bay-Cheng

Few concepts have been more influential over the past 15 years than the advance of computer technologies. As many have written before (too numerous to fully recount here), nearly every aspect of contemporary society has been affected. The earliest use of 'digital' in a computational sense was first recorded in U.S. Patent 2,207,537 (1961) for an electronic communications system that enabled the 'transmission of direct current digital impulses over a long line'.[2] Little more than 50 years later, a search for the phrase 'digital culture' registers many thousands of discrete citations.[3] The combination of digital, or computational, technologies within society and culture has been rigorously explored by scholars throughout the humanities. In *Digital Culture*, Charlie Gere argued for a reading of the digital as formative in our thinking about how we process culture: 'Digital refers not just to the effects and possibilities of a particular technology. It defines and encompasses the ways of thinking and doing that are embodied within that technology, and which make its development possible.'[4] More recently, N. Katherine Hayles has extended this consideration in *How We Think: Digital Media and Contemporary Technogenesis* (2012) to consider the effect within humanities research and scholarship, and her work joins many others exploring the impact of the digital humanities within academia and the effects well beyond college classrooms.[5]

Within theatre and performance studies, most studies have focused on the effects of new technologies within individual performances and how we perceive them. Andy Lavender's 'Digital Culture' in *Mapping Intermediality in Performance* (2010) provides an excellent overview, arguing for the ways in which new technologies shift the patterns and methods in performance practices,[6] one in a growing body of literature focused on understanding how performing artists across diverse genre – theatre, performance art, dance, installation, media, music, games, bioart – incorporate new technologies. The last 10 years have been particularly fruitful and we can point to a number of influential texts that have shaped our understanding of what Steve Dixon broadly referred to as 'digital performance'.[7]

Few of these, however, engage with the most recent evolutions of digital culture, namely social media and mobile computing, and there is still surprisingly little work on how performance studies methodologies are shaped by digital culture. Jon McKenzie's *Perform Or Else* (2001) remains one of the few to consider these effects, which he outlines as three interconnected threads within a larger theory of performance in the 21st century: efficacy, efficiency and effectiveness.[8] Jason Farman's *Mobile Interface Theory* (2012) offers an important insight to mobile technologies as both performative and embodied, although here we see performance studies applied to the understanding of locative media but not necessarily the reverse. Few collections on performance studies as a changing practice mention digital technology at all. This omission is striking in light of recent critical attention to the digital humanities and platform studies in other fields, where the term 'performance' occurs regularly. Lev Manovich, for instance, observes: 'In software culture, we no longer have "documents," "works," "messages" or recordings in twentieth-century terms. Instead of fixed documents ... we now interact with dynamic software performances.'[9] Elsewhere, historian Tom Scheinfeldt writes of digital technologies as part of the 'performative humanities'.[10] While we see numerous studies *of* performance and new technologies, very few reflect a change in the practice of performance studies as a mode of inquiry functioning *within and as* digital culture.

How then might we formulate a shift in our thinking about the role of digital media in and as performance studies?

Cesare Casarino's essay, 'Three Theses on the Life-Image (Deleuze, Cinema, Bio-politics)', offers one path through these relations of media and performance and how these dynamics affect performance studies practices.[11] Writing partly in response to the Guy Debord's critique in the *Society of the Spectacle* and Gilles Deleuze's arguments about representation in *The Logic of Sense*, among others, Casarino cites a prior conversation with Antonio Negri, who argues that:

> In the world of immateriality in which we live, reproduction – which is the first possible definition of biopolitics – and production can no longer be distinguished from each other. Biopolitics becomes fully realized precisely when production and reproduction are one and the same, that is, when production is conducted primarily and directly through language and social exchange.[12]

Responding to Negri, Casarino takes up this argument of biopolitics as a way of articulating the relation between contemporary capitalism and cinematic representation. For Casarino, the collapse between production and reproduction coalesces around and through post-Fordist capitalism, that is, an economy driven not by the manufacture and material exchange of commodities but by information and affect, what Paolo Virno calls 'the commerce of potential as potential'.[13] A particular marker of this economy is what Casarino calls the 'life-image', a function of the split between material life and immaterial labor power. Replacing 'life' in this construct is the 'lifestyle', a desirable but unattainable fetish object to be consumed, and to which labor power (newly divorced from life itself) is sacrificed and exploited. For Casarino, this manifests in what he calls the 'spectacularization' of AIDS as a reactionary attack on 1960s radicalism in general and Debord's critique of the spectacle, in particular.

This collapse has implications for performance studies. What happens if we acknowledge that, at least in the digital domain, the distinctions between production and reproduction have broken down? What does this mean for the animating theories of representation over the past decade – that perpetual debate often referred to as the 'liveness problem'?[14] If biopolitics constitutes itself primarily in and through social exchange, might we call this performance? And if so, where does performance studies fit within the landscape of biopolitics?

The immateriality that Negri associates with contemporary culture has a long history that we can locate perhaps first in the development of cybernetics in the 1940s, but which more fully emerges in the late 1960s and early 70s. This emergence is not linked solely to cybernetic systems, but also to the pervasiveness of those systems and their intersection with (and eventually replacement of) lived experience. While Debord may have railed against the society of the spectacle in 1967, we should remember that he lodged his attack primarily against the representation of media images through cinema and television, against what he called 'the technology of the mass dissemination of images'.[15] The willing participation of people – of society – in and through these images constituted the newest and most dangerous form of false consciousness. Yet, his response to this perceived threat was not only to write a book, but also to make a film, a film that you can now watch (like so many documents of the 20th-century's avant-garde) on YouTube.

While Debord continues to garner important attention for his early (and we must admit 'spectacular') critique of image-based late capitalism, as compelling is Marshall McLuhan's assessment of life in the age of satellites in *From Cliché to Archetype* (1970). What is striking about this book is that it surpasses, or rather envelopes and expands, McLuhan's earlier notion of the global village. McLuhan saw contemporary life as not only a global village – that is, social networks formulated laterally on the ground – but also as the product of a global theatre:

Since Sputnik and the satellites, the planet is enclosed in a manmade environment that ends 'Nature' and turns the globe into a repertory theater to be programmed. Shakespeare at the Globe mentioning 'All the world's a stage, and all the men and women merely players' (*As You Like It*, Act II, Scene 7) has been justified by recent events in ways that would have struck him as entirely paradoxical.[16]

McLuhan described the effects of this global, satellite stage as having particular impact on the youth, concluding that: 'The results of living inside a proscenium arch of satellites is that the young now accept the public spaces of the earth as role-playing areas. Sensing this, they adopt costumes and roles and are ready to "do their thing" everywhere.'[17] Sometimes reduced to the pithy 'after Sputnik there is no nature, only art', we might also understand his meaning here as, after satellites there is no living, only performance. Or rather, no *public* living, since McLuhan understands this global performance as emerging in specifically public spaces. In a book published several years later (1977), Susan Sontag first demonstrated the fragility of the public domain as such. Seeming to follow both Debord and Walter Benjamin's analysis of history in the excess of images, Sontag points to the power of representation to detach from politics (not unlike Casarino's argument) and to embed the repressed political in the ostensibly private realm of images. She argues:

> As we become further detached from politics, there is more and more free space to fill up with exercises of sensibility such as cameras afford. One of the effects of the newer camera technology (video, instant movies) has been to turn even more of what is done with camera in private to narcissistic uses – that is, to self-surveillance.[18]

Casarino's notion of biopolitics, through the lens of McLuhan's global satellites and Sontag's notion of self-surveillance, provides a compelling and disturbing context for analyzing contemporary social media. Though initially a product of it, online social exchange has evolved into the epitome of a post-Fordist economy based on the circulation of information, affect, potential and animated by images and self-surveillance. While we once feared Big Brother of 1984, we seem to have chosen to live in Aldous Huxley's *Brave New World*, a world in which the power of vision from above – the *sur*-veillance – pales in comparison with the data-mining from below and the self-extraction of biopolitical resources. Tracking the placement of our bodies in physical space (through CCTV, hidden cameras, external GPS devices) is not nearly as productive to contemporary capitalism as the aggregate of our digital movements, our 'likes', our 'friends', our bodily data, continually captured and wirelessly uploaded (e.g. Garmin training devices, Zeo sleep-monitoring systems, and our own enabled self-tracking GPS devices, also known as mobile phones).

Disturbingly, we participate in – even seek out – these modes of exploitation. When we upload, project and transmit our biodata, we trade our bioinformatics for … what? Badges, points, images, status? In an economy of social exchange, we are encouraged to provide biodigital assets (real physical measures that have hard currency value) for immaterial rewards. Is this not, to use Casarino's terms, the trade of labor power and life for 'life-style'? Another way to look at this is as a perversion of Pierre Bourdieu's notion of 'cultural capital', once the point of access of art to power, now cheapened to immaterial status points in an online forum. We give up everything for what is truly nothing, Benjamin's dwarf in the machine grown to impossible proportions. In the same paragraph in which Sontag identifies the effect of video as narcissistic self-surveillance, she further speculates that: 'Our inclination to treat character as equivalent to behavior makes more acceptable a widespread public installation of the mechanized regard from the outside provided by cameras.'[19] Although there is usually a brief concern when new surveillance cameras are installed, or we hear disturbing reports of drone activity in our neighborhoods, even the revelations of Edward Snowden and the massive National Security Agency's PRISM data collection program could not persuade the American public to change the way we share our private information online.[20] We have no fear of our own cameras, even in the wake of Edward Snowden's revelations on the NSA. On Facebook alone, over 200 million images are uploaded every day, with over 6 billion new images added each month. According to a Facebook engineer answering questions on Quora, there were over 90 billion images on the site in August 2011, making it the largest inventory of images in the world.[21] In a related move, Microsoft developed Lifebrowser – an embedded digital device capable of recording and rendering searchable all of an individual's online data, including searches, downloads and shared information. Such searches will allow the user (and potentially others) to analyze patterns of online behavior.[22] Or, consider Microsoft's 2004 patent 6,754,472, which protects the design for a method to convert human energy into a supply for electronic devices.[23] Even more troubling, perhaps, is the active patenting of the human genetic sequencing by international corporations.[24] The new iPhone 5s records an individual user's fingerprint for the purposes of unlocking the phone.[25]

Our daily devices – networked, biological, constantly self-monitoring and disseminating – have produced a fundamental confusion between not only production and reproduction and the public and private, but also between the biological and the technological. In an article I co-authored with Amy Strahler Holzapfel, we argued that theatre was not a body (in contrast to longstanding, popular metaphors) but a network. Now perhaps this distinction is less significant in present contexts.[26] In digital culture, our most private space, such as the area just in front of our eyes or within our own cells, has become the most public. This media landscape – for it is still, more or less, a mediated environment – exceeds what modernists such as Debord, McLuhan or Sontag ever imagined. Each of these writers, though eerily prescient in their own way, conceived of imaging within a discrete and unidirectional medium – cinema and mass media, satellites and video. Sent from producer – whether good or evil – to the passive, but hopefully critical receiver. We now know that contemporary media – particularly, the ironically titled 'social media' – absorb and embrace all these simultaneously and in every possible direction. And, more importantly, because such media networks are inherently social, they are perversely organic, capable of reproducing independently of any single agent or location. Hence, the proliferation of biological terms – e.g. viruses, memes – to account for digital functioning. Your typical social media site is both a diary and a megaphone, as loud and public as Times Square and as individual and intimate as your DNA. This ubiquitous, performance landscape *is* biopolitics. This is the moment, to return to Casarino and Negri, when 'production and reproduction are one and the same, that is, when production is conducted primarily and directly through language and social exchange'.[27]

This environment holds a number of significant implications for performance studies. Most salient perhaps is the idea that the distinction between reproduction and production has eroded. This distinction between ontology and reproduction – an argument that has animated so much of our recent theoretical attention in performance and theatre studies – no longer serves a contemporary understanding of relations among media and liveness, or between commodity and performance. Although this was obviously a compelling framework, the always migrating and mutating media have slipped, morphed and memed their way out of the 'liveness' construct into something just as interesting and much more dangerous. The question is not whether performance can be commodified; commodification itself now eludes materiality and instead takes on the hallmarks of performance – ephemeral, relational, transactional. Rather than serve as a potential political efficacy, performance functions in service to Casarino's lifestyle that circulates through social exchange. If we can set aside the distinction between performance production and media reproduction, performance studies might be able to respond to the rapid shifts of media, performance and politics, the fusion of which threatens to displace critical action and usurp all prior modes of resistance.

Whither resistance?

Some have located exceptions to this model in aurality, such as DJ Spooky's work, or in radical resistance to image, as in Derek Jarman's *Blue*, a 78-minute film showing only a blue field with accompanying audio. But even these gestures inevitably get recycled back into social media, which continually subsumes any and all image and audio production into its own ever expanding network. This is not an entirely novel mode of power production, but it is a peculiarly effective one. Although Michel Foucault argued that 'as soon as there is a power relation, there is a possibility of resistance', the biopolitical animated by self-surveillance and the translation of all lived experience (even the involuntary actions of the body itself) into disseminations of performance make such possibilities hard to identify and even harder to practice.[28] One might propose to go 'off the grid', but as drone attacks in remote villages (as well as closer to home) and pervasive satellite and ubiquitous data surveillance make clear, the grid is ubiquitous and inescapable. Indeed, it is so omnipresent that we might contend that nature – as an unaffected, digitally absent space – no longer exists. That is, it is impossible to locate a 'natural' space on earth independent from, or unaffected by, digital technology.

Both Debord and Sontag feared the political implications for excess images in capitalist society: 'The freedom to consume a plurality of images and goods is equated with freedom itself. The narrowing of free political choice to free economic consumption requires the unlimited production and consumption of images.'[29] Sontag's critique has been taken up in recent considerations of 'slacktavism', social activism reduced to simple and, often ineffectual, gestures such as 'liking' a social justice movement or reposting a political message via social networks.[30] While youth advocates and digital utopians have been anxious to define such gestures as potentially efficacious, most empirical data suggests that digital gestures have limited if any material effects, and that any political impact fades quickly. More often, such gestures produce a relatively superficial effect, but an outsized emotional affect. To cite only one example, the Youth Participatory Politics Survey Project – a project aimed at demonstrating the power of youth political movements online – opened the Executive Summary of its 2011 report with a compelling example of digital-political efficacy:

> Over a period of just three days in October 2011, 75,000 people signed a petition started by 22-year-old Molly Katchpole on Change.org to protest Bank of America's proposed $5.00 debit card fee. Ultimately, over 300,000 people signed and more than 21,000 pledged to close their Bank

of America accounts. The movement attracted national attention, and Bank of America reversed its decision to charge customers.[31]

The sensation of action and impact is profoundly underwhelming in comparison with the limited significance of the gesture itself. Yet, this is praised as contemporary participatory politics.

Or, consider the global Occupy movement, which in 2011 was hailed as the harbinger of global youth empowerment – a nonhierarchical, political challenge – and has since largely dissipated into online archives and forum debates. In a January 8, 2014 call to arms on the political site Daily Kos, Ray Pensador called for action to reanimate the Occupy movement in opposition to what he called, 'inverted totalitarianism'. His aim was specific:

> On Monday, January 27th, 2014, starting at 10:00 A.M. all people of good will who consider themselves part of the Occupy Wall Street movement will show up at specific locations at government and business nerve centers around the country.[32]

As of February 20, 2014, I can find no mention of any such action either in news publication databases or relevant online sites.[33] Appearances of revolutionary movements such as Occupy and the Arab Spring may be at best illusory and at worst deceptive. We should beware what Casarino defines as the 'paradox of bio-politics'. Dispersed

> throughout the myriad and ubiquitous networks of production; it finds its best determination in the absolute indetermination of the limits separating it from production; it is most discernible when it is not discernible from production – and when both reign omnipresent.[34]

That is, the possibility that these mediated protests, communicated through digital networks, become the very tools to limit real political change.

Social media, for all its apparent and real political efficacy, is performance, but it is a performance of mediation – self-replicating copies without originals – deeply imbricated within post-Fordist capitalist exchange. Critics have repeatedly drawn on various metaphors to explain this digital context, variously economic and ecological, but it is clearly both: the sine qua non of the biopolitical, a theoretical model that does not distinguish between life and mediation, nor between experience and image. Instead, we are in, to return to Sontag, the 'image-world', in which 'images have extraordinary powers to determine our demands upon reality and are themselves coveted substitutes for firsthand experience'; they are 'indispensible to the health of the economy, the stability of the polity, and the pursuit of private happiness'.[35] Given this state of affairs, perhaps it is the mission of 21st-century performance studies to recover the antagonism from the perversely (de)politicized, spectacular performance.

Notes

1 This essay draws on writing developed through invited lectures at ATHE's Performance Studies Focus Group pre-conference (2012), the University of Toronto Festival of Original Theatre (2013), and the University of Zagreb (2013). I also received the opportunity to discuss these ideas at length with colleagues through the support of the University of Vienna (2012). I am grateful to all the colleagues and students who provided me with generous feedback and ideas in the development of this work. I am also indebted to my collaborators in the International Federation for Theatre Research working group on Intermediality in Theatre and Performance, especially Klemens Gruber, Chiel Kattenbelt, Andy Lavender and Robin Nelson.

2 'Digital, n. and adj.,' *OED Online* (Oxford: OUP), accessed February 19, 2014, www.oed.com.gate.lib.buffalo.edu/view/Entry/52611.

3 My institutional library search engine provides nearly 8,000 individual citations, while Google Scholar records over 18,500.

4 Charlie Gere, *Digital Culture* (London: Reaktion Books, 2009), 13.

5 N. Katherine Hayles, *How We Think: Digital Media and Contemporary Technogenesis* (University of Chicago Press, 2012). Since 2002, the online group HĀSTAC (Humanities, Arts, Science, and Technology Alliance and Collaboratory, www.hastac.org) has provided an online resource for exchange and thinking about the impact of new technologies in teaching.

6 Andy Lavender, 'Digital Culture,' in S. Bay-Cheng, C. Kattenbelt, A. Lavender and R. Nelson, eds, *Mapping Intermediality in Performance* (Amsterdam: Amsterdam University Press, 2010), 134.

7 To cite only a few of the most salient examples, see Philip Auslander, *Liveness: Performance in a Mediatized Culture* (New York: Routledge, 1999); Jon McKenzie, *Perform or Else: From Discipline to Performance* (New York: Routledge, 2001); Gabriella Giannachi, *Virtual Theatres : An Introduction* (New York: Routledge, 2004); Matthew Causey, *Theatre and Performance in Digital Culture : From Simulation to Embeddedness* (New York: Routledge, 2006); Freda Chapple and Chiel Kattenbelt, eds, *Intermediality in Theatre and Performance* (Amsterdam: Rodopi, 2006); Steve Dixon, *Digital Performance: A History of New Media in Theater, Dance, Performance Art, and Installation* (Cambridge, MA: MIT Press, 2007); Susan Broadhurst, *Digital Practices: Aesthetic and Neuroesthetic Approaches to Performance and Technology* (Basingstoke: Palgrave Macmillan, 2011); Susan Broadhurst and Josephine Machon, *Performance and Technology: Practices of Virtual Embodiment and Interactivity* (Basingstoke: Palgrave Macmillan, 2011); Jennifer Parker-Starbuck, *Cyborg Theatre: Corporeal/technological Intersections in Multimedia Performance* (Basingstoke: Palgrave Macmillan, 2011); Steve Benford and Gabriella Giannachi, *Performing Mixed Reality* (Cambridge, MA: MIT Press, 2011); Gabriella Giannachi, Nick Kaye and Michael Shanks, *Archaeologies of Presence* (New York: Routledge, 2012).

8 Op. cit., McKenzie, *Perform or Else*.
9 Lev Manovich, *Software Takes Command* (New York: Bloomsbury Academic, 2013), 33.
10 Ibid.
11 Cesare Casarino, 'Three Theses on the Life-Image,' in Jacques Khalip and Robert Mitchell, *Releasing the Image: From Literature to New Media* (Redwood City, CA: Stanford University Press, 2011), 156–69.
12 Cesare Casarino and Antonio Negri, *In Praise of the Common: A Conversation on Philosophy and Politics* (Minneapolis: U of Minnesota Press, 2008), 148.
13 Paolo Virno, *A Grammar of the Multitude: For an Analysis of Contemporary Forms of Life* (Semiotext(e), 2003), 84.
14 Op. cit., Dixon, *Digital Performance*, 115.
15 Guy Debord, *The Society of the Spectacle*, trans. Donald Nicholson-Smith (New York: Zone Books, 1994), 13.
16 Marshall McLuhan, *From Cliché to Archetype* (New York: Viking Press, 1970), 9–10.
17 Ibid., 10.
18 Susan Sontag, *On Photography* (London: Macmillan, 1977), 177. I have written about this elsewhere more extensively. See Sarah Bay-Cheng, '"When This You See": The (Anti) Radical Time of Mobile Self-Surveillance,' *Performance Research* (forthcoming summer 2014).
19 Ibid.
20 Quite the opposite. The global 'Quit Facebook Day' from May 31, 2010 had, as of February 19, 2014, garnered only 40,755 committed Facebook quitters. By comparison, Facebook.com reached 1 billion users in October 2012. According to Pew Research Center survey findings, 17 percent of online adults are on Facebook and half of those users who are not on Facebook live with someone who does. See Aaron Smith, '6 New Facts about Facebook,' *Pew Research Center*, February 3, 2014, www.pewresearch.org/fact-tank/2014/02/03/6-new-facts-about-facebook/.
21 'How Many Photos Are Uploaded to Facebook Each Day?,' *Quora*, accessed February 22, 2014, www.quora.com/permalink/TmkFN4yMB.
22 'Lifebrowser,' http://research.microsoft.com/apps/video/default.aspx?id=159531, accessed February 22, 2014.
23 Lyndsay Williams, William Vablais and Steven N. Bathiche, 'Method and Apparatus for Transmitting Power and Data Using the Human Body,' June 22, 2004, http://patentimages.storage.googleapis.com/pdfs/US6754472.pdf, accessed February 22, 2014. See also Kris Verdonck's performance based on this patent, 'Patent Human Energy' (2007), www.atwodogscompany.org/en/projects/item/168-patent-human-energy.
24 Here, at least, there is some encouraging legal news. In a March 2012 decision, the Supreme Court declared that there should be some limits on patents for diagnostic tests using genetic material. However, corporations are still declaring patents on DNA sequences and are preparing a series of legal challenges to protect their research and development. See Heidi Ledford, 'US Supreme Court Upends Diagnostics Patents,' *Nature* (March 21, 2012), doi:10.1038/nature.2012.10270; Gina Kolata, 'Accord Aims to Create Trove of Genetic Data,' *The New York Times*, June 5, 2013, www.nytimes.com/2013/06/06/health/global-partners-agree-on-sharing-trove-of-genetic-data.html.

25 'iPhone 5s: Using Touch ID,' http://support.apple.com/kb/HT5883, accessed February 22, 2014.

26 Sarah Bay-Cheng and Amy Strahler Holzapfel, 'The Living Theatre: A Brief History of a Bodily Metaphor,' *Journal of Dramatic Theory and Criticism* 25(1) (2010): 9–28.

27 Op. cit., Casarino and Negri, *In Praise of the Common*, 148.

28 Michel Foucault, *Politics, Philosophy, Culture: Interviews and Other Writings, 1977–1984* (London: Routledge, 2013), 123.

29 Op. cit., Sontag, *On Photography*, 178–79.

30 See, for example, Kirk Kristofferson, Katherine White and John Peloza, 'The Nature of Slacktivism: How the Social Observability of an Initial Act of Token Support Affects Subsequent Prosocial Action,' *Journal of Consumer Research* (November 6, 2013): 1149–66, doi:10.1086/674137.

31 Cathy J. Cohen and Joseph Kahne, *Participatory Politics: New Media and Youth Political Action: Executive Summary*, 2011, 1.

32 Ray Penador, 'Occupy Movement Call to Action: The Time Is Now,' www.dailykos.com/story/2014/01/08/1267841/-Occupy-Movement-Call-to-Action-The-Time-is-Now, accessed February 22, 2014.

33 Coincidentally, January 27, 2014 was the same date that activist and folk singer Pete Seeger died.

34 Jacques Khalip and Robert Mitchell, *Releasing the Image: From Literature to New Media* (Redwood City, CA: Stanford University Press, 2011), 159.

35 Op. cit., Sontag, *On Photography*, 153.

5   Misperformance

Marin Blažević and Lada Čale Feldman

Expressed by a term coined with reference to the crowning concept of performance studies on one side, and various discursively well-adjusted, everyday mis-prefixed notions on the other (such as mistake, misunderstanding, misfit, misprision and so on), misperformance is proposed as a concept summarizing and adding to the already existent reflections and performative trials that point to the disturbing and potentially creative factors of failure. Offered as a topic for the 15th annual Performance Studies international (PSi) conference, which took place in Zagreb in June 2009, misperformance was argued to stem from a respectable theoretical genealogy comprising various attempts at destabilizing Western metaphysical dichotomies – from Freudian slips and Austinian misfires to Homi Bhabha's inappropriate signifiers and anomalous representations – with Erving Goffman's 'misframings' and Judith Butler's failed gender constitutions figuring as the most prominent forays in the field. The investigation of *misperformance studies* that was thus ceremoniously initiated now already relies on a discussion embracing several hundreds of conference interventions, as well as numerous different forms of experimental confrontations between theory and practice carried out within the format of so-called *shifts* inaugurated on the mentioned conference as a risky agency-pendant to the provisional conceptual scope of the leading term, as a (mis)performative frame within which to engage with its possible trajectories. An issue on misperformance was published by *Performance Research* 15.2 (2010), and a collection of essays continuing the debate is currently being edited by the authors of this entry. The fate of the concept almost runs the risk of its own easy-going pragmatic over-exploration – based on its assumed semantic flexibility – or, even worse, exhaustion. Nothing, however, could be said to be further removed from its potential and lasting *uncanniness*.

Freud's famous uplifting of an old Victorian notion of 'the uncanny' to the status of 'a master trope' of the 20th century is evoked here because its resonance pertains in many ways to the crucial components of misperformance. To concentrate on failures, non-functionality, futility or inoperativeness, on the inessential, the misguiding, the missing, on accidents, excesses and contingencies of various linguistic, cultural, organizational and political performances implies in fact, paradoxically – as it did for the *uncanny* – to touch upon the very essence of performing: its risky, precarious, unpredictable nature, which initially separated the interests of performance studies from more traditional focuses of theatre studies on all things (seemingly) fixed, from dramatic texts to directorial poetics, from documentary material to rounded histories. No wonder Nicholas Ridout reminds us that 'ontological queasiness' belongs to the very heart of modern theatre: the discomfort with its failure is the most precious origin of its true political value – the acknowledgement of its deeply compromising immersion in material conditions, whether the one concerning its capitalist foundations or the ones pertaining more to its human bodily investment (*cf.* Ridout 2006: 6–9). Misperformance is thus the necessary underside of any reliance on or striving for performance-as-representation: it cracks the mirror of representational illusion, not in the form of Brecht's intentional revealing of the actor's work – the never-to-be seen, repressed content of bourgeois aesthetic pleasure – but rather in the form of the irruption of the awkward or the embarrassing, the enlightening or the shocking reminders of what is at stake when we perform, actors and spectators alike. For, whatever our best intentions with respect to the audience may be, can anyone manage what Joe Kelleher (2010) termed to be spectator's 'infinite misattention'?

Misperformance would grow, however, into quite a misleading idea if it allowed for an uncritical enthusiasm for studying all the wrong tracks that performance could take to, as if the conceptual import of this notion were an irresponsible reveling in human, cultural, institutional, artistic and other fallibilities. If Jon McKenzie (2010) turned from the *Challenger* catastrophe to study natural disasters, it by no means implies that he gave up all hope in human remedies of such almost ungovernable outcomes of some bad environmental choices, but rather that he urges us to refigure the very notion of posthuman condition: above us not only Foucauldian power and Derridean language, but, as John Lennon sings, 'only sky' – and it is dark and gloomy. On the other side, what about cultures that are more predicated upon a completely different dilemma, the one that the Croatian anthropologist Ines Prica (2006) termed 'perform or not'? Are we, in fact, even capable of imagining a (utopian?) society, which would escape or challenge the very pressure to perform? The crucial motivating force here is to explore in which ways failing manages to produce something other than mere error, excess, loss, damage, waste or surplus, whether in cognitive, political or artistic spheres. Misperformance, we surmise, breaks the spell of representation: instead of panicking and avoiding it, can one attempt at inciting and representing it, or would one in that case inevitably end up merely miming it, repeating it, controlling it, engulfing its eventual creative and critical vitality, therefore missing the very misperformativity itself?

The search for *happy* theatrical *misperformatives* can take us all the way back to Stanislavsky (2008: 338) and his appreciation of the 'happy accident'. It is the accident that 'provides one true living note in the midst of the convention-bound theatrical lies' and serves as a 'new creative impetus' (ibid.: 163). In the same cultural and political environment, yet on the opposite side of the modernist spectrum, Daniil Kharms in his half-page performance script titled *The Unsuccessful Play* symbolically terminated the charge of historical avant-gardes on (the *off*-) theatre stages. After a number of gaunt characters appear and, unable to utter a word, vomit before they exit, a little girl turns up only to announce: 'Daddy asked me to tell all of you that the theater is closing. All of us are getting sick' (Kharms 2007: 70).

The two cases mark the two ultimate instances of theatre, or rather its performance. On one side, there is a (belief in) procreative potentiality of accidents in the *liminal* junctures of actor's – especially physical – actions. On the other side, there is a conceptual, if not actual capacity of actors/ performers (as/and authors) to decide upon and then perform the ending act of theatre. Both cases indicate that misperformance might be disassociated from failure or misfire. Stanislavsky relies on the adoptive efficiency of (acting) psychotechnique; Kharms discursively enacts an abortive act as a final moment of resistance against totalitarian (Soviet) regime. In between – to put it metaphorically – the whole project of historical avant-gardes lived and died. Its 'experimental *gestus*' (Adorno 2008: 23–4) nevertheless survived: 'the artistic subject that employs methods whose objective results cannot be foreseen' is likewise the subject that ventures upon the risk of misperformance. For better rather than for worse. In a short passage from the epilogue of *Postdramatic Theatre*, Lehmann (2006: 179) poses a rhetorical question regarding whether we should define the very theatre as *afformance art* and thus mark the 'somehow non-performative in the proximity of the performance'. It seems that the only thing left for postdramatic theatre to do is bringing to light what is already distinctive about theatre (the *afformative* dimension) and then radicalizing it in a performance that would do or mean *increasingly less*, all the way to undoing and no-meaning:

> Perhaps theater can never know whether it really "does" something acts, whether it effects something and on top of it means something. ... It produces increasingly less meaning because in proximity of the zero-point (in "fun", in stasis, in the silence of the gazes) something might happen: a now. (Lehmann 2006: 180)

The *affirmative* or at very least *doubtful performative* is embedded into the overall strategy of postdramatic politicality that Lehmann reduces to 'the suspension and interruption of the designating function' (ibid.: 179)

The Artaudian *cruel* necessity, the vital urge to perform, let alone semantic amplitudes and pragmatic functions of performative representation, are here again confronted with the promise of the *mis*-performative, moreover – *performative* closure, the *endgame*. *Afformance art* as idea echoes Beckett's maximally minimalistic scene, or rather installation – *Breath*. The *Breath* enacts ambivalence of the *zero* (of) performance, its – at the same time – initial and terminal, hence undefined, moment: *faint brief cry, inspiration, expiration, cry as before*, defined moments of silence to the very second and the stage 'littered with miscellaneous rubbish' which, in a free interpretative arch, brings us back to Kharms' *disgorged stage*.

At least attempted *afformative act* towards *dis/mis* or *zero* action/meaning, presumably emanates dramatic charge – or *tragic pathos*? – of the resistant gesture, against any symbolic regime, not only political. However, misperformance as *experimental gestus* generates more complex dramaturgies than the dual beginning-ending moment.

To begin with, the *mis-performative* thinking would reveal irony in the failure of the reductive conceptualism(s) and minimalism(s), especially with respect to performance vs. theatre contestations. The mere sound of the single breath is already a quite spectacular event. It comprises the potential to represent nothing but itself (the *breath*) just as much as it has the potential to represent everything (from a birth to …). So it is with the *zero*: the production of *increasingly less meaning* retroactively incites an overproduction of signifying operations on the semantic forte of the *zero's* paradoxical presence/absence, in performance or elsewhere.

Then, misperformance would wonder about the next act after breathing in/out as the opening/closure of the *zero moment*. Beckett requires two *cries* to frame the breath. And then? Is the breathing (some)body about to give a death rattle? Or just a yawn? What if that (some)body accidently coughs while performing the *breath*? Would Stanislavsky's psychotechnique be of any help? Or should the sound recording technology prevent any misperformance?

Rather than affected by the pre-arranged *miscellaneous rubbish*, misperformance is involved in the act of vomiting and the abject that remains. Misperformance marks the flow or the instant of performance when it finds itself beyond the already normative staging as well as just *liminal* state; when its course is suspended and any pragmatics – at least in the *mis*-moment – are missed. However, once it approached the *end(s)* of performance, misperformance resists the ontological retreat of the conceptual or factual demise, unless it wants to or has to betray the promises of its fallibility.

Misperformance attempts to go beyond the ultimate *disappearance* and the *perform or else* ultimatum. Instead, it enacts the vital and liberating *gestus* of puzzle and humor: *what else* – to fail and to fool? Surely, Lear's Fool embodies *misperformative gestus,* its (her? his?) missed (dis)appearance being a genuine misperformance, the one which foils the comfort of both normativity and liminality.

Sara Jane Bailes' recently published book *Performance Theatre and the Poetics of Failure* (2011) would unhesitatingly be listed as one of the crucial references in the formation of our imaginary *misperformance studies*. Bailes provides theoretical contextualization and further elaboration of what seems to be the leading notion in such *studies* (obviously, the *failure*), and then acts on the formal analysis and hermeneutic reading of the work of Forced Entertainment, Goat Island, and Elevator Repair Service. All three companies are regarded as instrumental in transfer and exploration of the 'discourse of failure' (Bailes 2011: 2) in the domain of performance-theatre. In life as well as in theatre, 'failure is a function of doing' since 'we cannot "do" without failure' (ibid.: 12): misperformance lurks in the wings of every performance as its defining, therefore constitutive in-/di-/sub-/per-version. In theatre, however, accidental failure gets additional function: to testify and amplify its aliveness. Furthermore, performance-theatre (like other experimental art forms) can 'adopt failure as a political and formal strategy' (ibid.: 10) and participate in mapping of 'a vibrant counter-cultural space of alternative and often critical articulation' (ibid.: 2). Bailes then argues for the *poetics of failure*, but misses the paradox of pairing the two concepts. While *failure* pertains to the realm of *liminal* occurrences and practices that ideally resist any framework and prescription, poetics already implies a certain degree of normative thinking, tested and accepted production-reception procedures. Poetics defuses the risk of the unknown, unfinished, unwanted in the performance of failure, thus progressively reducing its countercharge. Poetics indicates that the process of normalization (and eventual normativization) is already in progress. Failure turned into a constitutive element of a poetics presupposes a success that conforms and confirms that very poetics. And, in due course, constructions of theory and institution are built on and within the grounds of the – once *paradoxical* – 'architecture of ruin' (Bailes 2011: 22). What remains is failure that failed to fail, trapped in McKenzie's *liminal-norm* paradox.

Misperformance encompasses failure but attempts to go further than inscribing its aesthetic, social and even political countercapacity in the relatively safeguarded framework of poetics (plus related calculative economies, whether in the interest of symbolic cultural power or bare financial management.) That is why we propose a/to shift.

The PSi#15 conference in Zagreb took up the challenge of devising a format and a program structure that would allow misperformance to transgress its metaphorical virtuality and (local) historical realities in order to become conference's actuality, hence a constant threat to its efficacy. Curatorial strategy and its unfolding, (mis)performative participation and happenings in the shifting program were presented and discussed in the above-mentioned *Performance Research* issue on misperformance 15.2 (2010). In brief, PSi#15 conceptualized a *shifts* program as a sort of dramaturgical installation, multiple time-space for the experiments with shifting attention, expectations, choices, strategies, directions, formats, experiences, discourses, interventions, responsiveness; experiments with lost and gained time, inaccessible and found spaces, missed and discovered traces, aleatoric sequences and harmonized relations, impossible, temporary and broken connections, conflict and disintegrated situations; experiments with the complexities of interactions and mutual reflections between artists/activists and scholars/theoreticians, the dynamics of substitutability of their roles, functions and competences.

The overall (mis)performance of the conference was then defined as the *shifting dramaturgy,* a kind of perverted *rite of passage*, which – at least conceptually – should miss (to) pass, thus keeping its participants in potentially permanent liminality, *betwixt and between* art/act and (self)criticism, transition without imposed direction/directive/directing, since every such action would lead to the end of *shifting* in the interest of normative – even if failing – performance. *Shifting dramaturgy* is venturing upon an action that would not be motivated by the need or demand for rightful procedure, reaction, direction, relation and position: positions, relations, directions, reactions and procedures, failure included, are there only to be recurrently exposed to critical reflection – tested, altered, abandoned or transformed, dis-, mis- and re-placed.

Misperformance employs *shifting dramaturgy* as a constantly self-reflecting and reviving strategy that further complicates (and possibly overcomes) paradoxical coupling of liminality and normativity in the domain of cultural performance. It is not just *embracing failure*, enhancing the irony of the negative efficacy or intensifying resistant social and political force of the liminal act/action/acting/activism. It means/does all that, but also this: instead of maintaining the canon of once experimental and alternative performance, misperformance will not hesitate to turn normative practices into (now) liminal experiences; it will opt for mis-fail when failure misses to fool and foil its (mis)performative pragmatics (or *happiness*); it will keep *shifting shifts*, as one of the shifts at PSi#15 was called.

55

Works cited

Adorno, Theodor. *Aesthetic Theory*, ed. and trans. Robert Hullot-Kentor. Minneapolis: U of Minnesota P, 2008.

Bailes, Sara Jane. *Performance Theatre and the Poetics of Failure*. New York: Routledge, 2011.

Kelleher, Joe. 'Infinite Misattention', paper delivered at PSi#15 follow-up conference Misperformance: An Inverted Approach to Performance Studies. Rijeka, Croatia, 2010.

Kharms, Daniil. *Today I Wrote Nothing: The Selected Writings of Daniil Kharms*, trans. Matvei Yankelevich. New York: Overlook Duckworth, 2007.

Lehmann, Hans-Thies. *Postdramatic Theatre*. New York: Routledge, 2006.

McKenzie, Jon. 'Misperformance and the Posthuman', paper delivered at PSi#15 follow-up conference Misperformance: An Inverted Approach to Performance Studies. Rijeka, Croatia, 2010.

Prica, Ines. 'Perform or not!: Perfuming on Jon McKenzie's *Perform or else.' Frakcija* 41 (2006): 88–91.

Ridout, Nicholas. *Stagefright, Animals, and Other Theatrical Problems*. Cambridge: CUP, 2006.

Stanislavsky, Konstantin. *An Actor's Work*, trans. Jean Benedetti. New York: Routledge, 2008.

6 Interval

Dylan Bolles and Peter Lichtenfels

Interval is a word used more and more in performance criticism and performance practice. It has a history of use in music, and has found its way into film, stage and performance art. It locates the moment that time and space coalesce and expand, creating presence without coordinates. An interval is 'between the ramparts', an opening like a set of doorposts to let in light, or a place you can walk through. It creates space without coordinates, fissures, energy.

The interval, like Wittgenstein's logical proposition, can only show its sense, not say anything about it. In music, tuning the interval makes sense of sound in terms of both time and space. What lies outside the tuned interval is noise or silence: sound which 'gets into your head and won't go away' and which 'enables us to forget the larger world', or sound which 'catalyzes our powers of perception' and 'enables differentiation' (Prochnik 2010: 293–4). Sound contains a multiplicity of frequency relationships, sometimes called 'partials', whose relative complexity helps determine our experience of sound as consonant or dissonant. Though many attempts have been made to establish and prove a scientific basis for the hearing of consonant and dissonant interval relationships, it remains a highly situated practice with wide variations, even antitheses, among genres and cultures of music.

Composer James Tenney (1988: 18) traces a shift in the concept of consonance as melodic interval to simultaneous dyad (harmonic interval) to around the 10th century. This tension is now represented in the differentiation between melodic and harmonic interval, though these two poles, held tenuously apart, do not bear the separation: 'Rhythm cannot exist without tone, nor tone without rhythm. They are interdependent for their existence, and it is the same with time and space' (Khan 1996: 17). Melodic interval describes the passing of notes one after another in time, while harmonic interval considers notes that are played at the same time as in a chord. If we consider melodic interval to be an aspect of memory, while harmonic interval deals with simultaneity, a so-called 'slice of time', there would then be an interval that describes the quality of time in which an event becomes a series and ceases to be a singularity – a form described by its durational limit. This interval is always in play, depends largely upon the scale of our perception, what we are listening to and for, and bears directly on the uses of consonance and dissonance – what they do to and with the time of listening.

One of the challenges of tuning sounds to scores of other kinds of media involves tuning the intervals between different scales and materials in both time and space. There is often a dissonance of trajectories, an interval or spacing dissonance between sound and gesture, not a thematic one. Or, put positively, the spacings and rhythms by which something is made, if attended to on at least the same scale as its themes, will open new possibilities for collaboration. As in, 'what we don't notice – the visual/acoustic shape of letters, spaces, words, lines – in reading or listening to reading is exactly what delivers the things we do – image, metaphor, symbol, and so on' (Ratcliffe 2000: 4).

Musical tuning is literally active in the actor's or performer's voice. Bodies have wind, strings and percussion in speech with the resonating chamber of throat and mouth, the vocal chords and the percussive actions of teeth, jaw and tongue. For example, in Terry Riley's famous piece, 'In C', each instrument plays the same note, relying on the specific resonances of each individual instrument to create change and formal development. Each actor has a particular voice with its own tone and balance of partials creating different interval construction. For the musician, the partials are to do with pitch, rhythm and tone, while for the actor and performer, the partials are to do with an array of physical, bodily practices that generate intensity, rhythm and energy movement. Both work with scripts or scores, but the score does not fully determine the interval in performance. Something else always happens and there is always another term to tune. Instead, it carefully selects what will be left out, and that which is left out will be the measure of its potential as music and its method of connecting to the time of performance.

Often music in Western performance is used in descriptive ways that tune for consonance and ignore or eliminate whatever is thought of as noise, setting up a strict distinction between the musical and the unmusical sound, as between music and speech for instance. The high degree of intervallic specificity for both time and pitch in Western music notation and practice limits the flexibility of its texts, pushing interval play to a minute arena that struggles, at times, to remain music at all. Tuning for sound that increases dissonance, or expands the intervallic play, can create relationships without coordinates, to be negotiated in the time of performance. For example, the musical scoring in Noh theatre is an integral part of the ecology of the overall performance. The constant negotiation of interval relationships between the dancers and musicians, that each performer must shift between leading and following the flow of sound, creates a music that is always in a relationship of interdependence with other texts on stage. This kind of tuning for sound creates intervals that are attended to while they are happening to everyone in the performance, including the audience.

The text of any script/score isn't a closed event, you don't have to do it in a certain way. The words, like the notes, form a basis for a structure, but how you use them and what you do with them is as open as the cultural references they tie you to and how far you expand the dissonances. In performance criticism in the 20th century, we can read the experiments with defamiliarization in the Prague School theatre criticism, or those of Brecht with *verfremdungseffekt* (to make strange) as ways of testing or playing with the expansion of dissonance.

Take, for example, *Antony and Cleopatra* 4.3 (Arden Shakespeare 1995). In this well-known scene, there are four soldiers on watch, who are suddenly gripped with a feeling they don't understand. They all hear strange music playing, but music without a source or meaning, and the scene generates a sense of 'waiting', 'attending', but a waiting and attending that seem to have no beginning or end. A director or performer would take the script and start to read it for the consonances and dissonances in the text, listening for the places where openings could happen. Rhythm is vital to the process. The scene has a highly irregular number of beats in each line. While the typical in Shakespearean verse is 10 (Wright 1988), this scene has a minority of 10-beat lines and a lot of variation between 9, 11 and 12 beats. The lines themselves are unusual: there are a few short lines at the start, yet nearly all following lines are shared, speeding up the pace and impacting the words. The lines rarely consist of single sentences, more often they contain two or three – once four – or sentences followed by enjambements. The shortness and sharedness of the lines builds a sense of overriding voices.

In whatever edition used, there is a lot of punctuation activity, punctuation signaling discrete pieces of energy, and energy changes after each thought or partial thought. Punctuation can be for breath, mimicking orality, or for ordering (Graham-White 1995). Like 'pointing', the word that accompanies punctuation, the marks on the page indicate particular moments of thought, as in 'you've got a point there', or 'that's a pointed argument'. Sentences, or the early modern use of 'sentence', is much closer to the way we now use the word 'sententious', someone who rather ponderously speaks in a series of complete thoughts. The caesuras in this scene, while not set in stone, offer little breaks in a line. Shakespeare nearly always

has one, and sometimes two. They allow for comparisons, create differences for the ear (Wright 1988). They often happen at a foot ending, and
sometimes at a line ending. In this scene they occur at the end of sentence,
imparting a regularity or emphasis that is broken when they come half way
through a beat, making a little break in a rhythmic foot, creating irregularity at lines 5, 12 and 15.

At the level of consonants and vowels, which actors work with when
they are connecting verbal text to the body that physicalizes speech, actors
make choices about how words and sounds enter the air in which they
travel or resonate. By doing the vowel/consonant exercise, you learn which
parts of the actor's body are affected by a sound, and therefore have some
understanding of what the word generates within the body, where it comes
from, how it changes the rhythm of the body, and what your body wants
to do in response to a sound of movement on the stage. Sounds make part
of your response in that moment, and while they are partly cultural, they
go through your body choosing how to connect you to the scene in specific
ways. Take lines 7–8, in which the Second Soldier speaks with an inordinate
number of vowels to the usual ratios with consonants. It's not possible to
say what this 'means' but it is possible to mark out that this actor would be
having to deal with the way that vowels do not locate in the musculature
of the body the way consonants do, that this seemingly unexceptional line
'floats' in the actor's body, creating a physical sense of hovering or waiting
(Berry 1988; Rodenburg 1997; Steiner 1986).

Taking the scene in five-line sections, you can hear that the one-syllable
words get more frequent as it progresses, the two-syllable words remain
constant and the three-syllable words decrease, so that there are none in
the final section of five lines. Perhaps this is soldier's straight talking, yet
it's still eloquent and moving. It's extraordinary that out of a scene of 165
words, 136 are one syllable, yet there's the potential for great variation in
rhythm and stress.

Among many other techniques available to the practitioner working on
vocalizing scripted words is the search for keywords (Berry 1988; Linklater
1992). Not every word in a line can have equal value because then there'd
be no difference to direct the movement of the line. To make differences,
you choose words that you decide are more or less important to hear, and
these are keywords. They tend to be nouns and verbs, with adjectives and
adverbs being keywords of a lesser order, and conjunctions and prepositions
tending to get left behind. In this scene, there is a large number of keywords.
Usually, we have two or four in a line, but because these parts speak in
one-syllable words, short sentences and shared lines, it feels as if whole
lines are distilled into keywords. There are those that echo: 'good night',

'How now' and 'Do you hear?', repeating and beating out throughout the passage. One set of keywords is to do with the formality of address: 'Fare you well' (ie not 'thou'), 'sir', 'soldiers', 'watch', 'masters', reminding us of the location of these events in the context of the hierarchy of the military and the police. There are keywords that insistently recall around time: 'tonight', 'good morrow', 'tomorrow', 'good night', 'good day'. And the keywords that resonate around waiting, listening and seeing: 'heard', 'watch', 'noise', 'list list', 'hark', 'music', 'signals', 'peace', 'see', 'hear', 'hear', 'hear', 'hear','follow the noise'.

Amid all this mundanity, this soldiers' language marking time, waiting for something to happen, this small chat, suddenly the line ''Tis the god Hercules, …' . Where does this come from, this long, coherent, Latinate, regular, polysyllabic line that breaks into the dissonance of their talk and leaves it falling apart? From this line, they know Antony, their leader, will die – as if they are part of his body and the head has come off. Everyone on the stage, and potentially in the audience, hears the same thing at the same time.

These though are some of the techniques of the performer or actor in preparing to tune for interval. The openings do not define what happens in performance, they make possible the interval: the space-without-coordinates that lets the energy move, that generates presence. One of the first things the group of performers needs to do is decide on the task they will collaboratively undertake. They could, for example, agree that the task is waiting or attending, and then use the techniques to invoke strategies that keep them alive to the task. This could be through speaking to each other, or precisely not speaking to each other. It could be listening or seeing. It could be playing 'goodnight' – if it's night, is it dark? And what are the faculties of seeing, hearing, walking that are done in darkness. The task provides a landscape of energy and invites the performer to create interval, to inhabit the texts of the stage and thereby realize that space/time without coordinates where anything can happen.

The actor or performer, just as the musician, cannot play a technique. They need to have technique in their body so they can practice. Techniques provide anchor points that allow for things that are not anchored. They remind the body of consonance so that the little dissonances of consonance can be opened out and extended, depending on the energy that comes about with a particular combination of performers and audience members. As with a musical instrument, the performer plays the body, tunes the environment of the place, the other actors, the audience, through their own body to bring the energy up or settle it down, to move it. When performers become part of the ecology of the performance, they play on each other and on the bodies of the audience too, they tune the energy, play the interval.

61

The waiting here is not dramatic, simply inevitable, which is the mundane terror of it. The rhythms do not cloy or seduce. They are as uncaring as the drops off a slate roof after the rain. The music of the haut-boys enters from below the stage as both the physical manifestation of the god-essence of Hercules and an everyday element of the stage architecture, the given nature of the stage world. The sounds that precede this entrance should complement and amplify, make sensible, the stilted or suspended energy of the soldiers. We are not considering a soundless world that is interrupted by 'music'. We understand the music of the hautboys as inhab-iting only a different species or order than the music on-stage. Their music is not an imposition but a recognition, a making plain of that which is too painful to know or to admit to oneself.

The incompleteness and irregularity of the lines creates space for a marking of the unknown, its contours mapped by the rhythms of the speech. The silences speak, as when our lover's words do not flow freely enough, such that the music of the hautboys becomes excessive on two counts: one, for the sentimentality of the device, complete with its no-place and every-place locationality, and again for its blatant instru-mentalism, akin to the raising and lowering of a curtain or the wheel-ing in of a piece of set. The genius of the device, and its placement in the scene, is precisely this excess. That in failing to deliver by delivering too much it sets in clear relief the music which matters: ''Tis the God Hercules, whom Antony loved, Now leaves him.' As close as the scene gets to singing. Here, we might end the hautboys and resume our former music. As indeed the First Soldier, resisting any temptation to wallow in an uncomfortable truth, replies, 'Walk'.

The unheard music of the scene in *Antony and Cleopatra* is the sound of death, or, more precisely, the sound of presence leaving. The character-parts hear and attend at the same time, and the performers have to tune the parts so that they make the sound, make present, the leaving of presence. The scene is a bundle of dissonances, a lot of noise of simple ordinary words, which creates a poetry of everyday language, nothing apparently heightened, with a sparseness, a spareness. And the text tells us that they hear a 'hautboy', the 'music of the spheres', that suddenly the world is in tune, attending to the impending death of Antony. All the performers have to do is to tune the world so the performance can create an interval that makes the sound of the leaving of presence.

Performers have to have a practice, a long-term training in the tech-niques and strategies for tuning or playing, or they have nowhere to turn. For example, one strategy for learning how to get the energy moving, how to tune the interval in which time and space coalesce into presence, is to start with a script/score the performers are not fully in control of. Tell them to throw it away and play the text, knowing only little pieces of it. Over a period of time, you begin to remember more and more, and in the meantime you play like kids in a sandbox, who say: 'we're here, this is where we are now', who create parts of stories and when they get bored say 'we're now somewhere else'. Being 'here' is a kind of interval in which the energy moves, often becoming tired because it repeats and becomes consonant. Practice is constant repetition without falling into the expected. It depends on exceptional skill, so that it is always within the ecology of the moment, and never what happened before, even with minimal variation.

If noise for a musician is all the vibrations available to you, making sound into interval is tuning noise through expansions of dissonance. For a performer, noise is all they have in their body as well as any energy coming from things and people in the particular place they are. Techniques and strategies give the performer tools to try out expansions of dissonance, to test the tuning of the environment. Practice happens when this is so much in the body that you leave it behind and play. Practice is the skill to feel what's difficult, to make dissonance, to break down habit, and move the energy of that environment. The performer makes presence by directing the energy, going with it but shaping it, tuning it so interval happens.

In the current dispersal of geographically coherent communities and the penetration of the global, we need to know more about tuning and more about the interval. These days there is a lot of noise, less cultural expectation and more, and we need to learn how to tune for the interval not for complete consonance, to create presence rather than stereotype. It's an animal skill. As an animal you go around and you always have to listen to your body on some level. Listening to the body and tuning it all the time, attending to it. Sometimes, you are in awkward spaces, spaces with no habitual comfort, and need to know how to negotiate it, through the spine, skin, sentience, antennae, feeling, pressure. That's how you know you are in danger or relaxed, how you know your body's OK or not OK, how you know you're in the moment, how you know how to stay alive. Interval is a performative skill for life, as well as delivering vocabulary about presence to performance studies.

As Kara Keeling (2007) reminds us, Franz Fanon places the black body that goes to watch a film in the cinema, in the interval. It's as if the black body exists in a moment of coalesced time/space without coordinates that make sense in the cultural life of the rest of the non-black audience. For Butoh performer Tatsumi Hijikata, his movement is in Ma, the Zen concept of the interval between the body and the spirit, as he contemplates what 'rotting Ma' might mean. Trinh Minh-ha (1999: 72–3) turns to Zeami's 'concept of senuhima or "undone interval" of pause … to designate the moment of suspended action and of "no mind"' to describe a color: 'Rikyu gray is a manner of becoming'. She goes on to say:

> Since action and stillness mutually define each other; since a painting is determined as much by its filled-in surfaces as by those left undone; since a body can only structure space while being structured by it, a performance that includes no interval of pause is no doubt also one that "needs tuning". (1999: 90)

Interval is nondescript as an entity but has discernable shape. Like silence, it is a kind of measure for the relationships between non-silences, an echo, a wake of a movement.

Works cited

Arden Shakespeare. *Antony and Cleopatra*, ed. John Wilders. London: Routledge, 1995.

Berry, Cicely. *The Actor and the Text*. London: Harrap, 1988.

Graham-White, Anthony. *Punctuation and Its Dramatic Value in Shakespearean Drama*. Newark: U of Delaware P, 1995.

Hijikata, Tatsumi. 'Wind Daruma.' *TDR: The Drama Review* 44.1 (2000): 71–9.

Keeling, Kara. *The Witch's Flight: The Cinematic, the Black Femme, and the Image of Common Sense*. Durham: Duke University Press, 2007.

Khan, H. Inayat. *The Mysticism of Sound and Music,* rev. edn. Boston: Shambala, 1996.

Linklater, Kristin. *Freeing Shakespeare's Voice: An Actor's Guide to Talking the Text*. New York: Theatre Communications Group, 1992.

Minh-ha, Trinh T. *Cinema Interval*. New York: Routledge, 1999.

Prochnik, George. *In Pursuit of Silence*. New York: Doubleday, 2010.

Ratcliffe, Stephen. *Listening to Reading*. Albany: State U of New York P, 2000.

Rodenburg, Patsy. *The Actor Speaks*. London: Methuen Drama, 1997.

Steiner, Rudolf. *Speech and Drama*. London: Rudolf Steiner Press. 1986.

Tenney, James. *A History of 'Consonance' and 'Dissonance'*. New York: Excelsior, 1988.

Wright, George T. *Shakespeare's Metrical Art*. Berkeley: U of California P, 1988.

7   Neuroaesthetics, Technoembodiment

Susan Broadhurst

Performance, that extensive, but for some, challenging zone between drama, dance and happening, has entered new territory that reflects our enveloping experience of the contemporary world, capturing that primitive sense of interactive consciousness which Heidegger called simply 'being in the world'.[1] In a short period of time, there has been an explosion of new technologies that have infiltrated, and irreversibly altered, our lives. The consequences are not without problems, but these developments have given performance practice powerful new dimensions.

It is my intention to explore and analyze the effects these new technologies have on the physical body in performance. As a development of my previous theorization on liminality (Broadhurst 1999a, 1999b, 2004), I believe that aesthetic theorization is central to this analysis.[2] However, other approaches are also valid, particularly those offered by recent research into cognitive neuroscience,[3] which relate to the emergent field of 'neuroaesthetics', where the primary objective is to provide 'an understanding of the biological basis of aesthetic experience' (Zeki 1999: 2).

Whether intended to make experimental artworks or to amplify performances, it is my belief that digital practices serve both as critique of social and political conditions and as agents having an *indirect* effect upon them. When used in this way, they also question the very nature of our accepted ideas and belief systems regarding new technologies. The digital does what all avant-garde art aspires to do; it is an experimental extension of the sociopolitical and cultural themes of an epoch.

In performance and technology, instrumentation is mutually implicated with the body. The body adapts and, in effect, extends itself through external instruments. In this way, to use Merleau-Ponty's (1962: 146) phrase, 'the body is our general medium for having a world'. Technology can thus imply a reconfiguration of our embodied experience. When, to use the word non-semiotically, the meaning aimed at cannot be reached by the body alone, the body builds its own instruments and projects around itself a mediated world. Rather than being separate from the body, technology becomes part of that body, so altering and re-creating our experience in the world.

An example of this 'instrumentation' is magnetic or optical motion capture, which has been used widely in performance and art practices since the late 1970s. This involves the application of sensors or markers to the performer's or artist's body. The movement of the body is captured and the resulting skeleton has animation applied to it. This data-projected image or avatar then becomes some part of a performance or art practice. This motion tracking is used especially in live performances, such as Merce Cunningham's *BIPED* (2000), where prerecorded dancing avatars are rear-projected onto a translucent screen, giving the effect of a direct interface between the physical and virtual bodies. Within the dance theatre of Troika Ranch, a New York-based performance ensemble, live or prerecorded images thus captured freeze, fragment, speed up, slow down, or warp in a shimmering effect; all by means of Isadora software.

In Stelarc's performances, the body is coupled with a variety of instrumental and technological devices, which, instead of being separate from the body, become *part* of the body. One such performance is *Muscle Machine* (2003), where Stelarc constructed an interactive and operational system in the form of a walking robot. This intertwining of body, technology and world departs from the early supposition that robotics would somehow abandon the physical body, and in this instance extends it by altering and re-creating its embodied experience.

Artificial intelligence is also featured in some performance practices, where the challenge is to demarcate the discrete human body as against an artificially intelligent life form, such as Jeremiah the avatar from *Blue Bloodshot Flowers* (2001), which was developed from surveillance technology (Figure 7.1).

One of the most interesting aspects of this performance is how much the performer/spectator projects onto the avatar. This is not so surprising, since a substantial area of the human brain is devoted to face recognition (Zeman 2002: 216). This ability is so sophisticated that even very slight differences are noticed and made meaningful. By these means, faces such as Jeremiah's have a powerful and almost subliminal effect on the spectator. This response from the performer/spectator was unexpected since, initially, we were more interested in the real-time interaction between the performer and technology.

In similar fashion, the digital realm permits a proliferation of performances that utilize electronic sound technology for real-time interaction. A performance group that explores the use of this technology is Optik, who have performed at various national and international venues, and now prioritize the use of digitally manipulated sound in their movement-based performance.

Figure 7.1 Elodie and Jeremiah from *Blue Bloodshot Flowers* (2001). Director: Sue Broadhurst; technology: Richard Bowden. Image: Terence Tiernan

Optik is an independent company based in London that has developed a distinctive style of performance practice. The company was formed in 1981 by director Barry Edwards; today, the company's work ranges from minimal performance centring on simple physical movements, to an eclectic mix of sound, live music, video, theatre and dance. Their key precept is a compositional practice that is performer-centred. It engages three primary creative elements: live action (body, space and time); live and digital sound; and live video. The group concentrates on a performer technique that enables performers to improvise within a structure organized by specific conditions of body, space and time. The precise conditions are determined by what is present at each event. For Optik, the term 'improvisation' refers not to the notion of verbal improvisation as in the theatrical sense but rather working with key human actions with no preplanned spatial or temporal score given in advance. An example of this can be seen in Figure 7.2 in their performance of *Xstasis* (2003). Work on *Xstasis* took place over an intensive two-week development period hosted by Concordia University Music and Theatre Departments. The project culminated in three site-specific performances during Montreal's Festival of Theatre of the Americas.

Figure 7.2 Optik in Barry Edwards' *Xstasis* **(2003), Montreal, Canada. Photo: Alain Decarie**

Much of the technology used to create special visual and sound effects that interact in real time within these performances and art practices has been adapted from music technology such as MIDI (Musical Instrument Data Interface) and MAX, a real-time programming environment that has the special advantage of being interactive with visual and network technologies. The latter has also led to the development of OSC (Open Sound Control),[4] which is a protocol that allows the real-time control, by means of gestural devices, of computer-synthesized processes.

Palindrome is a performance group based in Berlin who focus on the interface and interaction between virtual sound and the physical body. Artistic directors Robert Weschler and Frieder Weiss have designed and developed interactive software and hardware, including Eyecon, a camera-based motion sensing system. Their choreography is affected by the live generation of sound through the use of sensors and real-time synthesis, and those movements in turn shape the resulting music.

Another use of EyeCon has involved Palindrome's 'shadow' performances, where, by using an infrared light source and infrared-sensitive camera, a performer's shadow is projected in different colours, with various amounts of time delay, position and orientation shifts (Figure 7.3). The shadows shift seamlessly between what is *known* and what is *surprising*, making 'the piece fascinating to watch' (Dowling et al. 2004: 5).

Figure 7.3 *Solo4>Three* (2003). Dance and choreography: Emily Fernandez; interactive video system: Frieder Weiss. Photo: Ralf Denke

When looking at objects in motion and therefore in performance, it is a matter of researched cognition that colour is perceived before form, which in turn is perceived before motion (Zeki 1999: 66). The consequence of this is that, over very short periods of time, the brain is unable to combine what happens in real time; instead, it unifies the results of its own processing systems, though not in the real time that runs concurrently with the stimuli it receives. Nevertheless, all visual attributes are combined to provide an integrated experience. Palindrome's shadow performances, as a result of their multilayered, distorted and delayed effects, challenge this 'integrated experience', while they ensure the audience's active participation in the production of meaning.

MIDI, MAX and OSC are central to the performances of Troika Ranch, who fuse traditional elements of music, dance and theatre with real-time interactive digital technology. They are pioneers in their use of MidiDancer and Isadora software, authored by artistic director Mark Coniglio, which can interpret the physical movements of performers, using that information to manipulate the accompanying sound, media and visual imagery in a variety of ways, therefore providing a new creative potential for performance. Troika Ranch's *The Future of Memory* (2003) explores memory and the act of remembering – 'how memories are created, stored, romanticized, repressed and lost' – by means of a multilayered collage of moving imagery and sound; the technology acting as a 'metaphor for memory' itself (Coniglio and Stoppiello 2002).

By contrast, in their *16 [R]evolutions* (2006), cutting-edge choreography and multimedia effects explore the similarities and differences between human and animal, and the evolutions that both go through in a single lifetime. The body, as it were, writes itself (Figure 7.4).

Figure 7.4   Motion tracking leaves 3D traces of the performers' movements in Troika Ranch's *16 [R]evolutions* (2006). Performers: Johanna Levy and Lucia Tong. Photo: Richard Termine

The physical and virtual interactions within these performance practices create inclusive, jarring metaphors. An aesthetic effect is produced, caused by the interplay of various impressions of different senses, which unsettle the audience by frustrating their expectations of any simple interpretation, and in turn produce a new type of synaesthetic effect, which is similar to the experience produced by cross-wiring or cross-activation of discrete areas of the brain in some perceptual conditions (Ramachandran and Hubbard 2001: 9).

Until recently, synasthesia was seen as a rare disease-like condition, but it is now known to be widespread, particularly among creative personalities. It was first brought to prominence in the critical writings of Baudelaire, and is a concept that effectively analyses the power of mixed sense impressions as combined components of Shakespearean metaphor. It may also be seen to underpin the ambition of that project loosely contemporary to Baudelaire: the multisensual total artwork, the *Gessamtkunstwerk*, of Richard Wagner. In a certain way, much performance technology developed now is directed to fulfilling that high Romantic ideal.

I would like now to discuss other forms of art and performance practices that directly incorporate biotechnology within their creative experimentation.

The artist Eduardo Kac (1998) investigates 'the intricate relationship between biology, belief systems, information technology, dialogical interaction, ethics and the Internet' and more recently 'transgenics'. In 2000, in his seminal project 'GFP Bunny', Alba, the GFP (green fluorescent protein) bunny, glows green when illuminated with the correct light following the introduction of a Pacific Northwest jellyfish gene into its rabbit DNA (Kac n.d.). This 'artwork' was a collaboration between Kac and INRA (National Institute of Agronomic Research) based in France, who had already integrated GFP into rabbit DNA.

It was intended that Alba would be taken home and become part of Kac's family. However, Paul Vial, the then director of INRA, refused to allow this, wanting the rabbit to remain in the laboratory. As one might expect, a wide debate ensued as to the implications of creating a living artwork, with Kac (2003: 102) carrying out an extensive media campaign to draw attention to Alba's 'situation and obtain her freedom'. At the same time, the international press were outraged by an artwork that 'fuelled existing fears of global genetic mutation'. Importantly also, 'Was Alba Art? What did she mean?' (Allmendinger 2001).

Another bioartist is Marta de Menezes. For her project *Nature?* (2000), she reprogrammed patterns on butterfly wings by injecting the pupa in development. These pattern transformations relate only to the phenotype and not genotype and disappear at the end of the life cycle. She has also applied various colors to elementary parts of brain cells and through projections in 3D has created live sculptures. Her work *Functional Portraits* (2002) employs functional magnetic resonance (fMRI), which visualizes the operation of the brain in real time (Figure 7.5). In so doing, de Menezes attempts to demonstrate the 'neuronal correlate of consciousness' (NCC), which generally refers to the correlation between neuronal activity and given sensations, thoughts or actions (Crick 1994: 208).

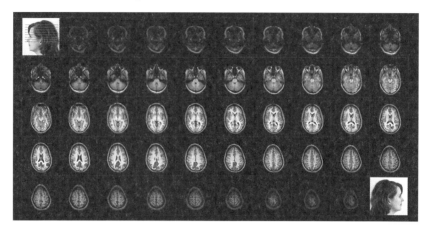

Figure 7.5   Portrait: Self-portrait while drawing. 2005
(© Marta de Menezes)

The search for the NCC is one of the last 'Holy Grails'. However, Semir Zeki (1999: 67) argues for a consciousness that is not one unified whole but is made up of various micro-conscious events; each one tied to the activity of different cells in the processing system of vision. A process where there is no final stage in the cortex of the brain but instead the generation of micro-consciousnesses at different times and locations, not to give a unified perception of an image, but rather to give us a unified percept of ourselves.

Although technology is central to its practices, the digital as a mode of discourse cannot convert phenomena directly but depends on a preceding production of meaning by the non-digital. For instance, Jeremiah the avatar in *Blue Bloodshot Flowers* emulates the graphic design and animation of a recognizable representation, in this case a human head. The digital, like all formal, and indeed logical, systems, has no inherent referring meanings unless these are added. Therefore, readings of digitally processed contents are different from ordinary readings since there is little distinction between the referring and the referent, between 'reality' and representation, or, you could say, between fact and fiction, since in digital, it is all the same.

It is important to note that much technology used in performance and art practices was originally devised for military applications; for instance, the equipment used in the Jeremiah project was developed from surveillance technology. Much of it is owned and controlled by multinational corporations. We must candidly acknowledge that the development costs of these were not borne for the sake of artistic research.

In conclusion, in digital practices, virtual bodies that are generated by physical movement through the mediation of digital technology are seen together with live performers. The performances, with their interface and interaction between physical and virtual bodies, can be seen to displace fixed categories of identity; each carries a 'trace' of the other, given that the virtual performers are the digital reincarnation of the human bodies. However, limits of the embodied self are not fixed, since embodied emotional response can also be due to the stimulation of external objects that have been appropriated by the body (Ramachandran and Blakeslee 1999: 61–2). Digital practices, with their use of motion capture and artificially intelligent technologies, take this appropriation further, since the motions of a performer's body have captured and so determined the motions of technologically featured avatars, such as Jeremiah and *BIPED*, resulting in a modified extension of the original physical body. The implication is that the embodied self, like any other aspect of the conscious self, is transitory, indeterminate and hybridized.

Finally, although much interest is directed toward new technologies in their informational uses, it is my belief that their most important contribution to art and performance lies in the enhancement and reconfiguration of an aesthetic creative potential that interacts with the physical body and does not do away with its endowments of experience.

Notes

1   'In understanding the world, Being-in is always understood along with it, while understanding of existence as such is always an understanding of the world' (Heidegger, 1978: 186).
2   Liminality (from *limen*, Latin: threshold) is a term most notably linked to Victor Turner (1990: 11–12), who writes of a no-man's-land betwixt-and-between, a site of a 'fructile chaos … a storehouse of possibilities, not by any means a random assemblage but a striving after new forms'. My own use of the term includes certain aesthetic features described by Turner, but emphasizes the corporeal, technological and 'chthonic' (Greek: back to the earth) or primordial. Other quintessential features are heterogeneity, the experimental and the marginalized. Therefore, *liminal* performance can be described as being located at the edge of what is possible (Broadhurst 1999a: 12).
3   'The term alone suggests a field of study that is pregnant and full of promise. It is a large field of study uniting concepts and techniques from many

disciplines ... At the heart of cognitive neuroscience ... lies the fundamental question of knowledge and its representation by the brain ... Cognitive neuroscience is thus a science of information processing' (Albrecht and Neville 2001: li).

4   Open Sound Control was created by the Center for New Media and Audio Technologies at the University of California, Berkeley in the 1990s.

Works cited

Albrecht, Thomas D. and Neville, Helen J. 'Neurosciences.' In Robert Wilson and Frank Keil, eds, *The MIT Encyclopedia of the Cognitive Sciences*. Cambridge, MA: MIT Press, 2001, li–lxxxii.

Allmendinger, Ulli. 'One small hop for Alba, one large hop for mankind', posted 31 May 2001, www.ekac.org/ulli.html, accessed 16 May 2014.

Broadhurst, Susan. *Liminal Acts: A Critical Overview of Contemporary Performance and Theory*. London: Continuum, 1999a.

– 'The (Im)mediate Body: A Transvaluation of Corporeality.' *Body & Society* 5.1(1999b): 17–29.

– dir. 2001. *Blue Bloodshot Flowers*. Performer: Elodie Berland. Music: David Bessell. Technology: Richard Bowden, University of Surrey. Brunel University (June); The 291 Gallery, London (August).

– 'Liminal Spaces.' In Nancy Bredendick, ed., *Mapping the Threshold: Essays in Liminal Analysis*. Madrid: Gateway Press, 2004, 57–73.

Coniglio, Mark, and Stoppiello. Dawn. 'Troika Ranch Fall Performances', 2002, www.scottsutherland.com/dancetechnology/archive/2002/0303.html, accessed 16 May 2014.

Crick, Francis. *The Astonishing Hypothesis*. London: Simon & Schuster, 1994.

Cunningham, Merce (Chor). 2000. *BIPED*. Computer-enhanced graphics: Paul Kaiser and Shelley Eshkar. Music: Gavin Bryars. Costume designer: Suzanne Gallo. Barbican Centre, London, October 11 (premiered at Zellerbach Hall, Berkeley, California, April 23, 1999).

De Menezes, Marta. 2000. *Nature?* Developed at the Institute of Evolutionary and Ecological Sciences, Leiden University, The Netherlands and exhibited at the 'Next Sex: Sex in the Age of Its Procreative Superfluousness,' Ars Electronica, Linz, Austria.

– 2002. 'Functional Portraits,' http://martademenezes.com/portfolio/functional-portraits/.

Dowling, Peter, Robert Wechsler and Frieder Weiss. 2004. 'EyeCon – a motion sensing tool for creating interactive dance, music and video projections.' Proceedings of the Society for the Study of Artificial Intelligence and the Simulation of Behaviour's convention: Motion, Emotion and Cognition at University of Leeds, England, (March): 1–7.

Edwards, Barry, dir. (2003) *Xstasis*. Collaborating artists: Howie Bailey (live video), Ben Jarlett (electro-acoustic sound), with Andrea-Jane Cornell, Kafri Rae Seekins, Philip Viel, David Zilbert, Clare Allsop, Simon Humm (performers). Curated by Kate Bligh and the Temenos Performance Group. In collaboration with La

Place des Arts and Concordia University. Performed outdoors in La Place des Arts Montréal and the Black Watch Drill Hall Montréal (May).

Fernandez, Emily (Chor). 2003. *Solo4>Three*. Interactive video system: Frieder Weiss from Palindrome. Berlin.

Heidegger, Martin. *Being and Time*, trans. John Macquarrie and Edward Robinson. Oxford: Basil Blackwell, 1978.

Kac, Eduardo. 'Transgenic Art'. *Leonardo* 6.11(1998), http://mitpress.mit.edu/e-journals/LEA, accessed 16 May 2014.

Kac, Eduardo. 'GFP Bunny'. *Leonardo* 36.2(2003): 97–102.

Kac, Eduardo. 'GFP Bunny', www.ekac.org/gfpbunny.html, n.d., accessed 16 May 2014.

Merleau-Ponty, Maurice. *Phenomenology of Perception*, trans. Colin Smith. London: Routledge, 1962.

Ramachandran, V.S. and Blakeslee, Sandra. *Phantoms in the Brain*. New York: Quill, 1999.

Ramachandran, V.S. and Hubbard, Edward M. 'Synaesthesia: A Window into Perception, Thought and Language.' *Journal of Consciousness Studies* 8(2001): 3–34.

Stelarc. 2003. *Muscle Machine* Performance Premiere. A collaboration involving the Digital Research Unit, Nottingham Trent University and the Evolutionary and Adaptive Systems Group, COGS at Surrey University. 291 Gallery, London, July 1.

Troika Ranch. 2003. *The Future of Memory*. Created by Mark Coniglio and Dawn Stoppiello. Performed by Dawn Stoppiello, Danielle Goldman, Michou Szabo and Sandra Tillett. Premiered at The Duke, 42nd Street, New York (February).

– 2006. *16 [R]evolutions*. Choreographer: Dawn Stoppiello. Music and video: Mark Coniglio. Set design: Joel Sherry. Lighting: Susan Hamburger. Performers: Robert Clark, Johanna Levy, Daniel Suominen and Lucia Tong. New York premiere Eyebeam Arts and Technology Center, Chelsea, January.

Turner, Victor. 'Are there universals of performance in myth, ritual, and drama?' In Richard Schechner and Willa Appel, eds, *By Means of Performance*. Cambridge: CUP, 1990, 1–18.

Zeki, Semir. *Inner Vision: An Exploration of Art and the Brain*. Oxford: OUP, 1999.

Zeman, Adam. *Consciousness: A User's Guide*. New Haven, CT: Yale UP, 2002.

8   Recursion, Iteration, Difference

Johan Callens

Independent of the theatre's vexed ritual origins in goat-song and mass and the medieval cycles' recursive figuration, repetition has been a constitutive aspect of the performing arts. The same or similar stories are retold, cultural traditions and disciplinary conventions transmitted, ideas and materials reworked or activities performed again, publicly and privately, in creative workshops and 'rehearsals'. 'To rehearse' in contemporary French is literally *répéter* or to repeat. What is repeated or re-presented can change, just as its relative importance depends on the artist, discipline, cultural tradition and historical period. In the Western performing arts of the 20th century, mimesis and the dramatic text have been demoted, first by the ready availability of analogue sound and image technologies of reproducibility, and then by the new digital media initially signalling a return to the creative animation logic of the pre-cinema era. These technological developments facilitated the emergence of a postdramatic theatre, increasingly devised and de-emphasizing linear narrative, though perhaps not the underlying principle of methods like Ibsen's retrospection. Rooted as it is in the mind's recursive operation, this cognitive principle gets manifested in what Freud called the secondary working through of dreams, memories and traumata, but also in the algorithms of mathematics or the control and search procedures of computers. In the postdramatic performing arts, recursion's operational logic foregrounds an ability 'to specify concepts by incarnating the differential relations and singularities of an Idea' conceived of as an '*n*-dimensional, continuous, defined multiplicity' (Deleuze 1994: 218, 182).

The repetitiveness of the performing arts is a variable on a scale in between minimized resemblance (e.g. the singularity of happenings) and maximized resemblance (from neoPlatonic Aristotelian mimesis, through Realism to Naturalism). The latter range includes traditional text-based theatre, but also documentary practices like verbatim theatre or the reconstructions of 'historical' dances. Technology theoretically allows for the pure seriality of extensive multiplicities in which additions do not change the nature of the whole, as opposed to the recursion of intensive multiplicities which do. In the case of the now omnipresent simulacrum, the copy has become indistinguishable from the original, thereby dissolving their conceptual difference and respective value, besides further reducing the pleasure of imitation, if we go by a (neo)Classical aesthetic criterion. In practice, repetition in the performing arts always proves iteration, i.e. repetition with a difference. In this difference resides a key to their critical potential, rather than in the return to some original state, as seems to be implied by the cybernetic 'loop', Hofstadter's related 'strange loop' or Richard Schechner's 'restored behavior'.

Given the theatre's live embodiment, the critical remediation of the re-enactment can never be as clearly defined as for the new media, whose goal is always an improved technological functioning to warrant the need and survival of the new media, either as a complement to or substitute for older media. But even onstage, each re-presentation is a renewed, open-ended investigation, as in the 'Canon per Tonos' from Bach's *Musical Offering* and earlier Baroque ricercars and their choreographic and theatrical offshoots (Forsythe, Tanguy). This musical genre, named after the Italian *ricercare*, meaning to seek out once more, consists of sectional or modular instrumental pieces, searching with more (fugue) or less rigour (the improvisational toccata) for the key or mode of the following piece, developing earlier motifs, or exploring techniques. Recursion, i.e. regression and progression combined, as a concept and practice, therefore recognizes the creative productivity of reproducibility, as well as its critical potential, which is enhanced by the reflexivity of non-coincidence, and even more so in the intermedial and interdisciplinary performing arts, compounding the inherent plurality of theatricality as a medium. But if reproducibility enables recursion, it also constitutes its limits beyond which lie, on the one hand, stasis, the impossibility of pure imitation or absolute reconstruction (maximized resemblance), and on the other hand, total deconstruction, the unrecognizability of what is repeated, self-erasure and the exhaustion of the original material (minimized resemblance). In the latter case, the presence problematized by the new media is reasserted by what is also known as machine failure, system errors, and the performing arts' eventuality or accidentality. If bodily time is unsustainable, so is the untimeliness of repetition, for in its accidentality or proneness to breakdown, the extreme of machinic reproducibility again meets the singularity of the performing arts.

The King Is Dead (Part 1)

The diverse modalities of recursion are well illustrated through *The King Is Dead (Part 1)* (1993) by the Stephen Petronio Dance Company, and the different circumstances in which it has been performed. Originally, the choreography appeared on an eclectic bill with two other premieres: *She Says*, a take on four 1970's songs from Yoko Ono, and *Full Half Wrong*, a revision of *Half Wrong Plus Laytext*, which already revised Stravinsky's epoch-making *Rite of Spring* (1913), in which Nijinski, the star dancer of the Ballets Russes and Diaghilev's lover, had caused such an uproar.

The King Is Dead (Part 1) consists of two parts. The first is a solo, created by the choreographer, in which he softly danced to 'Love Me Tender' (1956) by Elvis Presley, the king of crooners, his suave hip-swinging inviting the beholders to share his narcissistic admiration of his sexualized body. During the second part, set to Maurice Ravel's *Bolero* (1928), images of truncated and mummified bodies cross-faded on two panels suspended from the upstage wall. The macabre sphere of these images, made by Cindy Sherman, was maintained in the trailing bandages of the dancers' torn outfits (designed by Manolo) and Petronio's assuming the morality's allegorical figure of death or King of the Underworld, in a hooded costume sporting a ribcage on its torso and entrails on its abdomen. The October 1993 version ended rather conventionally in an orgasmic climax but in the spring 1994 revision, the entire company briefly disappeared right before the orchestra's cacophonic finale, only to re-emerge split up in two groups. And while Ravel's hypnotic rhythm kept pulsating through the air after the last notes had sounded, each group eased a dancer, one male, one female, onto the floor.

Elvis's pelvis

On the face of it, *The King Is Dead* presents itself as a contemporary version of the medieval dance of death invoking Elvis's lethal drug abuse of barbiturates and Demerol, though Elvis sightings fed the popular belief that 'The King' merely went into hiding, and the state of Tennessee in 1994 hired a doctor to review the autopsy report. Still, the origin of Elvis's sentimental song as the Civil War ballad 'Aura Lee' or 'Aura Lea' (by Poulton and Fosdick) gives the production a wider relevance that pertains to Bush Sr.'s first Gulf War (1991) as well. This wider relevance is underpinned by Sherman's related Civil War Series (1991), a photographic project that recalls Matthew Brady's earlier artistic venture on an industrial scale that seemed to replicate the systematicity of this precursor of modern wars, given the sheer numbers of soldiers mobilized and killed (half a million). Choreographically, Petronio's sexually energized gender-bending is comparable to Elvis's infringement upon racial, gender and social conventions. By helping rock and roll spread among white urban youngsters, Elvis was indeed taken to task for infusing popular social dancing with a 'primitivist' erotic appeal familiar from female burlesque, strip joint routines, male drag, and the African-American music and dance tradition (R&B, Snake Hips). His legs' 'erratic' swivelling and his hands' tense shaking, however, were also infused with 'angst-ridden' (white) teenage rebellion, embodied by hysteric female fans, James Dean and Marlon Brando, as well as the kind of delinquent school drop-out he plays in *King Creole* (1958, dir. Michael Curtis) (Hargreaves 1997: 5, 7–8). Either way, the difference from Elvis's models constituted the originality of his style, or its identity resulted from his not repeating the same.

On a deeper level, the narcissism of Elvis's and Petronio's public performances touches upon Freud's controversial understanding of it as a symptom of homosexuality requiring a working through of the 'ailment' by displacing it from the unconscious to the conscious level where it can be dealt with. This displacement, however, occurs not just once, but repeatedly, so that Freud's 'secondary revision' (*Sekundäre Bearbeitung*) is in effect a potentially endlessly recursive process, in which the originary experience is transformed to the point where it can no longer be recognized. Early psychoanalysis's discriminatory pathologizing of gay and female sexuality through the concepts of melancholia and hysteria, whose gendering had been a staple in medical and non-medical literature (Wald 2007: 164), helps to explain the revised ending of *The King Is Dead*, in which a woman and man appear to be collectively sacrificed. This interpretation seems to be supported by the dance company's somewhat cryptic programme statement that the production dealt with 'the symbolic death of the male figure' and 'the strength of the woman within the male, the redirection of aggression and the power discovered in retreat'.

Ravel's self-destructing dance machine

A similar gender tension appears at work in Ravel, a closet homosexual frequenting the unabashedly gay Ballets Russes, and in his *Bolero*, drawing on the flamenco and bolero, with its roots in Castillian and Andalusian courtship dances, as well as on the repetitive rhythms of factory machines. The sounds of modernity tended to be obscured in the 1928 premiere by Ida Rubinstein's troupe at the Paris Opera, set in a cavernous bar where the bystanders and female dancer (Rubinstein herself) mutually excited each other into an orgasmic climax, as in the first ending of *The King Is Dead*. Musically, however, Ravel's warhorse fuses the influences from his Spanish mother and French engineer father, two of his major self-acknowledged inspirations, besides Edgar Allan Poe (Orenstein 2003: 450). True, in the composition's fourfold repetition and orchestral expansion of the more melodic flamenco and the more tonic machine materials, the former are gradually stifled until the dance as a whole self-destructs and in a tutti orchestration crashes to a standstill. That the flamenco-related materials in the process descend an octave adds to the composition's recursive structure, in the sense of Hofstadter's strange loop. At the same time, Ravel's *Bolero* forms the concluding piece of a composite work, begun with a commission from Diaghilev, *Daphnis and Chloe* (1912), and pursued with *The Waltz* (1920). Together, this triad recursively explores the idea of 'mechanised (often high-speed) dance' across different genres and historical periods: the classical, romantic, and contemporary (Mawer 2000: 57). Small wonder that Petronio, whose work is often characterized by its self-destructive kinetic style, would be attracted to *Bolero*.

Poe's automata

Ravel's love of Edgar Allan Poe is due to the mathematical precision with which he arguably composed 'The Raven' (1845), a poem Petronio later incorporated into *The Island of Misfit Toys* (2004). According to Poe's companion essay, 'The Philosophy of Composition' (1846), the poem resulted from the careful deliberation with which he worked his way backward from the predetermined desired effect (the melancholy evoked by the death of a beautiful woman). What gets elided, though, in the retrospective presentation of the creative process as utterly rational and in the refrain's receiving ever new meanings through the slightly changed strophic context is the degree to which these subconsciously express and regulate Poe's obsession with his dead love. And this obsession threatens to overrule any aesthetic considerations over what effects make for the best poetry and how to achieve them. The vantage point of *The Island of Misfit Toys* leads me to suspect that Poe's 'The Masque of the Red Death' (1842) influenced the conception of *The King Is Dead* as a *danse macabre* with shroud-like costumes and a hooded figure of death. As is to be expected, this figure foils Prince Prospero's and his revellers' vain attempt at outwitting the plague, an attempt as vain as the ensconcement of Shakespeare's Scottish king in Dunsinane Castle, since Poe's story is indebted to both *The Tempest* and *Macbeth*. The dirge accompanying the queen's untimely death (5.5.17–18) actually encapsulates the relentless double-edged temporality of recursion, but with a twist, since the creeping petty pace of 'to-morrows' in its triple verbal repetition expresses and only stalls time's forward thrust (5.5.19) before it inexorably turns day to night, as evident in the inverted perspective of 'yester-days' lighting 'fools' to dusty death. Fascinated as Poe was by automata like that of the Three Kings paying tribute to the infant Christ in the original astronomical clock of Strasbourg Cathedral (1352–54), the American, with an equal twist, has his revellers (r)evolve in an abbey whose ground plan resembles half a clock face, and 'cease their evolutions' (256) every time the ebony clock chimes. Half an hour lasts their reprieve after they have been infected, and slightly less than half an hour is the time needed for Petronio and his dancers to get through 'Love Me Tender' and *Bolero*. Petronio's dance of death, combining Elvis's farewell song, Ravel's musical composition and Poe's story, is a composite, cross-generic time machine, a continuous, defined multiplicity, like Strasbourg's astronomical clock measuring different periodicities, all spelling loss, albeit at different rates.

Mourning Nureyev and Clark

If Poe's mournful subject, Lenore, stands in for his beloved wife, so does Elvis surrogate for two dancers, Rudolf Nureyev and Michael Clark; thereby turning *The King Is Dead (Part 1)* into a public and private memorial safeguarding the continuity of dance history or the prospect of further 'Parts' promised in the title's parenthesis. According to the doctrine of the 'kings' two bodies', his natural one is given to decay, his politic one meant to endure, as summed up in the ritualized public announcement at royal funerals: 'The King is dead, long live the King.' From this perspective, *The King Is Dead* inscribes itself within a recursive memorial chain begun by predecessors and prolonged with Petronio's own creations in a constant bodily rewriting or choreography. This again became clear in the May 2010 festive programme at the Joyce Theatre, New York, which concluded the Stephen Petronio Dance Company's 25th anniversary year with a premiere (*Ghostown*) and a selection of revivals (*#3*, *MiddleSexGorge*, *Love Me Tender*, *Foreign Import*). By itself, each represented a different period of the choreographer's career: his years (1979–86) with Trisha Brown, the roller-coaster artistic and private partnership with Michael Clark (1989–92), and his international ventures. Taken together, these signalled the recursive constitution of his artistic identity.

Apart from the fact that Clark and Petronio founded their respective companies in the same year (1984) and their sexuality borders on the exhibitionist and baroque, *Love Me Tender* must have been featured because

Clark in *Because We Must* (1988) made use of Elvis's 'Silent Night' and his pelvic movements in *Mmm…* (1992), short for *Michael's Modern Masterpiece…* . Notorious for the scene in which Clark's mother gave birth to him (again), this salute to Nijinsky's *Rite of Spring* formed the early start for a Stravinsky Project, prolonged with *O* (1994) (indebted to Balanchine's choreography for *Apollo*), and finished belatedly by combining revisions of the first two instalments with the creation of *I Do* (after *The Wedding*) (2007). The delay, as is common knowledge, was caused by Clark's nearly fatal methadone and heroin addiction, which strengthens the link with Elvis. For the rest, Petronio's dance vocabulary has been enriched by Clark's classical ballet training and his love of pop music, or perverted, going by proponents of the purist American postmodern dance vocabulary that Petronio inherited from Brown and Paxton. The latter's visit at Hampshire College caused Petronio to switch from nutrition studies to dance and subsequently to join his mentor at Channel Z, the New York collaborative devoted to contact improvisation.

The earliest impetus for Petronio's dance career, however, was Nureyev's *Sleeping Beauty* (1974) and Clark had worked with the Russian on *Angel Food* (1985), shortly after he had become dance director at the Paris Opera Ballet and been diagnosed HIV positive. This remained secret until his death of AIDS on 6 January 1993, aka Three Kings Day, although it must have been obvious for those witnessing his inept performance in a revival of *The King and I* (1989), no matter it fitted the part. At the time, Nureyev was heavily criticized for never using his artistic prominence to promote the cause of homosexuals or AIDS research. By contrast, in the late 1980s, Petronio had been involved in the AIDS Coalition to Unleash Power, and, shortly after its premiere, *The King Is Dead (Part 1)* featured in at least two benefit programmes, in the wake of the 25th anniversary of the Stonewall riots and the founding of the Gay Liberation Front. Unfortunately, 1993 was also the year in which the US military adopted the infamous 'Don't Ask, Don't Tell' policy, currently under revision thanks to President Barack Obama's initiative. Worst of all, the ravages of AIDS in the early 1990s had created a sense that the gay community, mourning those gone and about to go, was living in a post-apocalyptic or post-historic era, utterly warranting Petronio's decision to create a recursive dance of death whose outcome is as equivocal as Sherman's alternating slides. In production designer Tal Yarden's set-up, these hover in between the deadliness of animated stills and the liveness of cinema, between the singularity of the snapshot and the reproducibility of movies, creating the illusion that time is reversible and history might be rewritten.

Note

The research conducted for this article is part of the Interuniversity Attraction Poles Programme financed by the Belgian government (BELSPO IAP7/01).

Works cited

Deleuze, Gilles. *Difference and Repetition*, trans. Paul Patton. Minneapolis: Minnesota UP, 1994 [1968]

Hargreaves, Martin. 'The Pelvis Unbound.' *Theatre InSight* 8.2 (#18) (Fall 1997): 3–9.

Mawer, Deborah, ed. and intro. *The Cambridge Companion to Ravel*. Cambridge: CUP, 2000.

Orenstein, Arbie, ed. and intro. *A Ravel Reader*. Mineola, NY: Dover, 2003.

Poe, Edgar Allan. *Selected Writings*, ed. and intro. David Galloway. Harmondsworth: Penguin, 1967.

Wald, Christina. *Hysteria, Trauma and Melancholia*. Basingstoke: Palgrave Macmillan, 2007.

9   Living History, Re-enactment

Marvin Carlson

The activity now called 'living history' only became a major cultural activity in the 20th century, though one can trace certain features of it far back in theatre history. From the classic period onward, theatrical performances have sought to re-create historic events and scenes, sometimes, as in the Roman naumachia (full-scale re-enactments of famous naval battles), on a scale rivaling even the most spectacular military confrontations. The affirmation of cultural memory through historical re-enactment first became a central cultural concern during the French Revolution, when major events from the Fall of the Bastille onward provided inspiration for re-enactments, encouraged by the government as a form of public education. Nor was the new vogue limited to France. The same year that the Bastille fell, its spectacular storming was re-enacted by masses of actors at two different theatres in London. Europe even witnessed, as early as autumn 1792, an early example of the site-specific re-enactment of famous battles that would become a widespread phenomenon in the 20th century. On the actual battlefield of Jemmapes in Belgium, a company of Parisian actors staged a victory pageant only six days after the battle itself, with symbolic ballets suggesting the conflict and using soldiers who had actually participated in it.[1]

The rise of nationalism in 19th-century Europe encouraged the re-enactment of major national historical events both on the new national stages and in other public locales, and a growing cultural and theatrical interest in authenticity and realism encouraged attention to historical detail, even to the re-enactment of events in their actual historical surroundings. Victor Hugo, arguing for exact physical settings in historical drama, called the setting a 'silent character', without whom the scene was incomplete: 'Would the poet dare to assassinate Rizzo elsewhere than in Mary Stuart's chamber? ... burn Joan of Arc elsewhere than in the Old Marketplace.'[2]

Hugo meant his admonition to apply to the traditional stage, but, taken literally, it would argue for the sort of site-specific historical re-creation suggested by the Jemmapes project, which did in fact become increasingly common in Europe and elsewhere. In particular, in Germany the Franco-Prussian War inspired historical festivals that recalled the great civic festivals of the French Revolution. These spectacles anticipated and may in turn have served as the models for the civic pageants that became an important part of cultural life in England and then in America in the early years of the 20th century, when hundreds of pageants presented to hundreds of thousands of spectators all across America between 1905 and 1925 featured outdoor allegorical displays mixed with reconstructions of historical events such as revolutionary battles, often on the very sites where these events occurred.

One fascinated spectator at a number of the American pageants between 1914 and 1916 was Platon Kerzhentzev. His 1918 book *Creative Theatre* provided the intellectual basis for the great Russian mass spectacles of subsequent years, the most famous of them being Nikolai Evreinov's *The Storming of the Winter Palace* in November 1920,[3] which involved more than 8,000 participants, army units, armored cars and trucks, even the warship *Aurora*, anchored nearby on the Neva on its exact historical site, and with an audience of more than 100,000.

In 1960, as the centennial of the American Civil War approached, a number of local and national organizations became interested in celebrating that occasion with re-stagings of its great battles. The result was a series of carefully planned re-enactments, on their centennial anniversaries, of dozens of Civil War battles, from the most famous, such as Manassas and Gettysburg, organized by the National Park Service, to minor encounters scarcely known outside their sponsoring community. The official end of the Civil War centennial celebrations in 1964 saw no diminishing in such activity.

Scarcely had the official celebrations of the Civil War centennial concluded when plans began to be drawn up for the American bicentennial celebrations, then only ten years away. Almost every major military encounter of the Revolution was refought between 1975 and 1981, and as re-enacting continues to grow as a hobby, a tourist activity and, for many, a particularly effective way of presenting and understanding historical events, the scope of such activity, historically and technically, continued to expand. Battle re-enactments in America have covered almost the entire range of the nation's history and have ranged in size from the annual re-enactment of the opening skirmish of the Second Seminole War in Tampa, Florida, involving many more persons than the original event, to a 1991 re-enactment in Texas of the Japanese attack on Pearl Harbor, with Japanese and American aircraft, simulated bombing of the American fleet and huge numbers of American ground forces with meticulously authentic uniforms, gear, weapons and vehicles.

Nor has this activity been confined to the US. In England, one can now attend an impressive range of re-enactments, including Roman Army engagements in Shropshire, medieval combats and tournaments in many locations, the Battle of Hastings on its original site, sieges by Crusaders in Devon, English Civil War and Napoleonic battles in Cornwall and, for good measure, re-enactments of American Civil War battles as well.

Military encounters are surely the most spectacular sort of current re-enactment, but an even more widespread type of historical performance, dealing with domestic life, has developed alongside performed military history. A central model for this activity, at least in the US, has been the major American tourist attraction, Colonial Williamsburg, begun in 1927. The first example of what has come to be known as the 'living history museum' seems to have been established in Stockholm in 1891. This was Skansen, an ongoing exhibit of Swedish culture similar to the living ethnographic exhibits that had become popular features of the great international expositions of the late 19th century. At Skansen, actual historic structures housed fiddle players, Lapp reindeer herders and peasants in their mountain chalets. The Skansen idea spread all over Europe, but the idea of a museum village with living costumed inhabitants proved particularly attractive in the US. At first, there was no attempt to present these artisans, even in costume, as actual performers pretending to be historical figures, but this distinction was not a clear one, as can been seen in the comments of the 1951 Colonial Williamsburg *Official Guidebook*:

> Every effort has been made not only to exhibit all this evidence of the past, but also to re-create a living community. The blacksmith works with ancient tools in shaping his metal and the hostesses in the Exhibition Buildings wear appropriate farthingales.[4]

The next step in the performance of historical memory was taken at Plimoth Plantation in New England. Its assistant director articulated a new approach to the living history museum in a series of influential articles in the late 1960s and early 1970s. He argued:

> To function properly and successfully, a live museum should convey the sense of a different reality – the reality of another time ... It occurred to us that the live interpreters ought to be recreations at Plimoth too. We had them speak in period dialect, which we were able to research, in first person. At that point the visitors became the interpreters, and we started calling the interpreters informants. It was as if the visitors coming into the exhibit were anthropology fieldworkers going in to experience a community and elicit from it what they could.[5]

Gradually, more and more role-playing entered the experience until today almost all the town inhabitants that tourists encounter have assumed particular period roles and are carefully trained in the details of colonial life so as to give visitors the impression of actually meeting a person of that era. The same model has now been followed in Colonial Williamsburg and other living history museums across America. In addition to spontaneous interaction with visitors to these communities, these actor-inhabitants also stage elaborate historical re-enactments of community life: town meetings, festivals and, most famously and most controversially, a period slave auction in Williamsburg. From communities like Williamsburg, this historic role-playing has spread to countless individual locations, so that by the mid-1980s, there were over 650 living history homes and communities in America, and the number has steadily increased.

According to the supporters of this movement, 'living history' sites offer a holistic historic experience. Darwin Kelsey spoke of knowing history 'directly, through sight, sound, smell, touch, and taste',[6] and Jay Anderson has spoken of Plimoth Plantation as 'harshly realistic; it really *looks* and *feels* medieval'. The goal, he suggests, is that 'moment when you actually feel as if you are a part of a particular historical period or event'.[7]

Alongside these living history museums a parallel living history movement has grown, which is not based upon observation, but direct participation in historical culture. Again, the emphasis is upon the creation of historical memory through performance, but the phenomenological operations are very different, and considerably more complex. Colonial Williamsburg or Plimoth Plantation, insofar as they utilize performance, operate in certain basic ways like traditional theatre. An audience comes to a performance space to observe, in a relatively passive manner, performers who assume imaginary personae. In many re-enactments there may still be an audience, but the emphasis is upon direct participation. Normally, participants attend these manifestations not to observe, like Deetz's 'anthropological fieldworkers', a culture removed in time, but to attempt to imaginatively enter that culture, not as observers but as full participants.

Civil War re-enactments occupy a position with strong elements of both orientations. These activities were originally planned essentially as staged historical demonstrations, for the edification, entertainment and patriotic stimulation of the observers. Right from the beginning, however, the size of these events demanded a large number of active participants, whose background and motivation were very different from the quasi-professional historical performers in a living history museum or a kind of historical theme park like Colonial Williamsburg. Communities and the National Park Service turned for advice and participants to a variety of amateur organizations like the National Muzzle Loading Rifle Association, whose members were not actors, but hobbyists interested in certain historical activities. The Civil War centennial re-enactments turned the activities of these few scattered hobbyists into a national leisure time activity for thousands of Americans, and as time passed, for Europeans and Australians as well. Dozens of Civil War battles are now refought every year around the world. Most re-enactors, of whom there are an estimated 40,000 in the US, view this activity as the major ongoing occupation of their leisure time, serving as a combination of hobby, club, adult education and vacation.

Naturally, the degree of historical authenticity in these reconstructions varies widely, but many re-enactors, who call themselves 'hard cores', are deeply committed to making their activities as accurate as possible. Aside from historically accurate guns, costumes and hairstyles, they may gather a large collection of supporting gear, such as period toiletries, cooking and eating utensils, books, magazines, matches and trinkets of all sorts. Period vocabulary is studied, along with authentic accents. Not only are particular battles studied in great detail and carefully choreographed, but in some cases individual soldiers do not simply portray a member of a particular historical company, but pick a particular historical individual to play and do extensive research on him to be as authentic as they can.

The Civil War re-enactments, around which a whole cottage industry has developed in the US, are the most common form of actual participation in historical performance, but there are also living museums that go beyond simply demonstrating history for visitors, but provide opportunities for their visitors, like Civil War re-enactors, to actually assume historical personae. The Washburn-Norlands living history center in Maine, for example, offers guests an opportunity for a 'total experience of rural life as it was lived in northern New England a century ago'. Visitors are assigned the identities of actual historical dwellers in the area, whose homes and graves they visit, and they sleep in the dead of winter on cornhusk mattresses in bedrooms with no electricity, running water, or any hint of the 20th century. The aim is to provide a real and authentic experience of another era.

Historians, museum curators and administrators continue to hold a wide variety of opinions over such activities, ranging from enthusiastic endorsement of them as effective teaching tools, to heated denunciations of them as shams, charades and outright misrepresentations. The problem is not simply that the past, in all its complexity, can never be completely reconstituted, but that all living history is penetrated by what anthropologist Richard Handler and philosopher William Saxon have called 'dyssimulation'. Historical lives that would have been lived pre-reflexively or unselfconsciously are, by performance, bound to a 'necessarily reflexive operation' to a sense of reading, of narrative construction.[8]

What has been generally overlooked, however, in the continuing debate over the 'authenticity' of living history or historical performance is that from a postmodern perspective (which to date is almost completely lacking in this debate), 'living history' does not present problems that are different from traditional textual history. As Hans Kellner has argued: 'history is not "about" the past as such, but rather about our ways of creating meanings from the scattered, and profoundly meaning*less* debris we find around us'.[9] This postmodern perspective reminds us that all reconstructions of history are fragmentary, incomplete, subjective, colored by reflexivity, our own cultural context, and the desire to create narrative. The modern performed representations of history, whether one relates to them passively, as an observer, or actively, as a participant, do not create a new problematic relationship to the historical process, but merely call specific attention to a problematic relationship between present and past that has always existed. We, historians and laypeople alike, have always re-created the past in terms of our own needs, hopes and physical and mental modes of being in the world. The opponents of 'living history' are quite correct in condemning its more ambitious claims of a holistic recapturing of even a moment in the past, but that is far from the last word on such activity. Humanity has always been and will always be engaged in a negotiation with historical memory, a basic element of which will always be performance, either reflexively in the mind or literally, as some species of re-enactment or living history. A recognition of this dynamic will lead from too easy a dismissal of this modern performance phenomenon as naive or insufficiently reflexive to a more serious recognition of it as an important contribution to an ongoing and fundamental human project.

Notes

1 Eugène Hugot, *Histoire littéraire, critique, et anecdotique du Théâtre du Palais-Royal* (Paris: P Ollendorff, 1886), 55.

2 Victor Hugo, 'Preface to Cromwell,' in *Oeuvres complètes*, 18 vols (Paris: Club français du livre, 1967), 3: 63.

3 Frantisek Deák, 'Russian Mass Spectacles,' *TDR: The Drama Review* 19 (June, 1975), 22.

4 *The Official Guidebook and Map of Colonial Williamsburg* (Williamsburg, 1951), 7.

5 James Deetz, 'The Link from Object to Person to Concept,' in Z.W. Collins, ed., *Museums, Adults, and the Humanities* (Washington, DC: American Association of Museums, 1981), 8.

6 Darwin Kelsey, 'Harvests of History,' *Historic Preservation* 28 (July–Sept., 1976), 24.
7 Jay Anderson, *Time Machines: The World of Living History* (Nashville: American Association for State and Local History, 1984), 191–5, and *The Living History Sourcebook* (Nashville: American Association for State and Local History, 1985), 455.
8 Richard Handler and William Saxon, 'Dyssimulation: Reflexivity, Narrative, and the Quest for Authenticity in "Living History,"' *Cultural Anthropology* 25 (1989), 249.
9 Hans Kellner, 'Language and Historical Representation,' in Keith Jenkins, ed. *The Postmodern History Reader* (London: Routledge, 1997), 136–7.

10   Performance Philosophy

Laura Cull

From a 'philosophical turn' to performance philosophy

Interest in the relationship between philosophy and performance, including drama and theatre, has grown significantly, particularly gaining momentum over the past few years. At the start of 2012, I referred to this development as a 'philosophical turn' in contemporary theatre and performance studies (Cull 2012). In this case, my argument was that, following the so-called 'theory explosion' that affected US and European theatre studies no less than the other humanities from the 1970s and 80s onwards, contemporary Anglophone theatre scholars were now broadening the range of their philosophical engagement beyond those thinkers who had been embraced under the broad category of 'critical theory'. That is, while some described the theory explosion as having 'returned the humanities [including performance] to philosophy' (Reinelt and Roach 1992: 5), I proposed that it returned performance to some philosophies, but not to others – to Derrida and Austin, for instance, but not to Bergson or Deleuze; to Lacan and Foucault, but not to Spinoza or Nietzsche.

Now, however, myself and fellow conveners of a new professional association dedicated to the area are proposing that what we are currently witnessing might be better described less as a 'turn' within the existing field of theatre and performance studies, and more as the emergence of a new interdisciplinary field that we might call performance philosophy.[1] It is clear that the burgeoning literature and other forms of research activity taking place internationally now are not just the products of work being done by scholars based in theatre and performance studies. Rather, the relationship between performance and philosophy is attracting interest from a wide range of disciplines, including philosophy.[2] While analytically and continentally inclined philosophical aesthetics has, until recently, tended to prefer cinema, literature, painting and music as its objects of study, perhaps partly on account of the persistence of the 'anti-theatrical prejudice' of much Western philosophy, the nature of the specifically theatrical is beginning to be addressed by philosophers; for instance in Samuel Weber's *Theatricality as Medium* (2004), Rancière's *The Emancipated Spectator* (2009),

and Badiou's various theses on theatre, as well as in the work of Anglophone philosophers such as Simon Critchley, Noël Carroll, Tom Stern and
James Hamilton to name but a few.[3] We are not claiming, of course, that a
concern for the relationship between performance and philosophy is new,
given the philosophical reflection of theatre theorists from Artaud and
Brecht to Grotowski and Beckett, and the theatrical reflections of philosophers going back to Aristotle's *Poetics* and the *Natya Shastra*.[4] Rather, the
claim is that research into the performance–philosophy relationship has
intensified over the past ten years such that it might now be called a new
field, in ways that the inaugural conference of Performance Philosophy in
the UK in April 2013 interrogated.

Here, I would like to reflect on what this new field might become,
in the form of a discussion of two key ways of construing the perfor-
mance/philosophy relationship. The first of these relates to what I have
described elsewhere as 'the problem of application'; namely, the question
of the extent to which performance and philosophy tend to be set up
in a representational and hierarchical relationship in which philosophy
remains unaltered by its encounter with the event of performance. The
second is the idea of 'performance *as* philosophy' and related to this, the
particular question of how performance *thinks*, not only when or because
it is made by philosophically minded directors or addresses recognized
philosophical themes. This second line of thinking has already been well
established in other areas, such as film philosophy. As Robert Sinnerbrink
(2011: 7) describes:

> Film-philosophy argues that film should be regarded as engaging in
> philosophically relevant reflection via the medium of film itself, or as
> being capable of a distinctively cinematic kind of thinking … It is a way
> of aesthetically disclosing, perhaps also transforming, our experience of
> the modern world; one that prompts philosophy to reflect upon its own
> limits or even to experiment with new forms of philosophical expression.

Whilst for some, the notion of performance as thinking will only ever be
metaphorical, or an instance of stretching the meaning of the notion of
'thought' beyond any useful limits (as something of which the nonhuman is capable for instance), for many of us in the new field of performance philosophy, such an idea stages a critical challenge to philosophy's
presumption of itself as the discipline entitled to define what constitutes
'genuine' thinking, and what does not.

To philosophize otherwise, then. Of course, in the Preface of *Difference
and Repetition*, Deleuze (2004: xx) had predicted that: 'The time is coming

when it will hardly be possible to write a book of philosophy as it has been done for so long', going on to insist that 'the search for new means of philosophical expression … must be pursued today in relation to the renewal of certain other arts, such as the theatre or the cinema'. And while that prediction might have been somewhat untimely in 1968, this idea of finding new ways to do philosophy, to perform thinking, is precisely the project of the annual 'Performative Philosophie' Festival currently staged at Halle University in Germany. The festival encourages participants to focus on the performativity of the *how* as well as the what of the philosophical speech act, exploring such forms as what they call the 'Dead Philosophers' Café', in which 'living philosophers slip on stage into the role of dead philosophers to have discussions together, which history did not allow' (Totzke and Gauss 2012).[5] In turn, via the contemporary French thinker François Laruelle's notion of 'non-philosophy' or 'non-standard' philoso-phy (which is not a negation of philosophy but a performative mutation or expansion of it as material), we find the seeds of hope that performance philosophy might equally be embraced as an opportunity for the renewal of philosophy as much as of theatre and performance studies; or again, if this is not too grandiose, as an opportunity to reopen the very question of what counts as philosophical thought.[6] Better too grandiose perhaps than to settle for performance philosophy as that which merely renews the 'intel-lectual respectability' of performance studies or provides philosophy with little more than an 'enlivening pedagogical resource', such that performance is only understood as contributing to philosophical thought on the level of illustration or exemplar of a pre-existing concept (Sinnerbrink 2011: 119).

The problem of application

From the point of view of performance theory, one of the pleasures of the intensified interest in philosophy has been the exploration of how philos-ophy might provide alternative methods of performance analysis beyond the well-established frameworks of semiotics and phenomenology. But while we might wish to embrace these attempts to explore the implications of the various philosophies for our understandings of theatre and perfor-mance (and I might include my own past work on Deleuze in this category, despite its best intentions), we should perhaps also be wary of enacting a certain *philosophical disenfranchisement* of performance in a manner that echoes the broader tendency towards application in philosophical treat-ments of the arts (Sinnerbrink 2011: 128). For Martha Nussbaum (2008), for instance, it is all too often that art is 'simply being used as a primer for

Philosophy 101'. In particular, Nussbaum has suggested that while Stanley Cavell's readings of Shakespeare offer remarkable 'philosophical insights', 'his readings of Shakespeare tend to confirm the philosophical notions for which he has already argued independently, in readings of Wittgenstein, Descartes, and other philosophers' (ibid.). Similarly, in his 2006 book *Filmosophy*, Daniel Frampton (2006: 9) notes the way in which philosophy tends to use film, particularly as part of its pedagogy, but only insofar as it sees films as containing 'stories and characterisations that helpfully *illustrate* well-known philosophical ideas', rather than looking to the presentation of ideas by the cinematic form itself. Illustration is what Frampton calls 'film "plus" philosophy', a mode of relation he criticizes for its condescension and its failure to actually tell us something about film. Here, he argues, filmmakers are positioned as needing to learn from philosophers rather than as equal contributors to a two-way flow of ideas, albeit that they can also be back-handedly praised when they get a philosophical idea 'right', that is, when they illustrate it effectively.

In his work on film, John Mullarkey argues that it is largely the legacy of the Hegelian tradition within philosophy that can account for the persistent romanticism in philosophy in relation to the ineffability of art and the correlative perception of the incapacity of the artist to articulate the ideas immanent to their own art. 'Art only *becomes* philosophical' for Hegelians, he suggests, 'when a philosopher brings out its inner voice through translation and clarification. The Truth has a sensuous embodiment in art that needs to be told in words by philosophy' (Mullarkey 2009: xi). But does art really need philosophy in this way? Or is it more that, as Richard Lane (2002: 2) has helpfully suggested in relation to Beckett, that art 'always already communicates what it wants to say, but in a language entirely other to philosophy'.

(How) does performance think? Performance-as-philosophy and its critics

In what follows, I want to suggest that this 'otherness' of how art speaks, or better perhaps how art *shows*, does not necessarily mean that it should not be construed as philosophy. Indeed, this would be one alternative to the problem of application: to treat the artwork itself as capable of doing philosophical work, albeit in a different mode from conventional philosophy. As we've noted, the area of film philosophy has already gone some way to explore 'the idea that film does not simply reflect philosophical themes but can engage in philosophizing, broadly construed, in an independent manner' (Sinnerbrink 2011: 120).[7] In turn, might the idea of performance-as-philosophy be thought beyond the notion of 'influence', for example in cases where scholars have been able to evidence that a theatre practitioner has engaged with a particular philosopher's work (Ibsen with Kierkegaard or Eugene O'Neill with Schopenhauer)? Can it go beyond both the 'author' and 'interpreter' altogether: beyond the already relatively uncontroversial notion of 'Shakespeare as philosopher' or 'Beckett as philosopher' (and it is no coincidence that these accepted figures are arguably *writers* of theatre first and foremost) and indeed, beyond the perceived thoughtfulness of performance as merely in the eye of the already philosophically minded beholder?[8] In other words, might we say that performance *itself* thinks, that theatre *itself* philosophizes – not in a way that reduces theatre to being the 'same as' philosophy (as if philosophy was always the selfsame thing anyway) but in a way that enriches our concept of philosophy? On one level, we might propose that much of this thought has already been undertaken with respect to the notion of 'practice as research in performance', where university-based practitioners (perhaps particularly in the UK) have fought hard to have their practical work accepted as an equally valid form of 'research' and knowledge production as more traditional forms of scholarly output. But it could also be argued that it is too restrictive to construe how performance thinks solely in terms of 'the production of knowledge' (to cite the UK's Arts and Humanities Research Council definition of what constitutes research), which all too often must still be explicated with recourse to text. For contrast, in his work on music as philosophy, Andrew Bowie has suggested that the philosophical value of performance practice might lie precisely in its *resistance* to knowledge:

> It is when we don't understand and have to leave behind our certainties that we can gain the greatest insights. Given that this situation is in one sense almost constitutive for music, which we never understand in a definitive discursive manner, it is worth taking seriously the idea that such non-understanding might be philosophically very significant. (Bowie 2008: 11)

As we've already noted, there may well be those critics who will argue that to say 'performance thinks' or that theatre philosophizes in an independent manner is 'merely metaphorical', since performance cannot make logical and reasoned arguments (Sinnerbrink 2011: 117). Correlatively, in film philosophy, there are those such as Paisley Livingston (2006, 2009) who argue that 'any philosophy to be gleaned from a film is either due to the philosophical acumen of the interpreter, or else is confined to the expression of an explicit aesthetic intention on the part of its maker/s' (Sinnerbrink, paraphrasing Livingston, 2011: 117). In turn, Livingston argues that the claim that film can make an independent or exclusive contribution to philosophy will always be undone by ineffability on the one hand and paraphrase on the other. That is, unless the philosophical contribution of a film can be paraphrased (namely, articulated in words) it cannot be communicated, Livingston claims, but correlatively, if it *can* be paraphrased, it is, by definition, no longer exclusive to the medium of cinema; it has already been said or might now be said better by traditional philosophical discourse.

However, as Sinnerbrink (2011: 117) points out, such critiques 'often assume a too-narrow or reductive conception of what counts as philosophy' – defining philosophy in advance as that which necessarily excludes any non-linguistic form of expression, including theatre, which could be argued to think in images, sounds, colours, movements and so on as well as in words. Of course, for some this begs the question of how one should define philosophical thought anyway. For instance, Noël Carroll and Sally Banes (2001) begin their attempt to define what counts as a 'philosophy of theatre' with an attempt to define philosophy itself, arguing that Western philosophy since Socrates has tended to revolve around the interrogation of concepts such as 'justice', 'knowledge' and, indeed, the concepts of 'philosophy' and 'the concept of concepts'. Carroll and Banes (2001: 155–6) suggest that a 'preoccupation with concepts' (rather than, say, experience or the empirical) is what defines an activity as philosophical. In turn, they argue that 'what philosophers do is to clarify concepts, notably the deep concepts that we use to organize our practices, that is, the deep concepts that make our practices possible' (155). Based on this definition, Carroll and Banes are then dismissive of the possibility of construing theatre as a philosophical or a theoretical activity. For instance, while they note that '*Hamlet* is associated with the Oedipal complex', and the work of theatre director Richard Foreman 'is thought to deconstruct the boundary between theatre and reality', Carroll and Banes (2001: 161) insist that 'To illustrate – rather than to discover and argue for – generalizations, as some may claim that Shakespeare and Foreman have done, is no more ... philosophy than the illustration of Christian doctrine in a stained glass window is theology'. Theatre and stained glass amount to the same thing here then: mere illustration rather than discovery. For his part too, though for different reasons, Paul Kottman (2009: 17) suggests that we should resist the 'nomination of Shakespeare for the title "philosopher"', arguing that it is 'precisely insofar as they move us – insofar as they are dramatic – the plays are not themselves philosophy'. But is philosophy unable to move us? Is this moving not another way of describing how theatre philosophizes, how performance thinks? That is, we might argue that performance's philosophy can be specific to its own forms without necessarily being renounced as ineffable; it is, simply, a *different kind* of thinking and, indeed, one that challenges philosophy's tendency to conceive itself as the highest form of thinking and as the discipline that gets to decide how thought is defined.

At this point, I would like to return to the work of Laruelle (2012: 287), a critic of this 'superiority complex' in the history of philosophy, who argues that 'we must first change the very concept of thought, in its relations to philosophy and to other forms of knowledge'. Laruelle develops this call for change through the project he refers to as 'non-philosophy' or non-standard philosophy: a project which, as Mullarkey has made clear, is not to be understood as an anti-philosophy so much as one that aims to extend what counts as 'philosophy': 'It enlarges the set of things that can count as thoughtful, a set that includes extant philosophy, but also a host of what are often presently deemed (by philosophers) to be nonphilosophies and non-thinking (art, technology, natural science)' (Mullarkey and Smith 2012: 5). In turn, Laruelle insists that these thoughtful things should be construed not as representations of the Real but as material parts of it.[9] For all his engagement with the thought of artists, Deleuze's thought still privileges philosophical thought, Mullarkey argues, as that which ultimately explains the Real, including the reality of how theatre and performance think (ibid.: 6). In contrast, the non-philosophical project seems to call upon philosophy to engage in a kind of disappearing act – where it would no longer operate as a 'philosophy *of* …' (theatre, for instance) – whereby theatre is positioned as the object for a philosophical thought that is understood to take place outside it. Within the philosophy of theatre, theatre is constituted as the dominated object of knowledge rather than as a source or site of knowledge in itself; as Sinnerbrink (2011: 7) suggests: 'In the "philosophy of X" approach, philosophy conceptually analyzes and theorizes its object precisely because the latter cannot do so.' Or as Laruelle (2012: 284) puts it: 'To philosophise on X is to withdraw from X; to take an essential distance from the term for which we will posit other terms.' And so goes philosophy's anti-democratic history in relation to other forms of thought, Laruelle suggests. In contrast, according to a non-philosophical perspective, philosophy and theatre would be realigned as equal yet different forms of thought – embedded in the whole of the Real, with neither being granted any special powers to exhaust the nature of the other, nor indeed the nature of the whole in which they take part.

My concern here is not really a matter of trying to 'prove' that performance thinks or that theatre can be philosophical – and certainly not in any empirical sense. Yet, as Stanley Cavell concluded in relation to film though, perhaps the performance-as-philosophy argument cannot be made *in general*; it can only become convincing through the proliferation of analyses of specific performances, by performing the power of theatre to generate new thinking in writing, thoughts that are not the same as those constituted by its own events but are nevertheless produced by an encounter with them (Sinnerbrink 2011: 123). Or, again, we might draw from the American performance company Goat Island's notion of 'creative response' to suggest that performance's power to philosophize can be evidenced through the extent to which it provokes new forms of making and that we can respond to how performance thinks *in kind*. Or finally, perhaps we might equally conclude that theatre thinks in its own way precisely at those points when it resists our attempts not only to paraphrase it, but even to think it at all, at least according to an existing image of thought. In his discussion of Societas Raffaello Sanzio's piece 'On the Concept of the Face, Regarding the Son of God', for instance, Joe Kelleher (2013: 118) writes that:

> each performance is terminal, and terminally silent, as if somehow its thinking – the thinking of the performance – were calculated to resist the thinking – including the sort of productive consumption I am attempting here – that feeds upon it for its speech.

And to some extent, this is where both Deleuze and Laruelle situate the value of the encounter between philosophy and its other – whether that non-philosophy is construed as performance, science, or more broadly as the Real. Which is not to return to the notion of art or indeed life's ineffability. Rather, in Deleuze, non-philosophy is valued as that which challenges philosophy to go beyond received opinion or doxa, to create new concepts in response to that which it cannot recognize according to the formulations of common sense. In Laruelle, the Real – including the non-philosophy that is theatre and performance – is construed as a kind of inexhaustible excess to which no one ontology, no one philosophical account can lay claim. Relating to that Real, in turn, is less a matter of a pursuit of any one truth or essence, and more a matter of multiplying our perspectives – of 'seeing with as many eyes as possible', as Nietzsche would have it. And yet, this is not simply a reiteration of the postmodern maxim: 'anything goes, because nothing is real'; all philosophies are of equal value (or equally lack value) because none of them are true. Rather, Laruelle invites us to experiment with the hypothesis that all non-philosophies are equal because they are all part of the Real rather than more or less truthful representations of it. According to this democracy of thinking, the call is not 'to think without philosophy but to think without the *authority* of philosophy' (Laruelle, in Mullarkey 2009: xiii – my translation), including practising performance as an event of attending to its own plural ways of knowing and performing philosophy as the act of seeing new forms of thought in the non-philosophical realm of performance.

Notes

1 For more information on Performance Philosophy, the professional association, see http://performancephilosophy.ning.com/.

2 For instance, at the inaugural Performance Philosophy conference held at the University of Surrey in April 2013, while around 40 per cent of presenters were from theatre and performance studies backgrounds, the rest were from other fields including around 20 per cent from philosophy and critical theory.

3 The lack of exchange between analytic philosophy and theatre and performance arguably persists on the side of theatre studies, scholars of which still tend to prefer to work with continental thought. In 2001, David Saltz (2001: 149) argued that the Anglo-American tradition of analytic philosophy was 'one of the few major theoretical paradigms almost entirely absent from the discourse of contemporary theatre and performance theory and criticism'. Saltz cites J.L. Austin and Wittgenstein as two instances of 'cross-over' figures, who are referenced by analytic philosophers and theatre theorists; however, he also notes that one would be highly unlikely to hear any mention of 'seminal [analytic] philosophers such as Wilard Quine, Hilary Putman, Donald Davidson or Winfrid Sellars' in a theatre discourse (ibid.: 150).

4 Aristotle's *Poetics* is broadly considered 'the first philosophical account of Greek theatre' (Puchner 2010: 9), while the *Natya Shastra* (*Nātyaśāstra*) is an ancient Indian work on the performing arts, attributed to the sage Bharata and variously dated from 'about 500 BC to 300 AD' (Purohit 1988: 118).

5 For further information on the festival and other work being undertaken by colleagues in Germany in the area of performance philosophy, see www.sound-check-philosophie.de/ and http://performativephilosophie.wordpress.com/.

6 Readers interested in an introduction to the work of Laruelle might turn to *Laruelle and Non-Philosophy* (2012) edited by John Mullarkey and Anthony Paul Smith.

7 For instance, in Stephen Mulhall's work, it is proposed that '(1) films can reflect upon, question, even contribute to our understanding of significant philosophical questions or problems, (2) films can question or explore the nature of the cinematic medium in a manner comparable to philosophy ('philosophy of film'); and (3) films can reflect upon their own conditions of possibility or their own status as cinematic fictions' (Sinnerbrink 2011: 120).

8 In terms of recent texts on Shakespeare and philosophy, interested readers might look to Tzachi Zamir's (2006) *Double Vision: Moral Philosophy and Shakespearean Drama* (Princeton: Princeton University Press); Michael Witmore's (2008) *Shakespearean Metaphysics* (New York: Continuum); or Agnes Heller's (2002) *The Time Is Out of Joint: Shakespeare as Philosopher of History* (Rowman & Littlefield).

9 The relationship between these parts to the whole, or of the nature of this immanent rather than transcendent thought still needs work. But the point here is

that the notion of parts is less understood in a quantitative sense, but more as a critique of representation, where it is sometimes assumed that there is a privileged part (the image of philosophy as an exemplary form of reason) that can stand for the whole.

Works cited

Bowie, Andrew. *Music, Philosophy, and Modernity*. Cambridge: CUP, 2008.

Carroll, Noël and Banes, Sally. 'Theatre: Philosophy, Theory, and Criticism.' *Journal of Dramatic Theory and Criticism*, 16 (2001): 155–66.

Cull, Laura. 'Performance as Philosophy: Responding to the Problem of "Application."' *Theatre Research International,* 37.1 (2012): 20–7.

Deleuze, Gilles. *Difference and Repetition*, New York: Continuum, 2004.

Frampton, Daniel. *Filmosophy*, London: Wallflower Press, 2006.

Kelleher, Joe. 'The Writing on the Wall: Performances of Thinking, Terminal and Interminable', in How Performance Thinks conference proceedings, 114–22, http://performancephilosophy.ning.com/page/how-performance-thinks, 2013.

Kottman, Paul. *Philosophers on Shakespeare*, Stanford: Stanford University Press, 2009.

Lane, Richard. (ed.) *Beckett and Philosophy*, Basingstoke: Palgrave Macmillan, 2002.

Laruelle, François. 'Is Thinking Democratic?', in John Mullarkey and Anthony Paul Smith (eds) *Laruelle and Non-Philosophy*, Edinburgh: Edinburgh University Press, 2012, 281–95.

Livingston, Paisley. 'Theses on Cinema as Philosophy', in Murray Smith and Thomas E. Wartenberg (eds) *Thinking through Cinema: Film as Philosophy*. Oxford: Blackwell, 2006, 11–18.

Livingston, Paisley. *Cinema, Philosophy, Bergman: On Film as Philosophy*. Oxford: Oxford University Press, 2009.

Mullarkey, John. *Refractions of Reality: Philosophy and the Moving Image*, Basingstoke: Palgrave Macmillan, 2009.

Mullarkey, John and Smith, Anthony Paul (eds). *Laruelle and Non-Philosophy*, Edinburgh: Edinburgh University Press, 2012.

Nussbaum, Martha. 'Stages of Thought', *The New Republic*, available at www.tnr.com/article/books-and-arts/stages-thought, 2008.

Puchner, Martin. *The Drama of Ideas: Platonic Provocations in Theater and Philosophy*, Oxford: OUP, 2010.

Purohit, Vinayak. *Arts of Transitional India Twentieth Century*, vol. 1, Delhi: Popular Prakashan, 1988.

Reinelt, Janelle and Roach, Joseph (eds). *Critical Theory and Performance*, Ann Arbor: University of Michigan Press, 1992.

Saltz, David. 'Why Performance Theory Needs Philosophy', *Journal of Dramatic Theory and Criticism*, 16(1): 149–54, 2001.

Sinnerbrink, Robert. *New Philosophies of Film: Thinking Images*, New York: Continuum, 2011.

Totzke, Rainer and Gauss, Eva Maria. Unpublished abstract for What is Performance Philosophy? conference, 2012.

11 Translation, Cultural Ownership

Maria M. Delgado

I'd like to start with a story or rather a couple of stories; they take place about ten years apart. The first is in 1993 and I am in my first academic job; my doctorate is just completed and I'm networking at a conference. A senior academic in theatre studies/performance studies asks me: 'What am I working on? What are my areas of interest?' I reply: 'Spanish theatre.' 'Ah,' he nods earnestly, 'you should talk to David Bradby.' 'He works on French theatre,' I retort. 'Oh yes,' he replies 'but isn't it all European theatre?' I wanted to remind him that, to the best of my knowledge, and despite the then Conservative government's strong anti-Europe leanings, he too was based in Europe and working on European theatre. Or do theatre and performance studies scholars somehow think that the English or English-language theatres are somehow so pervasive that they exist outside the frame of geographic parameters?

Ten years on, I'm at an event organized by Lynette Hunter and Peter Lichtenfels at Shakespeare's Globe theatre in London, bringing together directors and academics who work on Shakespeare and a set of respondents whose job is to map the points of convergence and divergence between these encounters. I am talking to David Bradby – a fellow respondent and now one of my closest professional collaborators – when a UK-based academic comes bounding up to us and asks: 'What are you doing here, David? There's no French theatre here!' I respond: 'But surely, there's Shakespeare in France or does Shakespeare just belong to the Brits?' An embarrassed silence ensues.

My reason for beginning with these incidents is not about 'outing' colleagues or contemporaries in the discipline but about pointing to certain assumptions that shape the ways we look at theatre and performance in the UK. Yes, there is important Welsh-language work that takes place in a range of institutions in Wales, but this scholarship rarely 'speaks out' to scholars outside the Welsh language, in the way that Catalan-language work regularly published in bi- or trilingual journals does, and it represents a small percentage of the scholarship undertaken in the UK.[1] The

UK is an island and one that has not suffered occupation since 1066. The vestiges of empire, the world dominance of English, and the physical isolation from other geographical states has bred both insularity and complacency. Even in Wales, only 16.3 per cent of the population can read, write and speak Welsh.[2] 'Why bother learning other languages,' I am regularly informed, 'when the whole world speaks English.' But whose English are they speaking and what assumptions inform the structures through which the language is promoted and disseminated?

'Become less provincial' Marvin Carlson urged ASTR (American Society for Theatre Research) members in his contribution to the debate on 'Theatre History in the New Millennium' published in *Theatre Survey* in November 2004. Carlson (2004: 178) used North American government and economic policy, indifferent to or largely uninterested in matters outside its national boundaries (unless they impact on its corporate or monetary interests), as an analogy for a theatrical culture that he terms 'almost as provincial in its concerns and interests'. The power of the dollar has ensured that North American culture is the framework against which other cultural positions are defined. Its hegemonic power reaches across the developed and the developing world, the Northern and Southern hemispheres. Imperialism and cultural might go hand in hand.

Reading his comments, I found them equally applicable to the UK. We balked in embarrassment when George W. Bush and Tony Blair waxed enthusiastically about their 'special relationship', but it's possible to argue for a special relationship also in the sphere of theatre and performance studies. For many UK-based scholars, the US remains the ultimate aspiration. The ASTR and ATHE (Association for Theater in Higher Education) annual gatherings remain the pinnacles of the conference circuit; *Theatre Journal*, *Theatre Survey* and *TDR* the most prestigious journals in the business. It is to US scholarship that UK academics frequently turn when looking to conceptualize frameworks or critical discourses. The impact of Patrice Pavis and Hans-Thies Lehmann on scholarship in the UK comes largely by virtue of having their key critical texts translated into English. There are always exceptions, of course, but it's worth remembering that of the 125,000 or so works published in the UK in any one year, only 3 per cent are in translation. The proportion of translated works in Spain, for example, is nearer 25 per cent.

Theatre and performance studies in the UK looks, in methodologies and subject matter, to work occurring in English, with a particular gravitation around work occurring within these national boundaries. I am not suggesting that the privileging of the one's own national or cultural theatres should not happen, simply questioning the assumptions that ensue when that privileging inscribes a certain dominant order or hierarchy of theatrical cultures. The dominance of the English language effectively means that for many scholars in the UK 'international' means Anglo-American or Australian. English may be the world language but it is English as a second language, and it is marked, tainted and inflected through the discourses of colonialism. It accepts its own utterability as a given.[3] How many articles are published in English-language theatre journals from scholars writing in English as their second language? How much of the published scholarship is translated from another language into English?

Certainly, as journal editors – I write here as joint editor of Routledge's *Contemporary Theatre Review* – we have little practical assistance in facilitating that translation of scholarship into English. Funds are limited and so it's often a case of having to undertake the translation as part of our editorial duties. Translation is rarely recognized or respected as a scholarly activity and yet it is a constant process of negotiation and conceptualization; the transplanting of ideas, the re-situation of concerns. There is nothing imitative about translation. It is a process dependent on critical inflection and interpretation; indeed, the analogy with conducting a score or staging a script has been made on many previous occasions. Some languages have a wider vocabulary than others, some more rhetorical structures. There is sometimes no equivalent for particular phrases, words or sayings between languages. Walter Benjamin's recommendations that translators 'incorporate the original's mode of signification, thus making both the original and the translation recognizable as fragments of a greater language' (2004: 81) sometimes resonates as the art of the impossible.

Translation is always about interventions. Some might be invisible, others invasive. Translation can, as Lawrence Venuti (1995: 67) has observed, decontextualize (and domesticate) a foreign culture or keep it as something distant and different from the target culture (see Schleiermacher 2004). While there is, arguably, always an element of betrayal involved in the process of reworking a text into another language, it is nevertheless a process that allows my language, in the words of Rudolf Pannwitz, to be 'powerfully jolted' through the engagement with the 'other' language (cited in Venuti 1995: 148). Translation is indeed central to what I do as a scholar working largely outside English-language theatres. It shapes how I see, perceive, conceptualize and teach theatre. It allows me to bring the work of scholars and practitioners working outside the frames of the English language into 'the public domain' controlled by English-language scholarship. It allows me to consistently rethink the different patterns of exchange and assimilation that govern theatre making and theatre writing – what Marvin Carlson (2004: 179) has termed 'the increasing interconnectedness of our world'. It is also a means of locating dissonance and discontents. I am always disappointed when, usually in the name of 'saving space', I am asked by publishers and journal editors to 'cut' the language I am quoting from and simply provide an English-language version. I regard this as a process of erasure, of wiping the 'difference' of the original from the page: it doesn't allow for the reader to make certain connections, or follow my journey, and it imposes my translation without allowing it to function as the site of discussion. It erases the 'in between' of languages that functions, in turn, as a metaphor for the larger 'in betweens' within which I work: the state between reading and documenting performance, between conceptualizing and articulating, between theory and practice, between visibility and invisibility, between erasure and inscription. Barthes' *Camera Lucida* and Barthes' *La Chambre Claire* are two very different things. The moment you assume that they are one and the same, your attention to the arch, architecture and texture of the language shifts. It is as applicable to Ibsen, García Lorca or Brecht as it is to Barthes, Derrida or Pavis. We forget such difference at our peril.

While performance studies questioned the privileging of the dramatic text, thus allowing for a rethinking of theatrical language, it is still highly inflected through Anglo-American parameters and critical discourses. Performance studies has certainly opened up academic attention to a range of cultural phenomena and manifestations but it has also permitted and indeed endorsed particular colonialist assumptions around the availability and 'ownership' of the performance event. Ric Knowles' (2004: 181) important work on festivals as 'manifestations of a theatrical version of late-capitalist globalization, postmodern marketplaces for the exchange not so much of culture as of cultural capital' is a pervasive reminder of the economic imperatives that underpin theatrical exchange. I wonder whether his views on festivals as the sites for the exhibition of cultural objects decontextualized in the ways that 'modernist artists themselves pillaged African masks and "oriental" forms of ritual expression' is applicable in some way to certain strands of scholarship in our discipline (Knowles 2004: 181). In our supposedly global marketplace, in a voracious search for the new, how far are we, as performance scholars, cultural tourists searching to expand our own horizons and those of our discipline through contact with 'otherness'. If Chris Rojek's study of modern tourism points to its rise in the West over the past 50 years as tied to a belief that it would lead towards self-realization and fulfilment, it also signals the ways in which we cannot escape our cultural conditioning and assumptions. Tourism also inevitably reforms, taints and marks the landscapes it defines as 'pure', 'authentic' or 'untouched' (Rojek 1993: 5).

How far are Rojek's observations appropriate to performance studies? How far are we aware of the ethical implications of our scholarship? Of the responsibility that comes with the colonialist inflections of branches of our research? Or our privileged economic and cultural positions? Is theory the only necessary contextualization? I was once unceremoniously informed by a scholar working on the Catalan performance group La Fura dels Baus that he really didn't need to know Spanish or Catalan to undertake the proposed project: 'They're not making theatre, they're making performance that transcends literary language.' But, I ask, does it transcend a social context? And how is that social, political or economic context defined?

For those of us born into families fleeing political persecution, where travelling is a means of survival rather than an aesthetic choice, sometimes the metaphor of travel doesn't sit too easily as a form of defining how we approach performance. I am more comfortable with the trope of migrancy. My family were migrants, refugees who came to the UK and had to invent a new identity for themselves. Migrancy is who I am as well as what I do. I am reminded here of London-based director Jatinder Verma's remark that he considers

> that what the word migrant has given me in terms of theatrical sensi-
> bility is that what I think we *do* in the theatre is to translate; is to bear
> across to an audience a particular story or a particular work. And that
> seems to me to be what migration is all about, bearing from one world
> into another. (cited in Plastow 2004: 83)

Translation is, for me, irrevocably bound up with migrancy; it's about the need to work across languages, to propose hypotheses that articulate the shifting, indeed 'migratory' understanding of concepts that are being contested across the discipline, and undertaking reassessments of figures who have, for political, social or economic reasons, remained outside conventional historical narratives.

Harry Elam Jr's call for a 'creative, critical historicism' that recognizes our own complicity in the making of history seems to me particularly pertinent here. Elam (2004: 219) uses Walter Benjamin's suggestion of rubbing 'history against the grain' as a way of indicating the challenges that lie ahead for us as a discipline in historicizing our present; it involves interrogating

> the past in order to inform the present, remaining cognizant of the mate-
> rial conditions that not only shape historical production but the historical
> interpretations of production. It implies a need to work against conven-
> tional narratives and the ways in which history has been told in the past.

This is not to denigrate the incredible work that has been done in thea-tre and performance studies in the crafting of alternative histories, the issue of documenting ethically the recognition of the (sometimes) problematic position from which we read and interpret. The discipline now feels very different to the drama degree I encountered in 1983 when I entered the university system as an undergraduate student. I still think, however, there's a way to go. Some of the most vibrant research networks, clusters and asso-ciates I work with aren't based in the UK or the US. Many are situated across Spain and Argentina. They are among the 400 million inhabitants of the globe who count Spanish as their first language but an overwhelming proportion of these are in the Southern hemisphere: the cultural might of Spanish in no way relates to the proportion of the globe that speaks the language. English is spoken as a first language by 300 million and as a second language by a further 300 million. Diana Taylor's important work with the Hemispheric Institute of Performance and Politics has been hugely significant in shifting disciplinary understandings and broadening cultural knowledges of Central and South America, but it should not be seen as a substitute for further incentives or initiatives, and its impact in the UK is far less marked than in the US.

Multiculturalism is not simply about visiting a Thai restaurant, the local Chinatown's New Year celebrations, or the barrio's *Fiesta de la Virgen de Guadalupe* once a year. It is about recognizing our prejudices and the priv-ileged positions we often occupy through our geographical placing. It is about looking at what we do and how we do it as scholars and critics and thinking through the global and local consequences of these acts. How do they map out wider historiographies and canons? How can we support and disseminate broader bodies of knowledge around theatre and performance that draw on the findings and observations of academics working outside the English language? How can we ensure that performance remains an ethical mode of enquiry as much as the object of enquiry? How can we interconnect more productively with scholarship that is not disseminated through English-language journals? How can we facilitate the publication of more scholarship in English-language journals by scholars working in English as a second or third language? In the UK, the closing of modern language university departments and the government's position on the teaching of languages in schools looks likely to have implications on what is researched by future generations of graduate students.

We cannot ever hope to be comprehensive (and luckily few scholars position their work in this way, although the pressures of publishers still push towards *the* definitive textbook, *the* definitive guide, *the* most compre-hensive coverage, all in the most compact formula possible); *but* in our partiality, our specificity, we can aspire to the telling of stories and the documenting of practices that recognize overlap, intersections and connections in creative and multilingual ways. Translating, transposing, adapting and, to return to Verma's earlier remarks, 'bearing from one world to another' (83) should be central to both what we do and how we do it. I believe that we have ethical responsibilities to consider our own roles as makers, critics, archivists and historians of performance. Our choices have profound implications on how wider demographics of performance are constructed. In facilitating mechanisms that allow for the dissemination of research beyond the mainstream Anglo-American paradigm, perhaps we can attempt to create broader histories of performance that interrogate rather than accept the political hegemony of English and the implications of this for our understanding of the global village.

Notes

1   In Catalonia, for example, the journals *Pausa* and *DDT* are published in Catalan, English and Castilian.
2   In Catalonia, the analogous figure is nearly 50 per cent, with almost 95 per cent having an understanding of the language.
3   Much of the scholarship examining the refractions of English has come through its relationship to youth culture, issues of postcolonialism, and the language's relationship to Spanish in the US. See, for example, the works by Flores, Fusco, Gómez-Peña, Mercer and Stavans cited below. For a further commentary on this issue, see also Delgado and Svich.

Works cited

Benjamin, Walter. 'The Task of the Translator: An Introduction to the Translation of Baudelaire's *Tableaux Parisiens*.' In Lawrence Venuti, ed., *The Translation Studies Reader*. New York: Routledge, 2004: 75–82.

Carlson, Marvin. 'Become Less Provincial.' *Theatre Survey* 45.2 (2004): 177–80.

Delgado, Maria M. and Svich, Caridad. 'En Conjunto: from el performance to la performativa.' *Performance Research* 13.2 (2008): 37–8.

Elam, Harry J. Jr. 'Making History.' *Theatre Survey* 45.2 (2004): 219–25.

Flores, Jan. *From Bomba to Hip Hop: Puerto Rican Culture and Latino Identity*. New York: Columbia University Press, 2000.

Fusco, Coco. *English is Broken Here: Notes on Cultural Fusion in the Americas*. New York: The New Press, 1995.

Gómez-Peña, Guillermo. *Dangerous Border Crossings: The Artist Talks Back*. New York: Routledge, 2000.

Knowles, Ric. *Reading the Material Theatre*. Cambridge: CUP, 2004.

Mercer, Kobena. *Welcome to the Jungle: New Positions in Black Cultural Studies*. London: Routledge, 1994.

Plastow, Jane. 'Jatinder Verma: Encounters with the Epic – An Interview.' *Contemporary Theatre Review* 14.2 (2004): 82–7.

Rojek, Chris. *Ways of Escape: Modern Tourism in Leisure and Travel*. London: Routledge, 1993.

Schleiermacher, Friedrich. 'On the Different Methods of Translation.' In Lawrence Venuti, ed., *The Translation Studies Reader*. New York: Routledge, 2004: 43–63.

Stavans, Ilan. *Spanglish: The Making of a New American Language*. New York: Rayo, 2004.

Venuti, Lawrence. *The Translator's Invisibility: A History of Translation*. New York: Routledge, 1995.

Venuti, Lawrence. *The Scandals of Translation: Towards an Ethics of Difference*. New York: Routledge, 2004.

12   The Intense Exterior

Rick Dolphijn

How does the body move?

In a personal conversation with theorist Brian Massumi (2011: 140), choreographer William Forsythe stated that 'a body is that which folds'. Intrigued by returning issues like 'How can we tell the dancer from the dance?' (see Colebrook 2005), Forsythe's remarkable conceptualization of the body offered Massumi a starting point to differentiate contemporary from modern dance. Warding off any emphasis on representation and on using the body as a means to express an inner feeling, as happens in modern dance (Massumi specifically mentions Martha Graham's symbolic use of gesture; see, for instance, Graham 1937), he claims that contemporary dance intends 'to focus on pure movement' (Gil 2002: 121, quoted in Massumi 2011). Thus, whereas in modern dance the body dances (bodily movements create the dance), the dancer in contemporary dance comes to be *in* the dance (movements create a dancing body). An epic example of the latter would be Pina Bausch's *Café Müller*, where the chairs in the café did not surround the dancer creating the mise-en-scène in front of which the dancer danced: the chairs are involved in the dance no less than the dancer. The chairs, the bodies of the dancers and actually everything else somewhat complicit, make up for the raw material by means of which the dance (per)forms, from which the dance is abstracted.

Forsythe's definition indeed shows us that contemporary dance overcomes the dualisms that gave form to modernity/modern dance. On the one hand, it has no interest anymore in the opposition between the dancer and the world (which it was supposed to re-present or dance to). Contemporary dance does not consider the body 'already in existence', filled with potentialities to be realized whenever the situation (the dance) asks it to. On the contrary, the body is actualized in the dance, which means that it is *only* through the act of folding (the dance) that it (the body, the fold) realizes itself. On the other hand, this means that the folding actualizing a bodily whole is not consequential to (Aristotelian) memory or another agency from which the body is organized in advance. Rather, the body (plus the mind) happens *in* the fold, which is to say that it is only because of the folding that its unity appears.

To consider the body an immanent composition by movement reminds us of the work of Gilbert Simondon (1992: 311) on individuation, when he stated:

> Instead of grasping individuation using the individuated being as a starting point, we must grasp the individuated being from the viewpoint of individuation, and individuation from the viewpoint of preindividual being, each operating at many different orders of magnitude.

Directed against modernist philosophy (and physics, biology and psychology), Simondon's refusal of an anthropocentric genesis that works backward (presuming a history) in favor of an ontogenesis of works towards the realization of futurity makes a similar (contemporary) plea for pure movement, for immanence, and for thinking in terms of folds.

This refusal to start our thinking with modernist propositions is nicely conceptualized by Forsythe's use of 'the fold'. For isn't the fold, first and foremost, telling us that the body, even at the moment it appears to us (the realized moment of resemblance), is *not* to be considered an inside that can be opposed to an (or its) outside? Gilles Deleuze's (1988: 98) fold perhaps best tells us how to rethink the body as that which folds, when he states that:

> The outside is not a fixed limit but moving matter animated by peristaltic movements, folds and foldings that altogether make up an inside: they are not something other than the outside, but precisely the inside of an outside.

In his choreography *One Flat Thing*, Forsythe shows us best how dance can dissolve a fixed, geometric grid of tables into a topological surface in movement according to a series of synchronous folds and foldings (clustered bodies, contrapuntal bodies, complexes, differentiations).[1]

Rejecting the difference between inside and outside altogether is probably the only way to stress how radically contemporary dance is all about pure movement. Dance cannot be captured by bodily codes, its expressionism cannot be limited by signs, its movements to Vetruvian schemas. Contemporary dance is not about 'meaning' nor does it 'resist' anything, as Cooper Albright still claims (1997: xiv). In the early 1960s, legendary performer Merce Cunningham made it all too clear when claiming:

There's no thinking involved in my choreography. I work alone for a couple of hours every morning in the studio. I just try things out. And my eye catches something in the mirror, or the body catches something that looks interesting; and then I work on that … I don't work through images or ideas – I work through the body. (quoted in Tomkins 1965: 246)

More explicitly than Forsythe, Cunningham was very outspoken in his rejection of the modern tradition, especially its emphasis on schemes: 'That sort of A-B-A business based on emotional or psychological meanings just seemed ridiculous to me' (quoted in Tomkins 1965: 244).

Cunningham beautifully explains how contemporary dance does not start with the body but with the feeling of *all* matter, *every* form to be actualized and realized in the dance to come. Getting rid of modernism, then, also means getting rid of the body as the point of departure for dance to happen. Or, as José Gil (1998: 145) put it: 'energy circulates directly in space rather than from the body to things'. Contemporary dance is to feel the unforeseen, to allow the unexpected vibrations to kick in. Its point of departure should therefore be what Gil (2006: 24) later referred to as 'the intense exterior'.

Infinite experimentations

In the intensive exterior, all matter *has to be* opened up, one way or another, by a continuous myriad of forces that we could call 'the dance'. This is what Massumi refers to as the 'speculative' nature of contemporary dance. Every movement, every posture, is a movement to come, a promise never to be redeemed. For dance can no longer be a move from one gesture to the next, since in between, always already, something happens, a movement is broken up: unforeseen intensities keep on (un-)folding all matter into new bodies. Keeping this in mind, we must conclude that there is no reason to consider contemporary dance necessarily in its relation to the modern tradition. The intensive exterior is about the breaking up of *all* movement, transforming all geometrical surfaces into topological planes, and there is no reason to relate this solely to modern dance. Every possible tradition can be broken up and must be. If only because the intensive exterior refuses any predetermined relationality at all (creating connections *in immanence* is what it's all about), it can be – and must be – at work in all possible traditions.

In order to feel how the folding starts, how matter is opened up and (per) formed in contemporary dance, let us look more closely at a scene in contemporary dance practice in which this intense exterior is at work. I propose to analyze a scene from the performance *Ghost Track* by LeineRoebana. It is an intra-action between the dancers, Tim Persent and Boby Ari Setiawan, and the contemporary gamelan music played by Iwan Gunawan and his Kyai Fatahillah orchestra. The compositions and improvisations of Gunawan in many ways recall Karl-Heinz Stockhausen's orchestral works (the gamelan orchestra is as diverse as any contemporary symphony orchestra, with its woodwind, brass, percussion, strings and, today, electronics sections), though its emphasis on percussion (metallophones, xylophones and drums) proves how the history of gamelan (much more so than the symphony orchestra) always already comes with a history of dance (and with a history of martial arts, and a history of theater). Gunawan's rhythms are thus not the rhythms 'to be danced to', they do not set the body into motion: they *are* the rhythms always already traversing matter, the movements of the hands and of the eyes, the syncopating and polyrhythmic chants *are* the dimensionalities and directionalities according to which the rituals are set out in space. The acceleration and deceleration of the pulse keeps on altering qualitatively the proper intervals in which the body happens.

The pulses and peristaltic movements that dance the matters involved traverse patterns from modern traditions and Javanese traditions. In the beginning, the two dancers (slowly) skirt around each other. Facing the audience, standing belly to back, one dancer firmly attaches to the ground, slowly shifting his balance from left to right, while the other rises to the sky, searching for ways to fall into the emptynesses created while being pulled out of them. The former dances a *kreasi baru*, a 'new creation', which comes down to a re-creation of or improvisation upon (*nandhak*) all sorts of narrations (*greget*) found in the old Central Javanese and Sundanese traditions. The latter dancer was bound to rewrite the heritage of ballet, the relatively recent fulcrum of so many Occidental dancing styles. But as the experiment progresses, both traditions get tangled up into one another. Both styles turn out impossible to 'maintain'. Lines intertwine, the breaking up of movements is unavoidable, the one *has to* bleed into the other, and vice versa. And this is where the intense exterior kicks in.

During several of the public discussions I had with Harijono Roebana, one of the choreographers (the other being Andrea Leine), he kept on insisting that he (and his Occidental dancers) knew very little about all the different and rich traditions in Indonesian dance. Similarly, the Indonesian dancers were not aware of how modern dance worked. Themes were not copied, narrations were not retold. The pulses and the peristaltic movements, which became more and more forceful, more and more persistent throughout the dance, slowly but steadily broke open the traditions and all that they presumed. There was no pattern of interaction, no understanding, no anticipation possible. Something new had to step in, generated from the various individual movements as they clashed. A new system that *included* the dancers as well as the musicians and their instruments had to be actualized. And it had to be kept in movement not by the dancers or the musicians but by this larger entity, by the event, by the system itself. The new information causing this learning process came 'only from *within the system*'; as Bateson (2002: 130) says: 'There has been a change in boundaries.'

The abstract relations felt in the intense exterior modify a dance in every possible way. The two dancers extend each other's movements, folding and unfolding them, creating the unforeseen new bodies that make up the new dance, the contemporary dance. The old does not disappear but is fragmented and taken up into the new: the movements of the (over) stretching of the fingers (*ngithing*) aimed at creating figures such as 'the full moon' and 'the crescent moon' are now broken off only to be continued by the upper arm of the other dancer or in the sonorous sound of the gong. Still facing the audience, the two dancers, the two traditions, opened up, creating a vertical topological plane in constant metamorphosis. This happens through what Spuybroek (2011: 22) calls the 'stepwise procedure of iterative adjustments based on the minimalization of difference'. The smallest variation continuously makes entirely new figures arise – J-curves, S-curves, bodies that never happened before. The dance never follows the potentials of the body of the dancer, it does not respect what any body can do. On the contrary, oppositions between the important and unimportant, the approximate and the distant are all broken up *and* smoothened. Every dance creates a new diagram, a new set of functives, of textures *inhabiting* the matters involved, drawing them out anew.

The contemporary is already taking place

Ghost Track shows us that the intense exterior, as it signals contemporary performance, is at work everywhere. As may be expected, given its topological nature, it being unlimited, a transversal force through everything, the intense exterior has the potential of breaking up all matter, every aspect of that-which-is-about-to-happen. Its ethics is not that of 'opening oneself up' to the other, as Derrida (2000: 25, italics added) would have it (when he famously stated that: 'Absolute hospitality requires that *I open up* my home'), but rather of 'being opened up', as contemporary materialist philosophers such as Reza Negarestani propose. Being opened up by an outside force has nothing to do with having 'knowledge of' this force, this Otherness, it has nothing to do with respecting the Other or even tolerating her/him. To open up to the Other is, by its nature, a deeply conservative gesture, as it always departs from a self, from a humanism and thus shows us, once again, that postmodernist strategies are not too different from their modern predecessors. In the end, they propose the very opposite spatial politics compared to what Negarestani and others are after. Negarestani (2008: 199) puts it as follows:

> To become open, or to experience the chemistry of openness is not possible through 'opening yourself' ... Radical openness can be evoked by becoming more of a target for the outside ... one must seduce the exterior forces of the outside.

In the dance discussed above, this is precisely how the intense exterior is at work. A dancer or a tradition or any possible body becomes 'a target' not because it knows the Other, opens up or reaches out for 'it', on the contrary, radical openness is all about seducing the totality of exterior forces kicking in. The chemistry of radical openness is pure bodily experimentation, for only then can that radical change of boundaries occur, only then can folds or bodies happen anywhere. Then, it breaks open the dancers, the modern traditions, the traditions from Central Java and everything else to play a role. The intense exterior breaks open any dance. Its unforeseen new folds, its unknown new figures can be actualized everywhere, every time. For the intense exterior, although crucial to contemporary dance, is by no means limited to events that happen in our time. The intense exterior is a powerful transversal force that easily folds its way across time and space, breaking up all those bodies willing to become a target, willing to be broken up.

There is good reason why *Ghost Track* perseveres in breaking up the modern traditions *and* the Central Javanese ones. For as the intense exterior is invented time and again, this happens, par excellence, in Central Javanese performance traditions. In these traditions, there could never have been a *l'art pour l'art* movement (a tendency towards a purification of the arts). For it is not the melody and harmony but rather the tempo and (most of all) the density (*Irama*) of the performance that unites the music, the dance and the storyline. And this continuous acceleration and deceleration of the performance finds its fulcrum in the particular folded nature of the orchestra. Unlike the *doubled* Baroque orchestras (two halves that most of the time were identical to one another, 'knew' one another, responded to one another and thus played with the themes and variations so popular in the modern tradition), the two parts of the gamelan orchestra have no knowledge of one another whatsoever. They are two very different orchestras that fold into one another, that turn into one body because they move together. Known as the *slendro* (a five-tone tuning) and *pelog* (a seven-tone tuning) system, each ensemble consists of two uniquely tuned groups of instruments that only through the density of the composition break each other up. Indeed, they do not open themselves up to the Other system, they are *being opened up by* this unknown outside.

The intense exterior practices a politics of movement that, before being intelligible, before being interpreted, signals an 'elasticity of sensation', as Deleuze (2005: 29) once called it, that tells us a lot about life, a lot about the affects, forces and movements that do not reveal themselves in terms of words. What Bateson (2002: 130) referred to as a 'change of boundaries', as we used it above, is bound to happen many times a day. The experiment we conduct with the unknown, with the unforeseen, *is* 'the outside world as *I* live it'. This is precisely how Gil's (2002: 125) radical theories of movement, of the intense exterior, time and again tell us that 'the meaning of movement is the very movement of meaning'.

Note

1   See http://synchronousobjects.osu.edu/.

Works cited

Bateson, Gregory. *Mind and Nature: A Necessary Unity*. Cresskill: Hampton Press, 2002.

Colebrook, Claire. 'How can we tell the Dancer from the Dance?: The Subject of Dance and the Subject of Philosophy.' *Topoi* 24.1 (2005): 5–14.

Cooper Allbright, Ann. *Choreographing Difference: The Body and Identity in Contemporary Dance*. Middletown: Wesleyan UP, 1997.

Deleuze, Gilles. *Foucault*, trans. and ed. Sean Hand. London: Athlone Press, 1988.

Deleuze, Gilles. *Francis Bacon: The Logic of Sensation*, trans. Daniel W. Smith. New York: Continuum, 2005.

Derrida, Jacques. *Of Hospitality*, trans. Rachel Bowlby. Stanford: Stanford UP, 2000.

Gil, José. *Metamorphoses of the Body*, trans. Stephen Muecke. Minneapolis: U of Minnesota P, 1998.

Gil, José. 'The Dancers Body', trans. Karen Ocaña. In Brian Massumi, ed., *Parables for the Virtual: Movement, Affect, Sensation*. Durham: Duke UP, 2002, 117–27.

Gil, José. 'The Paradoxical Body', trans. André Lepecki. *TDR: The Drama Review* 50.4 (2006): 21–35.

Graham, Martha. 'Artist Statement.' In Jean Morrison Brown, Naomi Mindlin and Charles Woodford, eds, *The Vision of Modern Dance: In the Words of Its Creators*, 2nd edn. Princeton: Princeton Book, 1937, 49–53.

Massumi, Brian. *Semblance and Event: Activist Philosophy and the Occurent Arts.* Cambridge: MIT Press, 2011.

Negarestani, Reza. *Cyclonopedia: Complicity with Anonymous Materials.* Melbourne: Re.press, 2008.

Simondon, Gilbert. 'The Genesis of the Individual', trans. Mark Cohen and Stanford Kwinter. In Jonathan Crary and Sanford Kwinter, eds, *Incorporations.* New York: Zone Books, 1992, 297–319.

Spuybroek, Lars. *The Sympathy of Things: Ruskin and the Ecology of Design.* Rotterdam: NAi, 2011.

Tomkins, Calvin. *The Bride and the Bachelors: The Heretical Courtship in Modern Art.* New York: Viking Press, 1965.

13   Cosmopolitanism

Milija Gluhovic

Many political and social theorists are increasingly engaging a protean category of 'cosmopolitanism', which at the very least signals an attempt to rethink the scope and scale of moral and political obligations among human beings whose identities and loyalties are no longer coextensive with the modern nation state. Derived from the Greek words 'world' (*cosmos*) and 'city' (*polis*), cosmopolitanism describes a citizen of the world who partakes in a 'universal circle of belonging that embraces the whole of humanity, as a result of the transcendence of the particularistic and blindly given ties of kinship and country' (Cheah 2006: 21). The common association of cosmopolitanism with an intellectual genealogy that begins with the Stoics, proceeds to include authors such as Rousseau and Kant, and culminates with contemporary authors located in the modern West has been challenged recently by a number of scholars, who seek to understand cosmopolitanism not only as an idea with its own intellectual history but also as social, political or cultural practice. To Pnina Werbner (2008: 2), for instance:

> at its most basic, cosmopolitanism is about reaching out across cultural differences through dialogue, aesthetic enjoyment, and respect; of living together with difference. It is also about the cosmopolitan right to abode and hospitality in strange lands and, alongside that, the urgent need to devise ways of living together in peace in the international community.

This shift in the understanding of cosmopolitanism as practice rather than an idea makes it possible to register not only the existence but also political import of a variety of located and embodied cosmopolitanisms that can – and in many ways already do – serve as resources for the reworking of contemporary cultural imaginaries. I do not have space here to track the shifting fortunes of cosmopolitanism over time or to survey the various understandings of cosmopolitanism currently in circulation. Rather, in the first part of this chapter I approach cosmopolitanism as a political standpoint that extends the horizon of the polis from the boundary of the nation state to the world as a whole, and which has arisen mostly in response to the political, economic, legal, environmental and cultural problems generated by the forces of globalization, problems that no state can address alone. Then, in the second part I explore Anne Lise Stenseth's installation *The Kiss and Waste Project*, which brings into sharp relief the 'tension between promise of cosmopolitanism as the enactment of universal communitas and its limits as a theory of embodied material praxis' (Gilbert and Lo 2007: 4). Here, I focus in particular on the apparently seamless connection between Northern multiculturalism and cosmopolitan democracy, which remains largely unelaborated.

Factors such as massive cross-border capital flows, increased movements of people, the onset of globally shared risks such as climate change, disease, poverty, or international organized crime as well as the moral questions that these enjoin have opened a space for an active revival of cosmopolitanism as both a moral and a political project. Many influential thinkers, such as Derrida, Kristeva, Habermas, Beck, Held, Harvey and Brennan, to name a few, have written pervasively on the topic in recent years. Among them, Jürgen Habermas has offered one of the most thorough elaborations of the implications of these globalizing processes for the realization of a cosmopolitan political project for the contemporary world. Following Kant, Habermas (2006) calls for a move from classical international law, rooted in the model of independent nation states, to a new cosmopolitan order with a 'global domestic politics', implemented by global institutions and legitimated from within national public spheres. To achieve this goal, Habermas believes that we need the solidarity of world citizens that would exert pressure on already existing global institutions and actors to regard themselves as members of a cosmopolitan community who should act in cooperation and respect one another's interests.

In his excellent book *Inhuman Conditions: On Cosmopolitanism and Human Rights*, Pheng Cheah (2006: 105) convincingly argues that transnational forms of public debate, democratic participation and accountability are neither sufficiently mass-based nor firmly institutionalized for Habermas's cosmopolitical formulation to have weight. In his view, 'in the absence of a world state capable of ensuring an equitable international political and economic order, economic globalisation is uneven', which severely hampers any chances for the emergence of mass-based global solidarities and a sense of belonging to a shared world. Habermas, argues Cheah, overidealizes the First World welfare state as a prototypical prerequisite for cosmopolitan consciousness, ignoring the fact that Northern civil societies derive their prodigious strength from revenues generated through uneven global development, while he simultaneously underplays the role of the postcolonial nation state in providing an institutional locus for resistance to global capital. Ultimately, for Cheah, capitalism and the structural ineq-uities of globalization represent the unsurpassable horizon for thinking the limits of cosmopolitanism and human rights.

According to critical theorist Nancy Frazer, in order to build effective strategies for building cosmopolitan solidarity, we need a configuration of public spheres and powers that would overcome two key problems: a deficit of democratic legitimacy and a deficit of political efficacy. The former, for instance, plagues the European Union (EU), 'where existing transnational administrative and legislative bodies are not matched by a European public sphere that could hold them accountable' (Frazer 2007: 82). On the other hand, continues Frazer, at the global level, existing transnational publics such as the World Social Forum (WSF) 'are not matched by comparable administrative and legislative powers' (2007: 82), which systematically short-circuits the potential for their political efficacy.

To Boaventura de Sousa Santos, the transcontinental activist milieux of the WSF have become the most accomplished expression of counter-hegemonic globalization and subaltern cosmopolitanism in this century. He sees subaltern cosmopolitanism as 'the vast set of networks, initiatives, organizations, and movements that fight against the economic, social, political, and cultural exclusion generated by the most recent incarnation of global capitalism, known as neoliberal globalization' (2007: 64). Accord-ing to Santos (2007: 64), because

> social exclusion is always the product of unequal power relations, these initiatives, movements, and struggles are animated by a redistributive ethos in its broadest sense, involving redistribution of material, social, political, cultural and symbolic resources and thus based both on the principle of equality and on the principle of recognition of difference.

These goals also animate the feminist struggles within the WSF. According to Virginia Vargas (2003: 912), one of the leading feminists within the forum, they concern 'two types of injustice: the socio-economic, rooted in the political and economic structures of society, and the cultural or symbolic, rooted in the social patterns of representation, interpretation and commu-nication'. As Vargas reminds us, these are injustices that women share with other groups that are discriminated against based on their race, ethnicity, sexual orientation and so on.

Some of these issues also feature prominently in Seyla Benhabib's schol-arship. In her book *The Rights of Others: Aliens, Residents, and Citizens*, she examines the normative principles and legal practices to incorporate aliens, strangers, immigrants, refugees and asylum seekers into existing polities.

Ultimately, Benhabib (2004: 73) claims that 'the right to membership ought to be considered a human right, in the moral sense of the term. And it ought to become a legal right as well by being incorporated into states' constitution through citizenship and naturalization provisions.' Indeed, in recent years, some have argued that 'Refugees, peoples of the diaspora, and migrants and exiles represent the spirit of the cosmopolitical community' (Pollock et al. 2000: 582). However, the danger with this argument is that it tends to reduce the complexity of contemporary globalization to one of its strands – cultural hybridization in transnational mobility – or to charac- terize transnational migrant cultures as existing radical cosmopolitanisms that subvert national culture or localism. As Helen Gilbert and Jacqueline Lo (2007: 187) argue:

> such proclamations seem not only utopian but also curiously indifferent in so far as they demand no redress of capitalism's structural inequali- ties and no commitment on the part of its beneficiaries to enter into cosmopolitical community with those whose experiences of exclusion stand as historical witness to the system's failures.

Furthermore, the dispositions exhibited by the celebratory figures of the cosmopolitan, the privileged national who enjoys unfettered movement, shows an openness to the variety of global cultures, and freely proclaims multiple attachments and identities, are often 'treated with suspicion and hostility when demonstrated by minorities and migrants' (Kofman 2005: 92). Such double standards are at once enacted and concealed by top-down cosmopolitan projects such as the EU (often looked upon as some kind of Kantian cosmopolitan construction). Indeed, from the late 1990s on, public discourse and state policies in many European states have become more explicitly assimilationist, placing increasingly high demands on migrants to prove their belonging to the nation and their loyalty to the state, and, in some cases, exclusive allegiance. Now that the confrontation between the forces of political Islam and Western liberal democracies has come to dominate European discourse and politics, and mainstream politi- cians have come to consider particular forms of Islam as incompatible with the European secular tradition, Judeo-Christian heritage, and values, 'the fear of divided loyalties and transnational political participation falls in particular upon Europe's Muslim populations, who must demonstrate that they are not truly cosmopolitan' (Kofman 2005: 92).

In the Danish context, for instance, where policy developments have moved from liberal pluralism to communitarian assimilationism, the construction of Denmark as a culturally homogeneous nation (now under threat from globalization, the EU and 'alien' cultures) has been bolstered by a range of practices emphasizing the need to actively produce a stronger national identity and placing on migrants the demand for conformity to what are explicitly framed as 'Danish' values. Here, as in the rest of Western Europe, traditional gender equality politics has been 'replaced by a highly selective minority gender equality politics primarily targeting immigrant communities' (Siim and Skjeie 2008: 322). Focusing on certain immigrant women and certain issues, such as the hijab (Islamic scarf), forced marriages, female genital cutting and so-called 'honour killings', the media largely ignore the vast heterogeneity of backgrounds and experiences of immigrant women, tending to construct them either as prisoners of religion and the private-familial sphere (emphasizing their domestic roles in the family) or as agents resisting 'integration'.

Creating connections between women from the Black and North Sea regions, Anne Lise Stenseth's installation *The Kiss and Waste Project*[1] mirrors the complexity of these issues.[2] Traveling and investigating with a video camera and engaging in a cross-cultural dialogue with women from these two European shores, Stenseth has created a work of art that intervenes in prevailing perceptions of geopolitical, economic and subjective reality of East–West European migration. Via a sequence of 12 short videos, the project brings together narratives of women who come from socialist Eastern Europe and currently work in Western Europe, or come from immigrant families from the Black Sea region now living in the West, or have stayed resident in their homelands but have been involved in the vast processes of cultural mobility that have been taking place through Europe recently. Forging dialogues with these women across national, cultural, economic and generational lines, Stenseth has offered them a temporary platform to articulate their experiences of living and moving between and across borders, nationalisms, ideologies and histories. Raising questions about the actual or desirable relationship between the local and the global, rootedness and detachment, particularism and universalism, the project also lays bare the complex nexus of power, history and culture that differentially constrains potential participants to any cosmopolitan dialogue.

I focus here on Stenseth's then-minute video titled 'Now, Right Now, Yet Still' (2009), made during her visit to Helsingør, Denmark, and featuring Tülay Oguz, a young Danish woman of Turkish background. I chose it because it articulates well the geopolitical asymmetries of power that currently render certain kinds of cosmopolitanism a prerogative enjoyed only by a select few. The frames of the video show a heavily pregnant Oguz, in a red dress, a white blouse, and a red and white headscarf with touches of green, shopping for food in a grocery store, and then writing at a computer desk, perhaps at her home. The latter scene alternates with a scene of a ferry, flying a red and white Danish flag, sailing out of Helsingør harbour. The harbour imagery is accompanied by the joyous music of a marching band orchestra. In Denmark, where this colour combination is very much part of everyday life and 'the nation is flagged on a continual basis' (Wren 2001: 149), the prevalence of the colours red and white in the video's opening frames and seamless transitions between the two scenes would seem to suggest harmony and ordinariness. As Karen Wren (2001: 149) points out: 'This flagging is closely tied in with the concepts of home and garden (many contain flags), hospitality and comfort, all key symbols of "Danishness".' The semantics of the scene is made more complex by the fact that Oguz is wearing a headscarf, and that the Turkish flag is also red and white.

While to some viewers the headscarf may intensify awareness of the cultural hybridity that marks the scene and perhaps highlight Oguz's multiple belongings and overlapping allegiances, we may also recall that, in Denmark, the hijab is 'regularly framed as being juxtaposed to "Danish" majority culture, values and traditions' (Siim and Skjeie 2008: 329). Later in the video, we see Oguz sitting on an almost empty beach, gently stroking her pregnant belly. The scene exudes a sense of anxiety and uncertainty, reminding us of some other melancholy women from *The Kiss and Waste Project*. The following shot of her in a window of her apartment is also evocative of the image of '"the immigrant mother" (imagined as poor and illiterate but skilled at draining the resources of the state)' (Raissiguier 2010: 74), which circulates prominently in the West. However, through her address to her grandmother in Turkey – in the video we see her reading a letter she has written to her grandmother – we find out that she and her husband are from Denmark, and that she is highly skilled. Voicing her grievances to her grandmother, she says: 'I feel it has been difficult to find anything when you are an engineer called Tülay. Perhaps it would have been easier if we were in Turkey.' Then she adds, cautiously: 'But many other things would have been more difficult.' Oguz's complaint points unambiguously to discrimination against Muslim women in Denmark.

In Europe, where the post-9/11 surge in Islamophobia has redrawn boundaries of citizenship, and where the headscarf is increasingly viewed as a political symbol requiring state regulation, second- and third-generation Muslim women find themselves having to justify belonging to places and communities into which they were born. While in France and Turkey Muslim women are banned from wearing headscarves in public institutions for fear they might undermine the sanctity of secularism, in Denmark there are no general regulations that restrict the wearing of religious dress in public settings. However, 'a recent Supreme Court decision in Denmark rules that employers still, under certain conditions, are allowed to ban hijabs in the work place' (Siim and Skjeie 2008: 323). Hence, in Denmark, where 'the racialisation of the Danish ethnic minority population has led to institutionalized racism, rampant labour market discrimination and extremely high levels of ethnic minority unemployment' (Wren 2001: 158), Muslim women are locked into material realities that limit their agency and reinforce neo-Orientalist perceptions of certain immigrants and diasporas as unwilling or unable to integrate into Danish society.

While recent headscarf debates in France, Germany and Turkey view the headscarf as a political symbol requiring state regulation, in her article 'Islamic Cosmopolitanism: The Sartorial Biographies of Three Muslim Women in London', Emma Tarlo (2007: 143–4) shows that for some Muslim women the wearing of the headscarf may be the result of 'cosmopolitan lifestyles and attitudes in which concerns about fashion, religion, politics and aesthetics are interwoven in interesting ways'. Noting the ascendancy of a new Muslim cosmopolitanism and global Islamic feminism in the past two decades, Miriam Cooke (2008: 97) has somewhat contentiously argued that 'Muslim women are today's new cosmopolitans', pointing how they 'are constructing a cosmopolitan identity with local roots that unites them in a "shared culture, diffused by electronic media, education, literacy, urbanization, and modernization"' (2008: 98–9). Cooke shows how transnational organizing opens important avenues of empowerment for Muslim women, such as coalition building and sharing of information and resources.

While these cosmopolitan forms of solidarity among Muslim women are important, they are also fraught with internal challenges and external limitations. For instance, as Jasmine Zine (2008: 114) points out, the majority of Muslim women in the postcolonial South, 'dispossessed through the structural inequality and deep poverty that economic globalization and neo-imperialism have caused', are still unable to benefit from the kind of cosmopolitan mobilization Cooke advocates. Stenseth's video, however, does not tell us whether Oguz's choice to wear the headscarf is a direct result of her cosmopolitan outlook and orientation; whether it has been influenced by an experience of displacement and the feelings of difference it may have engendered; whether it is an expression of Muslim humility; or whether it symbolizes her embattled identity and public defiance. However, along with her complaint, it serves as a reminder of intensifying antagonisms concerning the integration of Islamic religious and cultural differences into modern liberal democracies. Pointing to the dark side of diasporas, Oguz's case exemplifies well how today in the West, Muslims, migrants and refugees are finding it more and more difficult to construct and inhabit cosmopolitan identities due to increasing stigmatization and racism.

Notes

1   You can find excerpts from selected video works at www.annelisestenseth.com/
video.html.
2   The installation was realized as part of a pan-European, interdisciplinary arts
platform called *The Black/North SEAS* project, 2008–10. See www.seas.se/.

Works cited

Benhabib, Seyla. *The Rights of Others: Aliens, Residents, and Citizens*. Cambridge: CUP,
2004.
Cheah, Pheng. *Inhuman Conditions: On Cosmopolitanism and Human Rights*.
Cambridge, MA: Harvard University Press, 2006.
Cooke, Miriam. 'Deploying the Muslimwoman.' *Journal of Feminist Studies in Religion*
24.1 (2008): 91–9.
Frazer, Nancy. 'The Politics of Framing: An Interview with Nancy Frazer.' *Theory,
Culture, Society* 24.4 (2007): 73–86.
Gilbert, Helen, and Jacqueline Lo. *Performance and Cosmopolitics: Cross-Cultural
Transactions in Australasia*. Basingstoke: Palgrave Macmillan, 2007.
Habermas, Jürgen. *The Divided West*. Cambridge: Polity Press, 2006.
Kofman, Eleonore. 'Figures of the Cosmopolitan.' *Innovation: The European Journal of
Social Science Research* 18.1 (2005): 83–97.
Pollock, Sheldon, Bhabha, Homi K., Breckenridge, Carol A. and Chakrabarty, Dipesh.
'Cosmopolitanisms.' *Public Culture* 12.3 (2000): 577–90.
Raissiguier, Catherine. *Reinventing the Republic: Gender, Migration and Citizenship in
France*. Stanford: Stanford University Press, 2010.
Santos, Boaventura de Sousa. 'Beyond Abyssal Thinking: From Global Lines to Ecol-
ogies of Knowledges.' *Review* 30.1 (2007): 45–89.
Siim, Birte and Skjeie, Hege. 'Tracks, Intersections and Dead Ends: Multicultural
Challenges to State Feminism in Denmark and Norway.' *Ethnicities* 8.3 (2008):
322–44.
Stenseth, Anne Lise. *The Kiss and Waste Project*. 2008–10.
Tarlo, Emma. 'Islamic Cosmopolitanism: The Sartorial Biographies of Three Muslim
Women in London.' *Fashion Theory* 1.2/3 (2007): 143–72.
Vargas, Virginia. 'Feminisms, Globalization and the Global Justice and Solidarity
Movement.' *Cultural Studies* 17.6 (2003): 905–20.
Werbner, Pnina. 'Introduction: Towards a New Cosmopolitan Anthropology.' In
Pnina Werbner, ed., *Anthropology and the New Cosmopolitanism: Rooted, Feminist
and Vernacular Perspectives*. New York: Berg, 2008: 1–32.
Wren, Karen. 'Cultural Racism: Something Rotten in the State of Denmark?' *Social
and Cultural Geography* 2.2 (2001): 141–62.
Zine, Jasmin. 'Lost in Translation: Writing Back from the Margins.' *Journal of Feminist
Studies in Religion* 24.1 (2008): 110–16.

14   Cultural Diversity

Lynette Goddard

Introduction

'Cultural diversity' has been a key concept in Arts Council England's (ACE) rhetoric since the late 1980s as a term that refers to policies and initiatives designed to encourage greater inclusivity, access and equal opportunity for 'Black' arts practitioners – defined as 'African, Caribbean, Asian, and Chinese' (ACE 1997: 1). A key objective of cultural diversity initiatives are to use casting, employment and wider programming of black plays to make the theatre industry more representative of the multiracial demographics of Britain's urban centres. British black and Asian theatre gained visibility during the 1980s through the work of companies such as Black Theatre Co-operative, Black Mime Theatre, Talawa Theatre Company, Tara Arts, Temba Theatre Company and Theatre of Black Women, who toured performances to studio spaces and arts, youth and community centres in cities with a significant black and/or Asian population demographic. Many of these companies lost crucial funding and closed down during the 1990s, signalling the demise of a dedicated black theatre sector. However, these potentially troubling times coincided with the Arts Council of Great Britain's (now Arts Council England, ACE) push towards cultural diversity through initiatives aimed to improve integration in the mainstream rather than maintaining the separatism of 'ethnic arts'. As Naseem Khan (2005: 23) highlights, ACE cultural diversity initiatives were important for looking at the very infrastructure of British theatre, and 'for the first time identified the causes of inequality as not just inequalities of funding but also organisational culture, tradition and privilege that restricted entry'.

Cultural diversity initiatives can be viewed either as an important move to integrate black practitioners into the mainstream, or, more sceptically, as an approach in which 'the Black Arts world is denied the ability to grapple for itself with issues of tradition and contemporary culture – this being seen as something which is the responsibility of the arts authorities' (King 2000: 28). This chapter outlines the trajectory of black British theatre alongside an assessment of Arts Council cultural diversity policy, to consider whether such suspicions are warranted.

Cultural diversity policy and black British theatre: moving from the margins to the mainstream

Debates about cultural diversity in the British theatre industry are presented in a number of key reports, which impacted on arts policy and practices. Naseem Khan's seminal report, *The Arts Britain Ignores: The Arts of Ethnic Minorities in Britain* (CRE 1976), highlighted the marginal position of African, Caribbean, Bangladeshi, Chinese, Cypriot, Indian and Polish community-based arts and recommended that funding was deployed to develop 'ethnic arts' as a professional practice. Khan's report resulted in the establishment of the Minority Arts Advisory Service, designed to foster training in administration for black arts organizations, and increased funding of black theatre. As Gavin Jantjes (1993: 64–5) remarks, the Arts Council 'responded boldly to a recognised need and desire by Black people to set up and run their own organisations ... not to distance themselves from the mainstream but to install a working platform from which to launch their particular art forms into it'. Such targeted funding coupled with the coming to voice of British-born black playwrights wanting to stage their own experiences were significant factors in the increased visibility of black British theatre during the 1980s. Black plays appeared primarily as the output of black and women's theatre companies, but there was an increasing sense that black practitioners wanted mainstream recognition. Winsome Pinnock (1999: 32) states:

> As one of the playwrights to emerge in the Eighties, I would say that I, like others of my generation, did not feel that my work should only be produced by the black theatre companies but that they should have a place within the mainstream.

Arts funding cuts resulted in the closure of a number of black theatre companies in the 1990s. However, these losses coincided with the Arts Council's ideological shift towards fostering cultural diversity, exemplified by greater acknowledgment of black British theatre as a professional practice that warranted inclusion at key mainstream venues. The publication of *Towards Cultural Diversity* (1989), *The Landscape of Fact: Towards a Policy for Cultural Diversity for the English Funding System* (1997) and *Cultural Diversity Action Plan* (1998) outlined the Arts Council's commitment to recognizing the fundamental role that black arts could play in diversifying British culture and society. *The Landscape of Fact* highlighted that 'Black arts have transformed popular culture ... brought with them specific value systems, practices and insights ... [and] new ideas about aesthetics' (ACE 1997: 5). Arguments for financially assisting black arts are stated with recognition that racism continues to affect black artists and black arts organisations who have less opportunity for business sponsorship, 'less access to prestigious venues and are less attractive to investors' (8). For example, the lack of a building for black arts groups limits possibilities for benefitting from National Lottery capital funds (8). *Cultural Diversity Action Plan* restated the Arts Council's commitment to ensuring 'inclusion and equal access' (ACE 1998: 7) through a focus on the four areas of 'access, advocacy, diversity and development' (5), which would monitor and respect diversity, increase awareness and inclusion through local, regional and national advocacy, ensure access through equal opportunities and develop strategies for sustaining diversity.

The long-term impact of cultural diversity initiatives gained further momentum during the first decade of the 21st century, firmly consolidating the shift in the profile of black playwrights in particular into the mainstream. Sir William Macpherson's inquiry and report into the investigation of the racist murder of black teenager Stephen Lawrence suggested damning evidence of institutional racism in the Metropolitan Police, which he defined as:

> the collective failure of an organisation to provide an appropriate and professional service to people because of their colour, culture or ethnic origin. It can be seen or detected in processes, attitudes and behaviour which amount to discrimination through unwitting prejudice, ignorance, thoughtlessness and racist stereotyping which disadvantage minority ethnic people. (Macpherson 1999: 321)

Macpherson's report led to other institutions identifying instances of institutional racism in their attitudes, policies and procedures, the urgency of which was underlined by the Race Relations (Amendment) Act 2000, which 'extends protection against racial discrimination by public authorities [and] ... places a new, enforceable positive duty on public authorities' (CRE 2000: 1).

The theatre industry's response to concerns about institutional racism were published in the 2002 *Eclipse* report, following a conference to 'devise strategies to combat racism in the theatre [and] ... explore ways of developing our understanding and knowledge of African Caribbean and Asian theatre' (ACE 2002: 4). Twenty-one recommendations restated the Arts Council's commitment to improving black practitioners' position within the industry, consolidating 1990s cultural diversity rhetoric in ways that have been fundamental to the rising profile of black theatre in the new millennium. A significant recommendation was that:

> By March 2003, every publicly funded theatre organisation in England will have reviewed its Equal Opportunities policy, ascertained whether its set targets are being achieved and, if not, drawn up a comprehensive Positive Action plan which actively develops opportunities for African Caribbean and Asian practitioners. (ACE 2002: 24)

An unprecedented eleven plays were produced in 2003 alone, creating an impetus that continued throughout the rest of the decade, with at least two black British plays staged in each year between 2003 and 2010.[1]

Two other important initiatives include the Arts Council's Decibel programme, launched in 2003 to promote diversity through regular show-casing of emergent artists, and the Arts Council-funded Sustained Theatre initiative, which was established to promote connections and collaborations for a diverse arts sector in Britain.[2] The Arts Council's *Race Equality Scheme 2004–7* set out further aims to eradicate racism in the British theatre industry by 'support[ing] Black and minority ethnic artists and organisations to enable them to create and develop projects that encourage confidence and self-sufficiency in developing arts for their communities and for society as a whole' (ACE 2005: 4).[3]

Black British playwriting in the new millennium

Barnaby King's response to *The Landscape of Fact* is wary of the term 'cultural diversity', which he claims 'can never depict all the voices that make up British society and, when unpacked, it turns out to refer to a mass of different groups with different aims and ambitions, both political and artistic' (2000a: 27). In a related article, King (2000b: 133) also implies that the move towards cultural diversity invigorates and empowers the mainstream, while black and Asian artists 'feel their autonomy being threatened, and therefore marginalized, by what should be an inclusive institution'. Indeed, one potentially problematic dimension of cultural diversity initiatives is that they place the onus on white artistic directors to determine the kinds of black plays that are produced and the roles that black actors are cast into, the danger being that they will programme plays that fulfil their own perceptions and biases of black Britain. Thus, we might consider whether an increased mainstream profile for black theatre comes at a cost to the kinds of representations of black Britain that are regularly staged.

The year 2003 was a groundbreaking one in black British playwriting, signalling one achievement of cultural diversity initiatives in the number of plays produced. The run of Roy Williams' *Fallout* (2003) was extended at the Royal Court, while Kwame Kwei-Armah's *Elmina's Kitchen* was playing simultaneously at the National Theatre and went on to become the first play by a British-born black playwright to be performed in the West End when it transferred to the Garrick Theatre in 2005. Both plays explored issues surrounding urban black masculinity, street crime and 'black-on-black' violence, themes that have continued in a proliferation of similar plays since, including Williams' *Little Sweet Thing* (2005), Levi David-Addai's *Oxford Street* (2008) and Bola Agabje's *Gone Too Far!* (2007) and *Off the Endz* (2010). In view of this pattern, Lindsay Johns (2010) controversially claims that 'black theatre is cruelly blighted by its ghetto mentality', in which 'urban' plays parade unhelpful stereotypes that are endorsed by a theatre industry infrastructure wary of being deemed racist:

> Contrary to the all-pervasive mood of multicultural bonhomie and self-congratulation, there is actually something rotten in the state of black British theatre, [which is] languishing in an intellectually vapid, almost pre-literate cacophony of expletives, incoherent street babble and plots which revolve around the clichéd staples of hoodies, guns and drugs … At best, these plays succeed by masquerading as the voice of the marginalized black underclass, which by dint of acute white guilt and a commitment to diversity get an immediate audience at the capital's most prestigious venues.

A more optimistic assessment of cultural diversity recognizes the extent to which black playwriting has become more prominent within the mainstream, which seems to be an acknowledgement that black plays that move beyond explicit concerns with identity politics have a wider audience appeal. Kwame Kwei-Armah's National Theatre triptych – *Elmina's Kitchen* (2003), *Fix Up* (2004) and *Statement of Regret* (2007) – were written as 'a catalyst for debate around themes that are pertinent to our communities and to our nation' (Kwei-Armah 2010). He takes inspiration for his subject matter from topical events as reported in the media, such as the increasing number of fatal stabbings and shootings in London, the bicentenary of the abolition of slavery in 2007, and the election of Barack Obama as the first African-American president of the US in 2008. Kwei-Armah represents rarely seen black professionals on the English stage, particularly in *Statement of Regret*, which shows a black political think tank debating a reparations for slavery agenda, and *Seize the Day* (Tricycle 2009), which contemplates the possibility of electing a black mayor for London. Kwei-Armah's plays attract new audiences to diversify the typically white, middle-class demographic of British theatre attendance, making it more inclusive for black spectators and suggesting shared cultural ownership of Britain's institutions. Staging them at the National Theatre is also an indication of their wider relevance, not just for black audiences but for British society as a whole.

Another important initiative is the National Theatre's quest to recognize Britain's increasing diversity through the creation of a Black Plays Archive instigated by Kwei-Armah, 'a major venture, in partnership with Sustained Theatre, to archive and record extracts from every African, Caribbean and Black British play produced in the UK in the last 60 years' (National Theatre n.d.). The housing of recordings as part of the National Theatre's Black Plays Archive gives it important credibility in the trajectory of contemporary British theatre, creating access for future generations to view black playwriting as an integral component in staging contemporary Britishness.

A further measure of the success of cultural diversity initiatives revolves around examining the extent to which black plays that do not address the typically expected subject matter or initiate new aesthetics of style and form are being produced. debbie tucker green's unique perspective addresses a range of issues, including domestic violence, incest, poverty and the AIDS crisis in Africa, female sex tourism, genocide, civil war and knife crime, and her experiments with form reject the linear conventions of social realism. *stoning mary* (2005) and *random* (2008) were both produced on the main stage at the Royal Court's Jerwood Theatre Downstairs and are indicative of contemporary black theatre's move beyond explicit identity politics narratives to tackle topical concerns in the UK and wider world. *stoning mary* depicts a couple stricken with AIDS, a child soldier, and a woman awaiting death by stoning, but tucker green troubles the typical association of these issues with Africa and emphasizes their urgency as a global concern, by instructing that '*the play is set in the country it's performed in ... all characters are white*' (tucker green 2005: 2), and projecting newspaper-like headlines to title each scene. *random* responds to the epidemic of teenage knife murders in London in 2007 and 2008.[4] Casting a solo black actress in multiple roles as Mum, Dad, Brother, Sister and Teacher, and focusing on the grief of a family whose son is murdered offers an innovative approach to exploring 'urban' violence in black British playwriting.

Conclusion

Black British theatre thrived during the first decade of the 21st century, which can be accounted for by the impact of cultural diversity initiatives throughout the 1990s and into the new millennium. The Tricycle Theatre's 'Not Black and White' season in 2009 mounted a trilogy of plays exploring black playwrights' perspectives on the state-of-the-nation at the end of the first decade of the 21st century. Artistic Director Nicolas Kent (2009: vii) outlines the motivation for the season as a recognition of changing demographics in which 'London's black and Asian children outnumber white British children by about six to four'. These figures also suggest the importance of cultural diversity initiatives for integration, equal opportunities and access for all in British theatre. Naseem Khan's 1976 report initiated many of the debates outlined in this chapter and her 2005 reflection on the inroads of cultural diversity hopes for times to come when the term itself will become obsolete within England's art structures.

> The distance travelled from the benevolent paternalism of a mere thirty years ago to today's more considered, informed and pro-active approach is considerable. But many questions now need answers: What role should ethnicity play within the broader concept of 'cultural diversity'? What is the right balance between policy that responds and policy that leads? How can the relationship between equality and quality be monitored? To what extent has Arts Council England's multi-million pound decibel programme succeeded in opening up the 'mainstream'? And, above all, when can we drop the term 'cultural diversity'? (Khan, 2005: 26)

Notes

1   See Deirdre Osborne, *Hidden Gems* (London: Oberon, 2008) for a comprehensive list of black plays produced between 2003 and 2008.
2   See http://sustainedtheatre.org.uk/Home.
3   ACE's *Race Equality Scheme 2009–11* updates the previous scheme and outlined the Arts Council's special focus on digital opportunity, visual arts, children and young people, and the London Olympics 2012.
4   27 teenagers were murdered on London's streets in 2007 and 28 in 2008.

Works cited

Arts Council England. *Towards Cultural Diversity.* London: ACGB, 1989.
– *The Landscape of Fact: Towards a Policy for Cultural Diversity for the English Funding System: African, Caribbean, Asian and Chinese Arts.* London: ACE, 1997.
– *Cultural Diversity Action Plan.* London: ACE, 1998.
– *Eclipse: Developing Strategies to Combat Racism in Theatre.* London: ACE, 2002.
– *Race Equality Scheme 2004–7.* London: ACE, 2005.

– *Race Equality Scheme 2009–11.* London: ACE, 2010.

CRE. *The Race Relations (Amendment) Act 2000: Strengthening the Race Relations Act.* London: Commission for Racial Equality, 2000.

Jantjes, Gavin. 'The Long March from "Ethnic Arts" to "New Internationalism."' In Ria Lavrijsen, ed., *Cultural Diversity in the Arts: Art, Art Policy and the Facelift of Europe.* The Netherlands: Royal Tropical Institute, 1993, 59–66.

Johns, Lindsay. 'Black Theatre is Blighted by its Ghetto Mentality.' *Evening Standard*, 9 Feb 2010, www.thisislondon.co.uk/standard/article-23803660-black-theatre-is-blighted-by-its-ghetto-mentality.do.

Kent, Nicolas. 'Introduction'. In Agbaje, Bola, Kwame Kwei-Armah and Roy Williams, *Not Black and White.* London: Methuen, 2009, vii–viii.

Khan, Naseem. *The Arts Britain Ignores: The Arts of Ethnic Minorities in Britain.* London: CRE, 1976.

– 'Arts Council England and Diversity: Striving for Change.' In *Navigating Difference: Cultural Diversity and Audience Development.* London: ACE, 2005, 21–6.

King, Barnaby. 'Landscapes of Fact and Fiction: Asian Theatre Arts in Britain. *New Theatre Quarterly*, 16:1, 2000a: 26–33.

– The African-Caribbean Identity and the English Stage. *New Theatre Quarterly*, 16.2, 2000b: 131–6.

Kwei-Armah, Kwame. MediaGuardian 100 2010: '96. Kwame Kwei-Armah'. *The Guardian*, 19 July 2010, www.guardian.co.uk/media/2010/jul/12/kwame-kwei-ar-mah-mediaguardian-100-2010.

Macpherson, Sir William. *The Stephen Lawrence Inquiry: Report of an Inquiry by Sir William Macpherson of Cluny.* Norwich: TSO, 1999.

National Theatre. 'Black Plays Archive,' www.blackplaysarchive.org.uk.

Pinnock, Winsome. 'Breaking Down the Door.' In Vera Gottlieb and Colin Chambers, eds, *Theatre in a Cool Climate.* Oxford: Amber Lane Press, 1999, 27–38.

tucker green, debbie. *stoning mary.* London: Nick Hern Books, 2005.

15   Citizenship, the Ethics of Inclusion

Nadine Holdsworth

Introduction

In 2002, Arts Council England (ACE) partnered Cardboard Citizens Theatre Company with the Royal Shakespeare Company (RSC) as part of its New Audiences initiative. Founded by Adrian Jackson in 1991, London-based Cardboard Citizens is Britain's leading professional theatre company working with artists, participants and audiences who have experienced homelessness. The RSC is one of Britain's flagship national theatre companies dedicated to productions of Shakespeare, other Renaissance dramatists and new writing. The ACE initiative aimed to support collaborations between companies experienced in theatre for social inclusion and those who had little experience of work in this field with a long-term objective to encourage attendance of excluded groups at mainstream arts venues.

Starting out on this creative collaboration, the RSC's director of education, the late Clare Venables, explained:

> not only is this a wonderful way for us to put together the artist at the centre of British culture with those who are most marginalized by that culture [but] this is also the RSC's opportunity to test our belief that Shakespeare does speak to, and for, all, whatever their circumstances or language. (cited in Draper 2003)

As such, Venables explicitly framed the project in terms of a citizenship agenda of equality of access, participation and representation, whilst acknowledging the significance of power relations that marginalize and exclude. Drawing on contemporary discourses around citizenship, this chapter considers issues emerging from this collaboration, which resulted in Jackson's site-specific production of *Pericles*, which premiered on 22 July 2003 in a disused warehouse in London that had last been used as a shelter for 500 rough sleepers at Christmas.

Citizenship, the homeless and Cardboard Citizens

In 1950, in a seminal text 'Citizenship and Social Class', T.H. Marshall outlined his conception of citizenship, which categorized the rights and responsibilities people have by virtue of their legal status as members of a nation state. He referred to rights as civil, political and social, including the right to equality before the law, the right to vote and the right to access social welfare provision, offset by responsibilities to the state such as observing the rule of law and paying taxes. But, as Hannah Arendt (1958) highlighted, rights associated with citizenship dissolve when a citizen ceases to be a member of a nation state that activates these rights, and for many years social scientists and political theorists (such as Benhabib 2004; Arnold 2004) have tussled with the limits of citizenship and the problems experienced by disadvantaged and marginalized groups such as the homeless, refugees and asylum seekers.

Rooted in the dynamic interactions of daily life, there is a developing awareness that citizenship is a much more complex social phenomena than the stress on rights and responsibilities implies. What it means to be a citizen has become a vexed question in a contemporary context dominated by the reconfiguration of national and international territorial borders of belonging and identity and the increasing global movement of people. This situation led Seyla Benhabib (2004: 144) to question how the status of citizenship functions 'in a world of increasingly deterritorialized politics?' Chantal Mouffe (1992) has developed a radical democratic citizenship model that extends Marshall's basic principles by stressing active citizenship and the potential for a more fluid and inclusive conception of citizenship. She proposes a complex understanding and negotiation of the relationship between the universalizing category of citizen, the particularities of individual experience and the shifting sands of contemporary globalized communities.

Above all, citizenship is a highly charged and politicized term that raises crucial questions around identity, power, access, exclusion and social participation. According to Werbner and Yuval-Davis: 'democratic citizenship is a dynamic and contested concept; a negotiated compromise, shaped by cultural and political elites, between forces of normalization and forces of difference' (1999, quoted in Rowe et al. 2001: 18). Certainly, citizenship simultaneously opens up access to rights and community membership whilst limiting access through contested legal, procedural and social channels that emphasis difference. Hence, access to citizenship is often more theoretical than actual – there is a difference between having rights and having access to rights, or the desire to participate and opportunities to do so. These issues are no more acute than when considering one of the most disadvantaged and vulnerable groups in society – the homeless.

The category 'homeless' suggests a problematic homogeneity that masks diversity through the unifying category of homelessness. In reality, the 'homeless' refers to an eclectic community that includes young people who have left a parental or care home, ex-prisoners, people with mental health problems, illegal immigrants, asylum seekers and refugees. They are people for whom citizenship is a fragile and often elusive concept, as they are remote from the state of legitimacy, status and dignity that the term suggests. If citizenship is tied to notions of belonging, of inhabiting, then homelessness is defined by a state of detachment or dispossession, whereby people are cast adrift from the structures and mechanisms that define citizenship. Indeed, the idea of homelessness encompasses both the physical dislocation and the social dislocation people encounter when estranged from their homes or homelands. State-sanctioned systems of criminalization or physical ostracism to temporary hostels and detention centres perpetuate the exclusion of the homeless and/or stateless, as they are defined, as problems to be solved or processed rather than as people with different personal histories and trajectories.

Theatre would seem to be an irrelevance for those struggling with homelessness and statelessness, but Cardboard Citizens combines a theatrical and social agenda to address citizenship-related issues for the homeless, refugees and asylum seekers through its use of forum theatre techniques derived from Augusto Boal's theory and practice of 'legislative theatre' (1998). With myriad national, political and domestic histories and various futures beckoning, the participants in Cardboard Citizens come together through their mutual experience of homelessness. These citizens are in various stages of travelling towards a revised conception of their own citizenship as it is resituated personally and/or geographically and/or nationally.

Cardboard Citizens provides opportunities for creative skills development and the chance to hear, see and voice stories in a public arena. More importantly, the company is dedicated to changing material conditions and explicitly connects creative processes to service referral. For example, in the Engagement Programme, Cardboard Citizens take a 'forum theatre' piece to hostels, shelters and day centres and after each show, trained actors mentor homeless clients and arrange one-to-one follow-up meetings, trying to ensure that the interest generated by the performance translates into positive referral to the agencies that may begin to activate or reactivate citizenship rights.

Pericles: an asylum seeker's fable

Retold as an asylum seeker's fable by a cast drawn from Cardboard Citizens and the RSC, *Pericles* was selected by Jackson because of the play's themes of geographical restlessness, exile, sexual exploitation, loss and reunion. He explained:

> It was easy to imagine Pericles or Marina putting their case for asylum to immigration officers; and, in these fraught and jumpy times, when politicians quake at the thought of being labelled 'soft on asylum seekers', it was also quite possible to think of either or both being turned down, on the basis of improbabilities in their stories. (Jackson 2004: 10)

With an asylum seeker in the lead role, the creative process began with a cut-down version of the play performed in hostels and day centres to a mixed audience of asylum seekers and refugees, including people from Iraq, Kosovo, Zimbabwe, Somalia and Albania.

After these 'show and tell' performances, audience members were invited to explore their experiences. 'The theatre became a meeting ground, a site of conversation; we told the story of Pericles, and they told us stories back, by turns amazing, shocking, unbelievable, painful, normal' (Jackson 2004: 10–11). The passage from exclusion to inclusion implied in the transition from marginalized, voiceless non-participant to engaged, vocal participant provides a symbolic model of the active citizenship Cardboard Citizens are keen to foster. Subsequent interviews developed conversations begun after the show and these oral testimonies were woven through the full-length production of *Pericles* to generate a creative collision between the fictional and the real world, the past and the present, the Shakespearean language and the languages of the displaced. Most reviewers found this an effective performance strategy that brought out 'the parallel predicaments of contemporary refugees [with] a piercing dignity [that] never feel[s] forced or pious' (Taylor 2003: 17). Nonetheless, some reviewers found these parallel narratives uncomfortable, with Michael Billington (2003: 18) arguing that: 'Treating Shakespeare's Pericles as if he were a prototype asylum seeker seems faintly spurious in that he is actually a prince protected by fate, not an impoverished victim of tyranny.'

In staging *Pericles,* Jackson evoked the refugee and asylum seeker experience. The audience arrived at an entry point to be greeted by officials demanding their names and town of birth before sitting them at school desks with 19-page asylum application forms. Five minutes of silent perusal gave way to real-life testimonies of fleeing homelands, physical endurance and survival against the odds. The central *Pericles* narrative emerged out of these stories as 'guards' herded the audience from scene to scene through a cavernous transit centre-style holding camp. Rows and rows of stretcher beds, tents, communal washbasins and garments hung out to dry powerfully captured the qualities of enforced cohabitation, dehumanization, lack of privacy and comfortless existence (see Figure 15.1).

Figure 15.1   From *Pericles* by Cardboard Citizens and the Royal Shakespeare Company (2003). Photo courtesy of Cardboard Citizens

One particularly important element involved a 'wedding dance' developed through collaboration between Cardboard Citizens and The Place Theatre formed for ACE's Dance Included initiative. This involved a series of dance workshops designed for the homeless and ex-homeless held at a Crisis Skylight centre. The 'wedding dance' performers were selected through an audition process that recruited eight participants and five others through outreach sessions in three refugee centres. The resulting celebratory dance visually captured the cultural collision and fusion that characterizes eclectic communities forged in the aftermath of displacement.

The ethics of a morganatic marriage

In terms of a citizenship agenda, it is possible to draw many positives from this production. The introduction of 'real-life' exclusion into the heart of the British arts establishment allowed a voice that is predominately absent or marginalized in public discourse to take centre stage. Access to institutions legitimizes different experiences through their public articulation and placing them alongside the authority of Shakespeare's texts symbolically implied the value of their personal narratives. Simply telling and listening to refugee experiences validates the refugee's personal narrative for the speaker and listener; and opening up these dialogical relations is a crucial component in encouraging understanding, positive integration and active citizenship. Individual members of the homeless and refugee community also gained immensely in terms of their self-esteem and confidence from the opportunity to interact with others, develop skills and work in a professional environment. The impact of regular engagement leading to a positive outcome in front of an audience should not be underestimated in the context of difficult and often chaotic lives. However, there are several notes of caution to add.

Jackson framed the benefits for Cardboard Citizens in terms of access to a specific skills bank in production and technical support, voice and verse speaking. But in his profile for the RSC's website, Jackson admitted that people are fascinated by the morganatic marriage of prince and pauper. The choice of the term 'morganatic' is revealing, as it refers to a marriage whereby a spouse and children have no claim to the possessions or title of the spouse or parent of a higher rank. This collaboration was an unequal partnership, culturally, socially, financially and, significantly, with no hope of future equality, which raises ethical issues around the production and reception of its outcomes to the extent that I question whether this 'marriage' actually undermines the radical democratic citizenship agenda pursued by Cardboard Citizens.

In the transition from the intimate sharing of the 'show and tell' performances in hostels and day centres to the high production values and RSC gloss of the final performance, a great deal was lost. Frances Babbage (2004: 70–88) and Helen Nicholson (2005: 120–5) both acknowledge the significance of context for negotiating meaning in Cardboard Citizens' work, drawing attention to the fact that when the work tours within its own constituency it provides a voice, a focus for identification and the potential for a change in material circumstances due to the stress on forum theatre techniques and agency referral. For Nicholson (2005: 125), this may enable participants to find 'creative ways to think differently *and* act productively in a wider social and global context'. In other words, an active citizenship is potentially fostered, but this defining aspect of Cardboard Citizens' work was absent from this RSC collaboration. Alternatively, real-life traumatic stories of loss and exile are dislocated from the contexts that give them meaning and they risk being appropriated to bolster a theatrical event. They become subordinate to the wider creative aim of refashioning Shakespeare and making him speak to 'our' times, in which questions of asylum and refugees are burning political issues. In other words, there is a danger that the 'real' refugee is reduced to a potent theatrical device, a marker of authenticity and political relevance.

Silvija Jestrovic writes about the way that the use of asylum seekers and illegal immigrants in performance can exemplify what she terms the 'hyper-authentic', drawing on Jean Baudrillard's notion of the hyper-real. For Jestrovic (2008: 160), 'hyper-authentic occurs when "real" people are expected to perform their own authenticity', which raises issues about the gap between actual experience and its representation in a theatrical frame. Arguably, the production commodified and repackaged these experiences, resulting in the danger that *Pericles* promoted a new form of cultural appropriation and tourism whereby the homeless person, refugee and asylum seeker becomes an exotic other to be consumed as they are mediated through a spectacular theatrical event.

By collaborating with the RSC, Cardboard Citizens entered an arena in which the audience experience is valued above an exploration of homelessness and laid themselves open to aesthetic criticisms about acoustics, disrupted narrative flow and uneven acting in a way that would be completely inappropriate in their more usual applied theatre contexts. There is also evidence that when held up against the force of the canon and the weight of the RSC, real-life testimonies are found wanting. As John Thaxter (2003: 959) insensitively put it: 'in the second half, when Shakespeare takes over from his lesser collaborators, the drama at last becomes more focused'.

Some of the ethical implications of embedding real-life stories into a theatrical experience relate to decisions about inclusion and exclusion. Jackson admitted to selecting and editing refugee stories, as some of the stories of persecution and torture were too painful to relate (Turner 2003: 5). Sufficiently compelling stories had to complement the theatrical narrative, but not be so gratuitously traumatic to put the audience off or promote compassion fatigue. So, audiences received a sanitized version of refugee and asylum seeker experiences made more palatable by the inclusion of feel-good stories of survival and family reunions against the odds that corresponded with Shakespeare's creative narrative. Even so, several reviewers, including Billington (2003: 18), referred to the show as something to be 'endured more than enjoyed'.

More worryingly, Dominic Maxwell (2003: 960) argued that: 'For all the good intentions, what comes across most strongly is not the horror of these people's experiences, but the distracting sincerity of the company's concern for them.' I find it hard to believe that accusations of 'distracting sincerity' would accompany Cardboard Citizen's work for and with its target constituency. Whilst the aims of the Arts Council's new audience agenda are laudable, I wonder if there is a danger that, without sensitive ethical consideration, this kind of collaboration risks falling into the trap of global citizenship gloss at the expense of promoting global citizenship rights. It would seem that issues of difference that define exclusion to citizenship were at the forefront of the reception of *Pericles* rather than the progressive consideration of more expansive conceptions of nationhood, belonging and citizenship that the opening up of Shakespeare might imply.

Works cited

Arendt, Hannah. *The Human Condition*. Chicago: University of Chicago P, 1958.

Arnold, Kathleen, R. *Homelessness, Citizens and Identity: The Uncanniness of Late Modernity*. New York: State U of New York P, 2004.

Babbage, Frances. *Augusto Boal*. London: Routledge, 2004.

Benhabib, Seyla. *The Rights of Others: Aliens, Residents and Citizens*. Cambridge: CUP, 2004.

Billington, Michael. 'Pericles'. *The Guardian*. 28 July 2003, www.theguardian.com/stage/2003/jul/28/theatre.artsfeatures, accessed 12 April 2014.

Boal, Augusto. *Legislative Theatre: Using Performance to Make Politics,* trans. Adrian Jackson. London: Routledge, 1998.

Draper, Michelle. 'The Perils of Pericles'. Arts Hub,16 July 2003

Jackson, Adrian. 'Pericles: Exile and Loss'. *Mailout*. February–March 2004, 10–11.

Jestrovic, Silvija. 'Performing like an Asylum Seeker: Paradoxes of Hyper-authenticity'. *Research in Drama and Education* 13.2 (2008): 159–70.

Marshall, T.H. *Citizenship and Social Class*. London: Pluto, [1950] 1997.

Maxwell, Dominic. 'Pericles'. *Theatre Record* xxiii (2003): 960.

Mouffe, Chantal, ed. *Dimensions of Radical Democracy: Pluralism, Citizenship, Community*. London: Verso, 1992.

Nicholson, Helen. *Applied Drama: the Gift of Theatre*. Basingstoke: Palgrave Macmillan, 2005.

Rowe, Michael, Kloos, Bret, Chinman, Matt et al. 'Homelessness, Mental Illness and Citizenship'. *Social Policy and Administration* 35.1 (2001): 14–31.

Taylor, Paul. 'Pericles, The Warehouse, London'. *The Independent*. 31 July 2003, 17.

Thaxter, John. 'Pericles'. *Theatre Record* xxiii (2003): 959.

Turner, Mandy. 'Dramatic Effect'. *The Guardian*. 23 July 2003, www.theguardian.com/stage/2003/jul/23/theatre.immigration, accessed 12 April 2014.

16   Installation, Constellation

Lynette Hunter

This chapter will look at four keywords in particular contexts: installing, constellating, performativity as a combination of these two, and a short note on articulation. The aesthetic background for these words lies within the nation state social contract politics of Western liberal states. The critical context is bounded by three rhetorical stances: ideology, hegemony and the 'alongside'. First, a few words about the critical grounds of these three stances.

Neoliberal ideology presents the fundamental 'universalisms' of the right to protection of property, and the responsibility to fight for the state: the state will protect your mortgage if you are prepared to die for the state, and in the meantime assume (in both senses of 'accepting' and 'taking on') its representations. Under modern liberal capitalism, the 'capital' part of this ideological agenda is based on the non-human expendability (to be spent) of the black body and the erasure of the female body. Liberal hegemony promises the possibility of equality and liberty as long as we remember that some people are more equal than others: every citizen has the right to acquire property but not if every individual tries to do so. The modern citizen has to remember and to forget the promise of equality and liberty. Yet, also under liberal capitalism, all people have lives that do not function according to the representations of the state. These non-representative lives are, to a greater or lesser extent, 'alongside' hegemonic and ideological pressures, and offer a source of energy that not only makes alterior value outwith the state but creates possibilities emergent into it, and change.

Liberal capitalism was built by a tiny proportion of the population in Western nation states, 5 per cent at best. Liberal assumptions appeared as 'universals' because everyone who held them belonged to the same group that controlled governing power, went to the same schools, owned the same kind of property (house, horse, servants), had the same kind of family, enjoyed the same structures of powerful institutions defending their ways of life, had the right to vote, and were citizens. The 20th century changed all that by giving the vote to just about everyone over 18 years old, although some had to wait a long time, e.g. Native Americans. This gave many more people the vote, and the claim on citizenship, but understandably these new citizens came from backgrounds valuing many different ways of life. Some of the new citizens did not even own property, some had different ideas of what family was. Given the reality of globalization and international movement, given the disunity of claims on power that have resulted from these franchises and the post/neocolonial withdrawal of many imperial powers, national communities acknowledging that they are built on universal assumptions are now not easy to find. Yet, many diverse groups have tried to claim power and cannot assume it.

What has this got to do with performance?

In the cultural contexts of social contract politics in Western liberal nation states, performance has become a place where people discuss the increasingly disunified aesthetics of democratic diversity. Many of the new citizens, having failed to assume political power, turned to cultural power as more effective for generating value for their 'alongside' lives. Performativity has become a word that indicates activity where the 'alongside' meets sociocultural representation.[1] Performativity is a situated textuality,[2] a textuality in any medium that enables situated knowing,[3] knowing as particular to space/time,[4] in the moment, practices of the everyday[5] (not the banal). Installating and constellating are distinguished from the similar words 'installation' and 'constellation' in ways outlined in this chapter, but primarily to emphasize that they are processes.

'Installating' is a word that delineates the performativity of aesthetic labour that goes on in *alongside* lives, making work that has not yet been said by representation. Apart from the work on this word in my own criticism, other performance critics such as Alan Read[6] also use 'alongside' to call upon the energy of performativity. This work is always in process, and to bring it into the sociocultural, the process has to be arrested into public performance, or installation. The ensuing experience of that *arrest* can be referred to as 'constellating'. In constellating, the alongside, as a process temporarily put into a place of resting, can emerge into hegemony where it may or may not be heard/seen/felt. If it is recognized, it moves into cultural *fit* or constellation, generates the adrenaline rush of fitting and the endorphins of completion. It becomes beauty – for a longer or shorter period of time.

Installating refers to what art makers do in rehearsal and at the moment of arrest, before what they make enters the public performance. Constellating refers to what audiences and performers do while they are part of the art-making process in public performance, and often generates recognition of something that has not been said before (hence the reluctance of art makers to tell you what their made art 'means'). The two words together make up the elusive concept of performativity. At the same time, constellating illuminates Laclau and Mouffe's idea of articulation[7] and the focus in performance studies on documentation.[8] Articulation can be thought of as made possible by the process of constellating and realized in performative documentation.

This chapter explores mainly the first two of these keywords and the work they can do to make political, ethical and aesthetic critique through performance. The grounds for the argument are drawn from the assumptions outlined above, which suggest that the performativity of installating/constellating in performance generates 'alongside' values, alterior to the hegemonic, and makes it possible to recognize them in discourse. Discourse recognizes performance through at least two rhetorical strategies: positionalities and sets toward hegemony. A 'set toward' hegemony signifies a disposition toward discursive structures. It is an ethos position taken up in reaction to a discursive field, and is characterized by a collective settling into a specific and repeatable behaviour toward an issue or element in hegemonic structure. In contrast, a positionaltiy is not a reaction to a hegemonic structure, but a conscious decision to position one's self or one's group on non-discursive grounds. A positionality is built not primarily in reaction to the subjection that results from hegemonic structure, but from valued elements in life alongside the discursive. This positioning may be recognized by hegemonic culture and become emergent into it. A set toward hegemony cannot be emergent because it is built on the grounds of the discourse it opposes or transgresses. But although emergent positionality may cause disruption, discourse may also ignore it, or simply not see it or hear it or sense it. The process of performance thought about in this way allows one the aesthetic experience of the feelings generated by the building of alongside worlds, their affects, their ethics, and the positionalities and sets toward hegemony they enable: in the work of installating. In constellating, this conceptual framework allows one to think about the interplay of differing positionalities with respect to hegemony, differing sets toward hegemonic norms, and the extents and possibilities for shift and fit – for fitting into cultural discourse, and for shifting it.

Installating

The making of things may happen along the path of the banal that joins the representations of the state. But this activity is not usually thought of as art making. At the very least, art making involves a twist to an idea or a tweak to a systemic structure that gets the audience thinking. A public performance that engages its audience usually draws on an installation that realizes non-discursive yet alternatively present structures of power. For example, in the context of the late 19th and early 20th centuries, Strindberg's plays were among a growing movement that enabled for the first time in a public audience (the novel had done this for a private audience a few decades earlier) cultural recognition of psychoanalytic traumas experienced by the middle class. These traumas were not 'talked about', they were definitely not part of the discursive field of European art, yet they were profoundly present in the alongside world not recognized by hegemony. In other words, I would argue that they were not repressed or suppressed but so alterior as to simply not be seen or heard.

In the modern Western liberal world, dramatic performance often displays the dialectical contradictions of capitalism in a moment emerging in slow time, arrested before its sublation, before we remember to forget the contradiction. Another turn-of-the-20th-century example could be Ibsen's plays and the way they made accessible to discourse vocabulary about the repressions of middle-class women. At the other end of the century, one could cite Robbie McCauley's performance piece *Sally's Rape*, which opens to cultural recognition the non-humanity accorded to African-American women.

At its most radical, performance can enable performativity particular to the time/space that materializes an alongside value. Here, one might think about Jess Curtis' and Maria Scaroni's 'Symmetry Project' series, in which formal but non-normative principles for symmetrical movement generate site-particular ritual that responds to the people gathered to watch (see Figure 16.1). For example, an audience member sitting on the floor or ground of a performance space might become the object over which the choreography has to move and negotiate. The inclusion in the dance generates engaged audience response.

In both rehearsal and public performance, texts acquire the materiality of systemic structures that have been learned since birth by those who rehearse the text and those who audience it. In installing the movements, sounds, words go through their bodies as if through a lens, rendering complex awareness that makes difference, or resists and diverts in various ways impelled by the energy of making different. Meg Stuart's work could be a case in point: choreographically a piece such as *Forgeries, Love and Other Matters* (2004–) continually moves past the edge of the discursive, past the place where recognizable narrative can happen. The dance theatre piece begins with a six-minute almost-but-not-quite slow-motion enactment by two people of consolation, and the refusal of consolation.

It moves through a series of body materials such as spat-up drink that one performer cleans up by licking it away and the other by rubbing it off and in, and possible rebuses such as the two tethering themselves together with a long rubber tube and pulling each other all over a brown faux-fur set. The point is not that narrative is broken down or challenged, but that something is happening that doesn't respond to 'recognition'. Emotions a Western audience has learned are carefully set up to identify with and then just as carefully dismantled into unpredictability. Audiences are frequently unnerved by the experience, sometimes destabilized to the point of nausea, and usually able to re-see the cultural narratives that do surface as absurdly random but simultaneously quite accurate collocations of social agreements. We do not yet know how to control emotions or classify feeling: however clichéd, we are still organized chaos to ourselves and others.

Figure 16.1   The Symmetry Project, Jess Curtis and Maria Scaroni. Credit: M.F. Scaroni, J. Curtis and hagolani.com

Installating expands time/space, generates an ecology in which things become present, we become aware of them and presence ourselves. The process depends on the performers making difference during rehearsal. Difference is not there before we make it so. In installating, because performers work together to generate affect and action that is appropriate to the moment, each apprehension or awareness of another person is an opportunity to make difference. In Stuart's *Forgeries*, one actor moves towards another and the audience has absolutely no idea what will happen because the performers are working from differences made during the rehearsal. In making difference, the performer acknowledges that they are not the same as the other person. They engage with some thing that they make, through the senses, radically alterior. In that making, they change their own self because the making of something radically alterior necessarily generates in the person making some thing that was not there before, makes it present. If nothing else, the intensity of the presence of the performers in Stuart's piece keeps the audience on the edge of their seats, deletes expectation. This making of difference releases the energy needed to net together ground, and neither the made differences nor the made grounds are there until the performer makes them.

Because each performer makes these differences, rather than finds differences that are already somehow 'there', the differences have happened because of their own actions. The differences are about the performer becoming present in a different way, rather than the other performers they work with being changed. Because the performers are changing their self, the work is vulnerable, and they know and/or choose these changes more easily in groups that have come together to support precisely this kind of work. These like-minded groups[9] offer collaboration that enables them to do this work so that they change, become present in a different way, and in the process prompt those around them to make further differences and change their selves.[10] Derrida speaks in *On Friendship* of the space of death as the place where we can for the only time know the friend: because friendship defines the process of change of our self that initiates a presence that enables the other person also to engage and make difference that changes the self that initiates a presence … the performativity of installating enables a change of our self that initiates a presence that in turn enables a collaborating person also to engage and make difference that changes the self that initiates a presence.

Installating is an ongoing process that we experience in the moment, so we cannot know what will happen next. The engaged rhetoric of installating is part of the process of being present. It is not collective action that aims toward a specific goal, but collaborative making that remains sensitive to/opens the senses to the interaction of people within an environment, to the ecological nuances that shift with every breath, to the varied etymologies and grammars with which we build our languages, whether in a visual, verbal, movement, musical, digital or other medium. Early showings of Keith Hennessy's *Turbulence* (2011–) allowed the audience the unique experience of installating by bringing similar rehearsal strategies into the performance. Performers in many different media – dancers, choreographers, musicians and others – melded onto a performance space where they enabled each other in getting to a point where they didn't know what

146

was going to happen next (see Figure 16.2). They then sometimes fell into an action they knew, or sometimes pushed on into apparent formlessness – structures that neither they nor the audience yet recognized – and sometimes hit, for a moment or so, some kind of emergent/turbulent form where suddenly there was a connection, a making present in the room. Hennessy himself usually nudged, shifted, shoved, split out the presence. At times, he would use other bodies as part of a trapeze, as if they were ropes or a bar. The actions began messily, as he found footholds or parts of anatomy around which to wrap his body. The movement quickly gained rhythm and surety – but just as the audience began to enjoy the repetition, commit to the expectation, Hennessy would move away from it. Not every performer was willing to let it go so quickly, yet time and duration slipped around each other a lot, and the different lengths or perceptions of length directed the energy around the space in unexpected ways.

Figure 16.2 *Turbulence* **(a dance about the economy), Keith Hennessy. Credit:** *Turbulence* **(a dance about the economy). Photo: Robbie Sweeney**

The process of installating becomes a contemporary mode of mimesis, in which we rehearse a text through the body and produce material difference. In making difference, we change our self, not others, but we do make available a different self to others. Difference generates a new presence that enables other people to engage, and engaging, they make difference and change self and initiate further presence. This mode of engagement is central to collaboration. Collaboration in rehearsal or performance becomes the process of valuing the differences/presences we make when working with other people. The concept of installating being here drawn from performance rehearsal has clear political ramifications. From the underlying assumption that difference is not there before we make it, our awareness of the differences we make alerts us to the values we generate when we do so. The generation of difference changes us because we make something that was not there before, and because we change our self we know we are responsible for the feelings, affects and effects that follow. And becoming responsible for making difference creates alterior value. The change to our self makes us present in a different way, and presence releases energy – energy that can be used to net together alterior grounds and generate alongside power that works alternatively, in long-term change. Those grounds allow us not only to value our particular lives, often lives that are not represented by the state, but also to build positionalities with respect to hegemony, as well as sets toward the state, each of which may change it.

In political life, the collaborative groups that support the performativity of installating in rehearsal coalesce around work on values that are not talked about by hegemonic culture and society. These groups have many rhetorical strategies that are not only topical but also schematic.[11] Topical strategies focus on issues such as environmentalism, poverty and sexuality. They create a set toward hegemony that insists on its alternative values and engages in negotiation through techniques such as compromise, opposition or resistance. Often a set toward hegemony makes direct, short-term articulations that critique and erupt into society and culture, disrupting representations. Schematic strategies that focus on structural or systemic principles and generate positionalities are more difficult to recognize.

A positionality exists firmly alterior to hegemonic structures, and generates an ongoing process of making difference that builds alterior grounds alongside hegemonic common grounds. The more radically alterior, the less hegemony will recognize critique, and the more long term that critique will prove. For example, the Afropessimist philosophy that has been put in place since the 1980s[12] is so radically alterior that many middle-class white critics cannot 'see' it. The Afropessimist positionality presents as the case the dependence of the civic state of liberal humanism on the non-humanity of the black body. Most liberal white people insist on empathy with this positionality, but empathy negates the argument – a human cannot be empathic with a non-human.[13] What is required is the aporia of nothingness, which is exceptionally difficult to bear. But then so is the history of slavery. Similarly, but for different reasons, women in Western states argued for women's 'human' status for centuries, but place after place and time after time, could not hear them. The radical alterity of the positionalities (and there are many of them) of women has generated an ongoing patriarchal critique. Positionalities are capable not only of long-term systemic change because the people involved have changed, but also of generating stances, rhetorical interactions, that can have a profound effect on hegemonic rhetorics.

In performance: constellating

Much of the potential that performance holds for political change in the liberal West derives from the moment of arrest, the moment at which those performers in rehearsal decide to arrest the ongoing process of installating and go into public performance. Its analogue in Derrida's philosophical commentary on friendship is death. This is the moment in performativity where constellating begins. Elin Diamond reworks Benjamin's 'dialectical image'[14] to foreground the way that 'constellation' catches the dialectical contradiction of capital before it sublates, before we remember to forget it. Brecht uses this structure to define the *verfremdungseffekt* (the so-called alienation effect) – the contradiction is arrested in time for the length of the play, enabling the audience to experience the implications in slow time that evacuates any attempt to normalize.[15] The conflicted and vicious assumptions of liberal capitalism are laid bare, agonizingly, and for a length of time that sinks into the somatic physiology and present memory of the audience as they attempt to make difference from it. The duration of that exercise in making different is vital to the audience's ability to continue to be alert to making different/making present once outside the walls of the theatre.

With constellating the question arises: can we even begin to converse with people in like-minded groups who are not of the same mind as our own? With a set toward hegemony, the issue is eased, since the specific conditions for the topic in focus may be held as common ground with another topic. For example, varied ability groups campaigning for recognition of bodily alternatives may be able to work with other groups, such as transgender lobbies, campaigning for similar recognition. In performance, one might look at Marina Abramović's well-known *The Lips of Thomas* in which she cuts a five-pointed star into her abdomen (1975, 2005). As Kriss Ravetto-Biagioli has pointed out, the performance may generate change around nationalism (the star being a comment on the former Yugoslavia), sexuality (the woman sacrificing herself), violence (as the primary medium available to those excluded from liberal discourse), or other topical fields.[16] A performance such as this encourages people in the audience with quite different topical focuses to talk to one another, to form a constellation of interests.

Yet constellating holds further potential for political change. In public performance, the audience and performers form a disunified group. Despite the coherence of many audiences, the underlying conditions for making different do not depend entirely on like-minded support, and public performance allows not only for negotiation between different topics, but also for engagement across positionality. And in politics, it is hugely difficult to work across positionalities. For example, how does a group focused on the complete exclusion of the black body from the liberal civic structure, with a particular systemic critique, converse with a group focused on the erasure yet enscription of the female body? There are no comparabilities. Or to repeat the comment above: how does a non-African-American even begin to approach the concept let alone deal with the affect of Afropessimism?[17]

Take the work of Frank Wilderson III, either the imbricated personal and political in the autography *Incognegro*,[18] or the searing effect of *Reparations Now*.[19] In the latter, a set of interviews of African-Americans in Oakland, talking about the way white people do not respect, see or acknowledge them as human, is juxtaposed with video of the African-American who has 'made it' into the middle class and found himself blanked out – literally, with reversed negative footage of a black middle-class male speaking of the invisibility of the African-American as human. As a white middle-class female reader, I cannot understand or empathize with the positionality offered by the feeling of burnt negative that I make present from the digital film. Yet, my making that difference changes me: the change to myself that it necessitates at the moment of *until*, the moment when I know that I cannot possibly know, the 'différance', the moment of aporia, of nothingness, that I fill with some thing I recognize as 'difference'. The performance Wilderson makes available allows me to feel the affect I have made across different positionalities, and to begin to work on values that recorporate my body and inexorably disturb normative representations.

Audiences with a specific set toward hegemony reach out for the cultural *fit* of constellation, performance events in which something unsaid by society but vital to the audience is made present, generating both the excitement and completion of the aesthetics of fitting, and a responsive ethics that attempts to change normative social agreements. This is one way of rethinking 'catharsis'. Such a constellation requires empathy, an emotional response tied to sympathetic affect that is dependent on hegemony providing the common ground linking different sets toward the state. So, feminist and neocolonial dramatic performance can constellate across topics in a play such as Caryl Churchill's *Cloud Nine*,[20] which currently layers, at the least, questions about the neocolonial and heteronormative sexuality, inviting common critique of a neoliberal ideology that informs both sets of issues, while generating quite separate responsibilities.

However, audiences that coalesce around positionalities rather than sets form a rhetorical stance that hears what has not been said before, but also realizes that the new thing that has just been said renders further lived experience unsaid. The aesthetics hold the moment in which each individual body recognizes its sociopolitical ecology through its feelings and senses, and makes itself present in that moment – even when what is made present is nothingness. The corollary ethics that is put into motion is an engaged ethics of an audience that may not wholeheartedly embrace a performance at its moment of arrest, but one that is precipitated into the self-awareness of the making of difference. For example, Ilya Noé's sequence of four large (4 x 6 foot) canvases *Palimpsests: the work of a scribe* (1994–2004), which repeat five pages from *Parcs Interiors. L'Obra de Set Despintors* by a Catalan eco-commentator Perejaume, are, on first look, simple representations and disturbingly arresting (see Figure 16.3). On the occasions I viewed them, other visitors were visibly intrigued but also often clearly unable to constellate, to pull into cultural recognition. Some visitors walked past, easily dismissing the work. Others were pulled back into engaging with it.

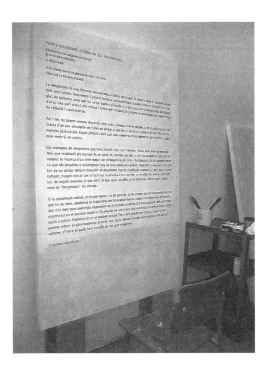

Figure 16.3 *Palimpsests: the work of a scribe*, Ilya Noé. Credit: Ilya Noé, with permission

For those who read Spanish/Catalan or who read the curator's notes to the exhibition, the social topic offered a spur to spend time interacting with the piece, for the words that were made present on the canvases concern ecological issues. Yet, once you allow yourself to observe, look, take part in the performativity of the piece, you begin to realize that each 'printed' letter is made by painting the white page with the black ink, that the care taken to ensure that each ascender, counter, bowl, tail and arc are defined within the font, each interlineal 'leaded' space is minutely observed, the kerning and the edge of the justification respected with a mathematical precision, then the apparently static becomes more and more engaging. You work with the art maker through the process of attending to the minute energetic balance of the handcraft and the large-scale architectural comprehension of these gigantic pages. They become a landscape with their own ecology, their own performativity. At that point, the topical and the schematic begin to contribute to the audience's capacity to bring into recognition, to engage in constellating.

Performance is one way that positionalities can interconnect: performance provides a place of invitation to make difference via performativity. Engaging in performativity in a performance establishes an ethics that allows us to change our selves while not changing others in doing so. As with the response above to Frank Wilderson's *Reparations Now*, empathy is not necessary, and affect is the result of our changes to our self not someone else. Performance becomes a gifting that we choose to do to our selves. This helps to understand why performers do not 'become' the thing they are perceived to perform, because perception is with the audience. And if the audience changes itself, enabling performers to respond and make their own differences to the new moment, those performers choose to do this to themselves. It helps to understand why performance is not persuasive in the same way as logic, for it enables choices within situated ecologies but does not define what those are.

Constellating around positionality has no need for identificatory empathy. The public performance gifts an audience with the embodied potential to make difference and change itself. Affect is the result of those individual choices and in Western liberal society is usually registered somatically or conceptually. The performer makes present something that has not been said before and encourages the audience to make difference and release energy. In performances with live audiences (in attendance or not), different positionalities are simultaneously releasing that energy, generating possible conversations across positionality. And as the audience makes difference/makes present something previously unsaid, the actor or performer has something to engage with, and make different. The audience becomes aware and attentive. Constellating puts into process a change that makes self present. It enables that change but does not define what it is, generating the hard work of engaged ethics. Audiences can make difference from other positionalities, and in doing so necessarily engage them. Public performance becomes a way that positionalities can interconnect, and, as such, it is an interesting place to do political study.

Note on articulation

Constellating experiences installating at its moment of arrest or installation, engages with the presence of performativity, builds varied aesthetics and ethics, and can make alterior values emerge into hegemony through articulation into constellation. Not all constellating articulates, but when it does so, it is usually critical because it articulates alterior values that come from alongside living. Even though Western theatre audiences are not encouraged to display physical or embodied change except through words, many will carry the change in their bodies for the rest of their lives. A relatively small number will use the conventions of representation to communicate the change. And even fewer audience members will attempt to document the embodied change in articulation. That articulation into what can be said can prompt further process. It works as an emergent or liminal form moving towards and challenging cultural fit and shifting assumptions, yet – depending on rhetorical drift – it can also join the representations of the state. When constellating articulates, it embeds itself into performative rather than representative documentary labour.[21]

The work of the performance critic as audience continues to recognize and document alternative values, not necessarily to agree with them. It can superimpose a presence onto a representation to transform its features and remind us of disunified aesthetics, and it can go much further and articulate the alterior values of disunified democracy, the difficulty of them, and that we make them so for particular reasons. This is a rhetoric of situated textuality that performance studies in the liberal West knows as performativity: the making of difference, collaboration, knowledge as process, temporary arrest, articulation of value, decision, action, and change to the state.

Notes

1   For example, on 'memory', Peggy Phelan, *Unmarked: The Politics of Performance* (New York: Routledge, 1993); on 'liminality', Jon McKenzie, *Perform or Else: From*

Discipline to Performance (New York: Routledge, 2001); on constitution and citation, Judith Butler, *Bodies that Matter: On the Discursive Limits of 'Sex'* (New York: Routledge, 1993).

2 Lynette Hunter, *Critiques of Knowing* (New York: Routledge, 1999), Chs 5 and 6.

3 Diana Taylor, *From Archive to Repertoire: Performing Cultural Memory in the Americas* (Durham, NC: Duke University, 2003), Introduction.

4 André Lepecki, *Exhausting Dance: Performance and the Politics of Movement* (New York: Routledge, 2006).

5 See D. Smith, *The Everyday World as Problematic* (Boston: Northeastern University Press, 1987).

6 Alan Read, *Theatre and Everyday Life* (New York: Routledge, 1994), used to distinguish from hegemonic culture, 43, 98–9.

7 Chantal Mouffe and Ernesto Laclau, *Hegemony and Socialist Strategy: Towards a Radical Democratic Politics*, trans W. Moore and P. Cammack (London: Verso, 1985); this book defines 'articulation' as the moment a relation with hegemony becomes possible.

8 See, for example, Matthew Goulish, *39 Microlectures: In Proximity of Performance* (New York: Routledge, 2000); Tim Etchells, 'On Documentation and Performance' and 'Repeat Forever: Body, Death, Performance, Fiction' in *Certain Fragments: Contemporary Performance and Forced Entertainment* (New York: Routledge, 1999); and Della Pollock, 'Performative Writing' in Peggy Phelan and Jill Lane, eds, *The Ends of Performance* (New York University Press, 1998).

9 These like-minded groups are more in tune with Dorothy Smith's concept of communities based on 'particularised ties', see *The Everyday World as Problematic* (Boston, Northeastern University Press, 1989, 3), than Hans-Georg Gadamer's small groups who practise consensual reasoning within their community, something he refers to as 'solidarity', in *Reason in the Age of Science*, trans. F. Lawrence (Cambridge, MA, MIT Press, 1981, 87). The former is collaborative, the latter collective.

10 L. Hunter, 'Installation in Ilya Noé's '*Deerwalk*' (forthcoming 2012).

11 This distinction draws from the rhetorical definition of 'topical' as 'related to content' (for example a simile) and 'schematic' as 'related to structure' (for example a chiasmus, or: part A, part B, part B, part A).

12 For example, Hortense Spillers, 'Mama's Baby, Papa's Maybe: An American Grammar Book', *Diacritics, Culture and Countermemory: The 'American' Connection.* 17:2 (1987) 64–81; and more recently, Jared Sexton, *Assimilation Schemes: Antiblackness and the Critique of Multiracialism* (Minneapolis: University of Minnesota Press, 2009).

13 Frank Wilderson III, 'Raw Life and the "Ruse" of Empathy' in Peter Lichtenfels and John Rouse, eds, *Performance, Politics and Activism* (Basingstoke: Palgrave Macmillan, 2012).

14 E. Diamond, *Unmaking Mimesis: Essays on Feminism and Theater* (New York: Routledge, 1997), 146–7.

15 Lynette Hunter, 'Installation in Ilya Noé's *The Deerwalk*', as above.

16 Kriss Ravetto-Biagioli, 'Marina Abramović', forthcoming 2013.

17 In criticism, one solution was the debate between partial knowledge in the 1980s – in which non-African-Americans simply didn't have to join the discussion – and the more alterior positionality of radical nothingness presented by

later Afropessimists such as Saidya Hartman or David Marriott. Yet their written criticism and poetry become performances that do invite an audience.

18 Frank Wilderson III, *Incognegro* (Cambridge, MA: Southend Press, 2008).

19 Frank Wilderson III, *Reparations Now*, produced by Anita Wilkins, Obsidian Productions, 2005.

20 Caryl Churchill, *Cloud Nine* in *Plays One* (New York: Routledge, 1985), c. 1979.

21 For more detail on articulation, see L. Hunter, 'Constellation: Engaging with radical devised dance theatre: Keith Hennessy's *Sol Niger*', in Peter Lichtenfels and John Rouse, eds, *Performance, Politics and Activism* (Basingstoke: Palgrave Macmillan, 2013).

17   Spatial Concepts

Silvija Jestrovic

In the late 1960s Michel Foucault coined the term *heterotopia*, while in the field of urban geography Henri Lefebvre (1992) wrote on the production of space and introduced the notion of *lived space*. These concepts have inspired more recent discussions on spatiality, including Edward Soja's version of the concept of *Thirdspace* and, in the field of theatre and performance, Una Chaudhuri's neologism *geopathology*. The keywords *heterotopia*, *lived space*, *Thirdspace* and *geopathology*, as well as other related terms, have at least one thing in common – they remind us that space is ideological and that performance could play a key role in the making and unmaking of its politics.

The notion of ambiguity is inherent in Foucault's definition of heterotopic spaces, described as those spaces 'endowed with the curious property of being in relation with all the others, but in such way as to suspend, neutralize or invert the set of relationships designed, reflected or mirrored by themselves' (1997: 352). Theatre is one of the examples that Foucault (1997: 354) uses to illustrate his concept, since, along with other heterotopic spaces, theatre 'has the power of juxtaposing in a single real place different spaces that are incompatible with each other'. Heterotopia suggests an inherent dimension of 'otherness' in both real and imagined spaces, even if we have initially recognized them as familiar.

Edward Soja, taking his cue from both Foucault and Lefebvre, points out that heterotopic space is indeed made/produced through action – whether the acting is physical, conceptual or symbolic. He works against the Lefebvrian binaries of *perceived space* (the directly experienced world) and *conceived space* (subjective, 'imagined' space), and draws from Lefebvre's concept of *lived space* – which operates between the dualities of subjective and objective – to introduce his version of the concept, which he calls *Thirdspace*. Soja (2000: 22, 21) defines it as a 'strategic meeting place for fostering collective political action against all forms of human oppression', and also as a 'distinctive way of looking at, interpreting, and acting to change the spatiality of human life'. The concept points to the inseparability of the historical, the social and the spatial, and promotes a 'third possibility' dialectics that does not culminate in synthesis but seeks instead 'to disorder, deconstruct and tentatively reconstruct the entire dialectical sequence and its logic' (ibid.: 21). Soja's Thirdspace is an open and inclusive space of action and intervention. It is the where and how of radical performance activity.

Inspired by Foucault and Soja, Una Chaudhuri (1995: 15) coined the neologism *geopatholgy* in the context of theatre and drama to theorize the notion of place as a problem that 'unfolds as an incessant dialogue between belonging and exile, home and homelessness'. Foucault's heterotopia is realized as a relationship among different and often incompatible spaces; Soja's Thirdspace is established through action – through becoming, rather than being, to echo Hegelian categories; while Chaudhuri's geopathology emphasizes the relationship between person and place. How are these spatial categories realized through performance? How do these terms inform our understanding and interpretation of certain performance practices? And how do performance practices and analysis confirm or broaden the meaning of these terms? In the following section, I examine two case studies – from Sarajevo and Belgrade respectively, during the Balkans War – that embody different, yet related, versions of the spatial concepts in question.

Performance activities

Example 1: Sarajevo cellist

The photo of cellist Vedran Smajlovic, performing among the ruins of Sarajevo's National Library, a casualty of the shelling, became an icon of the city's spirit of resistance and renewal (see Figure 17.1). The image was used to advertise the 1994 Sarajevo International Film Festival, held while the war was still going on. For the purposes of the festival poster, Smajlovic interrupted his performance for a moment and covered his face with his hands in an obvious gesture of mourning. Although the scene was staged, the idea came from an actual activity that took place daily from the beginning of the siege. More than a piece of festival memorabilia of Sarajevo under siege, however, the poster is a document that depicts a performance in which the very use of space was a political act. During the three-year siege of Sarajevo, Smajlovic played his cello every day in various locations throughout the city – from the promenade and cultural landmarks to ruins and graveyards. Dressed in a black tuxedo, Smajlovic performed his outdoor concerts even when there was no audience and when his music had to compete with the sound of gunfire. It is in this act/image of Smajlovic performing amid the ruins of the Sarajevo library that versions of Foucault's heterotopia and Soja's Thirdspace are embodied.

Figure 17.1   Vedran Smajlovic. Photo: Mikhail Evstafiev

Foucault (1997: 355) describes libraries and museums as heterotopias of time in which 'time does not cease to accumulate'. Sarajevo's ruined library, where hundreds of invaluable medieval manuscripts now lay entombed in ashes, adds a somewhat paradoxical twist to Foucault's point. The ruined library, however, does not necessarily embody the erosion of time as a direct opposite to Foucault's functional heterotopia. Rather, the ruins continue to signify the meaning and the memory of the space, even if the shape and function of that space has been transformed. Moreover, Smajlovic's performance on the library ruins confirmed the primary function of the destroyed building – its role as a cultural institution. Nevertheless, the image reveals other layers of this heterotopia, established through a violent assertion of another spatial and temporal dimension – the condensed present tense of the warzone.

The ambiguity of this space is evident in the contrast between the 'setting' and the person – the cellist performing on the ruins of a bombed city, dressed as if he were playing in a concert hall. The city is simultaneously a cultural centre and a warzone. Its libraries, museums, mosques and churches, buildings and streets are – in the moment of Smajlovic's performance – both repositories of cultural memory and death traps. Contrasts that render the performances of the Sarajevo cellist somewhat surreal also subvert expectations and make the familiar strange by inserting into the iconography of a warzone the images and sounds of a concert hall. Through the act of performing, Smajlovic temporarily produced an alternative space. The performance established Soja's notion of Thirdspace – a space of intervention and resistance through a symbolic act that subverted the finality of destruction. In Soja's and Lefebvre's terms, the performance produced an alternative to the first space – a site of erasure where all that remained of the National Library was rubble – and the second space – the representational, ideological and symbolic dimensions that the ruin evoked. Heterotopia here emerges as a space of defamiliarization and resistance, since the performance of the cellist produces an 'other' space at the very moment when 'otherness' and difference – whether it be ethnic, political, or cultural – is met with gunfire. The production of Thirdspace through performance asserts the idea of continuity into a context where rupture and destruction have been the norm and the modus operandi.

Example 2: Frozen Art

In May 1993, a group of artists came together in Belgrade under the name Frozen Art (Led Art) to express their revolt – through a series of performance activities – against the jingoistic and war-mongering politics of the regime in Serbia. The group staged its inaugural project, also entitled *Frozen Art,* in a refrigerated truck parked in the city centre opposite a well-known cultural institution – the House of Youth. The central metaphor of the event was that the citizens of Serbia lived in 'a time out of joint', where things froze in the middle of spring. The metaphor could be stretched farther to render the seemingly normal everyday life in Belgrade absurd in the light of a war raging only a few hundred kilometers away in Bosnia. The choice of the exhibition space and its positioning was not arbitrary. Despite a name that echoes the communist days of the 1980s, the House of Youth had become a venue for innovative and cutting-edge events ranging from exhibits and performances to rock concerts. By the early 1990s, however, state control of the venue was tightened and its doors closed for works that were in any way daring or subversive. When Frozen Art parked its refrigerated truck/mobile gallery in front of the building, it sent a clear message that embodied the group's perspective on cultural institutions, but it also created a dynamic urban environment of conflicting political and cultural tensions. In this environment, the refrigerated truck and the House of Youth traded places – the former acquired an aesthetic function, while the latter figured in the background as an empty shell – a haunted house of cultural memory.

With a crowd gathered in front of the truck waiting to get in, music and commentary emanating from the loudspeakers, the street turned into a stage. Each visitor was given an army coat to wear before entering the exhibit to keep warm. Inside the truck a display of objects stood captured in ice. The installations ranged from the overtly political and ironic, to personal, abstract and nostalgic. One installation displayed a kitschy Venetian gondola figurine[1] stuck in a frozen sewer pipe; in another one, entitled 'Summer Time Blues', a pair of old running shoes stood motionless.[2] An untitled ice sculpture captured a clock and a bullet from the latest war in Croatia,[3] while in the corner of the truck, an old Yugoslav flag sat stuck in a barrel of lard, refusing to freeze. The author, Rasa Todosijevic, named this one 'Gott liebt die Serben' alluding to fascist dimensions of Serbian nationalism.

The symbolism of these ice sculptures is twofold. On the one hand, freezing is a method of preserving something from decay. Frozen Art is a hibernation tactic– a strategy for lowering the temperature in order to survive the cultural, political and ethical ice age into which the former Yugoslavia had fallen. On the other hand, installations made of statutory flags and frozen bullets insert a blatant critique of war and the existing political situation. By offering army coats to protect visitors from the cold inside the truck, the artists suggested that everyone, no matter how uninvolved, was part of the war and implicit in the unfolding of the Yugoslavian catastrophe. Hence the hibernation metaphor turns full circle from having a positive connotation as a preservation strategy to standing for passivity and political cowardice that makes innocent bystanders complicit in the crime.

The *Frozen Art* project utilized the heterotopia of time, but added an ironic twist. The artifacts – as repositories of cultural, political and personal memories – were literally and metaphorically frozen in time but also made more vulnerable and dependent on space, since they could not survive outside the refrigerated truck.[4] The ambiguities of this Thirdspace unfolded along spatial and temporal axes. The former was embodied in the spatial and architectural relations among the refrigerated truck, the street and the House of Youth. Visual and verbal allusions foregrounded the contrast between the seemingly normal life of inner-city Belgrade and the neighboring warzone. The temporal dimension was established through a dialectic relationship between the outside and the inside – the springtime streetscape where the here and now of the event was taking place and the truck's interior where, in subzero temperatures, memories of the past and contradictions of the present confronted each other and turned into ice. This dynamic of outside and inside created an 'other space' that was simultaneously 'material and metaphorical, real and imagined, grounded in spatial practices yet also represented in literary and aesthetic imagery' (Soja 2000: 24). Through the contrast between outside and inside, as well as through their choice of artifacts within the refrigerated truck, the artists confronted different cultural and ideological spaces, revealing that in the given political circumstances, their relationship to place could be nothing but troubled. This relationship is geopathological as the performance exposes the problem with place and a 'sickness' of place.[5] The jingoistic ideology of Serbian officials, grounded in notions of tradition and continuity, created an illusion of normalcy where city life continued its everyday routine without interruption, as if Serbia had had no involvement in the Bosnian War, as if the citizens of Serbia had not been secretly drafted to fight in that war, as if oppositional voices had not been marginalized and silenced, and as if the country had not experienced one of the worst inflations in 20th-century history. The Thirdspace that this event carved out is one of rupture, discontinuity and transformation – a site of struggle with the problem of place. It is also a space where geopathological relations are revealed as a first step towards political critique and action.

Utopian performatives and synchronicity

Both examples embody versions of Jill Dolan's (2004: 165) concept of the utopian performative, described as allowing a

> fleeting contact with a utopia not stabilized by its own finished perfection, not coercive in its contained, self-reliant, self determined system, not messianic in its zeal for a particular social arrangement, but a utopia always in process, always only partially grasped, as it disappears before us around the corners of narrative and social experience.

Foucault (1997: 352) defines heterotopia against the concept of utopia – which represents arrangements that have no real space – as 'a sort of place that lies outside all places and yet is actually localizable' since it constitutes a 'sort of counter-arrangement' to 'all the other real arrangements that can be found within society'. Dolan's utopian performative is heterotopic in nature – not perfect, but realizable – and it comes with an expiration date, which could be only moments away. In the two case studies, utopian performatives are realized through dynamic relationships to place; through acts that challenge, negotiate and shape real spaces.

Moreover, the two case studies reveal another version of utopian performative that depends on synchronicity and yet is paradoxically delayed. Foucault (1997: 350) calls attention to the transition from time to space, from diachrony to synchrony, when he writes:

> We are in the age of the simultaneous, of juxtaposition, the near and the far, the side by side and the scattered. A period in which, in my view, the world is putting itself to test, not so much as a great way of life destined to grow in time but as a net that links points together and creates its own muddle.

The simultaneity that links the Frozen Art happening in Belgrade and the cello performance in Sarajevo is intriguing. Both events, as well as similar performances of Frozen Art, took place during 1993 and 1994 and were responses to essentially the same political problem and its geopathologies. Soja (2000: 22) points out that Thirdspace is 'a starting point for new and different exploration that can move beyond the third term in a constant search for other space'. The synchrony and simultaneity of the two performances creates an additional Thirdspace – a space other than 'other space'. This 'other space' is established through two acts of resistance taking place in two different (even incompatible) spaces (Belgrade and Sarajevo) at the same 'dramatic' point in history. Although derived from real spaces and actions, this 'other space' could be established only through discourse. Its utopian performative moment is, therefore, delayed, because it unfolds, *post festum*, in the process of writing on heterotopias – through comparisons, contrasts and analyses that intermingle seemingly distant spaces.

Notes

1   The Venetian gondola in Nikola Dzafo's sculpture used to be a status symbol representing the rise to working class to lower middle class in the 1960s, when the borders of Tito's Yugoslavia opened to the West and shopping trips to Trieste became common. The Venetian gondola, usually displayed on the shelf in the living room, was the main souvenir from these trips – a testimony of the first encounter between communist ideals and Western consumerism, as well as a memento of everyday life in Tito's Yugoslavia.
2   Author Jovan Cekic.
3   Author Milorad Cveticanin.
4   Although the state-run agricultural company that donated the refrigerated truck agreed to permanently house the exhibit, in the night after the opening, the truck's cooling mechanism mysteriously collapsed. The truck's owners claimed that the damage was beyond repair and nothing could be done. Artifacts were taken out on the street pavement and left to melt.

5   The 'sickness' of place was further emphasized in the performances of *Frozen Art*,
    which often used the term 'decontamination' of place to describe the political
    and cultural aims of their interventions.

Works cited

Chaudhuri, Una. *Staging Place: the Geography of Modern Drama*. Ann Arbor: U of
    Michigan Press, 1995.

Dolan, Jill. 'Utopia in Performance', *Theatre Research International* 31(2004): 163–73.

Foucault, Michel. 'Of Other Space: Utopias and Heterotopias,' in Neil Leach, ed.,
    Rethinking Architecture: A Reader in Cultural Theory. London: Routledge, 1997,
    350–6.

Lefebvre, Henri. *The Production of Space*, trans. Donald Nicholson-Smith. Oxford:
    Blackwell, 1992.

Soja, Edward. 'Thirdspace: Expending the Scope of the Geographical Imagination,'
    in Alan Read, ed., *Architecturally Speaking: Practices of Art, Architecture and the Every-
    day*. London: Routledge, 2000, 13–31.

18   Consensus, Dissensus[1]

Adrian Kear

In 1993, the South African photographer Kevin Carter published a photo-graph in *The New York Times* and *Johannesburg Mail & Guardian* of a famine victim in the Sudan. The analogue picture depicted a small starving child who had collapsed just outside a relief centre being watched over by a vulture stood a few feet away from her hopelessly exposed, emaciated body. The photograph, widely described as one of the 'photographs of the Century' (Rancière 2007a: 80) for its condensation of suffering into a tragic *image of* suffering, won Carter the 1994 Pulitzer Prize, and a good deal of notoriety for the detachment and calculation of its staging. Alternately derided for taking an exaggerated amount of time to compose the shot rather than indulging the immediate humanitarian impulse to intervene; or for having accentuated the scene's set-up by collapsing the distance between the vulture and the child by 'smashing' the foreground with a telephoto lens; the *ethics* of Carter's photographic act have remained the focus for discussions about the *politics* of the image's publication, circula-tion and impact.

In 2006, the Chilean artist Alfredo Jaar returned to the staging of this event in his installation work, *The Sound of Silence*. Rather than reproduce the content of the image and replicate its tragic effect, Jaar focuses on explicating the context of its production and the relational dynamics of its impact. The installation consists of a zinc-enclosed wooden box – perhaps reminiscent of camera obscura as the basic unit of photographic exposure – entry into which is controlled by red (horizontal) and green (vertical) lights at the aperture of the doorway. The back of the box is constructed as a picture frame surrounding a vertical arrangement of open white fluores-cent tubes that simultaneously functions as an image and as an *image of* the image-making process as the material framing, capture and contain-ment of light. The box is therefore quintessentially a light box: an illumi-nated space and a space of illumination. Yet once inside, the spectator is enveloped by silence and darkness – the conventional theatrical preface to the emergence of visibility and speech. The immersive environment is punctuated at first by the appearance of white printed words on a black screen, the typeface of which appears recognizably analogue. They mark the name of a figure called 'Kevin', silently calling out, and calling out to, 'Kevin, Kevin, Kevin'. The sentences – all short statements – gradually accumulate to provide a skeletal biography of this figure: a young South African news photographer and a member of the 'bang-bang club' collective responsible for documenting the brutal and brutalizing violence of the South African townships under the apartheid regime (Pollock 2012: 72). The narrative unveils the story of 'Kevin's' assignment to the Sudan and the immediate events leading to the photograph's capture, accounting for the processes of its 'staging' and their interrelation: the aesthetic juxtaposition of 'bare life' against barren ground; the photographer's watchful waiting for the perfect moment of the vulture opening its wings (and its recalcitrant refusal so to do); his parental concern for children at home whilst observing, within touching distance, *this* child's fate unfold. And only then the image appears, with shutter-speed suddenness as an interruptive burst of light, exposed to sight only for the same duration it takes to capture the image as the trace of light through the exposure of a frame of film. The reintroduction of temporality into the image – its *theatricalization*, so to speak – enables the spectator to focus not on the photograph as such but on the questions of politics and ethics it frames in its trace: the degradation of the human (black, female, child) to 'bare life', victim of the violence of capital and the vicissitudes of indifference; the limits of artistic detachment, implicating the observer in the thing observed, context in content, relationality in singularity; the self-regarding nature of the discourse of humanitarian intervention, supported by a tacit politics of spectatorship dominated by 'tragic' ways of seeing and a tendency to reduplicate the mimetic logic governing the commodification of suffering through the circulation of images of suffering in the economy of signs.

The interruptive burst of light in *The Sound of Silence* draws attention to the ontological appearance of the image within an ideologically 'determined regime of the perceptible' (Rancière 2007a: 78), exposing its conditions of visibility and destabilizing its status as spectacle. As the spectator learns of 'Kevin's' suicide within the space of a year of having taken the original photograph, and is informed that the destiny of the child remains unknown, the light box reverberates with nothing but the sound of our own investments in the aesthetic politics of the image and its framing of the reduction of human life to the very moment of its emptying.

Jaar's installation appears to demonstrate how the representation of the scene of suffering, so precisely and pitilessly undertaken by Kevin Carter's photography, continues to bear the traces of spectatorial co-presence within it. Its staging of the terrible exposure of the human being within the space and time of the exposure of the photograph not only exposes the (in)humanity on both sides of the camera but extends this thinking to the material relations of spectatorship inscribed in the installation. *The Sound of Silence* provides a theatrical context for thinking through the work of making and looking; for thinking the work of making and looking precisely *as* aesthetic practices of thinking. By staging the photograph within the mise-en-scène of a theatrical space designed for viewing, as illuminated by a burst of light lasting only the duration of the shutter speed with which the photograph was taken, Jaar identifies the political performativity of the image less with the narrative's illustration than its interruption. The image's moment of appearance becomes the point at which the activity of viewing is thrown into question, and the spectator is invited to occupy a different relation to the visible and its normative construction and distribution. As the perceptual apparatus is thrown open, however momentarily, an ethical and aesthetic thinking of the political logic of representation – and its disruption by the simultaneous co-appearance of presentation – is set in motion. In this sensate moment of fissure, this temporal burst of illumination, the political structure of spectatorship is opened up through a 'rupture in the relationship between sense and sense, between what is seen and what is thought, and between what is thought and what is felt' (Rancière 2010: 143).

Jacques Rancière (2004a: 12) identifies the experience of such moments of disruption and dissociation as being essential to the recognition and recalibration of the political 'distribution of the sensible'. He suggests that the aesthetic encounter's capacity to 'reconfigure the fabric of sensory experience' through altering the 'frames, scales and speeds' of perception, destabilizing the 'self-evidence of the visible' and making 'the invisible visible', exemplifies its operation as a practice of 'dissensus' (Rancière 2010: 140–1). For Rancière, the practice of 'dissensus' unites the domains of art and politics, albeit paradoxically, with the aesthetic reopening of the sensate experience of the visible qua 'distribution of the sensible' acting as an index of the reanimation of *political* processes of subjectivation. Although there remains a necessary 'undecidability' in the specificity of its organization, Rancière (1999: 37) argues that the aesthetic event operates as a key site for the *essentially political* 'manifestation of dissensus as the presence of two worlds in one'. Artworks such as Jaar's would seem to operate 'dissensually' by placing co-appearance into political tension, reopening the foundational gap between presence and representation at the heart of the 'fundamental grievance' articulated by politics as the locus of division and dispossession (Rancière 1999: 96–7). Experienced as 'a singular disruption', the aesthetic encounter takes place through the appearance of an image that '*interrupts* the smooth working' of representation and sets into play the recognition of the fact of presentation as 'a singular mechanism of subjectification' (Rancière 1999: 99). As a practice of dissensus, art – like politics – consists in revealing the distance, and the difference, between a social situation and its representation; the presentational appearance of the image functioning not simply as an ontological fragment of the visible but as a political *staging* of the conditions of visibility making manifest 'the separation of the sensible from itself' (Rancière 2010: 42). According to Rancière (2007b: 259), dissensual practices create 'a modification of the co-ordinates of the sensible' and an opening for political subjectification precisely by reopening the division, the foundational separation, between presence and representation.

Tellingly, Rancière (2010: 42) argues that the essence of 'democratic' politics resides in the practice of dissensus rather than in the attempted 'annulment' of the differences it reveals in the social field. With this reversal of the priority of dissensus over 'consensus', he effectively draws attention to the dialectical movement between them, thereby foregrounding the continuous reopening of the political divisions and ontological gaps that 'the practice of ruling relentlessly plugs' (ibid.: 54). In extending this critique from the domestic sphere to the domain of international politics, he notes that 'consensus' is the name given to the 'effective reconfiguration of the political field' conducted under the aegis of 'universal' human rights and citizenship, which in itself nominates 'an actual process of de-politicization' (Rancière 2004b: 306). For Rancière, then, the practice of 'consensus' is an attempt to delimit the possibilities of democracy whose productivity lies in the staging and enactment of 'specific scenes of dissensus' (ibid.: 304).

The term 'dissensus' is used by Rancière (2010: 14) to account for a division in 'the common experience of the sensible' or 'common sense', which is no mere 'conflict of interests, opinions, or values', but rather a fundamentally political 'dispute about what is given, about the frame within which we see something as given' (Rancière 2004b: 304). Consensus, as a representational practice, he argues, operates through a process of foreclosing spaces of dissensus in order to produce a social settlement, or ideological distribution, based on the economic coincidence of interests and identities. Accordingly, he suggests that consensus functions by attempting to excise the random element of participative politics – the presence of the 'surplus subject' whose affiliations, identifications and orientations are neither fixed nor coextensive with a 'definite collective' – and thereby exclude the opening of a juridical/political 'dispute' about their continuing representation (ibid.: 303). Substituted in their place are the 'representative' stand-ins of social groups attenuated to the state – 'stakeholders', 'community leaders', constituencies of identities and the like – whose role is to appear to legitimate the attribution of rights and demarcation of responsibilities within a stable cultural framework. For Rancière (2004b: 306), then, 'consensus is the reduction of democracy to the way of life of a society, to its *ethos*', achieved through the symbolic evacuation and exclusion 'the *political* core constituting it, namely dissensus' (Rancière 2010: 188, emphasis added).

'Consensus' is also the term adopted by Alain Badiou (2001: 30, 31), in the coruscating critique of the framework of human rights he advances in *Ethics: An Essay on the Understanding of Evil*, to describe the way in which the call of 'blind necessity' is staged in 'the spectacle of the economy' to produce passive acceptance of the 'logic of Capital'. He sees the neutralization of the idea of need in political economy as being coextensive with the valorization of suffering in human rights discourse, with both being directed, from the outset, towards the foreclosure of any form of dissensual politics. Badiou (2001: 32) insists that 'the very idea of a consensual ethics … is a powerful contributor to subjective resignation and acceptance of the status quo', whose aim is to provide a bulwark against the realization of possible alternatives and to secure the de facto recognition of 'necessity as the objective basis for all judgements of value'. Genuine politics needs must be excluded from this tight-knit relation because what it offers, Badiou (2001: 32) suggests, puts 'an end to consensus' through the irruption of the radically innovative and performatively resubjectivating.

Likewise, for Badiou, the contemporary 'turn to ethics' represents an abandonment of the foundational principle of equality and the reintroduction of an essentially abstract, faux 'universalism' at the expense of a concrete, socially situated materialism. He regards the philosophical underpinnings of human rights discourse as essentially Kantian, and the contemporary 'turn to ethics' as being, as Simon Critchley (2005: 222) has noted, essentially a 'return to Kant and to a Kantian conception of the subject of the moral law as universal and context-free and not situationally bound'. In *Ethics*, Badiou (2001: 2) rehearses a formalist reading of Kant's *Foundations of the Metaphysics of Morals*, emphasizing 'how subjective action and its representable intentions relate to a universal Law' and the imperative of judgement. He traces the extension of this position in human rights discourse to demonstrate how an 'ethics of judgement' correlates with an essentially negative conception of human beings and human actions (2001: 8). The external imperatives privileged by this framework not only conceive of the subject as 'incapable of thinking the singularity of situations, that is, of being orientated to praxis' (Critchley 2005: 222); they constitute a regulative matrix designed to guarantee obedience and – in cases of transgression – the justification of punishment and enforced compliance (which is especially important, given their extension into the codes of international law). Badiou (2001: 8) suggests that 'ethics is conceived here both as an *a priori* ability to discern Evil' – the acceptance of the *negative* as the fundamental consensual 'given' – 'and as the ultimate principle of judgement, in particular political judgement: good is what intervenes visibly against an Evil which is identifiable *a priori*'.

While it is clear that according to this assessment, neo-Kantian 'ethical universalism' acts as an 'apologia for Western ideology' (Critchley 2005: 222) – an ideology which determines *in advance* the criteria for what will count as morally acceptable, devoid of contextual/situational considerations – this is by no means the end of the matter. Badiou contends that the negative discourse of ethics positions human beings primarily as *victims*. More particularly, by adopting a certain figure from tragic performance, he suggests that the so-called universal 'subject of rights' is effectively split between a 'passive, pathetic, or reflexive subject' – a victim who suffers – on the one hand; and, on the other, an 'active, determining subject of judgement' who occupies a classical 'spectator' position in relation to suffering, exposed only to the vicarious experience of pity and fear. This latter position, Badiou (2001: 9) suggests, is by far the most important and powerful within this bifurcation, subordinating the politics of the situation to the 'sympathetic and indignant judgement of the spectator' and soliciting their concomitant desire for intervention. This formulation resonates with Jaar's questioning of relations of representation in *The Sound of Silence*, for example, and its opening up of the ethics of reproducing suffering through the image of suffering and the concomitant risk of reduplicating 'ethical' demands for intervention. Like Jaar, Badiou's provocation, in this context, is to remind us that the 'judgement of suffering' from the spectator's perspective serves not only to confirm the victimization of those being 'represented', but concedes, at the same time, a self-reflexive conception of the human subject as 'the being who is capable of recognizing himself as a victim' (2001: 10).

Here, Badiou is perhaps simply reiterating a certain Platonic antitheatricality in associating spectatorship with the scopophilic enjoyment of victimization and subjective *in*capacity, or, at least, with the structural impossibility of the spectator's intervention into the domain of the act. In an essay concerned with challenging the notion of the spectator's 'passivity' and accrediting the role with intellectual and political agency, Rancière (2007c: 272) characterizes this conception as asserting that

> the theatre is the place where ignorant people are invited to see suffering people. What takes place on the stage is a pathos, the manifestation of a disease, the disease of desire and pain, which is nothing but the self-division of the subject.

While this is also potted Plato, for sure, Rancière is at pains to indicate its intransigence in structuring the theatrical relation as a mode of appearance that produces a split between activity and passivity, capacity and incapacity, which remains evident even in forms of practice that celebrate their binary inversion. For Rancière, this structural bifurcation is integral to the theatre's role in maintaining a certain 'distribution of the sensible', which partitions capacity and incapacity, activity and passivity, knowledge and ignorance and attributes them to discrete social 'parties', with the gap between stage and audience serving as an 'allegory of inequality' imbricated in the play of 'domination and subjection'. So instead, he proposes a theory of emancipated spectatorship that 'starts from the opposite principle, the principle of equality'. This entails rejecting the association of looking with passivity and the bifurcation of capacity and incapacity, and recognizing that spectatorship is a critical and creative activity that confirms, contests and changes the 'distribution of the visible' with which it is presented (Rancière 2007c: 277). In this way, the theatrical relation may be reconfigured as a mode of *dissensual* engagement and *democratic* political participation.

It should be clear, then, that for both Badiou and Rancière, the question of human rights as the rights of the victim is a question of the conceptualization of the subject and the process of subjectification. Badiou (2001: 35) rejects the notion of an a priori universal subject and demonstrates how such a conception is both irremediably split and fundamentally nihilist, focusing on the negative construction of the victim and 'the underlying conviction that the only thing that can really happen to someone is death'. The key site of application for the discourse of rights is therefore the deciding of death: 'who shall die and how?' becomes the central touchstone in decisions about judgements of responsibility and the ethics of 'humanitarian intervention'. Badiou's analysis points to a certain 'sordid self-satisfaction' (2001: 13, 37) permeating the construction of the spectator/victim relation – an essentially *tragic* configuration irremediably concerned with the dispensation of *eudaemonia*, or 'happiness', as the ultimate social good, which leads him to conclude that 'every definition of Man based on happiness is nihilist'.

The reliance on an ethics derived from abstract universals is, then, for Badiou (2001: 13), both incapable of recognizing the fact that 'we are always dealing with a political situation, one that calls for political thought-practice, one that is peopled by its own authentic actors', and impervious to the recognition of its own reliance on representation. Rancière similarly notes the vacuity and lack of utility of the rights derived from such abstractions. Tellingly, he suggests that Western society dispenses these as it does whatever else is deemed empty or of no further use, by giving them to the poor:

Those rights that appear useless in their place are sent abroad, along with medicine and clothes, to people deprived of medicine, clothes, and rights. It is in this way, as a result of this process, that the rights of Man become the rights of those who have no rights, the rights of bare human beings subjected to inhuman repression and inhuman conditions. (Rancière 2004b: 307)

In other words, this process turns 'human rights' into 'humanitarian rights', and enables them to be remanufactured and returned to their sender. For if those who suffer – in the frame of the image – are regarded as incapable of exercising or enacting the rights afforded them, then it follows that these can be enacted for them on behalf of a certain gaze in the Other. This is what, for Rancière, forms the political and psychic fabric of humanitarian intervention – a non-reciprocal relation (a quasi-theatrical relation of non-relation), which refashions 'disused rights' and gives them a concrete new dimension, which amounts to the 'justification' of occupation. Rancière (2004b: 309) insists that this is in no way a matter of 'equality', as this new utility is instrumentalized on the world stage to achieve 'what consensus achieves on the national stage': 'the erasure of all legal distinctions and the closure of all political intervals of dissensus'.

Rancière is clearly on the same page as Badiou when it comes to recognizing that the reign of ethics secures itself by precluding any political conception of the human subject and foreclosing any space of genuine politics. Rancière (2004b: 309) further suggests that 'the "ethical" trend is in fact the "state of exception"' – the term taken up by Giorgio Agamben (2000: x) to describe the attempted temporary suspension of the rule of law that reveals itself instead as the foundational exclusion sustaining the structure of law – in that it seeks to ensure the erasure (not the completion) of the political and the forced identity of exclusion and law. In so doing, Rancière (2004b: 308) stresses that adherence to any sense of 'ontological destiny', in the Heideggerian stance adopted by Agamben, risks both privileging the inescapability of human animality and prioritizing 'faithfulness to the law of Otherness, which rules out any dream of "human emancipation"' or any possibility of a political process beyond the self-reflexive determinism of 'resistance'. It would seem that, for Rancière, resistance attenuates ethics to legalesque 'responsibility' rather than to the possibilities of politics. It should come as no surprise, then, that Badiou is equally hostile in his critique of 'ethical radicalism', which prioritizes the role of responsibility for the other in the construction of human relations and subjectivity. Although anti-ontological in orientation, Levinasian ethics, according to Badiou (2001: 19), ends up reproducing some of the mimetic plays of self-identity that were supposed to be avoided in the 'ethical opening to alterity'. Specifically, Badiou (2001: 19, 22) suggests that Levinas' 'fleshy epiphany' of the face-to-face relation can only side-step the narcissistic and aggressive logic of identification outlined by Lacan in the 'mirror stage', by recourse to 'a principle of alterity which transcends mere finite experience', namely the 'absolute alterity' and 'infinity' of God. This would appear to confirm Badiou's characterization of ethics as a moralizing and reactionary *ressentiment* – a practice of guilt and blame – which subordinates the stage of politics and aesthetics to the spectacle of religion.

Badiou's conception of an *affirmative* ethic of practices, in contradistinction to the *negative* ethics he discerns in discourses of 'human rights', 'respect for the other and for difference', and even good old-fashioned 'tolerance', starts out from a fundamentally *secular* position that takes *equality* as its foundational category. This is an *ethic of singular truths*, borne of singular situations. For Badiou (2001: 16), 'there is no ethics in general. There are only – eventually – ethics of processes by which we treat the possibilities of a situation'; or, as Rancière suggests, the reappearance of aesthetic political practices of dissensus through which to counterpoint the emergence of consensual ethics as the 'ultimate form of the will to absolutize this dissensus' (Rancière 2010: 201).

Perhaps Jaar's aesthetic practice should be seen, in this context, as engaging an *international* mode of dissensus disputing the politics of global consensus. If *The Sound of Silence* examines the fallacious presumption that the discourse of human rights and ethics can somehow cross the structural divide between spectator and tragic 'victim', or that the work of art can somehow do the work of politics sui generis rather than simply attest to the opening-up of possible spaces of political subjectivation, it does so by recognizing the inexorable foreclosure of the 'aesthetic cut' as a process of formalization internal to the work of the work of art itself. Accordingly, the installation's unpacking of the theatrical logic of the construction of the victim and attendant discourses of 'ethical responsibility' puts into question normative conceptions of relations of agency and action, making visible the traces of the acts, ethics and material relations of presence upon which representation builds its ineluctable political apparatus. By constructing a frame in which the activity of viewing is thrown into question, and the spectator is asked to occupy a relation to the visible and its normative construction and distribution, *The Sound of Silence* breaks open the perceptual apparatus of consensus, however momentarily, to show a political and aesthetic stage of 'dissensus' through which it might become possible to think the situation differently.

Note

1   A longer version of this essay, 'Traces of Presence', appears in Jenny Edkins and Adrian Kear, eds, *International Politics and Performance: Critical Aesthetics and Creative Practice*, New York: Routledge, 2013, 19–39. Short version published by permission.

Works cited

Agamben, Giorgio. *Means Without Ends: Notes on Politics*, trans. Vicenzo Binetti and Cesare Casarino. Minnesota: University of Minnesota Press, 2000.

Badiou, Alain. *Ethics: An Essay on the Understanding of Evil*, trans. Peter Hallward. London: Verso, 2001.

Critchley, Simon. 'On the Ethics of Alain Badiou'. In Gabriel Riera, ed., *Alain Badiou: Philosophy and its Conditions*. Albany: State University of New York, 2005, 215–36.

Pollock, Griselda. 'Photographing Atrocity: Becoming Iconic?' In Geoffrey Batchen, Mick Gidley, Nancy Miller and Jay Prosser, eds, *Picturing Atrocity: Photography in Crisis*. Lofnond: Reaktion Books, 2012, 65–78.

Rancière, Jacques. *Disagreement*, trans. Julie Rose. Minneapolis: University of Minnesota Press, 1999.

Rancière, Jacques. *The Politics of Aesthetics*, trans. G. Rockhill. London: Continuum, 2004a.

Rancière, Jacques. 'Who is the Subject of the Rights of Man?' *South Atlantic Quarterly* 103 2004b: 297–310.

Rancière, Jacques. 'Theater of Images'. In Alfredo Jaar, *Alfredo Jaar: La politique des images*, Musée Cantonal des Beaux-Arts, Lausanne: jrp/ringier, 2007a, 71–80.

Rancière, Jacques. 'Art of the Possible: Fluvia Carnevale and John Kelsey in Conversation with Jacques Rancière', in 'Regime Change: Jacques Rancière and Contemporary Art'. *Artforum International*, March 2007b: 256–69.

Rancière, Jacques. 'The Emancipated Spectator', in 'Regime Change: Jacques Rancière and Contemporary Art'. *Artforum International*, March 2007c: 271–80.

Rancière, Jacques. *Dissensus: On Politics and Aesthetics*, trans. Steve Corcoran. New York: Continuum, 2010.

19   Counterpropaganda, Resistance

Suk-Young Kim

In the scorching heat of mid-July, an angry blond man sits alone on a busy street of Seoul, facing the South Korean Ministry of Foreign Affairs and Trade. His scruffy face is baked under the merciless sun, and his sagging cheeks soaked in sweat, but the man's stern expression reflects the sign-board hanging on his ruddy neck: '50 Years Overdue: Freedom for North Koreans!' Accompanying the slogan is a lingering picture of a North Korean child whose agonized face painfully captures the dark reality of malnourishment. In fact, the child in the picture is not the only one suffering from starvation; this blond protester is also on the verge of collapse from an eight-day hunger strike and irregular catnaps in the nearby parks under the nocturnal monsoon rain.

Meet Doctor Norbert Vollertsen, a German citizen, who had spent almost a decade vehemently accusing North Korea for inflicting violence against their own citizens. At the same time, he has been criticizing South Korea for not intervening enough to stop the North Korean violation of human rights. His methods of resistance are so flamboyant that Vollertsen has been known as much for his performative insolence as for his political defiance. But Vollertsen's relationship with the two Koreas has not always been so confrontational. Prior to his media-attracting provocations against both Koreas, he had spent a year and half in North Korea as a humanitarian worker providing much needed medical aid to North Koreans, specifically in the area of skin grafting procedures. Vollertsen was so eager to fulfill his humanitarian mission that he even donated his own skin for one North Korean patient. The North Korean state took note of Vollertsen's selfless service to the country and rewarded him with a Friendship Medal – the highest honor that could be bestowed on a foreigner. Things were amicable between Vollertsen and the North Korean state for a short while until the doctor started to travel around North Korea and realized the subhuman treatment of the people by the same regime which had rewarded him. The winner of the Friendship Medal turned into a human rights activist, which eventually led to his expulsion from the country. Vollertsen did not go back to Germany, but moved his stage of anti-North Korean resistance to South Korea, where he unleashed a series of provocative demonstrations intended to reveal the North Korean state's subhuman treatment of its people and the South Korean government's lack of involvement, which ended in multiple arrests and banishments.

Vollertsen probed various strategies of talking back to state-sanctioned violence, resorting to a wide array of performative modes ranging from provocative agitation to more benign measures. This was not only about displaying performative versatility, but also about how eclectic choices of performance modes could enable certain political strategies and authenticate motivations for political action effectively. According to an interview with the online journal *The Daily NK* in 2006, he eventually learned that there is a variation to performing resistance, which could flexibly accommodate situational differences as far as those elastic performative strategies result in attaining his political aim:

> Vollertsen says he is 'Fed-up!' with the [South] Korean government. In the past, he has tried some 'crazy' protests, but with little success. He believes that now it is the time to take an approach on par with the [South] Korean government actions, passive and polite.[1]

Hunger strike for Vollertsen, in a way, is an adjustment in performance strategy, which tries to replicate the same 'passive and polite' modes of the state he tries to resist. This conspicuous mimicry in Vollertsen's hunger strike raises some questions about how performance and resistance form an effective yet underscrutinized alliance working towards the same mission of countering state machinery: Can every form of performance be justified solely because it resists any oppressive order? Can resistance employ the same performative strategy as its oppressor so far as the adopted strategy attains its goal? If the aim of countering the established order itself is a legitimate enough justification for resistance, then how is the ethical dimension construed between the modes of performance and the efficacy of resistance?

These questions carry much ethical weight as Vollertsen's default mission to resist both Korean states is predicated on performances appropriating the strategies of the same oppressive order. The potentially disturbing propagation of the oppressor's strategy by the rebels often dodged critical scrutiny, since there seems to be an irresistible urge for bystanders to protect David from Goliath when the two collide in sociopolitical debate: when a powerless individual like Vollertsen stands up against the oppressive North Korean state machinery, it sets up a perfect context for the performance of martyrdom, and thereby creates a justified aura of sacrifice and defiance around the brave individual. The dramatic nature of this confrontation could be so palatable that it could potentially take due attention away from scrutinizing the ethical dimension of performance as a tool of resistance. Countering state propaganda is prone to propagandistic urges, and consequently, in order to measure the ethical dimension of counterpropaganda, we must first examine the very object of Vollertsen's resistance – propaganda.

The word 'propaganda' originates from the Catholic Church, and its etymology embedded in religion illuminates the main objective of propaganda to 'convert' people. The Sacred Congregation for the Propagation of the Faith (*Sacra Congregatio de Propaganda Fide*), organized by Pope Gregory XV in 1622, attempted to train missionaries, or propagandists, to revive the Catholic faith in Protestant Europe and strengthen it in the new European colonies and Americas.[2] The religious tendency to convert has always been the defining feature of propaganda, as can be detected in some pre-Cold War era examples, such as World War I posters showing the Virgin Mary's advent to the Russian troops or Nuremberg rallies to deify the Nazi Party and its leader Adolf Hitler.[3] Perhaps this etymology itself explains why countering propaganda could well be projected as martyrdom, both in the literal and figurative senses, for the ultimate sacred form of religious resistance arguably was martyrdom.

From an outside point of view, North Korean propaganda presents a unique case, in a sense that it exists in a liminal time zone when the socialist ideals of the bygone era still have to authenticate the North Korean people's belief in the regime. The disparate realities of the utopian world projected in propaganda and the dystopian realities of everyday life have to be adjusted by means of propaganda.

On one level, North Korean propaganda performance reflects the state's wishful desire to cultivate its ideal self-portrait. David Holm, in commenting on the Chinese Communist Party's appropriation of folk art as propaganda, wrote:

> The general feeling is, of course, that propaganda is lies – in the words of Dr. Goebbels – and that therefore a study of propaganda will yield nothing of value except perhaps a moral lesson on the wickedness of the totalitarian regime. I would suggest that, on the contrary, propaganda is interesting – and revealing – precisely because it is an attempt to manipulate and persuade.[4]

In accordance with Holm's observation that propaganda is a transparent showcase of the regime's intentions, it is telling to look beyond the political façade and pay close attention to how North Korean propaganda productions manipulate and persuade. Behind the blatantly fictional representation of an ideal self-image lies the modus operandi of the state; therefore, propaganda is one of the available ways of understanding North Korea. What appear to be a series of one-dimensional campaigns actually have tremendous impact upon society. The inquiry into how and why propaganda works as a tool of manipulation and persuasion is a revelatory process through which the inner workings of North Korean society and culture may be unfolded.

While this may be true in theory, propaganda in practice is more unpredictable, often difficult to control once it becomes a part of social interaction. Vollertsen's own account of North Korean propaganda reveals such a discursive application of propaganda in reality. In a lecture he delivered in the US, he recalled how the aforementioned skin donation incident degenerated into gross state propaganda:

> We [the foreign aid workers] wanted to show that we are not only humanitarian aid workers, that we are not only donating food, but that we are real friends. That we wanted to be a member of the family. So we offered also to donate our skin. And this was accepted. There was a huge propaganda show about this because it was the first time that I learned about North Korean propaganda. They used this – our quite innocent intention to do something, to show friendship – they used this as their sort of propaganda. They made it up in order to create a story that we were donating our skin in favor for Kim Jong Il, as a tribute to worship Kim Jong Il and his socialist system. And there were even some stories, and I was suspect in the beginning, but I learned this is North Korean propaganda.[5]

While the North Korean state intended to appropriate the incident to evidence the greatness of its leader, what North Koreans intended as strictly controlled propaganda fails when an individual like Vollertsen reveals a different perspective of the same event to the public, thus revealing the unpredictable and uncontrollable nature of propaganda circulation.

Therefore, it is necessary to suppose another view of propaganda as a dynamic and dialogic process between creator and receiver. Laura Frost, in her study of the erotic fantasies of fascism in modern literature, delineates an alternative function of propaganda – complementing the aforementioned definition proposed by Holm – as 'a form of communication that can express its creator's inadvertent or unconscious investments (and fantasies) and that can also be read many ways and have unintended effects in its reception'.[6] North Korean propaganda can be a window into the agenda and inner workings of the state. However, such an instrumental approach is based on the naive belief that the state's intention to manipulate and persuade symmetrically translates into actualization of the master plan. The actual operation of propaganda, even in a rigidly controlled society like North Korea, is much more discursive; it does not simply conform to the state's intentions.

Resisting propaganda for Vollertsen is primarily a way of articulating the possibilities of unearthing the layers of monolithic propaganda of the North Korean state, but if we were to step aside from Vollertsen's countering act, there is yet another disturbing parallel between the original act (Vollertsen's skin donation), the distorted propagation of the original act (the North Korean state's creation of propaganda out of Vollertsen's skin donation), and countering that very appropriation (Vollertsen's resistance against North Korean propaganda). Just as there is an unexpected twist in the deployment and reception of state propaganda, so there is an element of subversion in counterpropaganda, illustrating another verisimilitude that exists between propaganda and counterpropaganda.

Going back to the earlier case of Vollertsen, his anti-South Korean hunger strike consciously emulated what he was opposing fundamentally, not by turning it into a parody, but by replicating it in a faithful manner. Prior to the hunger strike, Vollertsen attempted to enter North Korea as a tourist, with the aim of staging an anti-North Korean protest.[7] Even though the attempt was bound to be aborted because of his cantankerous revelation of the plan in advance, the provocative idea and the frenzied response from the media created enough performative impact. The South Korean government declared that it would prohibit Vollertsen from re-entering the country in case he attempted such sensational acts to incite the South Korean public. Vollertsen's strategies are based on agitation more than anything else, making a spectacle of resisting North Korean atrocities:

> Try to get the attention of the world – nobody knows – so nobody can care. When there is no normal way to get this attention try the unusual: hunger sit-in in front of the Chinese Embassy (Olympics!); set up refugee camps at the Chinese-North Korean border; take provocative acts at the border, jump over the fence, get arrested.[8]

Vollertsen's blunt agitation makes one revisit the same questions raised earlier: Does inviting attention have a value of its own, or does it merely demonstrate an empty propaganda strategy with no tangible reference to the actual issue? Human rights activists and theatre scholars will have different answers. From a performance studies point of view, such an action of creating the extreme version of what a conscious person should do, as demonstrated by Vollertsen, creates a simulacrum of impossibility, because staging an actual demonstration in North Korea would certainly result in his detention, or if he is lucky, his expulsion. Thus, Vollertsen is virtually rehearsing a show meant to culminate in the actual protest. However, in this case, the rehearsal process is much more significant than the actual, though paradoxically nonexistent, performance within North Korea.

Such a predominance of rehearsal over actual performance strikingly parallels the North Korean state's emphasis on creating theatrical performances rather than actual outcomes. In the coordinated and disciplined rehearsals for mass games[9] and parades, North Koreans learn to subordinate their individual voices to the commands of leadership. Thus, rehearsals are not mere preparations for culminating performances, but crucial pedagogical processes defining the fulcrum of North Korean society's seeming absence of individual opinions.[10]

However, transforming what started out as an anti-North Korean dissident performance into propaganda of its own is not the only disturbing feature associated with staging counterpropaganda. The most pronounced aspect of propaganda is arguably the lack of North Korean people's opposition, which appears in the form of complicity with the propaganda machine; without this silent complicity, the system could never have operated to the extent it has for half a century. In order to stage labor-intensive propaganda performances, the North Korean state has been using forcible measures to ensure people's participation.[11] In case there was a failure to send a required number of participants, the slackers were immediately punished by reduced food rationing and other means of withholding basic necessities. Despite these practices that stripped people of basic human rights and dignity, the North Korean people seem to have enjoyed the collective shaping experience of performance rehearsals.

To what degree people perform their compliance or dismissal is a difficult question to quantify, but it directs us to think about what kinds of critical filtering processes are at work in accepting or rejecting propaganda. The rejection of propaganda led to another kind of propaganda in Vollertsen's case, raising a critical query about whether counterpropaganda is just a subversive performance of complicity. Finding answers to these questions could be an elusive process, but the questions themselves cast profound doubts about the limits of resisting propaganda.

Moreover, Vollertsen's case illustrates how dogmatic principles could limit counterpropaganda, often canonized as sacred political martyrdom. Performance of counterpropaganda, then, becomes a furtive collaborator in camouflaging the dictatorial process of truncating the potentially dynamic interactions between the state and compliant citizens. Has this kind of distillation of an idealized resistance fighter figure not failed to address potentially diverse voices of silent North Koreans, who are often left out in Vollertsen's performance of resistance? Vollertsen certainly is a martyr who dedicated himself to the cause of suffering North Koreans as much as he is an agile performer who can obfuscate the ethical consequences of his protest.

Notes

1 Norbert Vollertsen, 'South Korean Government, Wake up to the North Korean Reality!', interview, *The Daily NY*, www.dailynk.com/english/read.php?cataId=nk02500&num=921.

2 Simons Adams, *Propaganda in War & Peace: Manipulating the Truth* (Chicago: Heinemann Library, 2006), 8.

3 Suk-Young Kim, 'Propaganda', in Ruud van Dijk et al., eds, *Routledge Encyclopedia of the Cold War* (New York: Routledge, 2008), 721.

4 David Holm, 'Folk Art as Propaganda', in Bonnie McDougall, ed., *Popular Chinese Literature and Performing Arts in the People's Republic of China 1949–1979* (Berkeley: University of California Press, 1984), 5.

5 Norbert Vollertsen, 'Human Rights Issues: The Case of North Korea', Institute for Corean-American Studies Lectures, 14 October 2003, Washington D.C. For the entire transcript of the lecture, see www.icasinc.org/2003/2003f/2003fnsv.html.

6 Laura Frost, *Sex Drives: Fantasies of Fascism in Literary Modernism* (Ithaca: Cornell University Press, 2002), 12.

7 For a more detailed account of Vollertsen's stance on the North Korean human rights issue, see James Brook, interview with Vollertsen, 'One German and his North Korean Conscience', *New York Times* 19 March 2002, A4; Hong Seok-jun, 'NK Human Rights Like Nazi Germany', *Chosun Ilbo* 8 May 2001; Vollertsen 'A Prison Country', *Wall Street Journal Opinion* 17 April 2001; Donald Macintyre 'Diary of a Mad Place', *Time Magazine* 22 January 2001.

8 Norbert Vollertsen, interview, *Joseon Journal* 30 June 2001.

9 The term 'mass games' refers to a particular genre of performance developed in North Korea. It involves a large number of participants, its number reaching 100,000 in case of the *Arirang* performance, which far outnumber spectators. Mass games incorporate various forms of physical performance, such as gymnastics, acrobatics, martial arts, dancing and card sections.

10 The analysis of Vollertsen's provocative countering act is based on Suk-Young Kim, 'Directing Tourists and Escapees: North Korea's Two Conflicting National Performances', in Jisha Menon and Patrick Anderson, eds, *Violence Performed: Local Roots and Global Routes of Conflict* (Basingstoke: Palgrave Macmillan, 2008), 317–37.

11 The way the North Korean regime ensures people's participation is to apply a quota system to draft from each *inminban*, the minimal social unit in North Korea, a certain number of people required for the given performance.

20 Ekstasis

Anthony Kubiak

Literary critic Murray Krieger's distinction between aesthetic and ascetic approaches to literary analyses – the former accentuating the interpretive possibilities of the text, the latter the 'factual' historical contexts of literary production – suggests a larger impulse within critical and literary theory, not simply the aesthetic dimension of art, but the role of the ecstatic in art and performance, and, more germane to the current discussion, the experience of the ecstatic in the *doing* of theory itself (see Clarke 2000). But I want, at the outset, to resituate this word, ecstatic: I do not mean here simple excitement, or mania, elation or even necessarily some hyperventilated state of emotion or perception. By ecstatic, I mean a state in which one is constituted by one's own experience of the ineffable and indefinable, by the true sundering of boundaries. *Ekstasis* here is a radically deterritorialized state of being, which may be expressed as often by deep quietude and equanimity as by excitement or frenzy. Ecstasy may, unlike the sublime, be either pleasurable or terrifying, and also, unlike the sublime, is not necessarily accompanied by later categorical or ethical definitions (I am thinking here largely of the Kantian sublime).

Something like the ecstatic suggests itself here as arguably the controlling context of all forms of art and theory: even those who embrace a more historical and empirical approach to theory and criticism do so because, in essence, such approaches initiate a kind of transport – a displacement outside or even beyond current trends and contexts, trying to find the limits and limn of 'current' theory, and projecting beyond this to a 'new' poetics. This new poetics will, presumably, be thrilling, enthralling and captivating, and will take us past the apparent theoretical stasis in which we seem currently stuck. Or, in the case of more sober reflections on the current place of theory that simply wish to re-delineate the proper concerns of criticism, these reconsiderations do what they do in order to carry us beyond the moribund state of current poetics, aesthetic, ascetic or otherwise.

This is the very definition of ekstasis – to take oneself beyond, to break the morbid bonds of stasis, to be 'beside oneself', or to break through the impasse of mind or ego into new modes of consciousness. This is consonant with the appearance of what I have called the New Aesthetics in more recent theory (or perhaps, dispelling the ghosts of the Frankfurt School, the 'new' New Aesthetics) – the trend toward the felt, experiential sense of art and performance not accounted for by the historical/historicist or formalist methodologies of recent decades. This work comes out of the theories of Teresa Brennan, Elizabeth Groz (herself derivative of Deleuze), Roland Barthes and others, echoing the theoretical and philosophical work of such early 20th-century thinkers as Maurice Merleau-Ponty, Gaston Bachelard and Henri Bergson.

Now, this invocation of the felt over and against the formal is nothing new in the history of literary critique. Indeed, one might be tempted to characterize the timbre of Modernist and poststructural criticism and its as-yet unbroken succession as a revolt against the too-sloppy excesses of late Romanticism and its tendencies to flights of rapture in praise of European (Western) culture (I am thinking here of 19th-century critic and philosopher Matthew Arnold. Of course, Modernist critics were, in many cases, even more likely to extol the superiority of European cultural formations over the 'primitivism' of 'less refined' cultures). Moreover, the realization that these 'new' aesthetics are really not new at all is perhaps apropos. The role of the experiential, the participatory, the felt in performance is, after all, apparently ancient. The aesthetic/ecstatic axis of critique suggests that the contours of the primal, the originary, may be the closest we come to a transglobal, transhistorical linkage among the different and differing traditions of art and performance, even those traditions that don't identify with the our insistence on the category of 'art' itself. Moreover, in the affective (Grosz, Brennan), and the ecstatic we are close to the untheorizable and the unpresentable – the ineffable here marking, perhaps, that which all human experience shares – moments of intensity and states of mind that surpass our ability to describe them. And yet, as Herbert Blau reminded us throughout his work, in searching for the linkages between epochs, cultures, even individuals, we may in fact be erasing them – that the linkage of culture to culture, historical period to historical period, subject to subject, play to play, performance to performance lies precisely in the impossibilities of those linkages, connections that do nothing more than supply the illusion of continuity, meaning and 'situatedness', the illusion of theatre's actual moment – an invocation, in the Blauian mode, to the ghost of Hamlet's father, 'Stay, Illusion.' Here, theatre represents, finally, exactly what cannot stay, what cannot be located, what cannot come to rest, that which is eternally displaced – the very poetics of ecstasy, engrailed in theatrical form, but straining at the invisible mind's invisible proscenium.

Along a different axis, Willis Barnstone's *The Poetics of Ecstasy from Sappho to Borges* (1983), a pretty much neglected work written before the firestorm of French post-theoretics hit Euro American shores in the early 1980s, is one of the few studies to seriously propose a theoretics of ecstasy in the understanding of literature, if not art and performance per se. And while it lacked a clear understanding of its own hidden historical and methodological suppositions, it nonetheless tried to move critical thought beyond the confines of the structural or functional, pointing to the ecstatic impulses of a wide range of literary tropes and types, including religious texts, political treatises, postmodern literary works, and philosophical exegesis. Through this panoply of texts, Barnstone suggests that the contours of the ecstatic are themselves wide-ranging and morally disparate: the spiritual raptures of the mystics (John Ruysbroek and John of the Cross) are juxtaposed with the political transport of the revolutionary spirit (Mao and Neruda), while the visionary and eschatological (Dante and Ramon Llull) are brought into conversation with secular excess and postmodern dissolution (Borges and Jorge Guillen). By examining works of such range and variety, Barnstone suggests that the ecstatic, as a register of intensities in critique, embraces the entire range of human aesthetic interaction – from spiritual rapture to murderous rage, from blood ecstasy to sexual transport. And behind each of these, lies the unspoken intimation that it is ekstasis itself that drives the human organism beyond, and beyond beyond.

What might we mean, then, by ekstasis? If there are such wide-ranging manifestations of these extremes of human behavior and emotion, what might link them all? There is, first of all, the emphasis on the experiential, the immediate over and against the merely thought, the glibly theorized, the typically analytical. Further, there is often an emphasis within the experiential on the felt, and following this, in extremis, on the insensate, the ineffable, the undescribable. In this state I enter the environs of the other, inhabit the body and time of the other, while the other, conversely, inhabits me, my time, my space. When one releases into the ecstatic, one begins to understand that the reality of self and identity is purely ephemeral, pure illusion. One understands experientially the permeability and edgelessness that constitutes the nonmateriality of the world, the solidity of identity and its matters merely an idea whose substance fades the moment it appears.

And then – inhabiting other, inhabited by the other – ecstasy melds quite seamlessly into animism, into the experience of the dissolution of boundaries, the dissolving of normal identity into an other. In becoming other, in entering and co-inhabiting with another, in being so co-inhabited, one further ceases to be as one has been. Here, thought process itself is purged. In the theatre we say that one undergoes catharsis, in theory one becomes queer, or, rather one (many?) experiences becoming-queer.

I would suggest that in recent performance work and the theories that trail, we follow the scent – the blood scent, if needs be – of the ecstatic as that which drives mind and the cultures it formulates. I suggest it is the ecstatic that has remained and continues to remain the unspoken impulse behind aesthetic and ascetic action (to return to the Kriegerian categories), and which remains untheorized or repressively desublimated. When we look back to the originary theoretics of Kirby and Schechner, out of the body-impulse work of Grotowski, and all that followed from it, we see that the ekstasis of theatre/critique has always been simply an attempt to embody the spiritual in the material, to trap the excesses of experience in the logos of 'theory'. Even such thinkers as Bataille, and Deleuze and Guattari have done little more than provide a means by which we might presume to understand the mystic fire, the ravages of maddened obsession, or the push toward ecstatic dissolution – the very forms of experience that truly threaten the power/structure itself – by transmuting them into ideas, thought, philosophy. The *elan vital* of the work itself, the experience itself, remains firmly outside the ken of all critical approaches of the past century, simply because theory itself has desired the transport of the ecstatic within its own movements – as if it were possible to think oneself into a state of ecstatic transport – whether that transport is seen, citing Barnstone, as mystic, aesthetic, or political. In passing into the ecstatic through catharsis, through the realization of what Buddhists call 'co-arising', through the shifting dissolutions of identity and the uncertainties of perception itself, one enters the theatre, sans mud, bare feet feeling the boards.

Works cited

Barnstone, Willis. *The Poetics of Ecstasy from Sappho to Borges* (New York: Holmes & Meier, 1983).

Clark, Michael P. 'The Persistence of Literature in Early American Studies.' *William and Mary Quarterly*, 3rd series, vol. LVII, number 3 (July 2000), 641, quoting Philip Gura. The reference to Gura is to an article by him in the same issue, 599–620.

21   Social Somatics

Petra Kuppers

Somatics: adjust how you sit. How do you hold this book? Where are you located in relation to what you are reading, which illuminations travel neuronally and which words fire you? With these questions, asking for personal attention, I open a chapter about individual experiences of embodied living, wrestling with writing, with the move from sensation to sharing. I have many resources to draw upon; there have been thousands of years of engagement with the challenges and opportunities afforded by the somatic. But the somatic evades, undermines or preens itself in the side-space to writerly practice, and many practitioners are fine with that. In this chapter, I connect somatic experience with bodily specificity through feminist thought at the site of writing.

In my embodiment/environment/community undergraduate class, my students engage with one historic lineage of 'the somatic' through an overview essay by Martha Eddy (2009). Eddy charts many influences and practitioners in the field, from Rudolf Laban, Moshe Feldenkrais and Ida Rolf to Anna Halprin, Joan Skinner and Bonnie Bainbridge Cohen. This is the way of thinking and charting somatics out of anti-industrialist, anti-Fordist, pro-personal empowerment movement practices that also shaped Thomas Hanna's (1989) naming of the field as 'somatics'. It's the lineage that influenced publications such as Don Hanlon Johnson's 1995 *Bone, Breath and Gesture*, one of the first academic introductions to many somatic practitioners.

Some of Eddy's arguments resonate deeply with my students: somatic education as a pathway to taking responsibility for one's self, in the absence of hard truths, in experimentation and playful process. The students make complex and useful connections between their classroom experiences of meditation, body scans, community performance exercises and visits in botanical gardens, being with plants, being with fellow humans. In our classroom, we acknowledge that the written word alone is not enough. In order to understand and feel our way into the somatic, we need to engage in exercise work, observing our own breath, and watch each other breathe. Embodiment becomes a form of reading practice, and informs attention to sounds and signs, a visceral close reading. After a few weeks of conscious attention to our 'bodyminds', we have trained ourselves to let poems glide over us and through us, to explore language as a homeopathy of influence, a cilial connection between breath and meaning. Breath breaks into sound fields. A sibilant induces vibration and travels across skin surfaces. Sounding words, deconstructed writing, become the basis for new, playful assemblages, liberatory somatic educational practices that can infuse patterns of living. Lying on their yoga mats, my students try out phonemes in their mouth, throat and thorax. They transfuse them through the torso, into bone oscillation, toward blood dispersal. Embodied labors of attention: that is one of my working definitions of the somatic field.

There are other ways of telling the narrative of the somatic. One pathway into the somatic would be through contemporary articulations of ancient practices. In the wider somatics field, people pay attention to yoga, chakras and Sanskrit, to Vedic prosodic vibration as life energy, to the hallucinatory or ecstatic properties of soma libations.

In my own performance work, I am drawn to the brain-altering effects of hymns, shaman rhythmicity and mass cycles, pagan ritual practice, and the mystery of transubstantiation. My atheist sensibilities are pressured by my lean into the efficacy of spiritual practice for performance work, and into the political potential of strategic essentialism. Something assembled under the sign 'I' calls, with yearning, for identificatory community and yet finds itself, again and again, alone in a skin sack.

The somatic, in this narrative, troubles, and troubles productively. It unmasks as undesirable, and as fantasy, the universal non-needy subject, the '(pure) disembodied a-historical structure composed of differences in which no-one actually differs at all' (to follow along with Christine Wertheim's introduction to *Feminaissance*, and its re-evaluation of strategic essentialism, 2010: xii). Revisiting foremothers' writings is a useful tactic for feeling one's way into the dynamic alignment of embodiment and writing. Writing on the (skin's) periphery, exploring the hollows of shame and pleasure, charting the terrain of sensation: these are moves that inform much writing on the yoga mat. This Cixous quote offers rich nourishment:

And why don't you write? Write! Writing is for you, you are for you; your body is yours, take it. I know why you haven't written. (And why I didn't write before the age of twenty-seven.) Because writing is at once too high, too great for you, it's reserved for the great – that is for 'great men'; and it's 'silly'. Besides, you've written a little, but in secret. And it wasn't good, because it was in secret, and because you punished yourself for writing, because you didn't go all the way, or because you wrote, irresistibly, as when we would masturbate in secret, not to go further, but to attenuate the tension a bit, just enough to take the edge off. And then as soon as we come, we go and make ourselves feel guilty – so as to be forgiven; or to forget, to bury it until the next time. (Cixous [1975] 2000: 259)

Somatic engagement allows us to take seriously the disavowed, to explore writing as a wayfarer, not as enemy. Claiming a space for the somatic scoops out a place of pleasure and connection, an island within the roil of disidentificatory tenuousness, a strategic location for a politics of tenderness, a (shifting) ground.

The manifestos of many political artists claim new bodies, new senses, new alignments between organs and energies. As a third narrative of somatics, I could discuss Joseph Beuys's social sculpture or Antonin Artaud's athletes of the heart, charting connections and erecting lineages, fields of influence, the fatherland and mother tongue, the oaken tree, the homeland's soil.

But notions of lineage and citational practice are themselves at odds with my understanding of the somatic as poetic method. The somatic is a perspectival investigation. It is dependent on the knowledge found in the subjective experience; it is first-person knowledge. This first-person wisdom is not the owned self of storytelling. It is itself queried into thin layers and skins, until the 'I' fragments into the sensate textures that phenomenologists like Maurice Merleau-Ponty explore as the source of subject development. Under the explorer's scrutiny, this 'I' becomes a shifting field of intensities. This is the terrain that practice-as-research artists' favorite thinkers Gilles Deleuze and Félix Guattari map and warp into a politics of energetics, dependent on and connected to bodily strata in *A Thousand Plateaus* (1980).

Mining Deleuzian thought for somatic thought brings up many treasures. In the following passage about painting, the point of entry is actually not 'the body', which is quite statically seen here as the finite other to the folding motions of painted garments. But it is easy to transpose this writing onto specific bodily sensations, to multiply the body away from the finitude with which Deleuze holds it here, and toward multiple openings and sense layerings, to juxtapose multitude and distension in an endless dialectic with the hidden unity (here, the body):

If the Baroque is defined by the fold that goes out into infinity, how can it be recognized in its most simple form? The fold can be recognized first of all in the textile model of a kind implied by garments: fabric or clothing has to free its own folds from the usual subordination to the finite body it covers. If there is an inherently Baroque costume, it is broad, in distending waves, billowing and flaring, surrounding the body with its independent folds, ever-multiplying, never betraying those of the body beneath. (Deleuze 1993: 139)

The image that emerges for me is akin to many of the exquisite sensory sensibilities dancers or somatic practitioners speak about: there is the space of the utterance, the self that narrates, this kernel of subjectivity that holds on to an idea of an 'I' – an island of questionable solidity within the fragmentation and generous weft of somatic dispersal. Skin, muscles, liquid sensation, bone sensoria, organ movement, fascia tensions: somatic awareness can train a garment out of everything, until the subject emerges as an undecidable but gorgeous mass of sensations.

Specificity, and the ethics of nuance. Here lies for me the politics of somatics, specific bodies, not 'the body', bodies in specific cultural alignments and webs, not 'just' bodies. Luce Irigaray ([1977] 1985: 29) reminds us of the requirement for location, nuance, the politics of specificity, and the processual character of recognition:

> One would have to listen with another ear, as if hearing an 'other meaning' always in the process of weaving itself, of embracing itself with words, but also of getting rid of words in order not to become fixed, congealed in them. For if 'she' says something, it is not, it is already no longer, identical with what she means. What she says is never identical with anything, moreover: rather, it is contiguous. It touches (upon). And when it strays too far from that proximity, she breaks off and starts over at 'zero': her body-sex.

Irigaray's call to specific and process attention reverberates for my understanding of social somatics. What does it mean to listen/read/view/witness differently, through touch, through the densities of embodied, enacted, gendered, raced, disabled flesh, to not confuse speaking with being, body or word with static meaning, but to be in touch with specificity? This is the philosophical lineage of Spinoza: 'what does a body do', not, 'what is a body?' Lines do not demarcate here: the border marked in flesh can be both violation and edge zone, in Gloria Anzaldúa's productive rereading of the hysterics of nation states. Bodies, in the plural, are on the line, and remake the line continuously in procedures of meaning-making: plurality within and without, intersected and interdependent. Subjectivity is not insular, or dependent on the happenings within one skin sack, but is always in relation, in contact zones, through the bodily imaginary that shapes how our bodily boundaries come to be thought. Our bodily imaginaries have histories, are shaped by cultural forces, by white supremacy and colonialism, by misogynistic, ableist or classist thought. How we live our somatic reality as social reality is as much shaped by the sensorium of our fingertips as by the images we inherit from biomedicine, as much by the textures and pleasures offered to us by popular media as by the culturally specific ways we establish intimacy with others, by the practices with which we weave ourselves into the internet or into the street scene. Imagining our somatic selves otherwise, understanding somatic knowledge as inauthentic, as discursive: that's the political charge of social somatics.

Engagement: breathe. Taste the air, experience the permeability, the vulnerability, the strength and the dissolving presence as an 'I' assembles around acts of breathing. This instruction is another narrative, an invitation to breathe, together, during a number of performance poetry events at the Subterranean Arthouse in Berkeley, California. Breath, pollution, toxicity, waste and surplus, division and decay, emergence: decline your breath through these words, taste their metallic residue, mouth their fatty feel on your tongue. These are some of the instructions that ushered a group of somatic divers into border states. We are in a participatory performance, an Olimpias happening (the artists' collective I lead), in a show called *Burning*, a workshop and performance series that investigated cell imagery, cancer imagery, and healing journeys through ritual-based happenings infused with poetry, dramatic scenes, dances, and live drawing. We are lying on the wooden floor of the Subterranean Arthouse, an old shop-front that is now a performance space daily infused with Butoh ritual. Community participants allow themselves to open their membranes to the gift of words. Lying among this group are autistic self-advocates, people with environmental toxicity syndrome, cancer survivors and others who find themselves interpellated into chemical relation. This connection between the somatic and the cross-boundary engagement with others, crystallized into temporary specificity, into this performance laboratory of alchemical encounters, offers another narrative for the somatic.

Much of my thinking about the social somatic's aesthetics and ethics occurred at Arnieville, a few blocks south from the Subterranean Arthouse. The activity of breathing tainted air, tainted by metaphor, image, word and matter, connect these two sites, *Burning* as an art-framed community performance and Arnieville as a political performance action. Arnieville was an activist camp and tent village erected by a coalition of disabled, poor and homeless people. Its tents stood on a traffic island in a busy street, opposite the Berkeley Bowl supermarket, during May, June and July of 2010. People slept in tents three feet away from roaring traffic, fast wheels and exhaust fumes. Activists used their physical presence in these precarious and polluted surroundings, their art, song and a large papier-mâché puppet of Arnold Schwarzenegger, complete with raised hatchet, to protest the ongoing dismantling of the social welfare system. Cuts kill, taxes save lives. Interdependence, not independence.

189

At Arnieville, we did create provisional community among people with mental health differences, addiction issues, physical disabilities and in poverty, we found multiple new alliances across racialization and impairment lines. Our activist chants engaged with the rhythm of the car wheels pounding by our island – our activist prosody, a healing magic for an ailing welfare state.

I remember: the poetics of street action played across my body, as we sat in our wheelchairs, scooters and loungers, huddled together to sun ourselves or shiver in the treacherous northern California spring and early summer, my senses alert to the infiltrations of temperature change, of migraines held barely at bay with ever higher doses of painkillers, of the cramp setting into joints. I also remember the scent offered by the warm food neighbors brought by each day, and the settling in each day for the sharing circle, to hear and bear the different voices, different cognitive frames. The bearing was not always easy: there were tears, and shouts, and accusations, arguments, ravings, these genres' boundaries often interwoven and undecidable. I also remember the renewed pleasures of the possibility of home when I did wheel home on many days, to connect myself differently, to plug into the electrical web and charge my wheelchair, fire up the computer, post photos on Facebook. I remember my few nights' worth of disrupted, poisoned sleep in one of the tents, the concentration of traffic fumes peaking in the morning commute, my light-headed writing in the gray light of early morning hours.

I am not sure that anybody can say that Arnieville had a significant impact on the legislature. Social welfare systems are crumbling everywhere, and the people of California keep voting down anything that would cost them. The democratic process is flaying vulnerable and poor populations. Maybe some drivers and shoppers got to think differently when witnessing us on our traffic island, think differently about what they might have assumed were silent and invisible populations. Bay Area public radio and quite a few newspapers came out, and there was a good show of disability agency and interdependent self-determination in the media. But did that reach anybody who was not already in our camp, not already on the side of welfare politics and a need for taxes? I am not sure, and am rather cynical. But 'politics' does not just mean effectiveness at the level of policy making. It can't be, or else many of us would have to pack up our 1980s and 90s' honed political tools and retire from the public arena. There is a politics of engagement and relationality, of embodied contact, of shared space and common ground.

We need to touch, and stay present to the multivalence of touch as violence, as tenderness, as invitation, as shifting border states. Audre Lorde

(1984: 54) writes, and I have to listen again and again to not fix what is said: 'We tend to think of the erotic as an easy, tantalizing sexual arousal. I speak of the erotic as the deepest life force, a force which moves us toward living in a fundamental way.'

And that is to me the politics embodied and instantiated at times, momentarily, during Arnieville: engaging embodied with difference, finding intercultural and intercorporeal resources for living, even if we know that some of us will wheel home to comfortable homespaces, and some of us will sleep on cardboard again when the tent village folds down. I can only speak about myself, in the end: but hanging out at Arnieville has changed my perspective on the homeless folk that I see around my home spaces, and I now know some of them by name. The class divide does not miraculously lift. But for moments at a time, over shared coffee, desirously, we engage in practices of artful living, embodied poetics, an erotics of encounter, practices that halt the flow of cars, of business as usual, of the visibilities and invisibilities, the glib narratives, the budget bottom line, if only for a moment, a shared breath. Arnieville offered a social sculpture, and a social somatics: a therapy for the world, an unhinging of space and time, for a moment. In that unhinged time, in the long duration, after those of us who talk are talked out, we can take shared breaths, with the tinge of exhaust on our tongue.

Note

Somatic work is exploration, and is also often shared work, as the energy of community enhances potential pathways toward experiencing oneself differently. I am grateful to my collaborators in *Somatic Engagement* (2011), a small artists' book full of material by poets and visual artists. The writing here also serves in a different form as the Introduction to this collection. Many of the collected writers met during the Olimpias events and at Arnieville, and we explored the different heritages of the somatic through reading groups and discussions.

Works cited

Cixous, Hélène. 'The Laugh of the Medusa' [1975]. In Oliver, Kelly (ed.) *French Feminism Reader*. Lanham: Rowman & Littlefield, 2000, 257–75.

Deleuze, Gilles. *Leibnitz and the Baroque*. London: Continuum, 1993.

Deleuze, Gilles and Guattari, Félix. *A Thousand Plateaus: Capitalism & Schizophrenia*. London: Continuum, 2004.

Eddy, Martha. 'A Brief History of Somatic Practices and Dance: Historical Development of the Field of Somatic Education and its Relationship to Dance.' *Journal of Dance and Somatic Practices* 1.1 (2009): 5–27.

Hanna, Thomas. *Somatics*. Reading, MA: Addison-Wesley, 1989.

Irigaray, Luce. *This Sex Which Is Not One* [1977], trans. Catherine Porter. New York: Cornell University Press, 1985.

Johnson, Don Hanlon. *Bone, Breath and Gesture: Practices of Embodiment*. Berkeley, CA: North Atlantic Books, 1995.

Kuppers, Petra (ed.). *Somatic Engagement*. Oakland: ChainLinks, 2011.

Lorde, Audre. 'Uses of the *Erotic*: The *Erotic* as Power.' In Audre Lorde (ed.) *Sister Outsider: Essays and Speeches*. Freedom, CA: Crossing Press, 1984, 53–9.

Wertheim, Christine (ed.). *Feminaissance*. Los Angeles: Les Figues Press, 2010.

22   Globalization, the Glocal, Third Space Theatre

Carl Lavery

Despite what Julia Kristeva once claimed, theatre insists on taking a place (1977: 131).[1] Theatre's spatiality, moreover, is never abstract spatiality; it always engages with whatever locality or environment it finds itself in. This is not to say that theatre is narrowly parochial or inherently place-bound. What I want to suggest is somewhat different. For me, theatre's ability to 'return us to the local' (Lippard 1997) is not incompatible, in any way, with its capacity for addressing global issues. Rather, theatre's spatiality is best understood in terms of what the geographer Edward Soja (1996) has called a 'third space', a heterotopic site or interplay where binaries give way to hybridity, and where the local is always already globalized.

If theatre is, as many critics have maintained, the spatial art par excellence, it is also, to appropriate the sociologist Roland Robertson's language, the 'glocal' art par excellence. Drawing his inspiration from Japanese business practices in the 1980s, which sought to customize capitalism for its own purposes, Robertson (1995) claims that globalization is a two-way process, whereby the particular impacts on the universal and vice versa. For Robertson – and this separates him from Marxist geographers and sociologists such as Henri Lefebvre, David Harvey and Fredric Jameson – globalization is not characterized by a simple top-down model, whereby one culture (the US) dominates another; on the contrary, it is inherently dialogic. For him, the local always particularizes the global, and, by doing so, produces new hybridized identities that oppose and subvert any simplistic notion of totalized hegemony.

Robertson's theory of the glocal is politically progressive insofar as it shows how cultural domination is always fraught with reversals and tensions. However, this ought not to blind us to its limitations. Robertson's insistence on diversity, along with his seeming reluctance to criticize capital, means that he has no way of accounting for the fact that alienation in Tokyo, while certainly different from alienation in London, is still ultimately alienation. To exploit the notion of the glocal for critical purposes necessitates, I think, a shift in emphasis. Instead of simply accepting that theatre's radical spatiality troubles homogeneity in and by itself, we need to think about how theatre can disclose what always remains the same under capitalism: inequality, exploitation, injustice. To put it otherwise, the political potential inherent in theatre's glocality resides in its ability to show how specific forms of oppression are enmeshed in, and related to, total forms of oppression. In this way, theatre might perhaps recover what Harvey (1990) and Jameson (1992) argue has been lost in postmodernity: metatheory, a critique of the whole.

That theatre's glocalism is not, by itself, synonymous with emancipation is underlined by the UK feminist geographer Doreen Massey. Massey (1995) argues that glocalism, like community, is not a common substance that all subjects experience in the same unproblematic way. For her, the glocal is always lived differently, and is determined by one's class, gender, sexuality and age. Speaking of what she calls the 'power geometry' involved in the 'global sense of place', Massey (1995: 149) insists that

> different social groups have distinct relationships to the [glocal]; some people are more in charge of it than others … some are more on the receiving-end of it than others; some are effectively imprisoned by it.

Massey's caution is important: it suggests that glocality needs to be qualified if it is to make politically progressive sense. To be somewhat blunt about it, theatre must engage, critically, with glocality. Only by engaging in such activity can theatre hope to become a practical mode of resistance. To say that theatre is resistant because it is a glocal practice is not, ultimately, to say very much. What we seem to be dealing with, when all is said and done, are modes of efficacy, ways of making theatre politically useful and evental. For the rest of this chapter, I intend to show how theatre might engage in a useful form of glocal critique by using Jean Genet's 1966 essay 'That Strange Word' as a theoretical case study in 'third space theatre'.

The time of empire

'That Strange Word' opens with a powerful and provocative statement, in which Genet claims that contemporary urbanism is the enemy of both theatre *and* death:

> That strange word urbanism whether it comes from a Pope Urban or from the city will maybe no longer be concerned with the dead. The living will get rid of their corpses, slyly or not, as one rids oneself of a

shameful thought. By hurrying them to the crematorium furnace, the urbanized world will rid itself of a great theatrical aid, and perhaps of theatre itself. (Genet [1966] 2003: 103)

In Genet's aesthetic, the stage is a special space where actors leave the world of the living and enter the world of the dead. As such, to go to the theatre, Genet believes, is to get a foretaste of non-being, to exist, momentarily, in a realm where conventional ideas of space and time have been placed on hold. If theatre is to rediscover its lost power as a kind of performative homeopathy, contemporary urbanists, Genet proposes, will first need to place a theatre in a graveyard and then proceed to locate that site in the very heart of the urban metropolis:

Of future urban planners we will demand that a cemetery be installed in the city, where the dead will continue to be buried, or to plan a disturbing columbarium, with simple but imperious lines, and then, next to it, in its shadow, or in the midst of tombs, the theatre will be erected. (Genet [1966] 2003: 103–4)

Looked at from this perspective, Genet's theatre in a graveyard appears to have little in common with politics, since it seems to be based on a quintessentially metaphysical or sacred relationship to time. Things are complicated, however, by the following long passage where he historicizes and politicizes Western concepts of temporality:

The Christian West, by dint of ruses, does what it can to glue together all of the peoples of the world in an era that has its origins in the hypothetical Incarnation. This is nothing other than the 'calendar trick' which the West tries to pull over the entire world. ... It would seem urgent, then, to multiply the 'Advents' starting from which calendars can be established, without any relationship to those that are imperialistically imposed. I even think that any event, private or public, should give birth to a multitude of calendars, in such a way to put the Christian era and what follows that counted time, starting from the Very Questionable Nativity, out of business. (Genet [1966] 2003: 104–5)

Genet's reference to imperialism politicizes, immediately, the function of theatre and, by association, death. By presenting spectators with another experience of time, one which has 'neither beginning nor end', Genet disrupts the chronology of what he refers to as the Western 'calendar trick'. In this way, Genet's theatre dissents from the idea, implicit in Christianity and Marxism, that the time between the beginning and end is somehow worthless and empty, a mere prelude to some dream of redemptive fullness. In 'That Strange Word', Genet argues that time, in its very facticity, its presentness, is a value in its own right. Such thinking explains his comment about how the strange temporality of theatre has the power to provoke what he calls earlier in the essay 'a breathtaking liberation', releasing the subject from the empty structures of historical and revolutionary time (Genet [1966] 2003: 104).

Although Genet does not state this explicitly in 'That Strange Word', his attack on imperialist time is, by necessity, an attack on globalized economics. Just as theological time, by placing its emphasis on a dubious *arche* and *telos*, devalues and defers the passing of time itself, so capitalist economics, by allying itself with the homogenizing logic of the commodity, produces a world devoid of events, a world where everything repeats. As a consequence of global capitalism's 'imperialist calendar', we are condemned to live a miserable and disenchanted reality, which, to cite Michael Hardt (1997: 76–7), is defined by 'the fixity of one immobile destiny'. For Genet, theatre has the capacity to resist what Hardt and Antonio Negri, in their book *Empire* (2000), see as the non-movement of capitalist or imperialist time in the extent to which it functions as a memory machine, in which the present is simultaneously haunted and disrupted by the past and future working together. As with Tadeusz Kantor and Heiner Müller, Genet believes that theatre is a site for revenants, a space where the dead can return as fleshy ghosts, and where the relentless flow of theological/imperialist/capitalist time is exploded. In this respect, theatre in Genet's view is a *topos uchronia*, a space where the homogeneity of commodity-based time is put out of joint and opened up to the possibility of a different future.

Glocal space

If there is, as Genet implies, something in theatre's ontology that has the potential to disrupt the global time of empire, such a disruption is always specifically located. In this respect, it is telling that the play Genet wanted to stage in the graveyard was *The Screens*, and the designated city, Paris. By attempting to ghost his host site with a work that celebrated the French defeat in Algeria, Genet sought to produce a complex enfolding of history and place, in which three competing notions of space – national, imperial and global – were brought together in one site. It is tempting to suggest that Genet was looking to produce a kind of performative cartography, what Jameson (1992: 54) might call 'a cognitive map', to account for Paris's specific relationship to the new form of globalized politics that was on the cusp of emerging from the ashes of European imperialism.

In *Fast Cars, Clean Bodies: Decolonization and the Reordering of French Culture*, the US cultural historian Kristin Ross (1995) contends that French modernization in the 1950s and 60s was marked by a contradictory attitude towards the nascent phenomenon of globalization. On the one hand, France was more than willing to exploit the new immigrant population that had flooded into the country in the wake of decolonization; but on the other hand, she was extremely anxious about the presence of so many black bodies on French soil. According to Ross, urbanism was used by the French government as a strategy for overcoming the conflicts between decolonization and nationalism that were threatening to tear the country apart. As Ross (1995: 151–2) explains it, rebuilding the city and relocating 44 per cent of the working classes to the new cities in the *banlieues* beyond the outer Paris ring road meant that the immigrant population needed to produce the French economic miracle was conveniently kept out of sight, denied entry to the city which, in many ways, it had built:

> French modernization, and the new capital city that crowned it, was built largely on the backs of Africans – Africans who found themselves progressively cordoned off in new forms of urban segregation as a result of the process.

For Ross, and it seems hard to disagree with her, decolonization ironically transformed Paris into a new Algiers, a city segregated economically and racially.

Placed within this spatial and historical framework, Genet's attack on urbanism in 'That Strange Word' takes on a very different meaning. The 'guilty secret' that urban planners were trying to repress is not simply synonymous with death; rather it is a metonym for the new immigrant workforce who, in the 1960s, were in the process of being expelled to the *banlieues*. This would appear to be substantiated by the fact that the play destined for the graveyards was *The Screens*. By staging a play about Algeria in the heart of Paris, Genet was effectively seeking to provoke an encounter with a reality that French nationalism refused to admit: namely, that the loss of Algeria was synonymous with the loss of France herself. In 1966, Genet realized that the decolonization of France's overseas empire signalled a shift in the geography and meaning of colonialism. Henceforth, colonialism was no longer simply a form of economics administered by a single nation state and exported aboard, but was now located in the very heart of the mother country herself: the exterior had migrated into the interior. This collapse of stable racial and geographical boundaries challenged the sense of French nationalism that President de Gaulle had been trying to cultivate since the late 1950s, with his policy of *rayonnement culturel*. To this extent, then, the provocation of Genet's desire to site *The Screens* in a graveyard starts to take on its full political significance: he is seeking to undermine – to bury – French nationalism and to show that a new global reality has taken place, one in which nations and places are no longer self-identical or essentialized.

Genet's critique of nationalism does not mean, of course, that he was willing to condone the nascent forms of economic globalization that were on the verge of coming into being in the 1960s. On the contrary, Genet's theatre in a graveyard is designed to call into question the very homogeneity that globalized economics invariably leads to. On this point, it is helpful to compare Genet's critique in 'That Strange Word' to Lefebvre's ideas about the colonization of everyday life in *The Critique of Everyday Life* (2005). In Lefebvre's view, the end of French imperialism intensified the colonization of *la vie quotidienne* in metropolitan France. Capitalism's need for new internal markets, contends Lefebvre, changed the spatial and temporal forms of everyday life fundamentally. With the construction of the superhighway within central Paris itself and the development of the RER network linking the urban centre to the periphery, Paris was rationalized according to the needs of capital in what Lefebvre referred to as the second stage of Haussmanization. As with the first stage in the 1850s, the objective was to guarantee the circulation of goods and people, and to ensure that the population was spatially disciplined and rendered politically passive. From Lefebvre's perspective, then, colonialism is not a historical process as such, something which, in a French context, began with the bombardment of Algiers from the sea in 1830 and ended with the return of the *pieds-noirs* from Algeria in 1962; it is a method for controlling space and time, a way of disciplining bodies for the sake of economic profit.

Lefebvre's ideas allow us to see how Genet's calls for a great 'festival of death' in Paris conceals an alternative type of everyday politics. For Genet, as for Lefebvre, festivity represents an example of a different economic relationship to the world, one in which the commodity is replaced by the potlatch, where quantity gives way to quality.[2] In this respect, Genet's provocative suggestion that theatre in a graveyard should 'have as much importance as the Palace of Justice' and 'the Chamber of Deputies' is a *plaidoyer* (a pleading) for a new form of non-alienated living, a desire to rehabilitate the spaces of everyday life ([1966] 2003:

108). Against the real-estate logic of urban development that so dominated France in the 1950s and 60s, Genet posits a useless space, a space that reveals what global capital seeks to veil: contingency, transience, history. In Genet's hands, then, the space of festivity is always temporalized, and the temporalization it evokes is, by necessity, opposed to the dehistorized time of capital. By pointing to endings, the spatiotemporal logic of the festival points, necessarily, to new beginnings, as well as the production of new spaces.

Conclusion

If I have concentrated uniquely on Genet's text 'That Strange Word' in this chapter, it is because it provides a perfect example of the political potential inherent to third space theatre. Not only does Genet's text offer us a heterotopia where antinomies between the global and national, and colonial and postcolonial, are deconstructed, but its 'disjointed spatiality' posits theatre as a magnet for memory, history and the production of alternative temporalities. Importantly, Genet is not content to let this third space theatre be regarded as a site of resistance in and by itself. On the contrary, he is always concerned to highlight the injustices, exclusions and inequalities of the new glocal order in a manner that is radically specific. In this respect, Genet shows us, in ways that I find hard to dispute, that third space theatre should seek to combine the ontology of theatre with the specificities of the place in which it locates itself. And as a final provocation, I would like to conclude by suggesting that such an approach problematizes unhelpful attempts to privilege either stage-bound or site-specific theatre. The key factor is how we use the locatedness of theatre to position ourselves in the world.

Notes

1   Kristeva is able to make this provocative, and largely counterintuitive, claim because she insists that semiology in the theatre is grounded in a demonstrative logic that would reflect a shared reality – a communal world – existing beyond the walls of the theatre. From Kristeva's point of view, theatre only takes (a) place when its signs are experienced as real, that is, when it manages to bind together author, actors and spectators as a community of believers. The problem with Kristeva's argument, as I see it, is that her central premise overlooks theatre's inherent and inalienable spatiality: the fact that the theatrical event is constituted by bodies taking place in actual space and time. The performer is

never simply a sign. On the contrary, they are always there, always in historical context, always in the world, not just a vehicle or conduit for some sacred,
transcendent truth to disclose itself on another stage.
2   In anthropological discourse, potlatch describes a social structure founded on
exuberant and often destructive forms of generosity. In this pre-capitalist form of
economics, power and sovereignty are dependent upon expenditure rather than
the accumulation of surplus value.

Works cited

Genet, Jean. 'That Strange Word' [1966]. In Jean Genet, *Fragments of the Artwork*,
trans. Charlotte Mandell. Stanford: Stanford University Press, 2003, 103–12.
Hardt, Michael. 'Prison Time'. In Scott Durham, ed., *Yale French Studies*, special issue,
Genet: In the Language of the Enemy, 1997, 91: 64–79.
Hardt, Michael and Negri, Antonio. *Empire*. Cambridge, MA: Harvard University
Press, 2000.
Harvey, David. *The Condition of Postmodernity*. Oxford: Blackwell, 1990.
Jameson, Frederic. *Postmodernism or the Cultural Logic of Late Capitalism*. London:
Verso, 1992.
Kristeva, Julia. 'The Modern Theatre Does Not Take (a) Place'. *Sub-Stance* 1977, 18/19:
131–4.
Lefebvre, Henri. *Critique of Everyday Life,* vol. 3. *From Modernity to Modernism (Towards
a Metaphilosophy of Daily Life)*, trans. Gregory Elliot. London: Verso, 2005.
Lippard, Lucy. *The Lure of the Local; Senses of Place in a Multicultural Society*. New York:
New York Press, 1997.
Massey, Doreen. *Space, Place and Gender*. Minneapolis: University of Minnesota Press,
1995.
Robertson, Roland. 'Glocalization: Time-Space and Homogeneity-Heterogeneity'.
In Mike Featherstone, Scott Lash and Roland Robertson, eds, *Global Modernities*.
London: Sage, 1995, 25–44.
Ross, Kristin. *Fast Cars, Clean Bodies: Decolonization and the Reordering of French
Culture*. Cambridge, MA: MIT Press, 1995.
Soja, Edward. *Thirdspace: Journeys to Los Angeles and Other Real-and-Imagined Places*.
Cambridge, MA: Blackwell, 1996.

23   Theatre of Immediacy, Transversal Poetics

Mark LeVine and Bryan Reynolds

Tarek al-Tayeb Mohamed Bouazizi was a street vendor in the provincial Tunisian town of Sidi Bouzid who, on 17 December 2010, sparked the Tunisian and broader Arab Spring revolutions when he self-immolated. After surviving in a coma for 18 days with severe burns covering almost his entire body, he died on 4 January 2011. Bouazizi's self-immolation was an act of radical anti-government performance activism staged in response to the emotional, political and physical injury he suffered at the whim of a municipal official named Faida Hamdi and two policemen, who supposedly attempted to extort money from him, beat him publicly, and confiscated his cart and scales. Right after the altercation, Bouazizi went to the office of Sidi Bouzid's governor to complain and request the return of his equipment. The governor refused to see him, even after, according to witnesses, he declared: 'If you don't see me, I'll burn myself.' Ignored, he soon departed, but quickly returned with a can of gasoline. Standing in the middle of the road, he drenched himself, shouted 'How do you expect me to make a living?!' and set himself ablaze.[1]

All these events, from Bouazizi's confrontation with police and municipal officials to his self-immolation, occurred in less than an hour. News of what happened spread like wildfire throughout Sidi Bouzid, and within hours angry protesters filled the streets. Given that Bouazizi's self-immolation was in fact the third one within the space of a few weeks across Tunisia, we wonder why his act sparked a revolution whereas the previous public suicides did not. Clearly, one reason is that his act was photographed by someone with a cell phone camera and then mass-circulated via cell phones and the internet in a swift flurry that completely escaped the control of the Tunisian government, one of the world's most notorious regulators of internet access. The images of the flaming man captured in the now iconic photos (see Figures 23.1 and 23.2) were quintessentially 'auratic', that is, exhibiting an affective energy that forges solidarities between and demanding a response from all those experiencing them: the power of the photos literally leapt from cell phones and computer screens, demanding a response from those who viewed them commensurate with the courageousness and agony of the victim/performer.

Figure 23.1   Mohamed Bouazizi in flames. Photo: Anon.

Figure 23.2   Mohamed Bouazizi visited by President Ben Ali. Photo: Anon. Source: Tunisian Presidency

To be sure, Bouazizi's self-immolation prompted many other men and women to carry out similar acts across the Arab world, none more important than that of Bouazizi's friend, Hussein Lahsin Neji, who, just a few days after Bouazizi's suicide, went to a protest at the local offices of Tunisia's state-sponsored labor union, snuck behind a police line, climbed to the top of an electricity pylon, and spectacularly electrocuted himself in protest against the government system that had done nothing to recognize the meaning of his friend's sacrifice.[2] While Bouazizi gets most of the attention, it could be argued that it was Neji's equally dramatic self-'martyrdom' (as many Tunisians describe these actions) that added enough heat for the revolutionary fire to catch. At the same time, the mise-en-scène of Sidi Bouzid, a rural hinterland at the heart of Tunisia's poorest and most agriculturally focused region, also provided the protests that erupted there with much greater saliency than if they had occurred in the capital Tunis or another major urban center. It was precisely the intimacy of the act, occurring in a small town where, as one activist put it, 'everyone is someone's cousin', that helped engender such anger and sympathy for the victims.[3]

In the weeks and months after Bouazizi's and Neji's deaths (and they were preceded and followed by other, lesser known self-martyrdoms, though most not acts of self-immolation), all sorts of phrases and intentions were attributed to their actions and to the protesters who took to the streets in defense of their memory. Bouazizi is supposed to have shouted *shughul, huriyya, wa karama wataniyya!* (work, freedom and national dignity) as he took his final steps, whereas the chants of the protesters that grew in the wake of their deaths marked the first utterances that people around the world can remember of the now celebrated demand that became the mantra that reverberated heroically throughout the Arab uprisings, beginning with the first protests in Tunisia: 'The people want the downfall of the system' (*ash-sha`'ab yurid isqat al-nizam*).

But even these actions and slogans were not merely spontaneous bursts of political genius. Rather, they were the result of a 'deep wave' of societal maturation, which saw a new generation come of age in Tunisia, and across the Arab world, that was no longer afraid of its aging and progressively more out-of-touch leaders. In the weeks between Bouazizi's self-immolation and his death, protests became increasingly aggressive and violent, and after he died they rapidly spread throughout the nation, including the wealthy areas of the capital. By January 14, a half-century old political order had largely collapsed, as President Zine El Abidine Ben Ali fled the country with his family after supposedly being tricked by the head of his presidential security team into thinking a coup was imminent.[4]

As their significance amplified through the media, Bouazizi's actions continued to inspire many self-immolations across the Arab world and Europe, with 107 taking place in Tunisia alone within the six months following his death. In Egypt, at least three self-immolations occurred in the weeks after Bouazizi's, including one in Cairo by a restaurant owner named Abdou Abdel Moneim Jaafar, whose Bouazizi-modeled self-immolation was rooted in a failure to get much-needed food coupons for his restaurant. As he burned, Jaafar purportedly screamed: 'The security of the State of the State Security, my right subconscious is lost by air (inside) of the State.' This was a powerful if seemingly unintelligible, but, if read a certain way, comprehensible attack on the manner in which what Giorgio Agamben described as the 'state of exception' imposed upon the vast majority of the population, in which individuals or groups of people are placed outside the normal bounds of protection, rights and citizenship and subject to systematic and dehumanized violence as a core process of state practice and preservation. And yet, as the quote demonstrates, the same citizens who are opened to being placed into this state can, as might an abused person, become more entangled with and supportive of the state possessing such power over them. As a result of being pulled in two or more directions at once, for and against the state, this schizoid dynamic moves the population towards the kind of break that, at least for a moment, has revolutionary potential.[5]

In the longer work from which this essay is excerpted, we explore the link between highly charged performative individual acts, like those of Bouazizi, Neji and Jaafar, more organized forms of protest epitomized by the actions of the fanatical Egyptian soccer fans turned frontline protesters, known as Ultras, and the Black Bloc tactics deployed by them and other anarchist-inspired groups, and the cultural creation and performance produced by various artists – music, theatre and visual arts – in the periods leading up to, during and after the core revolutionary protests in Tunisia and Egypt.[6] To do this, we employ the theory, terms and research methods of 'transversal poetics', which we briefly explain here as a means by which to engage analytically the marginalization and removal of a critical mass of citizens from the political body by authoritarian systems whose modes of governance are increasingly neoliberal.[7] We approach the performance of dissidence in the cultural, sociopolitical and economic environments that are our focus within the Arab world through the prism of what we call 'theatre of immediacy'.

We define 'theatre of immediacy' as artistic creation and performance for an intended audience that is not merely emergent – that is, in the process of formation – but what we refer to as 'emurgent' (emergent + urgent): developing rapidly and in the context of intense sociopolitical struggle that is at, or produces, a threshold (crossing), or transitional moment in which dominant, congealed structures and networks of power and identity destabilize and reconfigure. Moreover, theatre of immediacy must be experienced live and in real time. It is quickly produced (created, brought forth, staged) to embody and reflect the imminence and urgency of a particular, often radical moment. It also proves to be transversally empowered, insofar as it stimulates individual or group transformations that defy, exceed or undermine established systems and parameters for perceiving, experiencing, interpreting and reasoning, what, for transversal poetics, constitute the 'subjective territories', 'official culture' and 'sociopolitical conductors' that work together, separately and reciprocally to maintain them.[8]

We further see the practices surrounding theatre of immediacy as embodying and reflecting a crucial moment in the struggles for hegemony between power elites, the political and social institutions under their control, and various elements of the population who are attempting to challenge, subvert or even overturn the existing political order. Certainly, theatre of immediacy depends on actors and acts – the events they produce together – forceful enough to reappropriate meaning and valence for what Agamben has described as otherwise 'bare lives': lives without rights; lives vulnerable to the arbitrary power of the sovereign.[9] The practices constitute a level of immanent critique and epistemological and moral transcendence that violate and soon enough dissolve the boundaries between state and citizen, elite and subaltern, public and private, and political and cultural, without which the state of exception as a structural condition of subjectivity-as-subjugation, that is, the subjectification integral to subjective territories and the official culture they mutually support, cannot maintain coherence and so collapses.

According to transversal poetics, as developed by Reynolds, 'sociopolitical conductors' interconnect a society's cultural-ideological framework. They are mental and physical movers, orchestrators and transmitters, such as educational, juridical, religious and entertainment structures, multimedia broadcasting and information sources, and the institutions of marriage and family; they are the individuals with authority working separately and together within and representing these societal assemblages. Conductors affect the circulation of three types of relationally implicated and contested power: open power, state power and transversal power, as they promote or oppose partially or predominantly, and often contradictorily, the dominant ideology of the society in which they function. Open power is any force that cannot be categorized as state power or transversal power, that is, until it is activated, related, contextualized, differentiated. The power of Bouazizi's theatre of immediacy was open before he conceived of it and was therefore not yet influencing and influenced by discourse, not yet supporting, undermining or transforming a structure. State power is any force that works in the interest of coherence and organization among any variables, such as words in a sentence, images on stage or actions in the streets, and therefore builds and reinforces structures, whether semantic, material, social, cultural or political (whether mainstream, official or oppositional).

For instance, much effort on the part of various sociopolitical conductors (government representatives and factions, other dissident groups and information sources) has gone into trying to *grasp – make sense of* and thus *semantically reduce* – the implications of the groups using Black Bloc tactics that *emurged* transversally in early 2013 during anti-government protests as part of a broader indictment against the Muslim Brotherhood and, among other purposes, to demand justice from the government for crimes committed against people during the Arab uprisings.[10] Black Bloc tactics involve protesters concealing their identities – theatrically, mysteriously and ominously – with nondescript black clothes, ski masks, hats, scarves, sunglasses and so on, while engaging in violence against government forces and destroying targeted property (see Figure 23.3). The menacing and fugitive quality of the tactics provokes reaction by sociopolitical conductors in the interest of sense-making, control and political jockeying. Such examples of state power at work are typically discursive when engaging a potent, big news or hyped-up topic, which was the case for responses to the Black Bloc tactics, as the fraught topic circulates in the public sphere and in discourses generally in what we refer to as an 'articulatory space'. This is a fluid, multifaceted, primarily abstract, spatiotemporal realm in which disparate concepts and sentiments converse; ideational streams, discourses and performances negotiate and aggregate meanings, redefine their trajectories, boundaries and strategies, while orbiting and informing subjects of critical speculation. It is in such fields of semantic, perspectival and affective play that state power, conveyed through the operations of sociopolitical conductors, is often most obviously apparent. A 'disarticulatory space', for example, would manifest as streams of discourse on a topic convolute and disperse, language breaks down, semantic coding becomes indecipherable, and transversal power dominates.

Alternative to open and state powers, 'transversal power' is any force – physical or ideational, friendly or antagonistic – that inspires emotional, conceptual and/or physical deviations from the established 'norms' for any variables, whether individuated or forming a group. Operating as a field of instantiation and contestation for norms, articulatory spaces furnish connectivity to otherwise disparate elements, generating clusters of coherence out of multiple ideas, events, feelings, subjects and objects. Insofar as the deployments of Black Bloc tactics foster an articulatory space, what we call 'BlackBloc-space', rife with portholes though which transversal travel and revolution can happen, it is a source of transversal power. That is, the representation and extension of such deployments through various media, as in the case of Bouazizi, are the mechanisms of transversal power, and not necessarily the individuals using Black Bloc tactics themselves. They are anonymous and may be functioning in strict accord with the codes of the privileged society of which they are members, the society to which their subjective territory most adheres, whether dissident, subcultural, transgressive and so on.

Figure 23.3   Black Bloc tactics in Egypt. Photo: Amr Nabil

The same can be said for Bouazizi himself, who became a channeler of transversal power through his conduction of historical self-immolation as performance activism and transduction from individual to international celebrity and cultural/political icon. Credited as the inspiration of the Arab uprisings of 2011, and with a legacy of streets and plazas named after him, stamps with his photo on it, T-shirts, caps and buttons that say 'We are all Mohamed Bouazizi' (see Figure 23.4), films about him and accounts of him in history books, 'Bouazizi-space' will remain potent for years to come. It will be resurrected and the force of his actions laminated, to some extent, with every subsequent self-immolation protest performed in history, just as Vietnamese Mahayana Buddhist monk Thích

Quang Duc's famous self-immolation theatre of immediacy in protest of the Vietnam War on June 11, 1963 resonates and reverberates through Bouazizi's; as do all other self-immolation protests, inasmuch as their history is known, their aura present and affective – their 'affective presence' persistent. In effect, Bouazizi-space is a subset of, among others, 'self-immolation-as-protest-space', and powerfully so. The fact that fire is the instrument of suicide, a controversially loaded act in itself, also gives power to this mode of performance activism, since fire suggests danger, itself spectacularly sensational and one of the most unpredictable elements that humans often cannot control. Pyrotechnics has long been a tremendous source of entertainment and worry, precisely because of its combined effects and signification (consider the mesmerizing tranquility people enjoy when they marvel at fire *safely contained* within a fireplace in their homes).

Figure 23.4   We are all Mohamed Bouazizi. Photo: Anon.

In agreement with their investment in cultural, social, political and economic codes and determinations, sociopolitical conductors that reinforce the official ideology work over time and space, consciously and/or not, to channel and convert open and transversal powers into state power, thereby working discursively to give stability to a society's government. Put differently, the ultimate purpose of the organizing machinery – that runs on the state power it generates – is to configure society and manufacture 'the state': the totalized 'state machinery' that the conductors together comprise. Bouazizi's theatre of immediacy was a volcanic embodiment and channeler of transversal power that proved uncontainable by the state machinery of Tunisia and, by extension, the Arab world. His suicidal performance was especially radical. It was sacrilegious and eternally self-destructive as well as dissident, insofar as Islamic law forbids and condemns suicide, unless as martyrdom as part of a jihad, and Arab governments and societies are mutually grounded, with considerable uniformity, in the religion, ideology, customs, symbols and institutions of Islam. Bouazizi's theatre of immediacy continues to generate transversality circulating within and through the articulatory space it generated and continues to generate, Bouazizi-space, and the other articulatory spaces it informs and with which it overlaps, such as Arab Spring-space and self-immolation-as-protest-space, long after the live/immediate performance ended. The future of BlackBloc-space, less specific historically and individually to a person, may prove even less containable, not just as it is recorded in oral, literary and digital archives, these being the means by which state power is often most efficiently exercised (through the 'paper trail' that becomes history), but as Black Bloc tactics periodically reemerge in different locations and eras, and are converged upon by interested and invested sociopolitical conductors.

Reynolds coined the term 'state machinery' for a society's governmental assembly of conductors as a corrective to the political philosophy of Louis Althusser that has informed much Marxist scholarship over the past 50 years, particularly that of cultural materialists, new historicists, post-Marxists, materialist feminists and new materialists. With state machinery, a term that simultaneously connotes singularity and plurality, Reynolds adapted Althusser's conception of what he calls the 'repressive state apparatus', which includes the governmental mechanisms, such as the military and the police, that strive to control our bodies, and fused it with his subsidiary 'ideological state apparatuses', the inculcating mechanisms that strive to control our thoughts and emotions.[11] This fusion emphasizes that a society's drive for government coherence is always motivated by assorted conductors of state-oriented organizational power that are at different times and to varying degrees always repressive and ideological. This is a sociopower dynamic in which various conductors work, sometimes individually and sometimes in conjunction with other conductors, to substantiate their own positions of

209

power within the sociopolitical field. Hence, state machinery makes explicit the multifarious and discursive nature of state power, and thus prevents the misperception of the sociopower dynamic as the result of policies led by a monolithic state. This is not to say, however, that conspiracies do not occur and take the form of state factions. On the contrary, this must be the case for the more complex machinery to run.

The top components of the US's state machinery, for example, consist of the executive, legislative and judicial branches of the federal government, the armed forces and interest groups that influence public policy, such as religious, human rights and corporate organizations (versions of these categories operate on state and local levels as well). Both consciously and inadvertently, they have together manifested and continue to develop and enforce, with their respective legislation, disciplinary capacity and lobbying, a pervasive 'official' ideology and culture that is rooted in Christian mythology and morality. In turn, inasmuch as US citizens subscribe to and privilege Christian beliefs, the 'sacred' dogma of Christianity works to legitimate the power of these state-oriented apparatuses. Church and state attempt, together and separately, to reinforce and promote the existing sociopolitical hierarchy upon which their superior status relies. They do this notwithstanding internal contradictions and conflicts, such as those between and within the Senate and Congress, the Democratic and Republican parties, labor unions and corporations, public and private educational institutions, and the various denominations of the Christian Church. Nevertheless, no matter how apparently organized or coherent the dominant sociopolitical conductors become, and no matter how effective the democratic process, pure democracy (total consent of the governed) or an absolute state can only ever be a fantasy goal whose realization would preclude this sociopower dynamic. This is because 'the state', like the Marxist concept of historical totality, is impossible to achieve, or, at the very least, it is inaccessible and unobservable by even its most powerful conductors. Social systems continue to evolve in relation to ongoing natural processes, such as thermodynamics, chaos, environmental changes, genetic mutations and anarchist tendencies that remain uncontrolled by human intervention. Even the fundamental religious codes, threat of punishment, and the guilt, shame and anxiety that the mere thought of such an action could invoke in a good citizen with a large well-respected family could not prevent Bouazizi from self-immolating, his theatre of immediacy achieving 'emulative authority' (a person's or group's combined aesthetic, cultural, social and political energy that draws people to emulate them) in conjunction with transversal power capable of generating mass protests and copycat suicide performances by others.

The exceptionalism of Bouazizi's emulative authority and related affective presence gained through his theatre of immediacy (affective presence referring to the feeling-thought and power-to-influence together with dynamic occupation of space/time that his presence manifested in the popular imagination) is irreducible to the conditions of its emergence, and thus could not be repeated with identical impact, however 'natural' the process necessarily is, or however predictable it is, based on knowledge of the 'human condition'. Whereas research in many disciplines, both sociological and scientific, seems to have made significant progress in its quest to understand and influence natural processes, the organizing machinery of all modern states is still far from being able to account for all inconsistencies and ruptures in the *conduction* – the dissemination and management – of social order. Precisely for this reason, the machinery focuses on what it knows it must, and often can, control: the range of thought of the populace, their 'conceptual territory', which is typically sought through enforcement of ideological inculcation and, ultimately as the source of the ideology, religious creed, which is often fear-driven and with high stakes, like freedom of the body on earth or eternal salvation of the soul. More specifically, the machinery continually needs to reestablish the scope of personal experience and perception of the populace's members. This scope, their 'subjective territory', must be navigated so that notions of identity cease to be arbitrary and transitory, and acquire temporal constancy and spatiotemporal range for the subsistence of what is perceived to be a healthy individual and, by extension, a cohesive social body. Regardless of how originally or actually heterogeneous the subject population, genetically, ethnically or philosophically, the state machinery needs to imbue this population with a common state-serving subjectivity, indeed a shared ideology, that gives this social body the assurance of homogeneity and universality.

The massive ripple effects of Bouazizi's performance throughout the Arab world exposed the tenuousness of the mythologies on which the state machinery of different countries had been fabricated and sustained. Revelation happened. The population learned that the actions of one individual, a common person like themselves, can turn their world upside down, and they too can make a difference – not only does every person have agency, but the extent and influence of their affective presence is potentially far-reaching and impossible to predict. *Becomings-Bouazizi* became a common phenomenon as people tried to understand his actions and empathize with him by moving outside their subjective territory subjunctively 'as if' or 'what if' they were him or like him and had to contend with similar circumstances and situation. This identification and transference, as well as idolatry for some, all the result of his affective presence and corresponding emulative authority, led numerous people to try to become him physically as well as conceptually and emotionally by self-immolating, in other words, through performance. Comings-to-be-x are inadvertent becomings of something beyond or other than an intended becomings-x into which one can slip. Perhaps *comings-to-be-Bouazizi* superseded the original objective of empathy and consequently some of the copycat self-immolations resulted from a temporary loss of control. Such comings-to-be would be a byproduct of the 'transversal movements' inaugurated and eventually unbridled by the becomings-Bouazizi ignited by the radicalism and exceptionalism of his theatre of immediacy and how it was processed through Bouazizi-space, Tunisian revolution-space, and Arab Spring-space, among other related and overlapping articulatory spaces (consider Zine El Abidine Ben Ali-space and Hosni Mubarak-space).

Reynolds' term, 'subjective territory', refers to the combined conceptual, emotional and physical range from which a subject perceives and experiences the world; this applies to all individuals living in a society who are, consciously and/or not, self-governing in accordance with their state-sanctioned worldview. In other words, subjective territory accounts for the individual who has been subjugated conceptually, emotionally and bodily, that is, developed into a subject by the state machinery of any hegemonic society or subsociety, such as universities, criminal organizations, or religious societies. Therefore, the individual's subjective territory, and corresponding self-government, reflects their socioeconomic positioning. Subjective territory reinforces the society's sociopolitical conductors that work to inculcate individuals with the appropriate ideology, the ideology that in turn confirms for them their prescribed addresses, their subjective territory, within the society's hierarchical geography. The resulting determination is physical as well as conceptual and emotional; physical constraints (such as traffic laws, ghettoization and regionalization) influence the conceptual and emotional aspects of subjectivity, just as they are symptoms and extensions of these aspects. Subjective territory also accounts for the individual who steps out or against the network that works to strengthen and affirm it. This person's subjective territory fractures and refashions, which leads to either a reconfiguration of the official territory of which it is a part or the individual's marginalization from that official territory. Belonging to a group, culture, nationality, to any defined population with official territory, is always under pressure; the dominant structure remains susceptible to resistance, mutation or expansion, and the individual vulnerable to indelible marking, expulsion or extermination. Such 'pressurized belongings' characterize all affiliations, but are substantially more pronounced for individuals and groups associated with subsets of a dominant culture, particularly the subcultures and countercultures that define themselves by negation, through exclusionary logic, alternative and oppositional behavior, or by principle of specialness and privilege. Consider the categorical positioning of Egypt's Ultras and other dissident groups who use Black Bloc tactics, the pressure under which its members belong (commitment demonstrated by dangerous and violent performance activism), the structure of its own official territory, and the distinctive traits of the subjective territories required to support it.

'Transversal movements' are uncontrollable feelings, thoughts and actions alternative to those that work to circumscribe and maintain an individual's subjective territory, and, by extension, they are capable of undermining the parameters of belonging to a group, community or official culture and the pressures that attend to them. Most people engage in transversal movements to some degree, in one form or another, every day. People most often move transversally when they empathize or imagine they are empathizing with others. They may actually have no idea what someone else is thinking or feeling, but nonetheless they are still thinking and feeling atypically in their attempt to empathize, as if they are someone else, as theatre actors and audience members often do, which pushes them transversally. By occupying, if only imaginatively or ephemerally, the subjective territory of another, one's own subjective territory expands and reconfigures. Whatever the specific impact of Bouazizi's theatre of immediacy on individuals and groups, and its effects across different populations, a measureable impact on the subjective territories of a vast number of people was demonstrated by their anti-state, life-risking actions against the dominant official territory of which they had been a functioning component, and, however conflicted, possibly continued to be one in some ways while also being defiant in other ways.

Notes

1   Bob Simon, 'How a slap sparked Tunisia's revolution,' CBS News, February 22, 2011, www.cbsnews.com/news/how-a-slap-sparked-tunisias-revolution-22-02-2011/, accessed February 2, 2014.

2   For a description of Neji's death and the larger context in which it occurred, see Mark LeVine, 'What a difference a decade makes,' Al Jazeera, September 11, 2011, www.aljazeera.com/indepth/opinion/2011/09/201191174753518987.html, accessed February 2, 2014.

3   Interviews with local residents and activists by Mark LeVine, Sidi Bouzid, September, 2011.

4   This was reported by many news outlets based on an Associated Press story that ran on June 11, 2011. See for example, 'Ben Ali says he was duped into fleeing Tunisia,' Radio France International, June 20, 2011, www.english.rfi.fr/africa/20110620-ben-ali-says-he-was-duped-fleeing-tunisia, accessed February 2, 2014.

5 On 'bare life', see Giorgio Agamben, *Homo Sacer: Sovereign Power and Bare Life* (California: Stanford University Press, 1998); Achille Mbembe, 'Necropolitics,' *Public Culture*, 15.1 (2003): 11–40.

6 Ultras arose in Europe out of team fan clubs and have long been characterized by fanatical devotion to their teams as well as a propensity for violence. While not inherently political, various Ultras clubs have long reflected the local and/or class identities of their teams, and, along with battling rival teams' clubs, have, in Egypt, had long experience battling government forces, as football stadiums during the Mubarak era were among the few places where anti-government chants could be heard openly. The Ultras, and the Black Bloc tactics they adopted, were crucial to the early success of the Tahrir Square uprising because they provided seasoned frontline fighters during the early battles for control of Tahrir Square. For a brief history of Black Bloc tactics, see http://en.wikipedia.org/wiki/Black_bloc.

7 Transversal poetics was developed by Bryan Reynolds and a number of collaborators primarily in the fields of literary, cultural, theatre and performance studies, and is further developed by us here. See Bryan Reynolds, *Transversal Subjects: From Montaigne to Deleuze after Derrida* (Basingstoke: Palgrave Macmillan, 2009); *Transversal Enterprises in the Drama of Shakespeare and his Contemporaries: Fugitive Explorations* (Basingstoke: Palgrave Macmillan, 2006); *Performing Transversally: Reimagining Shakespeare and the Critical Future* (Basingstoke: Palgrave Macmillan, 2003); and *Becoming Criminal: Transversal Performance and Cultural Dissidence in Early Modern England* (Baltimore: Johns Hopkins University Press, 2002).

8 For more on transversal poetics and the associated terms, subjective territories, official culture and sociopolitical conductors, as well as terms that will be introduced later in this chapter, transversal power, state power, open power, articulatory space, state machinery, conceptual territory, transversal movement, becomings, emulative authority, and pressurized belongings, see the following works by Reynolds: 'The Devil's House, "or worse": Transversal Power and Antitheatrical Discourse in Early Modern England', *Theatre Journal* 49.2 (1997): 143–67; *Becoming Criminal: Transversal Performance and Cultural Dissidence in Early Modern England* (2002), 1–22; *Performing Transversally: Reimagining Shakespeare and the Critical Future* (2003), 1–28; *Transversal Enterprises in the Drama of Shakespeare and his Contemporaries: Fugitive Explorations* (2006); *Transversal Subjects: From Montaigne to Deleuze after Derrida* (2009). *Transversal Subjects* includes a 'Glossary of Transversal Terms'.

9 Giorgio Agamben, *Homo Sacer: Sovereign Power and Bare Life* (Palo Alto, CA: Stanford University Press, 1998).

10 On Muslim Brotherhood, see Mark LeVine, 'The revolution, back in black,' *Al Jazeera*, February 2, 2013, www.aljazeera.com/indepth/opinion/2013/02/201322103219816676.html, accessed February 2, 2013.

11 For Althusser, 'every State Apparatus, whether Repressive or Ideological, 'functions' both by violence and by ideology' ... [but] 'the (Repressive) State Apparatus functions massively and predominantly *by repression* (including physical repression), while functioning secondarily *by ideology*' ... [and] 'the Ideological State Apparatuses function massively and predominantly by ideology' (145). Louis Althusser, *Lenin and Philosophy and Other Essays*, trans. Ben Brewster (New York: Monthly Review Press, 1971).

24   Time in Theatre

Jerzy Limon

Time provides a complex theoretical issue, especially when dealing with the theatre where different time structures are at play. As usual, there exist many typologies of time in theatre, but in a brief chapter it is not possible to go deeply into the controversies and discussion of variant theories.[1] In literature, the written or printed text does not, in itself, contain any temporal value, with the possible exception of the measurable thickness of pages that have been read and those still to be read.[2] A literary text as a material object may, of course, signal the time of its origin, or time necessary for its reading, but cannot convey precise information concerning time as a physical phenomenon or the nature of time within the created fictional realm. In other words, in literature the material substance of signs carries in itself hardly any referential meaning. Moreover, the same literary text may be reproduced in different typographical layout, different size fonts, different colour of print, and the substantial meanings will remain the same. In the theatre the situation is strikingly different, for the substance of scenic signs includes a live human body, which contains its clear temporal value of the biological present time, shared with the members of the audience. Moreover, the substance of the performance (which may be called 'signalling matter') includes real objects, lights, music and other phenomena, which may be perceived by the senses and appear in different selections and modelling in every production, even if the same dramatic text is used. In other words, it is not irrelevant what substances are used in performance, what is their shape and mutual relationships. Contrariwise, as this chapter aims to show, meaning in theatre is not limited to the creation of fictional realms, but is generated through the relationship of the denotata to the material substance and its modelling on the stage. This means that the signs of the theatre reveal a double orientation: towards the denoted world, purely fictional, hence invisible and inaudible, which can only take the form of a mental structure in the spectator, and towards the material vehicles of the stage signs. This rule incorporates all components of the performance, including, for example, acting and the language used. In all these instances, the crucial role is played by the time structures involved.

To begin with, the biological present time of the actor overlaps with the fictional present time of the ensuing action and dialogues performed by the fictional figures,[3] which, as we understand, are set in historical past (taking as the point of reference the time of the spectators). This creates a paradox, typical for theatre, which the recipient must solve and accept in order to be able to understand the message. In theatre, therefore, we are dealing with two present times, which allows us to talk of five, instead of just four, dimensions. I am stressing the temporal aspect because in my understanding of theatre as an art, the basic difference between theatre and other means of human communication lies in the time structures employed. In other words, in theatre we observe all sorts of temporal relationships, combining real and fictional streams, and time flows with variable speed and in variable currents on both sides of what I call the 'fifth wall'.[4] It is the invisible boundary between two time streams, two present times, two temporal dimensions, separating the material substance from the fictional sphere; separating human bodies, props, costume, music and so on from what all this signalling matter denotes in the fictional realm. In addition, the fifth wall marks the division between the two spheres governed by different laws of physics, and that includes geometry (space) and – most importantly – time.

However, the simultaneous occurrence of two streams of time, and two present times in particular, is not a common feature of empirical reality, and thus it requires an acceptance on the side of the recipient who is expected to adapt their cognition of the world to the specific requirements and conventions of the stage. Even in those productions that imitate 'real life', which is a common present-day practice (especially in postmodern or postdramatic productions),[5] the borders of the work are clearly marked by the beginning and the end. There is no past before the beginning, and no future beyond the end.[6] This means that time is finite and within those time limits and within the space of the stage everything undergoes semiosis and is given a sign function, entering into some sort of relationships with everything else within the boundaries of the whole work. So, within the given time and the given space, an actor becomes a sign of a figure, his costume signifies real garment, his wig real hair, and the stage speech real language and so on. As soon as the show reaches its end, everything returns to its previous (and real) ontological status, loses its semiotic significance. A costume in an actor's wardrobe is not a sign of anything, it is simply a theatrical costume.

Thus, it becomes apparent that theatre arises from the appearance of discrepant time structures: the performer as a live actor, living in the same time as the spectator, pretends that they are someone from the past (or, more rarely, from the future), but behaves as if the fictional figure were living now, in congruence with the biological time of the actor and the spectator. This duality is perhaps the most important feature of stage time. However, in empirical reality, we cannot have two present times, each flowing within a different time stream.[7] But theatre is not an empirical reality, in which everything has to succumb to the laws of physics: in theatre, which is a work of art, the laws are based on a mutual agreement between the performers and the spectators, and the particular letters of the agreement are called 'conventions'.

Clearly, every performance is played out before our eyes and the time needed for its realization can be measured on our watches. We are, however, more concerned with fictional, scenic time. The simplest way of signalling its passage is through references to time arising from the dialogue. But, we might soon notice, when following the dialogue, that the time necessary for the actors to utter the lines differs from the time indicated in the ensuing verbal exchange. As noted above, most important in theatre is the duality of the present time. This does not have to be referred to verbally. The basic technique of signalling split present time is through the actors' habit of not noticing the spectators or the space of the theatre. In this way, we, the spectators, understand that the figure does not notice our presence simply because it is set in a time different from the present of the performance; and yet the actor pretends as if it were really our present time. The contradiction has to be treated as a convention marker, which may – but does not have to be – accepted by the members of the audience. We are thus constantly reminded that theatre is an art based on conventions, which depends on a mutual agreement between the performers and the spectators.[8] Let me repeat: the basic rule of that agreement (and of theatre) states that someone is pretending that what belongs to the past (from our, the spectators', temporal perspective) is their real present. It is a re-creation of the past as a continuous, evolving present of the recipient. This creates a separation of the three worlds: three because, apart from the 'real' world of the audience and the perceiving minds of individual spectators, the one on the stage is in fact dual in nature, material and fictional, with both spheres divided by the 'fifth wall'. So, during the performance, the dual world of the stage is created, with the concomitant division of time and space (and dual ontology, so to say), followed by the conspicuous emergence and juxtaposition of two models of perceiving reality, that of fictional figures and that of spectators (the actors' perspective is not part of the performance message). The figures see and hear what we, the spectators, do not see and hear, and vice versa. This enables us to notice the equivalences between the two worlds, and to recognize how fiction is created, which is essential to the aesthetic cognition.

The temporal paradox, mentioned above, may be treated as the essential conspicuous marker of the theatre as art, and distinguishes theatre from all other forms of human communication and behaviour.[9] In other words, whenever fictional time is created and is signalled by a live performer to a spectator, we can talk of theatre and *theatricality*.[10] In this sense, acting may be seen as the art of creating fictional time. Since the events concerning the fictional figure's past are presented within the actor's present time, it is logical that, by analogy, the same rule applies to the future. The present always seems to result from the future, and since the former is shared, so, we may surmise, is the latter. This logic fails, however, when the spectator is conscious of the fact of acting and knows that the actor on stage is not the figure enacted. This means that the agreement of the temporal present is only conventional; what follows is that the shared future (and past) is conventional too. Consequently, the stage figure as enacted by the actor does not reveal the actor's awareness of their past and future: the actor knows perfectly well what is going to happen and what their interlocutors are going to say and what they have already said (even in the scenes, in which a given actor does not take part); they also know what they are supposed to do and say. If the latter is forgotten, or the former is revealed, the basic rules of theatre are unveiled and undermined (as in the case of the mechanicals in *Midsummer Night's Dream*). So, another convention is constituted: namely, that the actor is not supposed to betray their (hence the figure's) awareness of the events to come and words to be uttered in the fictional realm. Hence, the actor signals constantly that the figure treats the future of the fictional realm as we treat our future – to some extent predictable, but basically unknown. This enables them to signal the fictional present as if it occurred in our real temporal present, stemming from a seemingly shared future, while signalling the fictional nature of everything that is being enacted and shown within the split present times.

The notion of memory comes into focus when discussing the complexities of time in theatre. One is the general memory of the spectators, of which the memory of the performance is only a part. The latter is, of course, essential to the proper perception and understanding of the work. One of the characteristic features of the 'memory of the performance' is that it is confined in time, it has a marked beginning and a marked ending. It is the memory of an artistic structure, which marks its separateness from the non-structured memory of our lives (of which it becomes part). Our memory, although 'edited', consciously or not, is not structured as an artistic work. Its particular components do not create mutual relations with all others. In theatre (in artistic texts in general), all components enter into closer or more distant relations with each other. One may also add that the spectators' memory naturally differs from the implied memory of the stage figures, for the figures, with rare exceptions of experimental works, are not presented as perceiving and memorizing the world around them as an artistic structure, with restricted time limits. Thus, the temporal structures employed reveal the conventionality of even those productions that pretend to be 'real life'.

It is significant that both of the present times – while appearing in the present time of the audience – belong to different streams of different nature and physical characteristics. The fictional time does not flow with the same pace as the real one, it is flexible, may be stretched or slowed down, may accelerate or be suspended, as, for instance, in 'freeze' scenes. The latter imply that although the actors are alive, the fictional time stops completely, at least for those figures whose actors freeze; those who do not, continue in a time gap, delivering, say, a soliloquy. Consequently, we understand that the utterance or behaviour (dance) occur in fictional timelessness. Time may even go backward, as in Irene Brook's *Tempest* (2010): in one of the scenes, Ariel wants to discover the plotting of Trinculo, Caliban and Stephano, which the audience had already seen. All of a sudden, he starts to move back in circles, waving his arms backwards, until he reaches a point in time when he reproduces, with mime gestures, the scenes involving the three plotters. The spectators recognize the meaning of the gestures, because they had already seen them in an earlier scene. Time may leak out between the scenes, as in Shakespeare's *The Winter's Tale*, where there is a gap of 16 years between Acts 3 and 4, which gives 'my scene such growing/As [if] you had slept between' (4.1.16–17). In *Titus Andronicus,* the lascivious Empress Tamora conceives in Act 2 and gives birth in Act 5, which, in performance time, means roughly two or three hours. In *Romeo and Juliet*, the ball at the Capulets begins at Act 1, scene 5, line 14 and ends at line 144: even if we include dances, this cannot take more than ten minutes of scenic time, but at least two or three hours is supposed to have passed. The flexibility of fictional time in theatre explains why within 'two hours traffic' we can have a whole life or generation presented on the stage, a scene lasting five minutes may be equivalent to five hours, and a three-day battle will be shown in three minutes of scenic time. That feature alone, which rests on the ability to model the fictional time, is the essential rule of the theatre, and it explains why the mimed performance of 'play-within-a-play' scenes, lasting, say, two minutes of 'our' time, becomes a sign of a performance at the Royal Court, lasting, say, an hour.[11] A hunting scene played out in a dance arrangement on the stage will take, say, three minutes, whereas it will be a sign of a day-long event.[12]

However, no matter what the time's pace is, it is always presented as our, the spectators', present. Time in theatre is not a narrative of the time past. Since it evolves in the real present time of the performer and the audience, it cannot be presented as a montage (a characteristic of cinematic narratives) of the time of the presentation. The present cannot be edited; if whatever is presented within one scene is a montage of temporal units, it has, by definition, to refer to the past, not to the present. It becomes a narrative, not a piece of theatrical presentation. This is why a film cannot pretend to be taking place in the present time of the screening, whereas in theatre, this is exactly what is happening. And even though one cannot employ a temporal ellipsis in the natural flow of the present, one can do that within the fictional time stream. To make things even more complicated, sometimes we may notice the presence of several different time streams operating on the stage, involving different figures, who, as a result, cannot see each other although they are present in the same space (as, for instance, in Tom Stoppard's *Arcadia*).[13] This means that we can have more than two present times presented on the stage simultaneously, the 'real' one (of the actors and spectators) and two or more fictional times that flow on the stage parallel to each other.

One cannot omit the use of media on the stage, which has become fashionable in the past 30 years. When stage directors decide to use the new media, what is introduced on to the stage is not only new technologies but also new geometries and temporal dimensions. The emergence of a different dimension and time is not the only consequence of using the televisual or cinematic (computer, digital etc.) media on theatre stage; another is the formation of a different, precisely delineated *point of view*, as well as the appearance of a new *way of seeing*. In traditional theatre, even if we are dealing with geometrical perspective, the point of view of the external creator of the stage picture is usually concealed. Theatre creates the impression that it is happening by itself, in our very own present. It does not want to be read as somebody else's creation, implying the existence of a pre-given way of seeing or point of view. Masking its subjectivity, theatre wants to be perceived as part of objective reality, without, however, attempting to achieve complete illusion (it constantly stresses its conventional character and material inadequacy). What is more, it gives the audience considerable freedom to 'frame' the stage picture by focusing on different parts of their own choice.[14]

Thus, the split present time, marking at least two different time streams flowing on the stage, has a fundamental impact on everything that appears on the stage. For every object, every sound and word, every human body, light and music, movements and gestures, all become entangled in these two streams and two present times. Consequently, what becomes essential is the need and ability to signal the fictional figures' way of perceiving the phenomenal world of the stage that is strikingly different from what we, the spectators, see and hear, and the rudimentary technique of achieving that is through the signalled spatial and temporal distance separating the two worlds.[15] On the basis of that juxtaposition, we learn what the fictional world denoted by the stage signs is like, what are the rules that govern it, who are the inhabitants and what their problems are. In this way, we begin to read the stage as a sort of text that describes another world to us. At the same time, we begin to understand that the 'description' is not only verbal, but consists of material components, human bodies and objects, light and movement, the sequences and compositions of which are significant. As indicated, the meaning of theatre is not just the creation of a fictional realm, but its relationship to the phenomenological reality of the stage. This is why theatre as art is not possible without the temporal hiatus sepa-rating the actor and the figure, which is essential for the creation of at least two confronting models of perceiving reality.[16] And the juxtaposition of the different models of perceiving reality is the key rule by which meaning is generated in theatre, whether dramatic, non-dramatic or postdramatic.

Even the most complicated theatre phenomena may be explained and elucidated by the analysis of the time structures involved, as this chapter attempts to prove. Take language as an example. Usually, in theatre studies, it is treated as a staged literary language of the drama, i.e. a scenic articu-lation of a literary work, dressed, perhaps, in theatrical costume. However, that 'costume' is essential here, for as all the other systems of signification employed on the stage, language also loses some of its intrinsic systemic features and becomes something else altogether. This 'something else' is worth a book-length study, but in a brief chapter I will just mention that it seems that 'language' is not the right word to be used in reference to what is being articulated on the stage.[17] To begin with, at every moment of the performance, every word enters into relationships of varying degrees with every other word spoken until that moment and following that moment, with every word spoken by the same figure and other figures, even if they never appear together in the same scene (paradigmatic equivalencies are created irrespective of the figures' configurations). This is the result of the literary selection and arrangement of words, their modelling as a piece of drama. However, in theatre the situation and relationships become more complex, because every word enters into a variety of additional relation-ships with the signalling matter, human bodies, light, costume, objects, movement and so on.[18] It becomes inseparably merged with its immediate material context and, in this sense, becomes unique in each production, even if the same dramatic text is used. This means that in theatre we are not dealing with natural language,[19] and so we should perhaps distinguish *stage speech* from language. Stage speech has a complex substance, because it is not only an acoustic articulation of phonemes, but also incorporates, through spatial and temporal contiguity, various objects and phenomena that appear simultaneously with it. *One does not only listen to stage speech, one also watches it.*[20]

In other words, stage speech, being of composite substance and modelled differently in every production, becomes a sign of the natural language that the figures use, the language we cannot hear and which is only implied, and from other signals provided by actors we come to understand what the meaning of the utterances in that language denote in the fictional realm. What we, the spectators, perceive as stage speech in our time becomes a sign of the language as used and perceived by the stage figures in the fictional time. This explains, among other things, why different substances, differently modelled, may denote the same fictional objects, human beings, their utterances and behaviour within the fictional realm. But it does not mean that their meaning is the same, for, as I have already indicated, in theatre the ultimate meaning is generated by the relationship between the denotata and the substance and modelling of stage signs. The substance of the sign not only carries meaning, but also plays an important role in the aesthetics of the show, even if the discrepancy between the substance and its denoted object is noticeable to the spectators. The latter justifies the selection of materials (casting, for instance), their modelling and the rules by which the performance was given its unique shape. Thus, the employment of different time structures is essential to the creation of the complex networks of relationships between the fictional and the real, unique for the art of the theatre.

Time is also essential to our understanding of theatre as an artistic phenomenon. The pleasure of understanding is part of communication in theatre: the common language has been found. However, understanding does necessarily mean emotional engagement, or, generally, emotional reactions of the spectators to the physicality, utterances and behaviour of the actors impersonating fictional beings, the scenic figures. Recently, scientists have discovered 'mirror neurons' and their role in the ability of humans to access and experience the emotions and intentions of others by watching them act. The latter phenomenon is sometimes called 'simulation', which, in the theatre, possibly rests on the ability of embodied emotions to produce corresponding emotional states in spectators. It is therefore plausible that spectators unconsciously mirror the actions of the actors and the figures they impersonate. This means that they react to the latter not only with their senses, but also with their bodies.

So, not only a performance artist, but also an actor in a theatrical performance has the ability, on certain conditions, to activate peculiar responses in the spectator, so that they experience, at least partly, some of the feelings and emotions accompanying those of the stage figures' (as signalled by the actors). It seems that the condition for this phenomenon is that the actor does not distance themselves from the role, and aims at creating oneness. This, in turn, is possible only when the two present times merge, at least seem to merge in the mental perception of the spectator, which is not the case when the distancing techniques are introduced. The other option, as often shown in postmodern theatre and performance art, is that actors/performers do not identify themselves with the fictional being, and concentrate on their own presence, remaining themselves throughout the artistic event.[21] The reactions of the spectators to the acts of performers have often been described in terms of some energy, often labelled as 'magic', passing between the participants. This was hard to prove and remained a metaphor rather than a scientific statement. However, now, with the help of cognitivism and neuroscience, it might just be possible to describe the phenomenon in scientific and, hence, verifiable ways. Again, time seems to play a crucial role in activating mirror neurons, leading to simulation, empathy and/or identification. Let me repeat: it seems to me that the condition sine qua non in activating mirror neurons in theatre perception is the subjective coalescence of the two present times in the mind of the spectator. Only this allows the sensation of oneness between the actor, the fictional figure and the spectator, in the sense of the unity of time and space. Otherwise, the temporal discrepancy makes it impossible for the spectator to identify with whatever the actor is saying or doing: the distance is marked by a clear division of time and space. Naturally, the activation of mirror neurons can only be temporary, and may therefore be related to the play of temporal structures in the evolving spectacle/event.[22]

The examples provided in this chapter have shown that the most important issues concerning theatre may be explained by the time structures employed. Time is crucial in defining and establishing the boundary between theatre, life and other artistic forms. Time is essential for showing the ways in which meaning is created in theatre, the ways in which it is perceived and experienced, and also for explaining all sorts of conventions that the theatre has developed.[23] In other words, theatre can be defined in temporal terms, which makes any analysis verifiable and not just based on somebody's subjective opinion. The study of theatre may eventually become a science.

Notes

1   It is sufficient to look at Patrice Pavis's *Dictionary of Theatrical Terms* to see how difficult it is to grasp the essence of the phenomenon under discussion. For an intriguing discussion of the ways we perceive time, see Vyvyan Evans, *The Structure of Time: Language, Meaning and Temporal Cognition* (Amsterdam: John Benjamins, 2004). Cf. also the chapter on time in Jerzy Limon, *The Chemistry of the Theatre* (Basingstoke: Palgrave Macmillan, 2010).

2   In this chapter, I am dealing with theatre, understood as an art form distinct from literature. For this reason, I do not consider drama as theatre, but as a literary genre, which loses a number of its literary features when incorporated into a stage performance; in fact, it ceases to be a merely linguistic phenomenon.

3   The actor is a human being for whom theatre is a profession or hobby, whereas the figure is a creation of the former. In other words, the actor is both the co-creator and the material substance of a sign of a figure which is immaterial and basically a mental construct. We have to remember, however, that the figure much more than an actor is capable of creating on their own: the fictional figure is a synthesis of the various relationships between fictional and material and verbal substances of the performance, and it does not exist in the material sense, for it is being created in the mind of the spectator by other factors, such as other figures' utterances, behaviour, costume, make-up, light, music and so on. It has to be said that the new wave of so-called 'postdramatic' theatre often attempts to break the boundary dividing the actor and the figure; consequently, the temporal and spatial split or hiatus is annulled. That may, of course, be a temporary feature of a production, but in its dominating variety it undermines the basic qualities of theatre as art, which inevitably becomes another type of art, such as performance or happening. Cf. Hans-Thies Lehmann, *Postdramatic Theatre*, trans. Karen Jürs-Munby (New York: Routledge, 2006).

4   I have described the concept of the *fifth wall* in Jerzy Limon, *Piąty wymiar teatru* (Gdańsk: Wydawnictwo Słowo obraz/terytoria, 2006), and in two recent articles, 'Theatre's Fifth Dimension: Time and Fictionality', *Poetica*, 41.1/2 (2009), 33–54, and 'The Fifth Wall: Words of Silence in Shakespeare's Soliloquies and Asides', *Shakespeare Jahrbuch*, 144 (2008), 47–65.

5   Op. cit. Lehmann (2006).

6   The performance, treated as a work of art, may be seen as evolving present (it does not have its past or future: both categories refer to the fictional plot, and not the work itself, which is real in the phenomenological sense).

7   The seeming physical and empirical impossibility of duality of the present time in theatre is one of the basic conventions and rules of the art, and distinguishes theatre from other signifying systems. Thus, of the many systems and practices of human communication, theatre is unusual in its ability to create a fictional (and usually past) reality as if occurring in the here and now of the performers and spectators. In other words, theatre principally creates a time gap between the fictional figure, the actor and the spectator, which consequently leads to their potential of creating fictional worlds. Without the time gap, no theatre is possible, although the rule is frequently violated through conventions and games with the audience.

8 In plain terms, the actors agree to behave and speak strangely and pretend that they are someone else somewhere else and at a different time (so, logically and consequently, they can neither see nor hear nor address the spectators), the spectators agree to treat this strange behaviour as an act of communication. In theatre, we understand that someone who is not usually present on the stage (the author and the director) is trying to communicate something to us, and for that purpose is using objects, human bodies, light, music and verbal utterances as the substance of their 'writing' (their communiqué).

9 In today's theatre practice, especially in so-called 'postdramatic' theatre, there is a tendency to abolish the conspicuous markers of the theatrical performance, so that the spectator remains uncertain as to what exactly they are experiencing. Cf. Lehmann (2006), op. cit.

10 For an intriguing discussion of theatricality, see Eli Rozik, 'Is the Notion of "Theatricality" Void?', *Gestos*, 15.30 (2000), 11–30 and 'Acting: The Quintessence of Theatricality', *SubStance*, 31.2 & 3 (2002), 110–24; cf. Samuel Weber, *Theatricality as Medium* (New York: Fordham University Press, 2004).

11 See Jerzy Limon, 'The Play-Within-The-Play: A Theoretical Perspective', in Jerzy Sobieraj and Dariusz Pestka, eds, *Enjoying the Spectacle: Word, Image, Gesture* (Toruń, Wydawnictwo Naukowe Uniwersytetu Mikolaja Kopernika, 2006), 17–32.

12 This same hunting could take place off the stage in a short break between scenes, then the saving of time will be even greater. From the dialogue that follows it could transpire that it lasted two or three or nine hours. This would mean that we are dealing with two distinct streams of time, the one operating on the stage, and the one off-stage.

13 Cf. Jerzy Limon, 'Waltzing in Arcadia', *New Theatre Quarterly*, 24.3 (2008), 222–8.

14 Directors can at most hint at what is important in a given moment, foregrounding the relationships crucial for the proper perception and understanding of the piece. For this to happen, they use actors, whose ostensive actions and utterances should be properly planned, as well as all the available scenic instrumentation and technology, including lighting, music, trapdoors, etc. Nevertheless, there will always be limits to the director's control of the audience's attention: the spectators usually tend to think that they themselves are the ones responsible for choosing what to focus on and what to neglect. And that conviction has an influence on the mode of perception of the theatre.

15 It is the actors who signal to us the way in which figures perceive the world. The figures do not see or hear anything on the stage, not even the actors who impersonate them. So, the true juxtaposition is between what the actors signal to us, being a sign of the figures' utterances and behaviour, and what we perceive as factual and real.

16 In the history of theatre and drama, we can find numerous examples of playwrights and directors playing with the rules and conventions of theatre, balancing on the boundaries separating theatre from non-theatre. Indeed, in many postmodern productions, the boundaries seem blurred, although I think it is still possible to distinguish theatre from other artistic systems by its unique use of temporal structures. At the same time, we are witnessing the appearance of a wave of performances that turn theatre into something comparable to movable installations, with conspicuous elements of body-art, multimedia, dance, perfor-

mance art and the like. This may lead to the appearance of new art forms that do not necessarily have to be labelled 'theatre'. This is too broad a topic for a detailed discussion here.

17 Cf. Limon (2010), op. cit.

18 See Eli Rozik, 'The Functions of Language in the Theatre', *Theatre Research International*, 18.2 (1993), 104–14.

19 Of course, the language used by the actors is not natural, because it has already been modelled by the rules of drama. However, the implication is that fictional figures, who are not engaged in staging anything, use natural language. This is why the verse speech of Elizabethan plays becomes the prose of the denoted figures.

20 A simple experiment will prove this point: when in the theatre, close your eyes and see if this does not make any difference to the perception and understanding of whatever is occurring on the stage.

21 Cf. Lehmann (2006), op. cit.

22 It is not enough to say that activated mirror neurons simulate the experience of corresponding states of emotions in spectators: according to the theory, this happens outside theatre, on occasions that do not have to be artistic at all. But, to my knowledge, neuroscience has not yet explained the unique experience of artistic texts and of theatre in particular, as opposed to the non-artistic ones. It has not explained the phenomenon of simulation when the observed object is fictional, as is the case in the theatre: naturally, we see the actor at work, but we experience the enacted person's emotions and feelings, not the actor's handling of the role, nor their technical skill, nor their emotions (of which we, the spectators, know practically nothing).

23 Cf. Limon (2006), op. cit.

25   Empathetic Engagement

Bruce McConachie

From the perspective of current cognitive science, empathy is generally defined as mind reading – the attempt by one person to understand the intentions, emotions and beliefs of another. Rooted in our evolutionary heritage as social animals, empathy helped our evolving species to survive and flourish by facilitating social cooperation and cohesion. Empathy is ubiquitous and commonplace; we engage in empathy hundreds of times every day. When we glance at the moving body of someone walking toward us to figure out if that person intends to pass us on the right or the left, we use empathy to do it. When we try to understand what a voice on a cell phone really meant by a particular tone and inflection, empathy is involved. Empathy works in our imaginations, as well; planning what you will say to a loved one and imagining their facial reaction is an exercise in empathy. As these examples suggest, the cognitive processes of empathy are mostly unconscious, although humans can (and do) educate themselves to improve their empathetic attunement.

Further, these examples underline the necessity of empathy for performance and performance scholarship. Without our evolved ability to engage in empathy, actors could not coordinate their performances and spectators would have little incentive to watch them, much less attempt to figure out what the actors were doing. Empathy also facilitates our ability as critics and historians to write about performances. Imagine an audience of intelligent lizards at a human performance of *Hamlet* who can understand Elizabethan English and critique it after the show. Lacking empathy, however, they would have no interest in the fate of the prince of Denmark and no reason to write about it later.

The contemporary scientific understanding of empathy differs significantly from most historical meanings of the term. Despite its etymology – *empatheia* means 'passion' in Greek – the current meaning of the term derives from a translation of the German word, *Einfühlung*. Nineteenth-century German romantics used the word and its cognates to mean the ability of individuals to project themselves into the situation of another person or into nature. How might a poet temporarily merge his identity with a famous Renaissance figure or a painter come to feel what it is like to be a gnarled tree on a hilltop?

These were the kinds of imaginative problems that the romantics believed *Einfühlung* could help them to solve. From their point of view, this aesthetic notion of identification and mystical merging involved conscious projection and the temporary loss of the self in another object or person. German aesthetic theory continued to deploy this vague concept of *Einfühlung* into the 20th century, when some began to use it more specifically as a psychological term and the German phenomenologist Edith Stein discussed *Einfühlung* as a means of losing the self in a different reality. As the term gained greater intellectual legitimacy, translators struggled to find an English equivalent for the German word. E.B. Tichener first translated *Einfühlung* as 'empathy' in 1909 and some of its German romantic connotations came with it. By the 1930s, however, most English speakers were using 'empathy' primarily to mean sympathy, and the romantic denotation of the word as mystical identification slipped into secondary meaning. Even today, if someone says, 'I empathize with you', they usually mean, 'I understand your situation and feel your pain.'

The derivation of 'empathy' from the German and its overlapping meanings in English have created multiple confusions in aesthetic and psychological discourse. In particular, English interpreters of Bertolt Brecht's epic theatre in the 1950s struggled to understand how the Marxist writer-director could be opposed to empathy. While most Anglo-American critics of Brecht connected empathy with sympathy, it is clear that Brecht's primary problem with *Einfühlung* in the theatre was the loss of agency among spectators that the romantic conception of the term entailed. Rejecting the loss of the self in another person or object as a recipe for spectator passivity, instead Brecht hoped to awaken his audiences to a rational understanding of the contradictions of capitalism and spark a socialist response. From his point of view, *Einfühlung* would 'wear down the capacity for action' in his auditors (Brecht 1964a: 37). Under the spell of *Einfühlung*, warned Brecht, 'nobody will learn any lessons' (Brecht 1964b: 26). Drawing on the German romantic understanding of *Einfühlung*, Brecht believed that empathy began as a conscious aesthetic choice and that spectators would turn away from empathetic engagement if induced to enjoy performances in other ways.

No current scientific definition of empathy assumes that spectators (or anybody else) can control empathetic engagement in this way. Nor do most definitions suggest that empathy involves a loss of agency and the mystical merging of the self with some Other. This is not to say, however, that cognitive scientists agree on a definition of empathy. In a 2009 survey of contemporary uses of the term, C. Daniel Batson singles out eight related but distinct understandings of empathy. Finding that researchers generally use 'empathy' to provide an answer to two very different questions,

Batson separates these definitions into two groups. Two of the eight link empathy to sympathy and, says Batson (2009: 3), attempt to determine 'what leads one person to respond with sensitivity and care to the suffering of another?' Most definitions, however, are responses to how one person can 'know what another person is thinking and feeling' (ibid.: 3). Within this predominant range of definitions dealing with empathy as mind reading, observers have noted two major approaches, which tend to emphasize different, though related aspects of the cognitive process. Neuropsychologist Simone G. Shamay-Tsoory (2009: 215–16) calls these 'cognitive' and 'affective' empathy and discusses the different research traditions and agendas that have informed them. As we will see, both kinds of empathy shape the creation of and the response to performance in significant ways.

Shamay-Tsoory notes that cognitive empathy is generally understood as perspective-taking. That is, the person engaged in empathy attempts to adopt the thoughts and feelings of another person in order to predict their future behavior. In the third act of Chekhov's *Uncle Vanya*, for example, Helena proposes to Sonya that she question Astrov about his possible affection for her. Sonya has watched the doctor over the course of the summer and knows that he is attracted to Helena, but does not know Helena's intentions towards him. Before allowing Helena to speak to Astrov on her behalf, Sonya tries to read Helena's thoughts and feelings about the doctor, but her own desperation for Astrov leads her to place her fate in Helena's hands before she can be sure of the other woman's motives and goals. In part, this is because Helena refuses to face up to her own desire for Astrov and adopts an attitude of sisterly helpfulness toward Sonya. Consequently, the scene between them is supercharged with perspective-taking, as each woman metaphorically puts herself into the shoes of the other in an attempt to figure out what the other person wants and intends to do. This presents some challenges for the actors and director, who must work carefully to determine each character's moment-to-moment relationships and intentions and whether they will choose to reveal or hide their face from the gaze of the other. Because this scene sets up the next one, when Astrov accuses Helena of hypocritically pleading for Sonya to signal her own desire for him, the actor playing Helena must make a complex interpretative choice. To what extent and when is Helena aware that she may be acting hypocritically towards Sonya? And, if there is such a moment, does Helena take Sonya's perspective in an attempt to discover if Sonya sees through her double-dealing? Then, what happens if and when Helena sees that Sonya sees that she may be a hypocrite? Although Chekhov's dialogue primarily encourages the spectators to focus on Helena's attempt at friendship and Sonya's desperate hope, an attentive audience will also be aware that each character is watching and empathizing with the other as they try to read each other's minds. The scene challenges audiences to do their own perspective-taking as well – to nimbly switch between the two actor/characters and attempt to adopt the perspective of each one in succession. The dramatic and psychological entanglements of this kind of theatre would be impossible for humans if evolution had never granted us the ability to process cognitive empathy.

Many psychologists researching the perspective-taking of cognitive empathy advocate a 'theory of mind' (ToM) approach to these cognitive dynamics. ToM research began in 1978, when two psychologists tested chimpanzees to discover if one chimp believed that other primates had minds like its own, that is, if chimps had a 'theory' about other chimp minds, and, if so, might engage in reading the minds of other primates to understand their beliefs and motives. Soon after they discovered that chimpanzees can readily process some low-level tasks through perspective-taking, psychologists began testing humans for the same abilities. Subsequent research has confirmed that humans use cognitive empathy all the time and we are much better at it than other primates; in fact, we cannot stop ourselves from reading others' minds in our ongoing attempts to orient ourselves within immediate social relationships. In this sense, however, the 'theory' part of ToM is misleading. Cognitive empathy is largely unconscious and proactive; humans and other animals do not consciously adopt some kind of 'theory' and then mentally apply it to others. It is also clear from the research that our imaginations are often busily engaged in ToM mind reading. Even when away from other people, we are trying to take their perspective to figure out their beliefs and feelings in our own mind's eye. This has led to the widespread application of ToM research to the process of writing fiction and the kinds of enjoyment readers take from fiction when they imagine characters' interactions, inner monologues and first-person points of view.

In contrast, affective empathy, as the name suggests, links the empathizer to the other through bodily emotion and movement. A series of experiments since the 1970s has validated and underlined the importance of affective empathy for social interaction. Researchers following this approach, also known as 'empathetic simulation', emphasize the embodied rather than the mental side of empathy. Simulation involves a kind of mimesis; the empathizer perceives and unconsciously embodies the emotional behavior of the target person at the neurological level. Perceiving the facial expression, muscle tension and physical posture of anger in another, for example, the empathizers will begin to feel anger in themselves. Alternatively, spectators watching a happy actor/character in performance will experience a degree of that happiness themselves. The operation of affective empathy is highly automatic and may result in 'emotional contagion'. When the home team scores a goal in ice hockey or soccer and fans immediately jump to their feet to cheer, their excitement usually results more from the 'contagious' emotions of the fans around them than from the goal itself. 'Entrainment' is an extreme form of emotional contagion, as when the driving rhythm of a rock band locks in motor and emotional responses among their rapt listeners. As these examples suggest, scholars in sports and music have often turned to the research in affective empathy to understand audience response to those kinds of performances. And, like cognitive empathy, a fictitious or imagined emotion in another can produce an emotion in the empathizer. Imagining the emotions experienced by their character will help actors to embody them themselves.

Most performances involve cognitive as well as affective empathy, for performers and spectators. Tennis players, for example, will often try to adopt the cognitive perspective of their opponents in an attempt to gain advantage during a point. Just as frequently, in an exchange of affective empathy, one player will pick up the intensity, frustration or joy of another in the midst of play. Players at the professional level often seek to entrain their competitors in a rhythmic exchange of volleys that may be to their advantage or, in an abrupt change of pace, 'stop the train' by slipping in a drop shot when their opponent is far behind the baseline. Perhaps because I am a tennis player, I usually watch the Wimbledon or US Open matches with avid concentration. In retrospect, I can sometimes tell when my response has switched from affective to cognitive empathy (or vice versa), but, for the most part, I jump freely between both. Or, more to the point, my mind and body unconsciously move me from one to the other as easily as Rafael Nadal executes a winning passing shot from a seemingly impossible position. Even players and spectators who know a performance genre well will not usually interrupt its flow to bring their empathetic engagement to the level of consciousness.

Because cognitive and affective empathy are genetically based, some people are more engaged by perspective-taking and individual emotions than others. At one extreme are socially attuned individuals very sensitive to what they take to be the thoughts and feelings of others. At the other are individuals who suffer from a degree of autistic impairment, from mild Asperger's syndrome to extreme forms of asocial isolation. According to neuropsychologist Simon Baron-Cohen (1995: 60), the symptoms of autism, 'lack of the usual [social] flexibility, imagination, and pretense', are apparent in children at around two years of age. Autistic children and adolescents have difficulty empathizing in cognitive and affective ways.

These impairments can be partly overcome; Temple Grandin's ability to educate herself in the expectations and feelings of others is a famous case in point. As an adolescent, however, Grandin was often at a loss in social situations and did not enjoy the imaginative engagements of fiction. For example, she told neuropsychologist Oliver Sacks (1995: 259–60) that she was 'bewildered by *Romeo and Juliet*' when she read it in school. 'I never knew what they were up to', she admitted. The research on autism and Grandin's case in particular suggest that empathetic engagement varies widely among people. Although some are more naturally adept than others at engaging in the mind reading that social interaction and performance entails, there are also ways of helping individuals toward more enriching forms of empathetic involvement.

Research into autism also implies that affective and cognitive empathy are related and probably derive from the same neurological and biological processes. The recent discovery of mirror neurons has given hope to those who are pushing for a unified theory of empathy. In brief, networks of neurons in our brains effectively 'mirror' intentional motor activity produced by another person and perceived by the empathizer. If one person watches another grasp a door handle, for example, the same group of neurons in the empathizer's brain is activated as in the grasper's brain; neurologically, it is as if the observer had grabbed the door handle. By working through our perceptions, bodies and minds, our networks of mirror neurons unconsciously attune us to each other. Neurobiologist and phenomenologist Evan Thompson (2007: 393–5) calls this process 'sensorimotor coupling' and understands it as the foundation of empathetic engagement. Thompson draws on the work of Vittorio Gallese et al. (2004: 5), one of the first scientists to investigate mirror neurons in monkeys, whose subsequent experiments validate the mirror neuron system in primates as 'the basis of social cognition'. From Thompson's perspective, mirroring puts humans in tune with each other and results in many of the unconscious affective links that are usually explored as a part of affective empathy, such as emotional contagion.

For Thompson, the sensorimotor coupling resulting from mutual mirroring may lead to a second, more complex form of empathy, which Thompson (2007: 395) terms 'imaginary transposition'. As the name suggests, imaginary transposition allows empathizers to attempt to place themselves into the mind of another; it is similar in most ways to what other psychologists mean by perspective-taking. To link sensorimotor coupling to imaginary transposition, Thompson draws on recent evidence about child development. Soon after they are born, infants are driven to mirror the intentional facial expressions of their caregivers and mutual mirroring continues between infants and mothers throughout early childhood (and much longer, in most cases). By nine to twelve months, the normal toddler can use other cognitive skills, plus the knowledge and memory that the child has gained from mirroring, to engage in imaginary transposition. This involves the toddler's recognition that other humans are intentional agents 'like me'. In this way, developing children can put themselves into the mind of a nearby adult and, later, even imagine what an adult may be thinking, feeling and intending when that person is absent.

Thompson's imaginary transposition helps to explain the common, though often unacknowledged use of empathetic engagement in performance criticism and history. Critics deploy Thompson's second level of empathy when they question the intentions and decisions of performers – from the latest blog on a new performance artist to the 'Monday morning quarterbacking' on a televised sports show. In performance history, historians may struggle to collect enough evidence to enable them to imaginatively reconstruct Garrick's Hamlet or Sophie Tucker's initial performance of 'Some of These Days'. A detailed, imagined reconstruction of past performance events is rarely the end product of such a history, of course, but if our understandings of performances are to be grounded in the intentional and embodied actions of artists, athletes and other performers, we must use empathy near the start of our historical investigations.

Works cited

Baron-Cohen, Simon. *Mindblindness: An Essay on Autism and Theory of Mind.* Cambridge, MA: MIT Press, 1995.

Batson, C. Daniel. 'These Things Called Empathy: Eight Related but Distinct Phenomena.' In Jean Decety and William Ickes, eds, *The Social Neuroscience of Empathy*. Cambridge, MA: MIT Press, 2009, 3–16.

Brecht, Bertolt. 'The Modern Theatre is the Epic Theatre.' In John Willet, ed. and trans., *Brecht on Theatre: The Development of an Aesthetic*. New York: Hill & Wang, 1964a, 33–42.

Brecht, Bertolt. 'A Dialogue About Acting.' In John Willet, ed. and trans., *Brecht on Theatre: The Development of an Aesthetic*. New York: Hill & Wang, 1964b, 26–9.

Gallese, Vittorio, Keysers, Christian and Rizzolatti, Giacomo. 'A Unifying View of the Basis of Social Cognition.' *Trends in Cognitive Sciences* 8 (2004): 1–8.

Sacks, Oliver. *An Anthropologist on Mars*. New York: Alfred A. Knopf, 1995.

Shamay-Tsoory, Simone G. 'Empathic Processing: Its Cognitive and Affective Dimensions and Neuroanatomical Basis.' In Jean Decety and William Ickes, eds, *The Social Neuroscience of Empathy*. Cambridge, MA: MIT Press, 2009, 215–32.

Thompson, Evan. *Mind in Life: Biology, Phenomenology, and the Sciences of Mind.* Cambridge, MA: Harvard University Press, 2007.

26   Theories of Festival[1]

Christina S. McMahon

If festivals are notoriously undertheorized in the fields of theatre and performance studies, it is likely because they are near impossible to theorize. What are the aggregate ideas that could link together the cacophonous strains of steel band competitions in Trinidad's vibrant Carnival season, the solemn air of a Japanese *matsuri*, and the trained silence of a Western audience paying premium prices to attend theatre at Scotland's Edinburgh International Festival?

Given the unwieldiness of the festival genre,[2] I have narrowed my focus here to international theatre and arts festivals, or what I call 'stage festivals'. I tend to other kinds of festivals – street, community and folk – where their conceptual paradigms overlap with stage festivals. While the 'stage' and 'street' festival separation may seem false, given their inherent intersections, I draw from Edouard Glissant's distinction of theatre from 'street scenes', or the folkloric performances, such as Carnival, that dominated the topography of his native Martinique. Glissant (1992: 200) asserted that incorporating folklore into staged theatre raised it to a new level of consciousness, prompting audiences to think critically about the street performances that shaped their cultural norms. By extension, we might think of performances on festival stages as twice subject to scrutiny: once by virtue of being placed onstage (Glissant 1992), and again by their insertion in an overarching festival framework, which invites audiences to draw comparisons and contrasts across the spectrum of events a festival encompasses (Schoenmakers 2007: 33).

To illuminate how stage festivals may heighten the reflexivity that theatre already demands of artists and spectators, I examine their performance dimensions in terms of *affect*, *schema* and *artist–spectator dynamics*.

Affect

Mood is seemingly indispensable to theories of festival. Writing about medieval carnivals, Bakhtin (1984: 238) described the metamorphosis of 'ordinary time' into 'merry' time. In stage festivals, this infectious celebratory mood can impact viewing practices. Fricker (2003: 82) asserts that local audiences experience local productions differently within the international theatre festival framework, since 'there will be a heightened atmosphere, that "extra something" that makes festival-time special'. In street festivals, 'joyous' time may be etched into a city's geography via banners, parade routes and food kiosks, as Cadaval (1998: 200) notes of a yearly Latino festival in Washington, DC. Yet this same festival also exposed political tensions among the diverse Latino nationalities represented.

The polemics that often erupt at festival events compel us to re-evaluate the primacy of celebration in theories of festivals. While festivals' impetus may be a utopian desire to unify a participating community, they also leave behind what I call 'aftermath' (McMahon 2014). This refers to the cultural tensions that arise in festivals' wake, such as new questions about collective identities or the artistic vexations that often accompany intercultural collaborations. Significantly, festival aftermath exceeds the 'here-and-now' moment privileged in recent festival theories,[3] since it may crop up in the vibrant afterlives that festivals generate in their communities: the verbal sparring of bloggers, reverberation of festival events in the media, or gossip among theatre artists. My own research into Portuguese-language theatre festivals suggests that participants may express sentiments of belonging to a transnational Lusophone community while they are among other artists at festival events. Yet in subsequent dialogue among friends in their hotel rooms or in their reports to colleagues back home, those same participants may protest the feelings of linguistic unity the festival enforced. Put simply, festival aftermath may directly counter the affective move towards unity and celebration that festivals cite as their raison d'être.

While some theorists correlate a festival's size and eminence to the level of tension it provokes about politics and control,[4] more pertinent seems to be organizers' strategies for cultivating group identities. Sauter (2007: 20) argues that a group identity or 'feeling' emerges when people begin to recognize each other as festival participants, which can be facilitated by a festival's 'density', or the 'location, duration and frequency of festival events'. An example is the Cape Verde Islands' Mindelact International Theatre Festival, which, according to many of my interviewees, fosters *convivência* (close contact) because of its minute structure: there is only one main stage performance per night, which permits all participants to see the whole festival program, and they all take place within the same small theatre venue, the 250-seater Cultural Center in Mindelo. Yet that kind of familiarity could also induce a 'too close for comfort' dynamic, which can become manifest in contentious dialogues about aesthetic differences and festival selection processes that may stretch across multiple years of a festival's existence.[5]

Lastly, it is crucial to address the relationship between affect and place within festival contexts. Holledge and Tompkins (2000: 154) note that what is specifically celebrated at international arts festivals is the cultural heritage of the host country,[6] which is often 'defined by national borders and/ or ethnic categories'. Thus, festivals can perilously 'celebrate' the ethnic exclusions that border politics and de facto racial segregation enacted in a nation space. Since participants have an unspoken prerogative to 'play' and 'improvise' at festivals,[7] it is possible for individual voices to subvert the ideological import clouding a festival's celebratory sheen. Yet, if such performance protests do not extend beyond a festival's temporal framework, they may leave exclusionary practices in place after its conclusion. Thus, any theorization of international festivals as 'global' performance events must also account for the restrictive national politics tempering their seemingly cheery, cosmopolitan air.

Schema

Perhaps the sheer magnitude of most international festivals mandates that their sense of 'joyousness' be eclipsed by that infamous killjoy, administration.[8] This was Adorno's stance in the 1940s, when he called European arts festivals prime examples of the 'culture industry', an insidious machine allowing managers and institutional affiliations to siphon the vitality from artistic expression (1991: 118). Meant to contrast the devastation of World War II with the promise of peaceful exchange among European artists (Harvie 2003: 14), events such as the Edinburgh International Festival were, in practice, chiefly driven by tourism (Knowles 2004: 181), one of the cogs in the wheel of Adorno's culture industry. How, then, might a festival's objectives be met or compromised by its *schema*? By this I mean administration, format, programming, funding, publicity and venue. Here, I focus mainly on issues of marketing and finance.

Elements of a festival's schema are meant to fit into a cohesive whole, which is often reflected in a theme or overarching title. Yet, as Hauptfleisch (2007: 42) attests, festivals comprise 'an uneasy composite of (potentially) competing activities' that may undermine the very notion of a festival's 'conceptual unity'. An example is Ghana's PANAFEST (Pan African Historical Theatre Festival), held every two years, which, despite its label, subordinates performance to meetings and ceremonies designed to draw visiting Diasporans into an 'African family' of Ghanaian communities (Campana 2003: 51). Yet, if PANAFEST's format is meant to unify Africans and Diasporans, its programming privileges wealthy Diasporans to the exclusion of local Ghanaians, who were actively omitted from a wreath-laying trip to a reverential garden at former slaves' tombs in 2009 (Adrover et al. 2010: 162). In this case, the specter of state funding for the 2009 festival, which came largely from Ghana's Ministry of Tourism and Diasporan Relations, created a social hierarchy that countered the egalitarian notions of family PANAFEST is meant to promote.

Funding has been central to theories of stage festivals in recent years, particularly since festivals' schemas are increasingly driven by the demands of a global arts market. Holledge and Tompkins (2000: 157) argue that arts festivals' dependency on government support and corporate sponsorship (in light of sparse ticket revenues) may lead them to 'isolate, frame, translate, and market culture as exoticized difference'. Female artists may be particularly impacted, since they may cede control over their own representation in the midst of a male-controlled festival market (ibid.: 152). From this vantage point, prospects seem bleak for individual artists to craft performances potent enough to spill out of a festival's predetermined marketing framework.

If this is so, we should take seriously Maurin's (2003: 11) concern that contemporary stage festivals privilege performances with mass appeal on festival circuits over genuine artistic innovation. What, then, does 'circulatable' theatre look like? Writing on the annual Singapore Arts Festival, Peterson (2009: 111) describes recent Singaporean productions as 'slick, glossy, and easily transferable across cultural and geographic boundaries', since troupes favored visual appeal and international themes over a 'rootedness' in lived Singaporean experiences. Peterson (2009: 122) attributes this partly to the festival's strategic alliances with other international festivals in Asia, Europe and Australia, which gave young Singaporean artists a glimpse of the kinds of visually stunning productions that traversed these festival routes. Calling such productions devoid of substantial content, Peterson (2009: 114) describes highly circulatable theatre as 'the globalization of nothing'.

If a globalized economy dictates that circulation is now the critical lens through which we must view cultural products (Gaonkar and Povinelli 2003), then performance studies scholars must conceive of methods for analyzing festival productions that account for circulation. My first proposal is that we push beyond lamenting how circulation may erode theatre's local specificity, which seems inevitable, given the prominence of stage festivals worldwide, and devote more analysis to the capitalist forces that now shape, for better or worse, the form that performance takes on festival circuits. Apter's (2005: 15) work on Nigeria's 1977 FESTAC (Second World Black and African Festival of Arts and Culture) is a good example, since he correlates FESTAC's grandiose spectacles – including colossal royal durbars for chiefs and elaborately staged regattas of war canoes – with a culture of conspicuous consumption and excessive government spending that Nigeria's oil boom ushered in. How, then, are current economic trends related to speculative capital, free trade and international regulatory bodies, such as the IMF and World Bank, sculpting the shape theatre takes on contemporary festival circuits?[9]

My second proposal is that we attend to alternative spaces in festival schemas wherein artists' protests against the festivals' larger hegemonic frames may leak out. We might also reconsider the potential for critical reflexivity in festival audiences' viewing practices. To this end, a closer look at the interfaces between artists and spectators within festival contexts becomes paramount.

Artist–spectator dynamics

Given the tendency of festivals to decontextualize, and then *recontextualize*, local performance, how may participants retain control over art presented for a festival public? Writing on folk festivals, Bauman and Sawin (1991: 289) explain that festival producers craft broader ideological fields for performances when they reframe artists' work in ways that are palatable to audiences. Yet they argue that folk performers often resist this repackaging of their work by asking questions back to festival presenters or making sly jokes to indicate their own collusion in constructing a false sense of 'authenticity', such as 'I have to stop lying to these folklorists' (1991: 304–5).

Is this same license available to participants in stage festivals? When productions hop on and off festival circuits, decontextualization may become a survival mechanism that allows theatre to travel. Knowles (2004: 189–92), however, proposes that a festival production's interventionist potential may be aided either by formalist devices such as meta-theatre (versus bland aestheticism), or unconventional performance venues, such as a city block or storefront window (versus a proscenium stage).

When a festival is situated within an embattled political context, such as apartheid era South Africa, the stakes for performers to enact social interventions are higher. South Africa's premiere theatre event, Grahamstown's National Arts Festival (NAF), saw a variety of protests in the 1980s for its privileging of European-derived arts forms over black African theatre. As Grundy (1993) notes, even after the festival began admitting black community groups performing politically charged plays, they were often relegated to the Fringe, which was not subsidized by the festival's two main sponsors, Standard Bank and the 1820 Settlers Foundation. Thus, the politics of funding, which itself represented deep racial divides in the country, allowed the festival to hold subversive theatre at arm's length while retaining ideological control over the main stage's content. About this impasse, one playwright advised political performers to stop staging protests and focus instead on developing theatre that could make these statements for them (Grundy 1993: 53–4). However, the apartheid logic informing the structure of the NAF could have defused any political statements artists made onstage. It is thus critical to investigate how individual performers might 'disidentify' with a festival's ideological underpinnings. Artists practising 'disidentification', as Muñoz (1999: 11) theorizes it, would have to work *within* the festival's cultural logic in order to transform it. For this to succeed, audiences would presumably have to recognize the production as a disidentification.

This brings me back to the question of audience reflexivity in festival settings. Given the unrelenting forces of the arts market and festivals' decontextualization of performance, it seems there are overwhelming odds against spectators' ability to appraise festival productions with a critical and informed eye. Can festivals truly render theatre productions 'twice subject to scrutiny', as I have suggested? I propose there are at least two kinds of spectators who can do this. The first is Schoenmakers' (2007: 30) 'festival participant', spectators who witness not one or two isolated performances but immerse themselves in the festival's program and understand its conceptual thrust. They are thus able to evaluate productions against each other and the festival's overall theme, critically assessing how events fit together as a whole. A 'festival participant' may be likened to a passerby in a street festival who opts to join in the procession and experience the event corporally. Stage festivals, however, introduce class barriers to spectatorship, since ticket prices are often targeted to the middle class and above.

There is another kind of audience member who blurs the lines between festival viewer and participant: the artist–spectator. In smaller-scale stage festivals, such as the ones I have studied in Brazil, Cape Verde and Mozambique, visiting artists do not simply perform and then hop to the next stop on the festival circuit. Rather, they may remain in residence for the festival's duration, often sharing common hotels and restaurants with other festival performers. Thus, they shift in and out of the roles of artist and spectator, performing on designated days and attending peers' productions on other days. The success of a Lusophone theatre festival may hinge upon *how much* these roles are combined. I have heard artists complain that when a festival's programming is too 'busy', with performances scheduled too close

239

together and spread out throughout the host city, it is difficult to attend productions outside one's own. Therefore, the artist–spectator thrives on what in Portuguese is called *intercâmbio*, or cultural exchange, within festival contexts, which only multiple experiences of spectatorship can feed. Since they have a personal stake in the festival's success, artist–spectators are optimally suited for critical reflexivity about its overall approach to performance and marketing, as well as individual production values and ideological nuances.

Conclusion: researching festivals

Since international arts and theatre festivals are inherently transnational, they are ideal venues for researchers to undertake what Marcus (1998) calls 'multi-sited ethnography', which situates local practices within the complex global vectors of finance, migration and sweeping ideological trends. Yet this same confusion of factors impacting festival frameworks may render holistic readings of festivals untenable, so that searching for a festival's overall 'meaning' may no longer be a viable option (Crespi-Vallbona and Richards 2007). If we must now divert our attention from meaning and redirect it toward circulation and its impact on cultural forms (Gaonkar and Povinelli 2003: 387), then performance scholars' mandate is to find viable ways to 'read' theatre in circulation that still honors local context. Ethnography is key here, since it helps us to investigate both the 'pre-lives' of festivals and their aftermath. By witnessing rehearsals with local troupes in the host country even before the festival begins, researchers can privilege 'place' and 'locality' within the festival mechanism. After a festival ends, researchers can then attend to its local and global resonances by tracking reception in community forums, the international press and blogs, following how festival productions transform as they move along festival circuits. In sum, contemporary theories of festivals may be enriched by ethnographers' abilities to weave local observations of performance into the tapestry of virtual reception sites that transnational media forces and cyberspace now offer.

Notes

1   I am indebted to Brian Granger, UC Santa Barbara Theater PhD graduate, who, as my research assistant, uncovered many of the articles I cite here on festivals.
2   John MacAloon (1984: 250) calls festivals 'megagenres' because of the wide variety of types the word encompasses (drama, religious, culinary, etc.), while Henri

Schoenmakers (2007: 28) uses the term 'meta-event' to denote the fact that festivals themselves comprise a multitude of individual happenings, such as staged performances, roundtable debates and workshops.

3 Both Cremona (2007) and Sauter (2007) emphasize the 'here-and-now' aspect of festival dynamics in their theoretical introductions to *Festivalising!*, and it is an underlying theme of many of the chapters in the book that examine individual case studies of festivals.

4 Writing about gargantuan folk festivals such as the annual Smithsonian Folklife Festival, Karp (1991: 284) notes that festivals purportedly celebrating diversity often result in 'disputatious performances'. See also Harvie (2003: 25) on how the Edinburgh International Festival garnered more criticism as it inflated in size and popularity.

5 See my analysis of one such dispute between a Portuguese and Cape Verdean director that occurred in the festival 'aftermath' surrounding Mindelact between 2003 and 2007 (McMahon 2009).

6 Indeed, two of the West's most renowned stage festivals, the Edinburgh International Festival and Canada's Stratford Festival, have faced harsh accusations of not being 'Scottish' or 'Canadian' enough (Harvie 2003: 13; Huffman 2003: 61).

7 Sauter (2007: 19–20) mentions the subversive possibilities of what he calls 'playing culture', or physical, non-literary theatrical expressions, at festivals, while Drewal (1992: 169–70) notes that within the context of a Nigerian festival, the Imewuro Annual Rally, Yoruba community members used improvisation to alter social conventions about who could perform Egungun masking.

8 See MacAloon (1984: 246) on the role of 'joyousness' in festivals.

9 Some promising examples from theatre studies are Peterson's (2009) analysis of the relationship between the Singapore Arts Festival and the economic forces that are making Singapore a global leader in high-tech production, as well as Knowles' (1995) analysis of the impact of free trade and multinationalism on Canada's Stratford Festival.

Works cited

Adorno, Theodor. 'Culture and Administration.' In J.M. Bernstein, ed., *The Culture Industry: Selected Essays on Mass Culture*. London: Routledge, 1991, 93–113.

Adrover, Lauren, Donkor, David A. and McMahon, Christina. 'The Ethics and Pragmatics of Making Heritage a Commodity: Ghana's PANAFEST 2009.' *TDR: The Drama Review* 54.2 (2010): 155–63.

Apter, Andrew. *The Pan-African Nation: Oil and the Spectacle of Culture in Nigeria*. Chicago: University of Chicago Press, 2005.

Bakhtin, Mikhail. *Rabelais and His World*, trans. Hélène Iswolsky. Bloomington: Indiana University Press, 1984.

Bauman, Richard and Sawin, Patricia. 'The Politics of Participation in Folklife Festivals.' In Ivan Karp and Steven D. Lavine, eds, *Exhibiting Cultures: The Poetics and Politics of Museum Display*. Washington: Smithsonian University Press, 1991, 288–314.

Cadaval, Olivia. *Creating a Latino Identity in the Nation's Capital*. New York: Garland Publishing, 1998.

Campana, François. 'The Africa of Festivals: Bringing People Together,' trans. Joel Anderson. *Contemporary Theatre Review* 13.4 (2003): 48–56.

Cremona, Vicki Ann. 'Introduction: The Festivalising Process.' In Temple Hauptfleisch et al., eds, *Festivalising! Theatrical Events, Politics and Culture*. New York: Rodopi, 2007, 5–13.

Crespi-Vallbona, Montserrat and Richards, Greg. 'The Meaning of Cultural Festivals: Stakeholder Perspectives in Catalunya.' *International Journal of Cultural Policy* 13.1 (2007): 103–22.

Drewal, Margaret Thompson. *Yoruba Ritual: Performers, Play, Agency*. Bloomington: Indiana University Press, 1992.

Fricker, Karen. 'Tourism, The Festival Marketplace and Robert Lepage's *The Seven Streams of the River Ota*.' *Contemporary Theatre Review* 13.4 (2003): 79–93.

Gaonkar, Dilip P. and Povinelli, Elizabeth A. 'Technologies of Public Forms: Circulation, Transfiguration, Recognition.' *Public Culture* 15.3 (2003): 385–97.

Glissant, Edouard. *Caribbean Discourse: Selected Essays*, trans. Michael Dash. Charlottesville: University Press of Virginia, 1992.

Grundy, Kenneth. *The Politics of the National Arts Festival*. Grahamstown: Rhodes University Press, 1993.

Harvie, Jen. 'Cultural Effects of the Edinburgh International Festival: Elitism, Identities, Industries.' *Contemporary Theatre Review* 13.4 (2003): 12–26.

Hauptfleisch, Temple. 'Festivals as Eventifying Systems.' In Temple Hauptfleisch et al., eds, *Festivalising! Theatrical Events, Politics and Culture*. New York: Rodopi, 2007, 39–47.

Hauptfleisch, Temple, Lev-Aladgem, Shulamith, Martin, Jacqueline, Sauter, Willmar and Schoenmakers, Henri, eds. *Festivalising! Theatrical Events, Politics and Culture*. New York: Rodopi, 2007.

Holledge, Julie and Tompkins, Joanne. *Women's Intercultural Performance*. New York: Routledge, 2000.

Huffman, Shawn. 'On and Off: A Tour of Theatre Festivals in Canada and the United States.' *Contemporary Theatre Review* 13.4 (2003): 57–65.

Karp, Ivan. 'Festivals.' In Ivan Karp and Steven D. Levine, eds, *Exhibiting Cultures: The Poetics and Politics of Museum Display*. Washington: Smithsonian University Press, 1991, 279–87.

Knowles, Ric. *Reading the Material Theatre*. Cambridge: CUP, 2004.

Knowles, Richard Paul. 'From Nationalist to Multinational: The Stratford Festival, Free Trade, and the Discourses of Intercultural Tourism.' *Theatre Journal* 47.1 (1995): 19–41.

MacAloon, John. 'Olympic Games and the Theory of Spectacle in Modern Societies.' In John MacAloon, ed., *Rite, Drama, Festival, Spectacle: Rehearsals Toward a Theory of Cultural Performance*. Philadelphia: ISHI, 1984, 241–80.

McMahon, Christina S. 'From Adaptation to Transformation: Shakespeare Creolized on Cape Verde's Festival Stage,' *Theatre Survey* 50.1 (2009): 35–66.

McMahon, Christina S. *Recasting Transnationalism through Performance: Theatre Festivals in Cape Verde, Mozambique, and Brazil*. Basingstoke: Palgrave Macmillan, 2014.

Marcus, George E. 'Ethnography in/of the World System: The Emergence of Multi-Sited Ethnography.' In George E. Marcus, ed., *Ethnography through Thick and Thin*. Princeton: Princeton University Press, 1998, 79–104.

Maurin, Frédéric. 'Still and Again: Whither Festivals?' *Contemporary Theatre Review* 13.4 (2003): 5–11.

Muñoz, José Esteban. *Disidentifications: Queers of Color and the Performance of Politics.* Minneapolis: University of Minnesota Press, 1999.

Peterson, William. 'The Singapore Arts Festival at Thirty: Going Global, Glocal, Grobal.' *Asian Theatre Journal* 26.1 (2009): 111–34.

Sauter, William. 'Festivals as Theatrical Events: Building Theories.' In Temple Hauptfleisch et al., eds, *Festivalising! Theatrical Events, Politics and Culture*. New York: Rodopi, 2007, 17–25.

Schoenmakers, Henri. 'Festivals, Theatrical Events and Communicative Interactions.' In Temple Hauptfleisch et al., eds, *Festivalising! Theatrical Events, Politics and Culture*. New York: Rodopi, 2007, 27–37.

27   Magic in Theatre

Mihai Maniutiu
Translated from the Romanian by Cipriana Petre

From a theatre practitioner's perspective, the stage is an ambiguous space, in which the world of the invisible offers itself to perception through image, symbols and bodily-figurative emblems. The temptation to objectify one's obsessively haunting ghosts, to exteriorize them, to give them a body, as well as the bewilderment generated through the incarnation and embodiment of such apparitions, are constitutive parts of the atmosphere of theatre, generally labeled as 'magical'. Because they are fugitive approximations of the unseen, the theatre's specters become credible only when they institute a relationship of high intensity between us (as practitioners) and their physical aura.

The scenic simulacra allow practitioners to experience in a poetical manner the adventure of the vertigo, of the excess. We simulate a certain action on stage in order to experience something different from the direct effect of that action: as a matter of fact, we do it precisely to provide ourselves with the occasion to rejoice in the sensuous halo created in us by this action. As a director, I realized that I share Novalis's belief that magic is the art of freely disposing of the world of senses, at one's own will.

In theatre, plausibility is in direct relationship with intensity: only that which is intense is verisimilar. The magic of intensity turns our make-believes to be neither mere artifice nor concealments, but sketches and prefigurations of a cathartic state. As participants in the theatre event, we (actors and directors alike) never return unchanged, and we cannot possibly come out untainted from the act of playing with the mask, and from the fictions in which we engage on stage.

The ability to absorb and irradiate vital energy is, for me, the highest virtue of a theatre practitioner. In a theatre performance, essentially one thing matters: whether or not it produces, throughout its duration, a genuine discharge and transmission of vital energy. It is important that the spectators feel their energy intensified as a result of their involvement in the theatre event. 'Good' theatre, theatre that does not betray its vocation, infallibly generates this type of energy, this efficient and intangible vital force (to use Bergson's terms), to some extent similar to what is referred to with the magical name of *Mana*, which specialists in the field define as the energetic feature of immaterial substance of a human body or object.

As a director, I am inclined to believe – much like a Ritual Man with magic beliefs does – that a symbolic action is self-efficient and resonates entirely within the spiritual realm. Ever since the first moments of its emergence in the theatre world, the stage director was in a process of incessantly reinventing what it means to be a stage director, because the very condition of this profession's survival was intimately related to a permanent, continuous and complex reformulation of the director's artistic and professional status as *internal* necessity of the theatre stage.

Although directors sometimes like to think of themselves – probably justly, the director in me would suggest – as inheritors (to a great extent legitimate) of an old tradition, it is only recently in theatre history that the stage director emerged as a visible presence; the director barely has a past of its own, a history of roughly 100 years. This may explain, I suppose, the existence of theatre creators who are obsessed with beginnings, and eager to project themselves onto an imaginary realm of the 'origins of theatre'. They wish to incarnate, in the most eloquent ways they could come up with, the self-consciousness of these beginnings. This is the source of their fondness, more or less visible, more or less camouflaged, towards rites, rituals and ceremonies. This could also be the reason for which they attempt to build their theatre poetics under the prestigious shadow of everything that is related, in one way or another, to the concept of sacrificial act.

The authentic artistic act is necessarily purified of the fright with which life is loaded. While working on a theatre performance, during rehearsals, I feel as if I am under an anesthetic, which does not impinge at all on my lucidity or my affective capacity. It is me, with something added to me, not something subtracted from me, it is me venturing without inhibitions into spaces where, in real life, inhibition and its deformations occur automatically. It is me starting playing with the limit and enjoying this game, without the risk of the limit spoiling the game, or unwinding it: that is to say, I am, during those moments, confounding myself with my ludic double. The magical ambiance from the duration of my work on a performance allows me to dispose of myself as if I were an instrument that can juggle with itself and with situations many times intolerable. The body of my ludic double is a therapeutic one, it is the fluid body of a ghost. And this ghost walks a step ahead of me, and in a sense shows me what to do.

Directing, as *ars combinatoria*, somehow relates to magic, because it initiates and invents symbolic relations between representations of objects, beings or things that do not communicate between them naturally or ordinarily.

What we call illusion, in theatre, is the very moment of transparence of scenic logos. Those who assimilate scenic illusion as a procedure of mystifying the spectator's perception seem not to know anything about the power of dreams and phantasms – namely the power to re-set ourselves in a lively and mystery-bearing relationship with ourselves and with the world. For the one who imagines that they need to go all the way to the last consequences of the playing – therefore, beyond play – the stage will, by necessity, constitute a falsified space, a space of mystifications. For the one, however, who presupposes that in the act of playing, and not in transgressing it, lays the truth of theatre, the stage will be a space of illumination and illuminated energies.

Spaces dream, too. They wait for the practitioner to enter into their dream. If one does not dream their dream, if one does not feel their breathing and does not capture it, one is bound to remain a foreign body in that space, a rejected body, and as a consequence bound to prove unable to model them, to transform them in receptacles of one's own visions. They refuse to consecrate themselves to you, and they refuse to assimilate your visions. Spaces have a memory of their own, which is not the same with the memory of the history inscribed in their matter and their pores – a memory that remains invisible and intangible at a first level of perception – a memory that could be fatal to any new element inserted in their territory. We see so many performances rejected, negated by the space in which they unfold, and we realize every time that the 'spirit of space' cannot be defeated; the stage is not a frame, but rather an internal medium and a symbolic center – precarious and transitory – of the outside world. For a moment, the practitioner must act so that the center opens towards that which surrounds it, and this opening up is emanation, it is irradiation.

Some say theatre practitioners are mirrors. Yes, we are mirrors of the world, but rebellious mirrors; irreality is the very spinal cord in the spine of what we call reality, and the phantasmic is not the reverse, but the coagulant of the reality around me. Therefore, what do I, theatre practitioner as mirror, reflect? Attracted by countless correspondences and rapports of mirroring in the world, attracted by this theatre of mirrors that multiply and reflect on and on, ad infinitum, I search the calm of a form in which, for a moment, chaos falls asleep, or at least in which it seemingly dissolves. I like to believe that directing is meant to guarantee the cathartic orientation of the theatrical act.

As a theatre practitioner, one can say 'myself' only when one possesses the key to his or her plurality. In theatre, one cannot be one's own self unless one is plural, that is, unless one is more than one, simultaneously.

Playing is based on the process of becoming multiple, and being-multiple is a condition of self-awareness: as the Ancient Greeks had it, 'know thyself.'

Theatre performance is a flux of energies to which moving architectures of sensations are added, which make the theatre director a poet of sensorial architectures; architectures that emerge, intertwine, fall down into pieces, self-destroy themselves. As long as the need for theatre makes itself felt, we know that the magical attitudes of the spirit are not bound to become obsolete, but, on the contrary, are as alive today as they have always been.

28   Animality, Posthumanism

Jennifer Parker-Starbuck

The announcement in May 2010 of the creation of a synthetic bacterium, nicknamed 'Synthia', marked a shifting notion of the 'posthuman' beyond the theoretical. Alongside experimentation such as artificial brain 'chips' (Geddes 2011) and the very real development of transgenic animals (Bobrow 2011), this synthetic DNA combines human, animal and technological resources to literally go post-, or beyond the human in creating new synthetic life.[1] This reading of the posthuman is one of human-driven 'progress', and the press release from the J. Craig Venter Institute (2010) promises that Synthia will

> undoubtedly lead to the development of many important applications and products including biofuels, vaccines, pharmaceuticals, clean water and food products. The group continues to drive and support ethical discussion and review to ensure a positive outcome for society.

The positive 'spin' within the press release is perhaps necessary to counter the trepidation associated with dystopic and futuristic posthuman worlds in which humans are replaced by machines. In contrast to these understandings, however, what I want to argue for in this chapter is the cautionary development of the term 'posthumanism' as an ongoing condition (theoretical and practical) that is expansive enough to include more complex considerations of non-humans as it reframes notions of 'humanity'.

Although variations of the term 'posthumanism' have filtered through the 20th century (posthumanist, the posthuman, the post-human),[2] as Cary Wolfe outlined in his 2010 *What is Posthumanism?*, the idea took firm hold in the 1990s with Judith Halberstam and Ira Livingston's *Posthuman Bodies* (1995) and N. Katherine Hayles' influential 1999 *How We Became Posthuman*. Emerging from shifting terrain in media and technology, cybernetic, information and systems theory, 1990's posthumanism's focal point was the body, largely concerned with identity and feminist politics following Donna Haraway's now seminal text 'A Cyborg Manifesto' ([1985] 1991). Halberstam and Livingston (1995: vii) introduce the posthuman as 'an open invitation to engage discursive and bodily configurations that displace the human, humanism, and the humanities'. Repeatedly, many of these writers caution, defend and explain that the post- needn't mean 'after human', and use it provocatively as a rethinking of the troubled historical condition of (an often white, male, hegemonic) 'liberal humanism', especially as it was being shaped by emerging technologies.

What also filters through the term's trajectory is a desire to question the anthropocentric notion of the 'human'. Maybe, as with all posts, the function of the prefix maintains and doubles a troubled relationship to the main word itself. How might scholars and theorists, especially in performance and theatre – significantly human-driven forms – think beyond the 'human'? In *The Posthuman*, Rosi Braidotti (2013: 104) suggests that:

> The posthumanist predicament, in both the post-humanist and the post-anthropocentric sense of the term, drives home the idea that the activity of thinking needs to be experimental and even transgressive in combining critique with creativity.

Braidotti (2013: 103) argues for new models and concepts to 'rethink links of affectivity and responsibility' for organic and technological 'others'. It is this activity of experimental and transgressive thinking that has propelled scholars and artists to engage beyond the human, and to explore encounters with non-humans that push performance in new directions.

The term 'posthumanism' is malleable enough to have raised a significant amount of debate over its usage. For example, Wolfe (2010) distinguishes between 'humanist posthumanism' and 'posthumanist posthumanism' (about which more later), while Braidotti (2013) differentiates between 'post-humanist post-humanism' and 'post-anthropocentric posthumanism'. These distinctions point to the interpretability of and tensions within the concept and its disciplinary lineages. Braidotti (2013: 57–8) explains that whereas post-humanism

> mobilized primarily the disciplinary field of philosophy, history, cultural studies and the classical Humanities in general, the issue of post-anthropocentrism enlists also science and technology studies, new media and digital culture, environmentalism and earth-sciences, bio-genetics, neuroscience and robotics, evolutionary theory, critical legal theory, primatology, animal rights and science fiction.

What seems at stake in the mire of these not always helpful distinctions are questions about bodies: What form do they take? Are they ethically cared for? How are they classified? Are they human or non-human? Will technologies override material realities? Braidotti ultimately proposes a 'critical posthumanism', a stance that can serve as a useful point of departure for performance and theatre scholars already well versed in collaborative and relational exchange. She defines it as being:

> within an eco-philosophy of multiple belongings, as a relational subject constituted in and by multiplicity, that is to say a subject that works across differences and is also internally differentiated, but still grounded and accountable. Posthuman subjectivity expresses an embodied and embedded and hence partial form of accountability, based on a strong sense of collectivity, relationality and hence community building. (Braidotti 2013: 49)

The question, then, becomes: If these distinctions continue to be, perhaps inevitably, human-driven, how can we, as humans, relinquish the power of the 'human' enough to form 'communities' with non-humans? How might performance and theatre offer a space for considerations of non-human others, for concepts of animality that transform anthropocentric concerns?

In the humanities (or post-humanities), posthumanism has been a generative umbrella term for research that encourages alternate modes of association with non-humans, and encompasses work on multimedia performance, bioart, interspecies performance, environmental and ecological concerns, and human and non-human rhizomatic and relational exchanges. It relies on the foundational work of Deleuze and Guattari, Braidotti, Latour, Wolfe, Hayles, Haraway and others in interdisciplinary conversations. In performance, other terms have been introduced to rethink human relations with the environment, with non-human animals and organisms. While 'animality' might encompass a general inclusion of non-human life and specifically non-human animals, the growing interdisciplinary crossing of performance and animal studies has prompted even more specific terms. Una Chaudhuri's important 'Zoöesis' (2003: 647), for example, proposes to better understand 'the discourse of animality in human life', or 'interspecies performance', the topic for the 2013 special issue of *Theatre Journal*, which is described by editor Ric Knowles (2013) as 'a horizontalist and rhizomatic project in which no one partner in the exchange and negotiation dominates'. The work I have done on the organic-technological cyborg and its move towards a 'becoming-animate' is an attempt to understand new corporealities that go beyond the exclusively human (Parker-Starbuck 2006, 2011). These terms mark an urgency for a response to the growing realization that we are not all that 'matters' on the planet.

While the word 'posthuman' can therefore signify multiple possibilities, these more specific terms and distinctions are needed to question the positioning of the non-human in relational contexts. Braidotti (2002: 2), for instance, proposes the term 'figurations' as 'alternative representations and social locations for the kind of hybrid mix we are in the process of becoming. Figurations are not figurative ways of thinking, but rather more materialistic mappings of situated, or embedded and embodied, positions.' Looking at Synthia as a 'figuration', for example, points to its complex mappings, which, while touted as human-directed evolution, should include the fact that the synthetic life form began as a bacterium, *Mycoplasma mycoides*, a parasite that has been known to infect goats, whose DNA was replicated synthetically and inserted into another bacterium (yeast) producing artificial multiplication (J. Craig Venter Institute 2010). Synthia also troubles the distinction Wolfe (2010: xv) makes between 'transhumanism', as 'an intensification of humanism' or the oft thought of transcendence of the body to technological advancements ('jacking in') and his reading of 'posthumanism', which, he explains, 'forces us to rethink our taken-for-granted modes of human experience ... by recontextualizing them in terms of the entire sensorium of other living beings' (xxv). While Synthia is, on one hand, a transcendence of human capacities, it also is, crucially, an amalgam of other living organisms. Wolfe's contribution to the term's expansion follows his earlier work on animal studies (*Animal Rites*, 2003, *Zoontologies*, 2003) to insist, like Haraway, Braidotti, Latour and others, on the necessity of openness between humans and non-human subjects. As the terrain of what it means to be 'human' expands to incorporate cyborgean and synthetic life, the terms, discussions and debates around these evolutions must also shift accordingly.

What does art add?

One goal of posthuman art and performance practices is to redirect attention outside an exclusively human sphere, to alter anthropocentric viewing positions. From experiments in bioart on a cellular level, to cyborgean intertwinement, to performances that feature living animals, non-humans are making an appearance in performance and art. In his chapter 'From Dead Meat to Glow-in-the-Dark Bunnies', Wolfe (2010) develops the distinction that one can be a 'humanist posthumanist' or a 'posthumanist posthumanist', posing differences in representation between artist Sue Coe's 'Slaughterhouse' series of paintings and the ongoing bioart practices of Kac, well known for his glow-in-the-dark rabbit Alba, which was conceived using green fluorescent protein (GFP) (www.ekac.org). For Wolfe (2010: 152), Coe's paintings are 'humanist posthuman' thinking because although she addresses the ethical use of non-human animals in her 'melodramatic' slaughterhouse series, she ultimately seems 'to form a kind of theater calculated to produce a "surefire effect" … by playing to the audience'. Wolfe's Fried-based critique argues that Coe's representation of animals being slaughtered 'invites a single, univocal reading' (154), which blames the forces of capitalism and maintains a separation of humans and non-humans. Wolfe (2010: 152) finally asks: 'why not just show people photographs of stockyards, slaughterhouses', adding: 'what does art *add*?'

It is this question that haunts my considerations of animality and posthumanism. If non-humans are drawn into 'communities' and spaces of performance, is it possible for humans to slowly relinquish centrality enough to form more balanced alliances? As a counterpoint to Coe, Kac successfully provides for Wolfe a decentered viewing position, one that begins to merge and shift the positionality of humans and non-humans alike. Wolfe (2010: 166) explains that Kac's work:

> lead[s] the viewer to the realization that the only place the meaning of the work may be found is no place, not where the viewer irresistibly looks … but rather … precisely where the viewer does not see – not 'refuses to look' or even 'is prevented from seeing,' but rather, cannot see.[3]

A later Kac work not mentioned by Wolfe, 'Cypher' (2009), serves here as a parallel, and preemptive reflection on contemporary posthuman thought in relation to Synthia's public emergence. In 'Cypher', viewers become 'users' and are given a portable mini lab to perform an experiment in creating synthetic 'life':

> The kit contains Petri dishes, agar, nutrients, streaking loops, pipettes, test tubes, synthetic DNA (encoding in its genetic sequence a poem I wrote specifically for this artwork) … The work literally comes to life when the viewer/reader/user follows the protocol in the booklet and integrates the synthetic DNA into the bacteria … After the transformation, the poem will be fully integrated into the bacteria's cellular machinery and therefore will be present in each newly reproduced bacterium. (Kac n.d.)

By exploring the creation of a synthetic life through art and performance practices, this work raises questions about who has access to these technologies and how they are manipulated. Kac (n.d.) explains that 'the key poetic gesture in "Cypher" is to place in the hands of the viewer the decision and the power to literally give life to the artwork'. Long before Venter's creation of Synthia, Kac evoked a poetic synthetic life, a precursor of what might be possible through a critical posthumanism that raises questions about the human, rather than merely holds up its achievements. As users follow instructions to integrate the synthetic life – and poem – into a bacterium, an artistic rationale is presented that precedes Venter's science. Kac and other artists working at the crossroads of biotechnologies, such as Critical Art Ensemble, ORLAN and Kira O'Reilly, might be the clearest examples of post-humanist performance studies practices, and I would argue that it is within the metaphoric possibilities of these works that posthumanism might begin to better explore the ethical and political repercussions of 'progress'.

The subversion and/or resituation of traditional modes of visual representation, especially when addressing the non-human subject, runs thematically through the work of many art and performance practition-ers and scholars invested in posthumanism and animality. Through its interdisciplinary nature, performance studies has been a productive site for scholarly and artistic intersections between bodies and science, bioart and technology, and, more recently, questions of non-human animals.[4] While animals have historically been exploited for performance, they have less frequently been a focus of study in performance studies, but by working with the expanding field of 'animal studies', performance studies' scholars and artists have extended the fields of performance and ecology, cyborg studies, multimedia performance and live art to begin to analyse and include animality.

In addition to the subversion and decentering of an anthropocentric viewing position explored through works such as Kac's, 'posthuman' animal bodies in art and performance practices challenge material understandings, and suggest alternate physical affiliations between human and animal. For example, in 'Falling Asleep with a Pig', artist Kira O'Reilly spent 36–72 hours in a pen with a pig named Delilah investigating daily patterns and relations between herself and the pig. O'Reilly, whose widely diverse work ranges from biotech explorations following an artist's residency at SymbioticA, the art and science research lab in Australia, to acting as a performer in Robert Wilson's *The Life and Death of Marina Abromović*, in this piece explores a more literal decentering of human positionality in an attempt to find an a new 'placement' with an animal. O'Reilly (2010: 47) explains that:

> I didn't think of falling asleep with a pig as cohabitation or occupying a domestic register. It was more to do with placement. In many ways it is disarmingly simple and clumsy to feel for a kind of poetic language; two

253

bodies sleeping next to one another and the possibility of dreams, both materiality and metaphorically; where words are at the tips of tongues and language and material meet and enmesh across bodies and the most ancient narratives of metamorphosis can come into play in a contemporary context. Somehow I am trying to find that language – a poetic one perhaps that is not reductive in the art work or my commentaries that can facilitate another kind of spaciousness.

O'Reilly's work exemplifies an approach to engaging animality that attempts to place the human and non-human animals in communication with each other for extended periods of time.

The work of French performance artist ORLAN perhaps best exemplifies an ongoing attention to posthuman practice. From her early masked 'body sculptures', which often featured an inclusion of manikin body parts in addition to her own form, to her 'Carnal Art' practice famously transforming herself through plastic surgery, to her recent exploration of hybridized co-cultured cells from different species in her *Harlequin's Coat*, her work has never hesitated to challenge viewers to reconceptualize what not only human, but non-human bodies might mean. ORLAN's work exhibits what Simon Donger et al. (2010: xv) described as a 'restless hybridity' that has grown more literal over time. During a residency with SymbioticA in 2007, she created the ongoing *The Harlequin's Coat*, exploring practical ideas of hybridization and skin grafting processes. It is a patchwork coat comprised of petri dishes containing the remains of multi-species, co-cultured cells grown in a custom-made tissue culture bioreactor, which acts as the head of the harlequin. The cells that originated the project were a hybrid of her own mixed with those of other species and humans; she writes: 'I am interested in undoing the biological and symbolic unity of the skin' (ORLAN 2010: 117). ORLAN's posthumanism perhaps facilitates another connotation of the term, more akin to an avant-garde, always using her own body to lead an exploration that ventures provocatively beyond traditional, stereotypical and actual human limits.[5]

ORLAN and O'Reilly are among a growing number of artists and performers whose work falls under the rubric of posthuman performance, also frequently engaging with issues of animality. Others work to expand the boundaries of the human to include animals, organisms, hybrids and machines. For example, Bryndís Snæbjörnsdóttir and Mark Wilson's installation and art practice explicitly sets out to engage notions of non-human animals. Their website explains that their work 'sets out to challenge anthropocentric systems and thinking that sanction loss through representation of the other, proposing instead, alternative tropes of "parities in meeting"' (www.snaebjornsdottirwilson.com). Patricia Piccinini's mixed-media sculptural works depict alien-esque hybrid bodies situated in a space between biotechnological casualties and domestic or family spaces (www.patricia-piccinini.net); the performance company osseus labyrint (Mark Steger and Hannah Sim) transform their corporeality in performance, moving naked and hairless in a seemingly impossible non-human physicality (Cheng 2001); the collective Critical Art Ensemble has, since the late 1980s, worked with themes of electronic disturbance, emerging media/technological practice, and civil disobedience, and is at the forefront of performance experimentation with processes of biotechnology (www.critical-art.net); and artists Olly and Suzi create paintings of and with a range of often endangered animals in their habitats, producing a hybrid animal-human process of art-making (www.ollysuzi.com; Baker 2000); these and many other artists and performers are taking risks, challenging boundaries, and reframing a human relationship to the non-human. In these works, it is the *thinking*, and thereby the thinking about seeing, that must shift so as to avoid reproducing, as Wolfe (2010: xvii) reminds us, 'the very kind of normative subjectivity – that grounds discrimination against nonhuman animals' in these posthuman times. What appears on stage is often what just eludes vision; artists often reflect the ungraspable, what isn't quite on the radar, yet.

In a time that is being called the Anthropocene – a term proposed across philosophy, animal studies and environmental studies to show how completely humans have changed and dominated the planet, a potent reminder that there is no going back – the term 'posthuman' might well produce a turning forward through the post-. In posthuman art and performance practices, bodies from human to cyborg to animal exemplify the possibilities and the problems of technological, interspecies incorporation – and while thus far the 21st century has not quite yet experienced 'jacking in' à la *The Matrix*, it is a time when iPhones arrive complete with Siri, an artificial intelligence, pig heart valves are placed into human bodies, and cloning techniques are growing more advanced. The human hand at the creation of the synthetic cell Synthia reminds us of the long history of the 'human' in posthumanism, and hopefully the possibilities of the terms 'post-' being investigated by art and performance practitioners will remain open enough to allow for multiple species, shifting terrains, and a greater animal–human awareness, Synthia's creator Venter is reported to have said:

> this cell we've made is not a miracle cell that's useful for anything, it is a proof of concept. But the proof of concept was key, otherwise it is just speculation and science fiction. This takes us across that border, into a new world. (Fatimathas 2010)

255

I suggest that the arts have shown that we are already in this new world, our realities are catching up to our imaginations, and as synthetic cells undoubtedly evolve to life forms, what is at stake in this evolving, perhaps, post-posthuman are still bodies, both human and non-human.

Notes

1   Much of what was widely reported about this breakthrough is taken directly from the press release of the J. Craig Venter Institute, which is reported to be a not-for-profit genomic research organization with funding from Synthetic Genomics Inc., which has been funded by the US government, BP and Exxon. To see the research making up this breakthrough, see Gibson et al. 2010.
2   The hyphenated term, 'post-human', may or may not signify a conceptual philosophical or analytic stand. We (humans) cannot literally be post-'hyphen'-human (and, of course, there is no 'we', considering how many people worldwide are without access to even basic technologies), but perhaps the 21st century brings with it a posthuman aligned more with Hayles' (1999: 5) hope of embracing 'the possibilities of information technologies without being seduced by fantasies of unlimited power and disembodied immortality'.
3   What might problematize Wolfe's argument is that Kac's work has been critiqued for using actual organism/animals in his practice, something Coe does not do.
4   See work by scholars such as Una Chaudhuri, Laura Cull, Baz Kershaw, Lourdes Orozco, Michael Peterson, Alan Read, Nick Ridout, Erika Rundle, Peta Tait and myself as a few of a growing number of scholars working across performance and animal studies.
5   See Parker-Starbuck, 'Reflective Viewing: ORLAN's Hybridized Harlequin, Banksy, Bacon, and the Animal-Human Divide,' in Fintan Walsh and Matthew Causey, eds, *Performance, Identity and the Neo-Political Subject*, London, Routledge, 2013.

Works cited

Baker, Steve. *The Postmodern Animal*. London: Reaktion, 2000.
Bobrow, Martin. 'The Future of Animal-Human Hybrids.' *The Mark*, September 28, 2011, http://pioneers.themarknews.com/articles/6809-the-future-of-animal-human-hybrids/#.UvTyEvvcfYQ, accessed 7 February 2014.
Braidotti, Rosi. *Metamorphosis: Towards a Materialist Theory of Becoming*. Cambridge: Polity, 2002.
– *The Posthuman*, Cambridge: Polity, 2013.
Chaudhuri, Una. "Animal Geographies: Zooësis and the Space of Modern Drama," *Modern Drama* 46.4 (2003): 646–62
Cheng, Meiling. Cyborgs in Mutation: osseus labyrint's Alien Body Art,' *TDR: The Drama Review* 45.2 (2001): 145–68.
Donger, Simon, Shepherd, Simon and ORLAN (eds). *ORLAN: A Hybrid Body of Artworks*. New York: Routledge, 2010.

Fatimathas, Lux. 'First Synthetic Cell Created in a Laboratory,' *BioNews* 559, 24 May 2010, www.bionews.org.uk/page_61470.asp, accessed February 7, 2014.

Geddes, Linda. 'Rat Cyborg Gets Digital Cerebellum,' *New Scientist*, September 27, 2011, www.newscientist.com/article/mg21128315.700-rat-cyborg-gets-digital- cerebellum. html, accessed February 7, 2014.

Gibson, Daniel G. et al. 'Creation of a Bacterial Cell Controlled by a Chemically Synthesized Genome,' *Science*, 2 July 2010: 329.5987 pp. 52–6, available at www. sciencemag.org/content/329/5987/52.full, accessed February 7, 2014.

Halberstam, Judith and Livingston, I. *Posthuman Bodies*. Indianapolis: Indiana UP, 1995.

Haraway, Donna. *Simians, Cyborg, and Women: The Reinvention of Nature*. New York: Routledge, 1991.

Hayles, N. Katherine. *How We Became Posthuman: Virtual Bodies in Cybernetics, Literature, and Informatics*. Chicago: U of Chicago P, 1999.

J. Craig Venter Institute. Press Release, 'First Self-Replicating Synthetic Bacterial Cell,' May 20, 2010, www.jcvi.org/cms/press/press-releases/full-text/article/first-self-replicating-synthetic-bacterial-cell-constructed-by-j-craig-venter-institute-researcher/; see also www.jcvi.org/cms/research/projects/first-self-replicating-synthetic- bacterial-cell/faq/#q9, accessed February 7, 2014.

Kac, Eduardo. 'Cypher, A DIY Transgenic Kit', www.ekac.org/cypher.text.html, n.d., accessed February 7, 2014.

Knowles, Ric. 'Editorial Comment,' Special issue on Interspecies Performance, *Theatre Journal*, 65.3, October 2013.

O'Reilly, Kira. www.kiraoreilly.com/blog, accessed February 7, 2014.

O'Reilly, Kira, 'Falling Asleep with a Pig,' interviewed by Snæbjörnsdóttir/Wilson, in *Antennae: The Journal of Nature in Visual Culture*, 13, Summer 2010, 38–48.

ORLAN. 'In Retrospect: The Poetics and Politics of the Face-to-Face,' trans. S. Donger, in *ORLAN: A Hybrid Body of Artworks*. New York: Routledge, 2010.

Parker-Starbuck, Jennifer. 'Becoming-Animate: On the Performed Limits of "Human,"' *Theatre Journal*, Special Issue on Film and Theatre, 58.4, December 2006.

– *Cyborg Theatre: Corporeal/Technological Intersections in Multimedia Performance*. Basingstoke: Palgrave Macmillan, 2011.

Wolfe, Cary. *Zoontologies: The Question of the Animal*. Minneapolis: University of Minnesota Press, 2003.

– *Animal Rites: American Culture, the Discourse of Species, and Posthumanist Theory*. Chicago: University of Chicago Press, 2003.

– 'From Dead Meat to Glow-in-the-Dark Bunnies,' in Cary Wolfe, *What is Posthumanism?* Minneapolis: U of Minnesota P, 2010.

29   Postdramatic Theatre

Patrice Pavis

More than ten years after its appearance in 1999, Hans-Thies Lehmann's *Das postdramatische Theater* (*PDT*)[1] continues to enliven debates on contemporary theatre. 'Postdramatic theatre': no other term since the 'theatre of the absurd' in the 1950s has emerged that encompasses the vast majority of experimental theatre production or 'research'. This 'umbrella idea', this general term inclusive of everything emerging from its universalizing blender – that also reduces complexity to simple, digestible ideas – seems to leave no one indifferent: Lehmann's important reflections stimulate as many polemics as counterpropositions or correctives; indeed, Lehmann himself has 'corrected' a number of his original claims in his most recent articles and his book *Das politische Schreiben*.[2]

Origins of the idea and the term

Although Lehmann did not invent the term 'postdramatic theatre', he deserves credit for systematizing it and grounding it on a set of observations and hypotheses. Andrej Wirth, for whom Lehmann worked as an assistant in the new department of *angewandte Theaterwissenschaft* (applied theatrology) at the University of Giessen in the 1980s, had already referred to 'spoken theatre (that) had lost its monopoly on the use of post-dramatic forms of sound-mixing, spoken opera, and dance theatre';[3] Wirth, who, according to Elinor Fuchs, started using the term in New York in the 1970s,[4] called attention to the oxymora pervading PDT. When Richard Schechner took up the term 'postdramatic' (or alternatively 'posthumanist'), he did so in a superficial and journalistic way, echoing Foucault's antihumanistic theories then in vogue in the US, declaring the avant-garde to be – according to Schechner – on the verge of disappearing. Helga Finter, who since 1985 has used the term 'postmodern' instead of 'postdramatic', has been much more precise and constructive than either Schechner or Wirth, perhaps because she has seen the *connection* between the postdramatic (PD) and the postmodern (PM), while Lehmann – as Jacques Derrida was doing elsewhere with deconstruction – established a distinct *difference* between PM and PD (*or* deconstruction).

In any event, 'postdramatic' initially modelled itself on 'postmodern', and, at the historical moment when theory was having difficulty renewing itself, tried to account for new experiences by ubiquitously pressing 'post' into service, with all that has followed, in something like the sense of the expression *après moi le déluge*. The postdramatic is, moreover, a 'tactic', since it was universalized in a cumulative series of conceptualizations including 'poststructuralism' (after 1968), 'post-history' (after 1989), and 'posthuman' (after 1999, with Katherine Hayles' *How We Became Posthuman*).[5] This idea of 'post' quickly became a paratactic accumulation of practices that Lehmann then reconfigured, sometimes hastily, often through a parenthetical insertion or a list, à la Jacques Prévert. It is almost simpler to identify Lehmann's pet peeves: literary and logocentric theatre, for which staging is a mere decorative formality; political theatre that underlines its own polemics and is thus nothing but a 'confirmative ritual of foregone conclusions' (*PTD*: 451); and intercultural theatre, given that we should not 'hope to find in interculturalism a new space for political public opinion' (*PTD*: 453).

These few exclusions, which are thus all the more radical and remarkable, do not, however, come without several ironies emerging from the 'trademark' PDT. A certain uninvited humor marks this strange trinity, 'postdramatic theatre':

1   The 'post' never actually indicates whether the distinction is temporal or purely theoretical, a distinction unnecessary to structuralism and semiology; Lehmann makes a non-contradictory principle out of it: 'The idea that PDT existed from the beginning, so to speak, and the idea that it defines a specific moment of theatre after/beyond drama, are not mutually exclusive but coexist.'[6]
2   Since the 'dramatic' is precisely what is left behind, even rejected, one might wonder that Lehmann still uses it despite its negation, perhaps suggesting that no other category – epic, lyric, philosophical, etc. – could follow it, even in other forms.
3   The word 'theatre' is certainly not obscene, but its Greek origin and its use strictly in the Western (or Westernized) world makes it suspect and of only minimal use if one's interest is non-European cultural practice, let alone non-aesthetic or non-fictional cultural performance going beyond the horizon of avant-garde theatre and research.

The meaning and objective of PDT

The objective of PDT seems to be universal, in extent and comprehension. Lehmann promises to define it but quickly forgets his promise through his enthusiastic discovery of new forms: 'only in the course of explication itself can I give a justification – even a partial one – for the criteria that have guided my choices' (*PDT*: 19). But his choices certainly go beyond many frontiers of intellectual and literary culture, leading him toward popular media culture, the visual arts and spectacles of all kinds. Dance, the new genres of circus, video art, visual arts, installations, and musical theatre all find a home there.[7]

Although according to Lehmann, forms from the 1950s and 60s, such as the happening, performance art, environmental theatre, body art and Viennese Actionism, should be distinguished from PDT, early on these forms wove themselves into the broad fabric of the postdramatic. And it would be incorrect to reproach Lehmann for not providing a narrower definition, given the immensity of the field and the hybrid nature of its various elements. Suffice it to say that any such criteria might be seen initially as those against which the postdramatic rose up, and would then provide certain perspectives on the new postdramatic values and fields.

The principal enemy of PDT is representation: the longstanding ambition of the dramatic theatre to represent, through text or acting, a conflict between two characters, a place and time distinct from the scenic event in any specific staging. In place of figuring forth what the text is saying, PDT prefers to exhibit, to expose, the mechanisms of language, to treat the text as a sound object rather than being concerned with the words' direct references. It thus interrogates the fragile theatrical equilibrium between the mimetic and the performative, what Martin Puchner calls 'theater's uneasy position between the performing and the mimetic arts'. Indeed, for Puchner, 'as a performing art like music or ballet, the theatre depends on the artistry of live human beings on stage. As a mimetic art like painting or cinema, however, it must utilize these human performers as signifying material in the service of a mimetic project.'[8]

PDT privileges the performative without becoming enmeshed in cultural performances. These cultural performances remain, from the perspective of the postdramatic, symbolic actions exterior to the aesthetic sphere of theatre.

What results is a clear preference in the postdramatic for live theatre, 'performed', emancipated from the dramatic text and asserting an absence of hierarchy between scenic systems and props, and most importantly between stage and texts. Its texts will not be 'scenic' (seen as easily acted and spoken), but, on the contrary, hostile to the stage, perhaps even written *against* it. In fact, the playwrights often cited by the postdramatic, such as Müller, Jelinek, Goetz, Polesch, Kane, Crimp, Duras, Bernhard, Vinaver, Fosse, Lagarce, etc., are thought of as not writing for the stage but against it, or, at best, despite it: such staging does not illustrate nor explicate the text but rather stages a mechanism for opening texts out to new perspectives, not within a sociopsychological framework but in one of play, of gestural and visual impulses bringing about a rediscovery of text and stage and provoking a confrontation between them. Certain directors or writers are known for their fascination with rhythmic structures: Wilson, Régy, Kriegenburg, Thalheimer, Etchells, Lauwers, Fabre, Castellucci, Lepage among the writers, Koltès, Lagarce, Gabilly, Handke and Foreman among the authors.

The unfindable object of PDT is thus located more in practical staging than in any kind of writing, though it is sometimes difficult to know whether one is dealing with research into writing or with actors at play. Perhaps this is why Lehmann rarely talks about 'staging', apparently finding this notion too closely linked with traditional writing and 'classical' staging, as in Copeau, for example. This 'classical' staging first examines the passage from text, seen as a stable entity, to stage, seen as unstable and unpredictable. It claims to be the work of a director who is simultaneously a creator and faithful to the text. According to Lehmann, however, the modern theatre's staging 'is generally nothing but the declamation and illustration of dramatic writing', a position that seems both unfair and oversimple to Jean-Pierre Sarrazac,[9] and not without justification. Lehmann's radical turn can be explained in part by the lassitude of the German *Regietheater* of the 1960s, which was often seen as being too focused on the artist-director's ego (e.g. Zadek, Stein). In countries such as France and Italy during the 1970s, however, staging was already being conceived as the best means of deconstructing a play or a performance: Vitez, in a series of exercises followed by performances of such classics as Molière and Racine, and Carmelo Bene, through his radical rewritings of Shakespeare in his style of histrionic play – both, well before the postdramatic, engaging in deconstructions of text, staging 'before and above' the text, using simple but radically destabilizing techniques for actors' and audiences' experience. They thus contributed to the exposing and exhibiting of textuality, as if they were dealing with an installation or plastic artwork. In place of the observer for whom the classical and modern theatre imitates and represents a reality, PDT and its deconstructed staging (deconstruction before it existed as such) asks what actors do with texts and actions, and through what mechanism they should intervene in that process.

Distinguishing the actor (postmodern) and the actor's double (postdramatic) helps us discern the differences between the two theatrical forms:

Dramatic theatre	PDT[10]
Actor	Performer
Dialogue	Choral ensemble, disposition
Dialogue and conversation	Impersonal address to the public
Dialogue and exchange	Uncertain address and reception
Representation	Presentation, presence
Body expressing emotions and interactions	Neutralized body
Einfühlung (identification)	*Ausführung* (disidentification)
Theatrical illusion	Sporting event

The postdramatic actor is a performer who does not attempt to construct nor imitate a character; located at the interaction of a choral ensemble, in a process restructuring the totality of his actions and physical performances. What is central is the simple presence of the person having abandoned the character, as though in a vocal or physical endurance test (Pollesch, Castorf). He no longer has to enter into the emotions of the spectator through the imitation or even the suggestion of his own emotions (*Einfühlung*) but, according to Roselt's formulation, he departs from all identification (*Ausführung*) and leaves behind the swamp of simulated emotions in order to rediscover his own, like an athlete, a musician, a singer, a technician in service not to imitation of the human nor to theatrical illusion, but to a collective enunciation.

Historical moment of PDT's appearance

In a search for the origins of the PD, of the historical moment at which the idea as well as its scenic practice appeared, it is difficult to differentiate the theoretical idea and the concrete object it describes. Changes in production are tied to historical changes, and the postdramatic is nothing but a reaction to such changes. And yet in order to understand them, we must develop a conceptual apparatus as precisely as possible.

Lehmann observed this change in the shows and performance art he saw in the 1970s and 80s, notably in Frankfurt (Theater am Turm), Germany, the Netherlands and Belgium. These performance pieces, created as reactions to absurdist literature, were linked to a philosophy and a literature that did not in the end lead to new theatrical practice but were situated in the drama's continuation and the symbolism of thought. Beckett is a kind of transition between dramatic literature and abstract, non-symbolic stage practice. The purely visual aesthetics (Wilson, Kantor, and later Tanguy, Gentil, etc.) appeared as much in reaction to 'art theatre' or staging as against dramatic literature.

However, in other countries, such as France in the 1980s (Vinaver, Koltès, Novarina) and 90s (Gabilly, Lagarce), this dramatic writing maintained a certain autonomy with regard to the reinvigoration of theatrical writing and publishing. Theoreticians of drama like Vinaver (with his charts analyzing global theatre) or Sarrazac (with his idea of rhapsodic theatre) in no sense inscribe themselves in an anti- or postdramatic reaction. They both still consider staging to be a lever with which to deconstruct, displace and divert classic canonical texts. They thus leave the field free for PDT to make alliances with media, the visual arts, popular performance and variety shows. They maintain their confidence in the power of mise-en-scène as the extension of the 1960s and 70s. The only thing they share with PDT is a certain blindness, or even a demonstrated indifference, to intercultural experiences and the expanding of theatre studies to performance studies and cultural performances.

This historical evolution coincides with changes in methodology and even epistemology occurring between 1968 and 1980: the end of dramaturgical analyses inspired by Brecht, the end of semiological imperialism, the beginning of the poststructuralist era. Adorno's work – his *Aesthetic Theory* (1970) or 'Trying to Understand *Endgame*' (1961) – is the essential reference point for an understanding of PDT. Adorno's idea that form is nothing but sedimented content helps us understand the theory of the evolution of forms and the connection between form and content. Regarding the dramatic as defined by Peter Szondi, or the postdramatic as defined by Lehmann, the difficulty is not to locate nor to describe textual or scenic forms; rather, the difficulty is to know and analyze the social and philosophical contents of one's age, which have somehow found refuge in these dramatic and theatrical forms. The PD plays with this difficulty by no longer needing to theorize. It gives up seizing on all those views of the real that theatrical forms can no longer manage to cover. But can it be reproached for that?

There is still one last, fundamental reason for the unprecedented rise of PDT in Germany, and then in other forms in France and elsewhere: the research theatre, powerfully subsidized by individual cities and the state, which is itself artificially supported, cannot survive without this aid. In Germany, *Stadttheater* (municipal theatres), very rich and powerful, have quickly adopted, reinforced and institutionalized it. The retreat of the state and its institutions means the risk – even the probability – that PDT will disappear or be transformed into a more marketable product, and the revival of a 'more accessible' theatre, 'well-made' plays, middle-class theatrical conformity, or more intelligent mainstream theatre (Reza, Schmitt). This restoration can be seen in a number of recent theatre pieces.

Thus, PDT is already, perhaps, an endangered species, at a time when we have just begun objectively to appreciate its virtues without ignoring its problems and challenges.

Problems and challenges of PDT

Some problems

Peter Szondi's incomplete project is the point of departure for postdramatic reflection. In his *Theory of the Modern Drama* (1956) studying European dramaturgy 1880 to 1950, Szondi lays out the evolution of dramaturgy through a crisis of drama (II), attempts to preserve dramatic form (III), and attempts a solution. In the conclusion of his historical survey, Szondi imagines what might or should become 'a new style'. By the mid-20th century, according to Szondi, both dramatic form and its tradition had become problematic, so that it would be necessary, were we to construct a new style, to find a solution to the crisis, not just for dramatic form but for its 'tradition'.[11] By 'tradition', Szondi means acting itself, in the manner of acting transmitted by tradition; Szondi realizes that the theatre to come must be theorized not only as dramatic text but as stage practice. But there is no longer a preserved tradition, a general model, a uniform performance style, since that stolid tradition of acting disappears simultaneously with the appearance of directorial staging around 1880, and in a renewed, post-classical, even postmodern form in the 1950s. Emphatically, with the PD, no tradition of acting or of interpretation is there to guarantee any stability. Staging is not a simple, traditional package; it is a vital element in the production of a performance's meaning. After Jacques Copeau, who never hesitated to disrupt and decenter texts, post-classical staging became a significant and autonomous practice, a way of staging and acting, of making comprehensive theatre: PDT says nothing else, except that it does not concern itself, or only rarely, with the details of staging processes.

In any event, this is the staging variable by which theatre evolves, and no longer, or no longer only, changes in dramaturgy, as was the case in the second half of the 20th century. Henceforth, dramatic writing has meaning only in its link to the stage, to mise-en-scène defined only by its connection to the stage, to staging itself defined as production and its effect on meaning, as the introduction of textual potentialities or external practices engaged in by the actor, the director and all their collaborators.

More challenges

PDT represents many challenges that are, at the same time, opportunities:

1 *Heterogeneity*: the dramatic and the stage are clearly imbricated; the result is an artistic object and a theoretical notion (the PD) that are rather heterogeneous, though generally adapted to works and a world familiar to us. No theory of dramatic genres, let alone stage practices, can include all these performances.

    The widely differing performance pieces of PDT cannot be defined with regard to any essence or specific common characteristics, but only through radically differing scenic and social practices. It is not only representation that is the heterogeneous totality of the arts and their materials and discourses; they are themselves heterogeneous and non-specific: 'The use of arts coming from other fields is a sign of this rhapsodic impulse which challenges dramatic form.'[12]

2 *The spectacular or performative object* itself is also ungraspable: it is impossible to distinguish between dramatic text, staging, devised theatre, and political or militant action, not to mention the countless cultural performances taking place worldwide.

3 PDT sees no clear-cut distinction between *text-based theatre* and *theatre without words*. The difference is, rather, between a text pre-existing production, its staging as such, on the one hand, and on the other, a text created in the course of rehearsals by a team more or less closed around a leader, who could even be the playwright – or by these two at once (i.e., 'devised theatre'). It is thus imperative that we examine the status of the text in the context of its staging.

4 *The text and its analysis* must be re-evaluated: the tools of classic dramaturgy need to be revised and adapted, not simply inverted. It is important not to confuse the various levels: the dramatic text is not the story, nor the narrative, nor the narration. The ultimate and principle difficulty is to understand the links between various dramatic or postdramatic forms to 'reality', since, as Lehmann correctly states, we are in the midst of a 'drifting apart of dramatic form and social reality' (*PDT*: 41). But are we still capable of establishing a link between the dramaturgical or scenic forms and our analyses of reality?

These challenges taken up by PDT show us that the problems Lehmann emphasizes are all too real and that they bring together all the interrogations of contemporary theatre. To reconnect the idea of the postdramatic to that of the postmodern and deconstruction (which would involve going in different directions from Lehmann's) would be, to some degree, to confirm some of Lehmann's contentions, and to verify them within the framework of deconstruction.

5   There exists no conceptual world adapted to new scenic and extra-scenic experiences after 1970: not structuralism, semiology, nor reception theory. Given that the work of art is itself fragmented, deconstructed and unfinished, the spectator or theoretician can no longer call on concepts or other tools that are broad and relevant. The only thing Lehmann's postdramatic can do is to refer in an eclectic way to notions borrowed from philosophers such as Derrida, Lyotard, Deleuze, Baudrillard, or Rancière. It must often do so through opposing concepts: event/situation, parataxis/hierarchy, space/surface, representation/presence, etc. These contrasting concepts help Lehmann organize the mass of observations and test the great dramatic/postdramatic dichotomy. This binary division is, however, too reductive to be able to explain phenomena that escape a clear-cut dichotomy.

Toward a postdramatic and deconstructed staging?

Lehmann often refers to Derridean deconstruction but without clearly differentiating it from his own conception of the postdramatic. It seems, however, necessary to distinguish between the postdramatic and deconstruction, in Lehmann and Derrida, while explicitly dissociating both from postmodern thought.

Deconstruction in theatre might be defined as the way in which mise-en-scène alternatively manifests and destroys itself before us. It locates and conducts its own fragmentation, highlighting its dissonances, its contradictions, its decentering. A single detail in the performance can deconstruct the entire narrative structure, ruin any claim of the production to represent the world or build a character. This becomes a matter of operating on meaning itself, and not simply through superficial stylistic procedures. More importantly, here lies the whole difference with postmodernism, which acknowledges its taste for the hybridity of form and an extremely developed intertextuality.[13]

Going beyond the classic examples – such as Vitez's exercises, the work of the Wooster Group, Katie Mitchell's filming sessions (*Some Trace of Her,*

2008), stagings of Shakespeare by Jan Decorte during the 1980s, Jan Lauwers in the 1990s or Ivo van Hove (*Roman Tragedies*) in 1997, the staged adaptations of novels by Proust, Musil or Guy Cassiers – there are very few examples of deconstruction, *sensu stricto*, that can claim to be philosophically inspired by Derrida; nonetheless, certain principles often seem to rise up, giving some commonality to the field:

1 *Decentering through mise-en-scène*, given that a globalized or universalized staging discourse – at least a clear or explicit one – no longer exists. The director is no longer the authorial instance, the central subject controlling everything. The actor, the creative ensemble in its entirety, technology, the media – none are still required to obey an artist-demiurge.
2 *Fragmentation* of prior forms of classical mise-en-scène resulting from the fragmentation of the subject has led to new work methods, such as what Martin Puchner calls 'collaborative production' and 'collaborative reception'.[14]
3 *Overt staging* of the theatrical process, the performative presentation of an event, has taken the place of representation, figuration and sometimes even signification.
4 All staging, especially all deconstructive staging, is a 'poetics of *derangement*',[15] but which nonetheless does not exclude the idea of regulation and adjustment.

The return of mise-en-scène?

If Derrida's deconstruction gives PDT its conceptual framework, it also encourages philosophical generalities, frequently departing from any grounding in a concrete analysis of performance. Lehmann's book, along with his disciples' and other artists' thoughts on postdramatic staging, attempts to return to more precise technical descriptions of performance, to recenter their work on a more classical idea of staging that is already in the process of being forgotten or neglected. Staging itself is the sole concrete place where theory and practice confront each other, calling for a wide variety of choices, including the refinement and correction of examples of PDT.

Along with these staging factors, in the 'Continental' sense, we must still pay attention to the idea and the practice of performance art itself, and play with the opposition of these two models.[16] These two paradigms in fact structure the international field of performance, most notably the Continental, European world and the Anglo-American English-speaking world: these two worlds still ignore each other to some degree. However, these different directions, even oppositions, through which to see and analyze theatre converge in a single hybrid practice: we may be moving toward some kind of 'performise', of 'mise-en-perf'.

PDT, in its desire to completely abandon the mimetic for the solely performative, leaving behind the story, history, action and characters, can result in something good or something terrible. Its tendency toward self-reference is soon exhausted, mimesis returns, the character is reborn from its ashes. And postdramatic theory does not impose its reflection extensively on the performative, given that it is not able to account for the performance work of the 1990s and 2000s, most notably Judith Butler's and Elisabeth Grosz's feminisms. However, the current questions over identities of all sorts may lead to a better understanding of ways of making and embodying all the elements of a performance.

Could bringing the general aesthetic of the postdramatic and the recent history of staging closer together provide foundations for a theory of a deconstructive (or postdramatic) staging? Only if we pay close attention to the following tasks:

1 *Historicizing staging practices*, contextualizing and comparing them, and inscribing them more clearly within a larger framework, as a theory of media or cultural practices.
2 *Analyzing their strategy*, their combination, their polemical value, their cultural dimension. And we must remember that within each cultural and linguistic context, identifying examples of the postdramatic and evaluating PDT differ. Thus, connections to classical texts are very different in the Netherlands, in France, or in England.
3 *Updating examples* of this kind of theatre from the past 30 or even 40 years, examples that Lehmann first began to analyze 20 to 30 years ago. This practice has now evolved and experiments in it diversified, even if certain artists such as those of the Rimini Protokoll have claimed for themselves the label of postdramatic, while others, such as Ostermeier, have kept their distance:

> The postmodern theatre is part of decadent and satiated era that is now extinct. The spectator I was in Berlin at the beginning of the 90s no longer has the kind of cynicism regarding the kind of theatre done, say, at the Volksbühne, that the critics defined as "deconstructivist," declaring that the "great stories" no longer had anything to say to us.'[17]

Can the dramatic/postdramatic duality perhaps be overcome? We are now a long way from the direct confrontation between the dramatic and the epic that Brecht was still able to theorize in the 1920s, within the tradition of the Platonic opposition between *mimesis* and *diegesis*. The postdramatic can contain both dramatic and epic elements, naturalistic or theatricalized. The opposition between a modern rejection of theatricality and its postdramatic acceptance is no longer valid: the same staging could be passed from one to the other, given the postdramatic principle of heterogeneity.

A comparable duality, which can also be overcome, is that between a realistic style (concealing the marks of representation) and a theatricalized style (accentuating them). A director like Chéreau, for example, is able to alternate psychological moments with very theatrical, stylized and intensified ('heightened') ones.

General conclusions: the case of dramatic writing

With the ending of an era marked by the disappearance of irreplaceable artists such as Cunningham, Bausch, Grüber, Zadek, Gosch, or Schlingensief, have we entered into a new era – a true post-postdramatic one? Can we now emerge from the postdramatic? Is it not going to be difficult to leap out of its shadow? Will we leave the postdramatic behind only to return to the dramatic? This seems hardly probable.

It is good in any event to return *in fine* to the question implied by the term 'postdramatic' when we consider it literally: *what* writing, then, *what* dramaturgy 'after' the dramatic?

It probably does not make much sense to speak of a contemporary post-dramatic writing, in that most writer/playwrights have integrated and absorbed the larger anti-textual tendencies of PDT while being able to remain readable, not only in the sense of 'decipherable', but publishable as dramatic literature can be. Thus, Koltès has at least partially integrated a stage-specific aesthetic into his writing; this mixture of mimetic authenticity and theatrical artificiality by Chéreau, his director, who in his turn knew how to detect this dichotomy – one not always perceived by some other directors between 1980 and 2000 – in a piece of writing, making his productions into naturalistic documents on marginalized youth. This 'circularity' of writing and staging has become increasingly frequent in theatrical production, not only in the 'devised theatre' – theatre conceived without a text or script prior to studio improvisations – but in a conjunction of writing and staging: a playwright like Falk Richter, in his work with Stanislas Nordey,[18] writes something, then quickly stages the text after an immediate translation before rewriting certain passages and giving them back to the translator, then to the director and the actors.

269

Such a circularity lasts as long as the production conditions and the artists' patience allow; it reaffirms the practical and theoretical imbrication of text and play, it encourages us to reflect on all the mechanisms of staging; it reminds us tangentially that the text that, 30 or 40 years ago, might have been called 'the theatrical text that is no longer dramatic'[19] has once again become the 'newly dramatic' text (allowing us not to have to say 'post-postdramatic'). Following the period of what Lehmann calls the 'retreat from representation', which is both a 'retreat from' and a phenomena of 'disaccustoming' or severance (*PDT*: 443), texts have once again begun telling stories (without once again becoming 'well-made plays'), representing elements of the real and lending themselves to the effects of character. This return is not at all a reactionary restoration; it is simply an increased awareness that all human works and all human discourses always recount something. The theatre, certainly the contemporary theatre, is always, according to Sarrazac, 'rhapsodic'. The notion of rhapsody is 'linked to the domain of the epic: to that of chants and Homeric narration, at the same time that it contains writing processes such as montage, hybridization, patchwork, chorality'.[20] This idea can be applied to the totality of staging, and thus it can be seen as on the level of the postdramatic.

The difference, however, is that the theory of contemporary texts, and above all its mode of analysis, remain to be established. This analytical theory must be integrated into the parameters of the dramatic and the postdramatic. Tools such as action, dramaturgy, intrigue, story and ideology remain pertinent, existing only in order to state their absence or their mutation.[21]

Could PDT stand in the way of the evolution of dramaturgy and writing for the theatre because of its new norms, its new *doxa*? According to Sarrazac, such a blockage is real, since the postdramatic misunderstood dramatic writing and its intrinsic evolution, which was not subjected to all the risks of the staged. Sarrazac calls what he wishes for a reaction against the postdramatic; he opposes a 'reprise': 'this moment – which is the opposite of a restoration – in which the drama is reconstituting and revivifying itself under the influence of a theatre that has become its own Stranger'.[22] There is indeed a genuine risk: the complete inversion of the text–stage relation. Previously dominated by the text and logocentrism, this relation, under the 'scenocentrism' of the postdramatic, finds itself entirely subsumed by the stage and scenic practice, leaving no chance for the text to be read or even written by a playwright. The new master is no longer the director, now seen as too logocentric, but the 'writer *from* the stage' (*écrivain de plateau*), who is seen as being simultaneously director and creator of the text/stage assemblage, and thus of a hybrid entity, an all-around athlete on the boards and on the page, (re)writing its texts in the light of the projections of the stage.

This 'stage writing', which has become more common, if not dominant, in the theatre of research, coalesces in PDT like two drops of water. The idea is that all creation emanates from the stage, out of concrete work with actors in the concrete space and time of the stage. In this sense, this 'stage writing' (not a very good name, since it is about neither writing nor the traditional stage) rejoins the British tradition of 'devised theatre', which has the annoying tendency to devour other forms of theatre of research, most notably dramatic writing and 'director's theatre', the theatre whose staging is inspired by the Continental tradition. Basically, three kinds of experience – PDT, devised theatre, and stage writing – meet to avoid, if not to liquidate, the tradition of artistic staging founded on the rereadings of plays, most frequently classics. Since the German *Stadttheater* could not easily renounce the classic repertory demanded by a traditional and petit bourgeois public, it integrated research into the postdramatic by applying it rather mechanically through invited directors or employees of the theatre. They did this with Robert Wilson, and are currently doing so with former postdramatic avant-gardists like Jan Lauwers, Jan Fabre, Luk Perceval, or Thalheimer. These same powerful, established institutions in Germany and elsewhere, which throughout the 1970s and 80s encouraged the beginnings of the postdramatic, are perhaps now in the process of recuperating, adapting, commercializing, completing and destroying them. The future of theatre probably resides more in systematic subvention in its mode of subsidizing than in the elaboration of new forms, whether dramatic or postdramatic.

Thanks to Lehmann's thoughtful commentary, as well as that of his students and now numerous artists who have spread his thought throughout the world, PDT has had the immense value of formalizing a living, regenerative current in world theatre, though certainly one with all the contradictions and imprecisions of our times, and with a skepticism as cynical as it is despairing toward dogmas of the past and easy promises for the future. PDT is far from having given up its secret: not simply style, theory, nor method, it is a ploy for moving beyond deadlocked contradictions. Its survival or disappearance depends not at all on a return of the dramatic and a neoclassical dramaturgy, but rather on the strengthening of a writing that has not completely severed its ties with art and dramatic literature. In the battle of the dramatic and the PD, the dramatic has certainly not said its last word.

Notes

1   Verlag der Autoren.
2   *Theater der Zeit*, no. 12, 2002.

3 Cited by Christel Weiler in 'Postdramatisches Theater,' *Metzler Lexikon Theatertheorie*, 2005, 245.

4 *Drama Review*, 52.2 (T198), 178–83.

5 University of Chicago Press.

6 *Contemporary Drama in English*, vol. 14, *Drama and/after Postmodernism*. Trier: Wissenschaftlicher Verlag, 2007, 44.

7 According to Jerzy Limon, PDT has a distant but clear ancestor in the form of the masque (e.g. the Stuart Masque) at the beginning of the 17th century. Cf. 'Performativity of the Court: Stuart Masque as Postdramatic Theatre,' in Paul Cefalu and Bryan Reynolds, eds, *The Return of Theory in Early Modern English Studies*. Basingstoke: Palgrave Macmillan, 2011.

8 *Stage Fright: Modernism, Anti-Theatricality, and Drama*. Baltimore: Johns Hopkins UP, 2002, 5.

9 *Etudes théâtrales*, 2007, 9.

10 From Jens Roselt, 'In Ausnahmezuständen. Schauspieler im postdramatischen Theater,' *Text und Kritik*, 166–76.

11 *Theory of Modern Drama*, The Age of Man, 1983, 135.

12 Sarrazac, 16.

13 Pavis, 2007, 159–60.

14 *Stage Fright: Modernism, Anti-Theatricality, and Drama*. Baltimore: Johns Hopkins UP, 2002, 176.

15 Hans-Thies Lehmann. *Postdramatisches Theater*, 1999, 266.

16 See Pavis, *La Mise en scène contemporaine*, Armand Colin, 2007, 43–71.

17 Thomas Ostermeier and Sylvie Chalaye, *Thomas Ostermeier*, Paris: Actes Sud-Papiers, 2006, 53.

18 E.g. *My Secret Garden*, Avignon 2010.

19 The title of a book by G. Poschmann (*Der nicht mehr dramatische Theatertext*), 1997.

20 Sarrazac, *Lexique du drame moderne et contemporain*, Paris: Circé, 2005, 183–4.

21 Pavis, *Le Théâtre contemporain*, Paris: Nathan, 2002.

22 Sarrazac, 2007, 17.

30   Evo-Neuro-Theatre[1]

Mark Pizzato

The term 'theatre' comes from the Greek *theatron*, a seeing place, which also gave root to the word 'theory'. But theatrical elements of performance, in life and art, emerged much earlier in human evolution, structuring how our brains experience and express actual and possible worlds, through current neural and interpersonal networks. The primal drives of our animal ancestors, to survive and reproduce, became extended toward ego powers, mythic names and soul ideas, as the struggle for existence shifted into a meta-awareness of self, other, mortality and a potential afterlife, in earthly and cosmic theatres. Environmental and sexual selection continued to play biological roles in our evolution. Yet various cultural stages transformed the environment for human survival and changed the inner theatres of our brains (Pizzato 2011), which structure today's performance realms of perception, fantasy, memory, dreams, daily interactions, group politics, child's play, sports and art.

In recent decades, scholars have stressed the textual, gendered and multicultural aspects of theatre through poststructuralist theories, or the broadest senses of theatre in performance studies. Diversity was favored, 'essentialism' critiqued. Now the other side of the coin deserves consideration. An evolutionary, neuroscientific approach can help us to explore the roots of human performance (and Western notions of 'theatre') through our species' prehistory and our brain's anatomy.

Some advocates of applying cognitive science to theatre, such as Bruce McConachie (2007), argue that it should replace postmodern approaches, because it is based in objective research with 'falsifiable' experiments, although still vulnerable to subjective concerns and interpretations. I would argue, however, that Lacanian psychoanalysis, which influenced various postmodernist theories, connects very well with a neurological approach to theatre today – providing a phcnomcnological complement to empirical discoveries about the brain, regarding scientific theories on the co-evolution of nature and culture (Pizzato 2006). I will make brief references to such connections here, involving animal drives that extend, through distinctive brain functions, into theatrical modes of performance: orientation and pattern-finding, playful mirroring, and self-/other consciousness.

Orientation and pattern finding

For millions of years, organisms competed and cooperated to produce further generations of genetic experiments as nature's artworks. Pleasure seeking and pain avoidance verified the biological value of certain physical orientations, locations and patterns for survival and reproduction – from animal instincts to human ideologies. Particular neural circuits have now been found for primal emotions in humans and other mammals, expressing such biological values: rage, fear, panic and seeking systems in the brain, which involve fighting, fleeing, calling/hiding, foraging, lust and nurturing drives (Panksepp 1998; Solms and Turnbull 2002: 115–37). But why do humans add to their survival and reproduction stress by valuing fictional displays of rage, fear, panic, seeking and lust?

There may be some pleasure (in the brain's dopaminergic reward circuits) to dangers and desires that are experienced and resolved, or made ridiculous, through vicarious conflicts and climaxes, on-stage or on-screen. Yet theatre, as an art form, seeks to provide more than just thrill-ride entertainment and illusory laughter. Theatre offers a 'threat rehearsal' space for the inner theatres of many brains to interact – as dreams do for individual brains, according to current research (Revonsuo 2003). Through the art of theatre, individuals and groups can reorient their priorities, gaining insights about the views of others, even those who are alien and perceived as threats. But theatre also bears a dangerous power to promote racist and sexist views, shown in popular melodramas from stage to screen, with binary depictions of good versus evil characters, or stereotypes of male heroes and vulnerable females (Pizzato 2005). Theatre may increase collective patterns of cooperation within a group through competition against others, focusing the cruelty of primal passions – desire, fear and rage – on certain scapegoats. And yet, theatre can also evoke the catharsis of such feelings, perhaps involving a prefrontal cortex (PFC) 'regulation' and 'reappraisal' of limbic emotions (Schore 1994; Kim and Hamann 2007; Beauregard et al. 2001; Schaefer et al. 2002; Urry et al. 2006; Ochsner et al. 2002).

Humans share with other mammals the emotional functions and basic structures of the limbic system at the center of the brain, resting on the brainstem and spinal cord. Such areas are much older than the human neocortex, which greatly expanded in our ancestors' evolution, with distinctive functional structures, especially in the PFC (inside your forehead). The parietal and occipital lobes (at the top and back of your head, for spatial negotiation and vision) also developed through our earlier primate and hominid ancestors, as they moved from tree to land environments, eventually with bipedal locomotion, which allowed for much greater gestural and tool-using skills. The temporal lobes (at the sides of your head), which are considered part of the limbic system, evolved to find survival meanings in genetically programmed and socially learned patterns, through primal emotions, memory circuits and the potential for ecstatic visions and inner voices – offering transcendent hopes in a divine theatre beyond mortality (Ramachandran and Blakeslee 1998; Persinger 2001).

All animals seek to orient themselves in their environment, recognizing certain patterns of threats, pleasures and survival benefits. Mammals use the emotions of their limbic systems to focus on survival and reproduction, as competitive and cooperative drives, from deeper and older brain structures (the brainstem, basal ganglia, cerebellum and the body's entire nervous system, including the 'second brain' in the gut). In humans, too, emotions communicate from the 'theater of the body' to more conscious, higher order feelings in the 'theater of the mind' (Damasio 2003: 28). The art of theatre extends this orienting of immediate and long term, emotional priorities, from mammalian play and imagined actions to the 'what if' and 'as if' of playing with feelings, gestures, words, ideas, characters and plots onstage. Patterns are not just reacted to, in the given environment, but radically transformed – in potential and reflective spaces. Humans evolved as extensive pattern finders, as diviners of signs beyond nature (Burkert 1996: 161–2), projecting 'faces in the clouds' (Guthrie 1993). Humans of many cultures created relationships with supernatural characters in animistic, cosmic or virtual theatres, as if needing superior species (as brain extensions) to contain their own. The human PFC and limbic system are still evolving to handle our primal drives in the new environments of language and culture that we create (Deacon 1997: 420–37; LeDoux 2003: 322). Theatre and other arts use these brain areas collectively to create new characterizations of space, frames, objects, time, plots, movement, beauty, truth, good and evil, political and metaphysical hierarchies, mortal meanings and natural or supernatural forces. Theatre is needed today, with or without the gods of the past, to develop further reflections and ethical patterns, despite the dangers it represents.

Playful mirroring

In evolutionary terms, the human animal extends mammalian play far beyond the youthful purposes of experimentation and skill learning. Human egos and groups continue to fight for survival, dominance and reproductive rights far into adulthood – using the 'what if' spaces of spontaneous play, or more formal sports and games, as well as stage and screen media – to practice and reflect upon potential or historical conflicts. Such competitions often involve the brain's 'binary operator' (in the left parietal lobe) with good versus evil, or 'us' against 'them' patterns (Newberg et al. 2002: 196). But theatre can also help us to perceive more complex relationships, clarifying the primal emotions that melodramatic stereotypes evoke, through a tragic (or tragicomic) catharsis of fear, sympathy, panic and rage – at the 'stimulus barrier' of the ventromedial (lower inner) PFC, where it connects with the limbic system (Kaplan-Solms and Solms 2000: 276; Solms and Turnbull 2002: 104, 136, 287–8).

The left and right hemispheres of the neocortex (including its prefrontal, frontal and parietal lobes) function in distinctive ways. The left, which also controls the right side of the body, is a rational, verbal, sequential thinking, executive interpreter and maintainer of beliefs and expectations (or a 'war-room General') often inhibiting, yet sometimes influenced or overwhelmed by the more emotional, intuitive, holistic anomaly detector (or 'Devil's Advocate scout') in the right (Ramachandran and Blakeslee 1998: 135–6; McGilchrist 2009). Thus, the playfulness of humans, especially through theatre, extends the functional influences of many right hemispheres together, through trickster figures, heroic rebels and new movements. Traditionalists may view the new radicals as dangerous or evil – as a binary threat to their own way of life, feared as being lost. And destructive revolutions may occur beyond the play. But artistic experiments of the right brain's Imaginary realm can also be cathartic (in a Lacanian sense) for the revision of social norms and language networks in the left's Symbolic order, through the continued evolution of brain areas and human cultures – regarding the Real of remnant, subcortical drives (Pizzato 2006: 62; Fink 1995: 71).

The recent discovery of 'mirror neurons' – involving an inner 'simulation' of the other's mind (Gallese and Goldman 1998) – confirms the significance of Lacanian ideas about the mirror stage, the Imaginary and the Other's desire, embedded in various poststructuralist theories. It also reveals more about the interplay of the brain's inner and outer theatres in everyday life. First discovered in other primates, mirror neurons fire when a monkey performs a certain action, such as picking up a peanut, and when it watches another monkey performing the same act. But humans have evolved their mirror neurons to fire, unlike the monkey's, when an action is pantomimed (Iacoboni 2008: 26, 228, 257; Keysers and Gazzola 2009: 19–20). Human mirror neurons are also tied to intuition neurons, in the insula and cingulate cortex of the limbic system (Blakeslee and Blakeslee 2007: 187–9). These are related to the emotional contagion that can be observed in other animals, when individuals react to subtle cues, producing spontaneous collective behaviors that ripple through the herd or flock (Hurley and Chater 2005: 9, 15).

Some mirror neurons, called canonical neurons, fire when the object involved in a typical action is observed, with or without the act. Echo-mirror neurons are triggered by words, stimulating the tongue to speak (Iacoboni 2008: 102–5; Rizzolatti and Sinigaglia 2008: 168–9). Thus, visually and orally, a 'chameleon effect' can be produced with spontaneous imitations of stereotypical behaviors (Hurley 2004: 171) – becoming compulsive in those with 'echopraxia' due to damage in their frontal lobe 'braking mechanism' (Rizzolatti and Sinigaglia 2008: 151). In all of us, the activation or inhibition of mirror neurons changes depending on the context of a scene (Iacoboni 2008: 6–7). Yet, signals are sent from mirror neurons to mimic the actions, facial expressions, gestures and words of others – even when other brain areas inhibit the mimicry (as is expected for conventional Western theatre spectators). We use mirror and intuition neurons, mostly unconsciously, to simulate one another's mental states, to interpret similar or different views (as a 'theory of mind'), and to share or counteract the ideas, desires and feelings of the other's inner theatre. Especially with the kinetic imagery and intense emotions of theatre as an art form, these Imaginary and Real, right cortical and limbic/subcortical dimensions of our collective neural networks play with Symbolic, left hemisphere rules – to reorder the ways that primal drives are expressed.

Self- and other consciousness (all merely players)

Another mode of animal to human theatricality, in our evolution and brains, is self- and other-consciousness, which extends from a basic spatial awareness (in the left and right parietal lobes) to ideas of ego, self-sacrifice, alienation and various identifications with and against others, on-stage or in life. Cognitive psychologist Merlin Donald (2001: 261) charts the evolution of such self-/other-consciousness from the 'episodic' awareness of our primate ancestors (concerned mostly with the present moment and instinctual goals) to 'mimetic' communications by *Homo erectus* two million years ago, involving conscious control and action planning, which 'enabled playacting, body language, precise imitation, and gesture'. *Homo sapiens* then developed 'mythic' cultures of verbal narrative communication about a half million years ago and the 'theoretic' technologies of tool use and further artistic sharing, starting about 40,000 years ago, as evidenced by fossilized skulls and archeological artifacts. These stages are the inherited layers of performance today, involving basic brain areas and Lacanian orders (subcortical/limbic Real, right cortical Imaginary, and left Symbolic), plus various technologies of stage and screen media.

277

Neuroscientist Bernard Baars (1997) uses theatrical terms, supported by empirical research, to explain the staging of consciousness by the 90 percent of brain activity that remains unconscious. Concepts and perceptions are like actors and scenery in a 'spotlight' onstage. Working memory is like the stage itself, with its sense of recent experiences. The rest of the brain's activity involves unconscious agents, competing and collaborating to focus on particular perceptions and ideas. There are deep goal and conceptual contexts, like 'directors' backstage, along with immediate expectations and intentions as stagehands, plus automatic skills, motivational processes and long-term memory systems as the interpretive 'audience', affecting what appears in the brain's inner theatre. These backstage operators form an implicit sense of self as 'the framework' of consciousness, 'the deepest layers of context ... largely unconscious' (Baars 1997: 145), and thus the unconscious subject (in Lacan's terms) behind the fragile mask of ego and its autobiographical scripts. They also interact with operators in others' brains, interpreted through external performances as allies or antagonists – for cooperation, involving reciprocal altruism and self-sacrifice to a 'kin' group (as with other primates), or the opposite.

According to Baars (1997), the players inside the brain's theatre, competing for the limelight of consciousness, include various bodily senses, inner imagery and speech, dreams, imagined feelings and verbal ideas. There is also a 'fringe' consciousness at the edges of the spotlight: intuitions of familiarity, beauty and goodness. Yet, what we accept as reality beyond the brain is actually constructed on its inner stage from various sense perceptions, confirming or changing our expectations and intentions. For example, after our eyes invert the images of the world outside, neural signals travel to about 40 areas in the occipital lobes at the back of the brain, each specialized for a different aspect of vision, such as motion, contrast, orientation, color and shape (Baars 1997: 65–6). Circuits then reconnect these aspects into a unified experience of vision, through secondary association areas and memory systems, in the parietal and temporal lobes (Solms and Turnbull 2002: 23–5). The inner theatre also fills in the gaps and disruptions of vision – from blind spots (where the eyes attach to the optic nerves), saccades (the normal flickering movement of the eyes) and other obstacles – creating the appearance of a full visual world (Ramachandran and Blakeslee 1998: 88–112). Yet, these same neural circuits are used for fantasies and dreams, giving scientific evidence for the postmodern notion that 'reality' is really a personal and social construction, a simulacrum projected upon the Real by the Imaginary and Symbolic orders within and between brains.

Conclusion

An 'evo-neuro-theatre' approach to performance studies offers tools for exploring theatrical structures in and between brains today. But it also extends our understanding of performance drives, from the animal heritage within us. When aligned with and not simply rejecting prior approaches, it points to a new era of values, built on both the universal aspirations of modernist art and the postmodern sensitivity to diverse cultural views. It shows how far we have evolved from, and yet continue to evolve through, the animal within the human brain: fueled by survival and reproduction drives, biologically and culturally, cooperatively and competitively.

Note

1   I have coined this term to reflect other new interdisciplinary fields: evolutionary psychology, neuroaesthetics, neuroeconomics and neurotheology. My thanks to David Bashor, Professor Emeritus of Biology at University of North Carolina at Charlotte, for years of discussion that were crucial to my understanding of evolution and neurology.

Works cited

Baars, Bernard J. *In the Theater of Consciousness: The Workspace of the Mind*. Oxford: OUP, 1997.

Beauregard, Mario, Levesque, Johanne and Bourgouin, Pierre. 'Neural Correlates of Conscious Self-Regulation of Emotion.' *The Journal of Neuroscience* 21 (2001): RC165.

Blakeslee, Sandra and Blakeslee, Matthew. *The Body Has a Mind of Its Own*. New York: Random, 2007.

Burkert, Walter. *Creation of the Sacred: Tracks of Biology in Early Religions*. Cambridge, MA: Harvard University Press, 1996.

Damasio, Antonio. *Looking for Spinoza: Joy, Sorrow, and the Feeling Brain*. Orlando: Harcourt, 2003.

Deacon, Terrence W. *The Symbolic Species: The Co-Evolution of Language and the Brain*. New York: Norton, 1997.

Donald, Merlin. *A Mind So Rare: The Evolution of Human Consciousness*. New York: Norton, 2001.

Fink, Bruce. *The Lacanian Subject*. Princeton: Princeton University Press, 1995.

Gallese, Vittorio and Goldman, Alvin. 'Mirror Neurons and the Simulation Theory of Mind-Reading.' *Trends in Cognitive Neuroscience* 2.12 (1998): 493–502.

Guthrie, Stewart Elliott. *Faces in the Clouds: A New Theory of Religion*. Oxford: OUP, 1993.

Hurley, Susan. 'Imitation, Media Violence, and Freedom of Speech.' *Philosophical Studies* 117 (2004): 165–218.

Hurley, Susan and Chater, Nick. Introduction. In Hurley and Chater, eds, *Perspectives on Imitation*, vols 1 and 2. Cambridge, MA: MIT Press, 2005, 1–52.

Iacoboni, Marco. *Mirroring People*. New York: Farrar, 2008.

Kaplan-Solms, Karen and Solms, Mark. *Clinical Studies in Neuro-Psychoanalysis*. London: Karnac, 2000.

Keysers, Christian and Gazzola, Valeria. 'Unifying Social Cognition.' In Jaime A. Pineda, ed., *Mirror Neuron Systems*. New York: Springer, 2009, 3–38.

Kim, Sang Hee and Hamann, Stephan. 'Neural Correlates of Positive and Negative Emotion Regulation.' *Journal of Cognitive Neuroscience* 19.5 (2007): 776–98.

LeDoux, Joseph. *Synaptic Self*. New York: Penguin, 2003.

McConachie, Bruce. 'Falsifiable Theories for Theatre and Performance Studies.' *Theatre Journal* 59.4 (2007): 553–77.

McGilchrist, Iain. *The Master and his Emissary*. New Haven: Yale University Press, 2009.

Newberg, Andrew, d'Aquili, Eugene and Rause, Vince. *Why God Won't Go Away: Brain Science and the Biology of Belief*. New York: Ballantine, 2002.

Ochsner, Kevin N., Bunge, Silvia A., Gross, James J. and Gabrieli, John D.E. 'Rethinking Feelings: An fMRI Study of the Cognitive Regulation of Emotion.' *Journal of Cognitive Neuroscience* 14.8 (2002): 1215–29.

Panksepp, Jaak. *Affective Neuroscience: The Foundations of Human and Animal Emotions*. Oxford: OUP, 1998.

Persinger, Michael. 'The Neuropsychiatry of Paranormal Experiences.' *Journal of Neuropsychiatry and Clinical Neurosciences* 13.4 (2001): 515–23.

Pizzato, Mark. *Theatres of Human Sacrifice: From Ancient Ritual to Screen Violence*. Albany: SUNY Press, 2005.

– *Ghosts of Theatre and Cinema in the Brain*. Basingstoke: Palgrave Macmillan, 2006.

– *Inner Theatres of Good and Evil: The Mind's Staging of Gods, Angels and Devils*. Jefferson, NC: McFarland, 2011.

Ramachandran, V.S. and Blakeslee, Sandra. *Phantoms in the Brain: Probing the Mysteries of the Human Mind*. New York: William Morrow, 1998.

Revonsuo, Antti. 'The Reinterpretation of Dreams: An Evolutionary Hypothesis of the Function of Dreaming.' In Edward F. Pace-Schott, Mark Solms, Mark Blagrove and Stevan Harnad, eds, *Sleeping and Dreaming*. Cambridge: CUP, 2003, 85–111.

Rizzolatti, Giacomo and Sinigaglia, Corrado. *Mirrors in the Brain: How Our Minds Share Our Actions*. Oxford: OUP, 2008.

Schaefer, Stacey M., Jackson, Daren C., Davidson, Richard J., Aguirre, Geoffrey K., Kimberg Daniel Y. et al. 'Modulation of Amygdalar Activity by the Conscious Regulation of Negative Emotion.' *Journal of Cognitive Neuroscience* 14.6 (2002): 913–21.

Schore, Allan N. *Affect Regulation and the Origin of the Self*. Hillsdale, NJ: Lawrence Erlbaum, 1994.

Solms, Mark and Turnbull, Oliver. *The Brain and the Inner World*. New York: Other Press, 2002.

Urry, Heather L., van Reekum, Carien M., Johnstone, Tom, Kalin, Ned H., Thurow, Marchell E. et al. 'Amygdala and Ventromedial Prefrontal Cortex Are Inversely Coupled during Regulation of Negative Affect and Predict the Diurnal Pattern of Cortisol Secretion among Older Adults.' *The Journal of Neuroscience* 26.16 (2006): 4415–25.

31   International/ism

Janelle Reinelt

A cluster of terms crop up whenever scholars try to discuss the exponential changes occurring at lightning speed worldwide. Words such as globalization, internationalism, transnationalism, cosmopolitanism and worldly (used as an adjective) are just some of the terms circulating through discourse as scholars attempt to find a suitable concept to describe a lived phenomenon and an object of study. I intend to make an argument for the value of 'international(ism)' as the key term for the scholarly field of theatre and performance studies, although my assessment may be surpassed by the changing state of what is, before this chapter even sees print.

In the past decade, our field was preoccupied with attempts to articulate the relationship between the cultural and artistic practice of performance and the emerging phenomenon of globalization. In 2005–06, three Anglo-American journals published special issues on these topics – *Theatre Journal, Modern Drama* and *Contemporary Theatre Review*. The word 'globalization' appeared in the title of two, while 'transnational' and 'diaspora' appeared in the third. International conferences featured themes as overt as 'global/local' at the international Federation for Theatre Research (Helsinki 2006)[1] or as subtle as the Performance Studies international theme (#14, 2008): 'Interregnum: In Between States'. In 2009, Dan Rebellato's *Theatre & Globalization* contributed a succinct and insightful treatise on the linkage between terms.

The disciplinary project is to understand and interrogate our scholarship in relation to the vastly different worldwide topography that shapes our contemporary experiences of performance. Recognizing that performance practices everywhere are affected by global cultural flows and what Arjun Appadurai (1996) has dubbed scapes – ethnoscapes, technoscapes, financescapes, mediascapes and ideoscapes – scholars struggle to find appropriately fluid ways to study these processes without becoming entangled in the neoliberal strategy of abstraction that so often underpins globalization itself (Koski and Sihra 2010: vii). Appadurai (1996: 37) coined his terms to emphasize what he perceived in 1996 as 'cascading phenomena' (a computer word as well as a geological one), characterized by the 'sheer speed, scale, and volume of each of these flows', so great that he argued we were experiencing a rupture.

Fifteen years after the publication of Appadurai's influential book *Modernity at Large: Cultural Dimensions of Globalization* (1996), most of his arguments remain bold and relevant although the withering of the nation state, which was the central prediction of the volume, has not taken place. Before discussing this book in more detail, I want to linger on theatre and performance studies as they take up the challenge of understanding and interpreting global change and the discipline's place in it.

In *TDR: The Drama Review* (2007), I participated in a dialogue began by Jon McKenzie, later followed up by Richard Schechner with a forum of scholars, under the title, 'Is Performance Studies Imperialist?' I advocated 'international performance literacies' as our disciplinary goal:

Believing that the nation continues to play a central role in both globalization and movements of transnational capital, goods, and information, I prefer the older, even old-fashioned term 'international', understanding international to mean pursuing interconnections and cooperation across cultural and national lines, fostering comparativist research, developing cosmopolitan methodologies and perspectives with regard to our national and local scholarship, and seeking to understand and critique the complex and ever-shifting global context within which we live and work. (Reinelt 2007: 7–8)

The choice of terms reflects an attempt to parse how these words currently signify and to develop a rhetoric that can carry a politics: a value-invested interpretation of these words leads to a particular preference for using them to chart a terrain that would neither affirm globalization's predations nor easily embrace the newer term 'transnationalism', but carry the older cluster of terms around 'international' precisely because it refers to a historical project and a contemporary predicament between nations.

To begin with globalization, this volatile term has settled down a bit in the time since the journal special issues were published, and Jen Harvie and Dan Rebellato (2006: 3) wrote in their editorial in *Contemporary Theatre Review* that 'what marks the globalization debate is, at the very most fundamental level, uncertainty about what globalization is and how we should respond to it'. If there is less anxiety now about what it is, perhaps there is more about how to respond to it. Globalization is primarily seen through an economic lens, the result of capital working in a transnational arena increasingly complex and multivalenced, producing consequences for every aspect of life on the planet, often through but also beyond nation states or territorial borders. It is also increasingly perceived through an ecological lens, which fixes on the interdependencies of the biosphere and the effects, most often negative, of said transnational capitalism on key aspects of the planet – weather, water, agriculture, energy, biodiversity, population, to name the obvious. In the realm of culture, it most often implies highly mediatized circuits of communication and representation, leading to fears of a homogenized and commodified world culture.

In other words, globalization is mostly perceived in terms of negative effects. That it is much more than these things and that often positive new developments grow out of globalizing forces has not offset its negative valence. This is especially true in the arts where the history of debates about high culture, popular and mass culture come back again like the return of the repressed to worry the question of aesthetic value anew, indicative in the particularly banal but ultra-present phrase, 'world-class culture', which is a favorite of funding bodies, corporate investors and many arts institutions and patrons. Calling an academic program in our disciplines 'globalization and performance' or worse 'globalized performance and culture' would create a narrow conception of events and processes that should be able to be thought in a resistant, even counterintuitive mode as a wedge against the already seemingly monolith. In social sciences, on the contrary, a 'center for the study of globalization' seems justified beyond question as a project coming from economics or sociology. In the arts, however, we need acts of naming that gesture beyond the limitations of this term and recall the qualitative and disaggregated indicators of sweeping social change.

The obvious opposition of global to local has often dominated scholarly discourse. The binary creates a problem because while the terms are held in conceptual opposition, local artistic practices are indigenous and simultaneously saturated with global materials. As Eng-Beng Lim (2005: 383–405) argued about gay performance in Singapore, Asian queer culture is a specific phenomenon, embedded in time and place, quite local, and simultaneously existing in relation to and influenced by Western commodification and representational styles. This complexity moves beyond categories of global and local, and indeed, becomes occluded by Western hegemony when the emphasis is placed on its relationship to First World queer cultures, or alternatively becomes subsumed by conservative or romantic ideas of ethnic or folkloric purity that emphasize the local and particular. For this reason, the neologism 'glocal', favored by Lim and which entered circulation through sociology in the mid-1990s, does not quite solve the problem as the two terms remain latent within the new term.

With regard to 'transnationalism' as a term, the potential for expressing new modalities of experience seems much better, and, indeed, it may be the most prevalent term in our field to embrace a trajectory that moves across and beyond borders, especially of the nation state. Coming to prominence in the late 1990s, especially in the work of people like Appadurai and Saskia Sassen, this term attempts to describe the heightened mobility of capital, information, images and people across traditional borders, rendering them less important than charting the flow of movement itself. The Transnationalism Project at the University of Chicago, led by Sassen, would be an example of a research center on this theme, and in our field, Diana Taylor's Hemispheric Institute of Performance and Politics uses the Americas as a transnational organizing point. Yan Haiping's title for her special issue of *Modern Drama*, 'Other Transnationals: Asian Diaspora in Performance', explicitly signaled her desire to focus on 'the process by which immigrants make their social relations across the established borders between their societies of origin and of settlement' (2005: 232).

Although it is useful, transnational should not be the primary descriptor for our scholarship or our objects of study, in that it tends to overrate the strength and extent of the 'trans', and it also dissembles the ongoing strength of the nation state – in particular, in relationship to performance. The history of world theatre depends on geographic, national and regional identity for the maintenance of its archives, even the contestatory archives of embodied performance such as precolonial performances in Chris Balme's study, *Pacific Performances: Theatricality and Cross-Cultural Encounter in the South Seas* (2007), or precolonial performances of Taylor and Juan Villegas's *Negotiating Performance: Gender, Sexuality, and Theatricality in Latin America* (1994). The circuitry of contemporary performance also still functions primarily in relation to national formations (such as national theatres). When a region or locality sets out against the state to specifically produce a dissident corpus of work, as in Catalonia for instance, it is the contrastive relationship that helps define the alternative form. S.E. Wilmer's collection on national theatres in Europe thus attends to (glossing Raymond Williams) 'the role of the National Theatres in negotiating between the residual values of the nation-state, and the emerging values of a pan-European culture' (2008: 2).

Geopolitically, I think Appurdurai was right about many things, but not about the speed with which we would move to the 'post-nation', a term he coined in *Modernity at Large*. He wrote (1996: 169): 'We are in the process of moving to a global order in which the nation-state has become obsolete and other formations for allegiance and identity have taken its place.' Critics seized on and debated this highly categorical statement. Appurdurai (1996: 169) delineates another entailment of the post-nation: 'the possibility that, while nations might continue to exist, the steady erosion of the capabilities of the nation-state to monopolize loyalty will encourage the spread of national forms that are largely divorced from territorial states'. This idea has seen some manifestations in the past decade as the war on terror has raised the threshold of anxiety about security, while what Seyla Benhabib (2006: 45) calls the 'disaggregation of citizenship' separates collective identity formation, the privileges of political membership, and the entitlements of social rights and benefits. This high mobility of the ethnoscape produces communities that are not stable, or if they stabilize, may not carry the attributes of membership and belonging expected of citizenship. So, while on the one hand, nation states are still extremely powerful structural units, on the other hand, the multiple identifications and loyalties that individuals develop as they exist in increasingly mobile and plural localities have changed the way subjects experience belonging and identity formation. Iwa Ong (1999: 11) explores the emergence of this new concept in *Flexible Citizenship: The Cultural Logics of Transnationality,* but she is careful to critique Appadurai's notion of the post-nation too, writing: 'He ignores the fact that nations and states are still largely bound to each other, and he ignores the need to consider how the hyphen between the two has become reconfigured by capital mobility and migration.' Appadurai himself acknowledges his critics by 2006, but does not back down from his argument that nation states are in decay, driving the social uncertainty and anxiety of incompleteness that fuels large-scale, culturally motivated violence of our time (2006: 5–23).

In the best part of Appadurai's earlier book, he speaks of a revolution in the social imagination, and here lies the real legacy of the book:

> The world we live in today is characterized by a new role for the imagination in social life. ... the imagination has become an organized field of social practices, a form of work (in the sense of both labor and culturally organized practice), and a form of negotiation between sites of agency (individuals) and globally defined fields of possibility. (1996: 31)

The highly mobile and interconnected world enables people to imagine alternative worlds, even if they are not living in them, and thus to contest the administered world or resist homogenization because of the freedom to invent alternative conceptual and affective possibilities. There is, of course, something utopian and even disingenuous in this claim, given that the imagination itself can be colonized, a critique long since established by feminists and postcolonial critics and not necessarily made irrelevant because the speed and scope of contemporary life has increased exponentially. Yet it is an important claim for those of us who dwell in artistic practice and scholarship because the training and cultivation of the social imagination is basically our raison d'être: it is the claim for art's utility (for those of us who do not mind talking about utility), and if we have an increased role in the production of culture in this brave new world, it is an identifiable task we can tackle.

To do that, I prefer internationalism and its family of terms. To start with the genealogy of the term: 'International' first appears around 1780, apparently coined by Jeremy Bentham from inter plus national. The same Jeremy Bentham who developed the panopticon, here he was acting as a legal scholar to suggest a replacement for the traditional term 'law among nations'. In jurisprudence, there was a sharp distinction between domestic or national law and international law because the latter was not made by any established authority, since the international sphere – the space between, among or outside nations – was essentially one of anarchy or, perhaps better, improvisation. Trade and travel practices developed without any central authority, such that practices and customs sedimented over time into law, taking account of heterogeneous participants. Not that power differentials did not influence these practices, but, nevertheless, international law did not develop in response to any single sovereign authority, and it tended to be descriptive of practices rather than prescriptive. This strand of early history featured improvisatory negotiations that resulted in ongoing practices, which retrospectively become identified as law. Cornell University Law School (n.d.) describes this in their online discussion of international law:

> Customary law and conventional law are primary sources of international law. Customary international law results when states follow certain practices generally and consistently out of a sense of legal obligation. … Conventional international law derives from international agreements and may take any form that the contracting parties agree upon.

The legal aspect of the term 'international' supports a description of politics conceptualized in relation to neighborhoods, regions, or nations as well as between nations, and thus avoids the trap of already containing within its concept what it purports to describe. The view of politics I invoke here comes from conservative political theorist Michael Oakeshott (1962: 123): 'Politics is the activity of attending to the general arrangements of a collection of people who, in respect of their common recognition of their manner of attending to its arrangements, compose a single community.' To find ourselves engaged in 'attending' to a number of these social arrangements seems to describe not only peculiarly local efforts but also the broadest aspects of what we now call 'global society'. This suggests a certain improvisation, or at least investment and struggle among a number of social agents, who may or may not be recognized under terminology such as 'citizen'. 'Cosmopolitanism' has been purposely retooled by scholars in our field (Rebellato 2009; Rae 2006; Gilbert and Lo 2007) to function as a description of this sort of behavior, although it can be a slippery term with an elitist past, as Helen Gilbert and Jacqueline Lo (2007: 5) point out: 'For some theorists, cosmopolitanism operates as a prescriptive vision of global democracy and world citizenship while, for others, it offers a theoretical space for articulating hybrid cultural identities', in other words, a space for the social imagination. With this background of the term and a political entailment in mind, we can consolidate 'international' as a term that signals more than one nation, and implies cooperation or at least negotiation between and among multiple entities called nations. 'International' may be suffused with power relations, but in its genealogy from law, and in its literal preposition 'inter', it does not presuppose or structure the primacy of one term over the other. Not a perfect term, it nevertheless offers a terrain for struggle that seems to gesture to history and the future, without a foregone conclusion. What, then, might it mean?

'International' can become both a descriptor and a political commitment. Many performances circulating now are 'international' in form and substance. As Marvin Carlson (2006: 179) pointed out in his book on polylingual performances, contemporary artists often now 'create with materials from different cultures to play against materials from different cultures, without necessarily privileging the material of any one culture, even that most presumed to be familiar to a presumed majority of the audience'. Paul Rae (2006: 8) also notes: 'increasing numbers of performances are being made by artists whose cultural affiliations and implicitly informing national imaginaries differ both from those of their collaborators, and of their audiences'. Along with these clearly polynational performances, others are aligned with specific national traditions or positioned in international festivals to occupy historically national positions – our work as scholar critics could be to facilitate comparativist lines of inquiry and to point out the constellation of hybridized ingredients in these performances. 'International performance scholarship' would then pursue interconnections and cooperation across cultural and national lines, developing cosmopolitan methodologies and perspectives with regard to our national and local scholarship, and seek to understand and critique the complex and ever-shifting global context within which we live and work.

Note

1   A volume of essays grew out of the Helsinki conference: *The Local Meets the Global in Performance* (Koski and Sihra 2010).

Works cited

Appadurai, Arjun. *Modernity at Large: Cultural Dimensions of Globalization*. Minneapolis: University of Minnesota Press, 1996.

– *Fear of Small Numbers; An Essay on the Geography of Anger*. Durham: Duke University Press, 2006.

Balme, Christopher. *Pacific Performances: Theatricality and Cross-Cultural Encounter in the South Seas*. Basingstoke: Palgrave Macmillan, 2007.

Benhabib, Seyla. *Another Cosmopolitanism*. Oxford: OUP, 2006.

Carlson, Marvin. *Speaking in Tongues: Language at Play in the Theatre*. Ann Arbor: University of Michigan Press, 2006.

Cornell University Law School. 'International Law.' n.d., http://topics.law.cornell.edu/wex/international_law, accessed 5 October 2010.

Gilbert, Helen and Jacqueline Lo. *Performance and Cosmopolitics: Cross-Cultural Transactions in Australasia*. Basingstoke: Palgrave Macmillan, 2007.

Haiping, Yan. 'Other Transnations: An Introductory Essay.' *Modern Drama* 48.2 (2005): 232.

Harvie, Jen and Rebellato, Dan. 'Editorial'. *Contemporary Theatre Review* 16.1 (2006): 3–4.

Lim, Eng-Beng. 'Glocalqueering in New Asia: the Politics of Performing Gay in Singapore.' *Theatre Journal* 57.3 (2005): 383–405.

Koski, Pirkko and Sihra, Melissa, eds. *The Local Meets the Global in Performance*. Newcastle upon Tyne: Cambridge Scholars Publishing, 2010.

Oakeshott, Michael. *Rationalism in Politics and Other Essays*. New York: Basic Books, 1962.

Ong, Aihwa. *Flexible Citizenship: The Cultural Logics of Transnationality*. Durham, NC: Duke University Press, 1999.

Rae, Paul. 'What is the Cosmopolitan Stage?' *Contemporary Theatre Review* 16.1 (2006): 8–22.

Rebellato, Dan. *Theatre & Globalization*. Basingstoke: Palgrave Macmillan, 2009.

Reinelt, Janelle. 'Is Performance Studies Imperialist? Part 2.' *TDR: The Drama Review* 51.3 (T195) (2007): 7–16.

Taylor, Diana and Villegas, Juan. *Negotiating Performance: Gender, Sexuality, and Theatricalty in Latin/o America*. Durham, NC: Duke University Press, 1994.

Wilmer, S.E. ed. *National Theatres in a Changing Europe*. Basingstoke: Palgrave Macmillan, 2008.

32 Transculturation[1]

Jon D. Rossini

In thinking about transculturation it is important to think about process – the doing that happens in the space of trans, of moving across. Transculturation emerged in opposition to a logic of acculturation or assimilation and serves as a conceptual fixture of philosophical and cultural reflection of power dynamics of the Caribbean, Mexico and their diasporas in the US. Though deployed critically to reimagine the supposedly unidimensionality of acculturation, what seems most powerful and simultaneously exhausted about the proliferation of transculturation as a critical framework is its sense of reciprocal process that transforms cultures or agents on both sides. This conceptualization is an accurate reflection of Fernando Ortiz's first definition of his neologism. According to Ortiz (1947: 102–3):

> the word *transculturation* better expresses the different phases of the process of transition from one culture to another because this often does not consist merely in acquiring another culture, which is what the English word *acculturation* really implies, but the process also necessarily involves the loss or uprooting of a previous culture, which could be defined as a deculturation. In addition, it carries the idea of the consequent creation of new cultural phenomena, which could be called neoculturation. In the end, as the school of Malinowski's followers maintains, the result of every union of cultures is similar to that of the reproductive process between individuals: the offspring always has something of both parents but is always different from each of them.[2]

This biological sense of cultural encounter tropes well on to intellectual projects invested in borders and margins, the haunted intersections of colonial and imperial encounters.

Ortiz's goal is to illuminate the complexity of the constructive influences in Cuban culture through an account of the material history of tobacco, its production and translation into new cultural spaces. Tobacco becomes a material symbol of Cuba's complex cultural history, a celebration of artisanal labor that serves as a nostalgic counterpoint to the homogeneous colonialist capitalism of the sugar industry. The complexity and darkness

of tobacco becomes a means of connecting Cuban identity to the indigenous and African traditions, establishing a complex genealogy predicated
on the recognition of multiple threads of interconnection and influence.

The idea of a mutually processual exchange of conceptual frameworks
and material practices is one manifestation of a cultural logic of postmodernism founded on the performative, and because of its implicit ubiquity in contemporary thought, an already understood product of cultural
encounter. Within the logic of progressive models of postmodern cultural
studies, the processual serves as a means of local resistance that provides
for an alternative reading of the intersections of power in the encounter of
two or more cultures. Ironically, this sense of the processual was already
present within the definition, if not the deployment of the term 'acculturation', the term 'transculturation' is intended to shift. As Silvia Spitta (1995:
3) reminds her readers, the operative employment of acculturation within
anthropological literature did not necessarily imply the one-way cultural
transmission that it currently signifies:

> Whereas the theorists of acculturation had envisioned that process as one
> of interaction and mutual influence between cultures, Ortiz understood it
> from a Latin American perspective as a theory that described the one-way
> imposition of the culture of the colonizers. In fact, 'acculturation' was first
> systematically defined by Redfield, Linton, and Kerskovits in the 1930s
> as follows: 'Acculturation comprehends those phenomena which result
> when groups of individuals having different cultures come into contin-
> uous first-hand contact, with subsequent changes in the original culture
> patterns of either or both groups. Note: Under this definition, accultur-
> ation is to be distinguished from culture-change, of which it is but one
> aspect, and assimilation, which is at times a phase of acculturation.'

Spitta, however, supports Ortiz's critique of the term through reference to a
standard Spanish dictionary; the *Oxford English Dictionary* is equally useful
in this regard since the first standard definition of the term is 'the adoption
and assimilation of an alien culture'. Used in the abstract, transculturation
provides the means of thinking through interchange and mutual (though
not reciprocal) influence. But for this term to help the thinking of performance, there must be more.

In Alicia Arrizón's (2006: 5, emphasis added) project on *mestizaje*, she
suggests: 'as a formulation of cultural hybridization and mixed-race identities, transculturation *dramatizes the in-between site in narratives of encounters
and confrontations*'. These encounters are implicitly predicated as colonial
encounters, moments of conflict, contestation and negotiation that Mary

Louise Pratt influentially articulated as 'contact zones'. Ironically, in Pratt's (1992) work, transculturation, which serves as a significant term of her postcolon(ial) title – *Imperial Eyes: Travel Writing and Transculturation* – is only defined and historicized in one sentence and a brief footnote. This is symptomatic of the emerging ubiquity of the term and its generally perceptible function within literary and cultural studies, a saturation that threatens to exhaust its possibility to generate revelatory thinking.

What seems both necessary and problematic in analyzing the genealogy and the future conceptual deployments of transculturation is a careful attention not to the interdynamics of transformation that make it such a compelling concept through which to argue for local resistance, mutual resistance and multidirectional (though not necessarily equal) flows of power, but the 'ation', the doing of the thing that yet retains its status as a noun. While the adjective 'transcultural' can and has been widely deployed to think about complex cultural interrelationships with mutual influence, the verb, 'to transculturate', is much less often deployed. In this sense, the process of transculturation is subtly shifted to, at best, a state, or a process describable precisely because of its completeness, and at worst, a static historical formation. The sense of completion or stasis is completely antithetical to the notion of process in an ongoing sense. 'Trans', a crossing that subsumes, both enables and limits this mode of thinking.

This problem arises differently in the 1990s when transculturation becomes one means of thinking through the issues of intercultural exchange in performance. One problematic use of transculturation is articulated in the work of Patrice Pavis, where he argues for it as a description of a cultural intersection that moves towards the universal. In their attempt to systematize a 'Topography of Cross-Cultural Theatre Praxis', Jacqueline Lo and Helen Gilbert (2002) present Pavis's point of view, citing the influence of Peter Brook and the relevant work of Eugenio Barba. Lo and Gilbert (2002: 37) argue:

> *Transcultural theatre* aims to transcend culture-specific codification in order to reach a more universal human condition. Transcultural directors are interested in particularities and traditions only insofar as they enable the directors to identify aspects of commonality rather than difference (Pavis 1996: 6).

Tamara Underiner (2004: 79) representatively critiques Pavis for emptying out the concept of culture in the very process of transculturation through his insistence on the universal. Through Pavis's shift to the universal, the transcultural becomes a way of leaving things behind and moving forward.

In thinking transculture as 'across' culture or 'through' culture, there is inevitably a sense of movement and this movement is crucial, but the utopian politics of Western European thinking are predicated on a fundamental unwillingness to reconstruct the terms of cultural exchange. In counterhegemonic thinking, this encounter is imagined as emerging from colonialism, a site of palpably assymetrical relationships to the representational machinery of power. In this case, there is no desire for disappearance on the part of either participant but rather assimilation or exchange. What is not emphasized sufficiently, however, even in this space is the idea of *deculturation*, of loss, as Diana Taylor (1991: 103) insists:

> while the insertion of black and Hispanic culture into the U.S. certainly qualifies as an act of transculturation, the hegemonic resistance to accept these 'minor' discourses, and the hostilities these intercultural relationships provoke, point to the important facet of transculturation that is completely missing from most analyses: the sense of loss.

This sense of loss serves to temper the potentially counterhegemonic euphoria of the transformation from the margins suggested by a real practice of transculturation. Yet even this sense of loss is not enough to avoid the reduction of the thinking of transculturation to a thinking of borders. Another powerful trope and crucial material site of political and economic contestation, the border, in both its paradigmatic and literal manifestations is a fundamentally unsatisfying location for thinking differently in a cultural moment in which the border is consistently staged as a form of crisis. Arrizón avoids this sense of crisis by recuperating the space of *mestizaje* as a way of thinking other, but this sense of crossing and mixing in the biological sense (and even the cultural) always seems to stop at a point of intersection rather than continuing through the encounter. The failure to extend this processual analysis may be a legacy of resistance to the telos of homogenization as everything becomes 'mixed', but it presents a static end point that can only be changed in a new space whose very condition is shifting.

Importantly, although Arrizón's sense of the 'in-between' can be argued as the general condition of a postmodern subject, her formulation of generic shifting suggests an alternative and more effective space for thinking. If one begins to attend to the 'dramatization of the narrative', shifting to a language of performance and perhaps to Diana Taylor's model of the scenario as an embodied representation, then the potential presence of the dramatic moment retains the sense of transculturation as always shifting in the present. But, to read this sustained and constant process as equivalent to occupying the space of the border is potentially to implicitly refuse the violence that exists within the border space.

In perhaps the most important, careful and extended specific deployment of transculturation in relationship to performance, Alberto Sandoval-Sánchez and Nancy Saporta Sternbach (2001: 97) argue that:

> The heterogeneity, partiality, fragmentation, and multiplicity that give transculturation its theoretical apparatus are precisely those that also define performance and that are evidence of the fluidity of the transcultural protean subject herself or himself. It is in performance where not only the contradictions of transculturation become evident, but also its essence and nature ... In Latina theater and solo performances, the third interstitial space – that culture in-between – becomes a site of resistance inscribed in the body of the performer and the performative space where the theater also functions as a border, a space not here or there, but rather a neither/nor location.

This formulation closely echoes that of Spitta (1995: 24), who insists that:

> The transculturated subject, then, is someone who, like Arguedas, is consciously or unconsciously situated between at least two worlds, two cultures, two languages, and two definitions of subjectivity, and who constantly mediates between them all – or, to put it another way, whose 'here' is problematic and undefinable.

While these studies are explicitly mutually influenced – Spitta thanks Sandoval-Sánchez and the authors of *Stages of Life* (Sandoval-Sánchez and Saporta Sternbach) carefully attend to Spitta in their introduction – both formulations result in a non-definable space that verges on the absent rather than the present. Within this abstract space of the border, its violent reality can be elided, and this absence serves to protect the subject from a specific material encounter. I am not insisting here that any of these critics have a naive relationship to the border as a lived geography, but rather that their formulation of it as a conceptual field shifts the nature of the political claims they make within a thinking of performance. If one shifts from 'neither/nor' or 'problematic and undefinable' to a language of 'both/and', a supplementary excess, then there is a presence that must be dealt with in multiple ways. Given the reality of loss, the border can only serve as a marker for the in between when this loss can and is acknowledged. And yet even this process of acknowledgement runs the risk of enacting a transformation in which rather than the formation of newly necessary epistemological frameworks, one simply shifts into pre-existing subject positions. What is exposed in this formulation is an incommensurable shift between the putative transculturation of a subject and transculturation of the object of the self. After all, Ortiz's example is tobacco, not himself, and his example is not intended as a mere allegory but an account of the translation of cultural practice that brings into being new forms of action and new means of doing. Taken in its most radical form, this is precisely what a counterhegemonic interpretation such as Arrizón's is striving for, but the fundamental difficulty of conceptually charting a new thinking is forgotten in the assumption of a resistance in the interstices.

As an example, I would like to look briefly at Evangeline Ordaz's play *A Visitor's Guide to Arivaca (Map Not to Scale)*, premiered by Borderlands Theater in Tucson and staged at Teatro Visión in San José, California during the fall of 2007. Intended to chart the multiple rhetorical and subject positions in and around undocumented migration in a location in the Arizona desert just miles from the US–Mexico border, the play employs a range of characters whose political positions are troubled by their actions and experiences throughout the play. On the political right is an unemployed worker from the Midwest, John Lambert, who adopts a vigilante position on the border to proactively (in his mind at least) improve the possibility of his own re-employment through a violent containment of economic migration northward. On the political left is a lawyer who wants to use a good Samaritan as a test case to press for limits on the prosecution of workers aiding undocumented immigrants. The defendant Iris, an older single woman rancher arrested for transporting an undocumented migrant to the hospital after he ended up dehydrated at her house in his attempt to move northward, is not necessarily sympathetic or willing to participate in this venture. At the same time, she is very clear about the real utility of migrant workers. In Kerri Allen's (2006) description of the Borderlands production, she punctuates one of these moments between Iris

> and an out-of-work auto plant supervisor, John Lambert (Roger Owen), who is explaining why he signed up with the Border Keepers, Ordaz's version of the Minutemen:
>
> JOHN: Figured I could address the unemployment situation from a different angle – really get at the root causes, you know? If immigrants weren't willing to work for so cheap, there might be a job for me out there.
>
> IRIS: Why? Do you pick lettuce?
>
> … At both performances, the audience's applause after Iris's retort momentarily stopped the show.

This 'visceral' (Allen's word) reaction is symptomatic of pro-immigrant partisan politics happy to see the complexity of the situation staged while maintaining a progressive stance towards the cultural debate.

While *Arivaca* is an effective political and pedagogical drama, it also points to the possibility that the borderlands are not necessarily the geography of transculturation, but increasingly a fixed and reified site of recognizable political contestation. While in the end a number of the characters have undergone a personal journey that underscores the multifaceted complexity of the issue, and reiterates the humanity of the individual actors in the face of the machinations of politicized rhetoric, the success of the play rests in its willingness to speak the complexity of the border, but in the end it does not offer anything new conceptually. While the mere act of nuancing political debate is a crucial function of the performance event, and one that emerges in few other embodied spaces, there is nothing new here when imagined outside the individual perspective of the characters articulating political and national subjectivities.

The only potential moment of transculturation in the creative sense is present in the potential of the unborn child who has been carried across the border. Linda Sanchez, the surviving migrant, the wife who follows her husband with little knowledge of the harsh desert environment and a pregnancy he is unaware of, vows to continue her journey in order to make her unborn child a US citizen. While this cliché harbors both a historical romanticization and a manifestation of real practices of cultural mobility through new forms of citizenship, the unborn child forms the potential dramatization of transculturation. Rather than a subject, for the baby remains only a potential in this space, this potential unknown becomes the possibility of a real alternative thinking, though a thinking that extends beyond the play. Rather than a typical narrative of a successful, or failed, dream of mobility represented by this future child, one can instead think about the forces of exchange and the work of the imagination that shape this life, reflecting on the institutional and state geographies that extend beyond the individual, psychological experience. While this demand might alienate the politically sympathetic liberal spectator, this process is necessary for a transculturation that is not 'neither/nor', but actually here.

Notes

1   Research for this essay was aided by a faculty grant from the University of California Institute for Mexico and the United States.

2   The term 'transculturation' has been developed by a range of scholars, including most prominently José María Arguedas and Ángel Rama. For more complete and complex genealogies of the term, see the first chapters of Spitta (1995) and Sandoval-Sánchez and Saporta Sternbach (2001).

Works cited

Allen, Kerri. 'Drama on the Border: A Feisty Arizona Theatre Dives Headlong into the Immigration Debate.' *American Theater* December 2006, www.tcg.org/publications/at/dec06/borders.cfm.

Arrizón, Alicia. *Queering Mestizaje; Transculturation and Performance*. Ann Arbor: University of Michigan Press, 2006.

Lo, Jacqueline and Gilbert, Helen. 'Toward a Topography of Cross-Cultural Theatre Praxis.' *TDR: The Drama Review* 46.3 (2002): 31–53.

Ortiz, Fernando. *Cuban Counterpoint: Tobacco and Sugar*, trans. Harriet de Onís, Intro. Bronislaw Malinowski, prologue Herminio Portell Vilá. New York: Alfred A. Knopf, 1947.

Pratt, Mary Louise. *Imperial Eyes: Travel Writing and Transculturation*. New York: Routledge, 1992.

Sandoval-Sánchez, Alberto and Saporta Sternbach, Nancy. *Stages of Life: Transcultural Performance & Identity in U.S. Latina Theater*. Tucson: University of Arizona Press, 2001.

Spitta, Silvia. *Between Two Waters: Narratives of Transculturation in Latin America*. Houston: Rice University Press, 1995.

Taylor, Diana. 'Transculturating Transculturation' *Performing Arts Journal* 13.2 (1991): 90–104.

Underiner, Tamara L. *Contemporary Theatre in Mayan Mexico: Death-Defying Acts*. Austin: University of Texas Press, 2004.

33 Social Practice

Maria Shevtsova

A truism of theatre and performance studies is that theatre, while concerned with aesthetics and so with art forms, is an active doing, a practice through and through. What the discipline has failed to recognize adequately, however – and this despite the work of sociologists of the theatre – is that theatre practice is not solely a matter of acquiring skills, developing crafts-manship and realizing the latter effectively in the making of pieces of theatre. This cumulative process of training, research, creation, rehearsal, presentation (or rejection thereof in laboratory conditions) together with repetition and continuity is 'practice' in the most basic sense of the term. Yet theatre practice, regardless of its technical-artistic specificity, is, at the same time, a *social* practice, and it is necessarily social for several reasons. To start with, it relies for its very execution on plural forces. It is not, in other words, the exercise of a single will, no matter how gifted, exceptional and inspired or inspiring this or that individual doing theatre may be.[1]

The first principle, then, that makes theatre a social practice is its collec-tive agency, based on a dialogical relationship, which is dialogical across the numbers of people involved, as in a network, in any given time, space and place. Performers and directors, choreographers, coordinators or project leaders come together with designers, composers, musicians, technicians and other collaborators to make something, usually with the intention of engaging spectators in that 'something' emerging from their work. These are group-made performances of whatever denomination, depending on their makers' conception and perception of generic categories – thus 'devising', say, or 'dance', or 'text-based interpretation', or 'participatory', or 'interac-tive' performance, where the spectator largely determines the performance, sometimes in a one-on-one, intimate encounter with the performer-initiator.[2] But there are, as well, varieties of solo performance, including 'performance art' or 'body art', this genre having been considerably shaped by women using such non-theatre-dedicated spaces as art galleries, clubs, ordinary rooms and so on. Among them are Marina Abramović, Carolee Schneemann and ORLAN, to name but three well-known pioneers. The notion of agency called upon here, whether agency is collective or singular, implies not only the exercise of will referred to earlier, but also a consciously assumed motivation and desire to fulfil the task at hand. By the same token, it suggests that the 'doers', who are agents of action, have a degree of freedom and choice in their actions, notwithstanding the rules, regulations and norms of societies.

These agents are human beings – in the phrase of everyday rather than sociological language. Yet it is vital to benefit from sociological thought and observe that human beings are social by the very fact of their living and working in groupings to which the word 'society' still pertains. 'Society' has not yet become an irrelevant point of reference, regardless of the fact that contemporary social structures are increasingly unstable, whether primarily for economic and political reasons (witness the current world recession), for reasons to do with globalization (hence the alleged disintegration of national communities) or because of those ideological and cultural pressures that favour entities smaller than the state (or fiefdom) in the name of groupings by religion or ethnicity. In whichever way a society is identified, its social character is derived from the relational character of the beings who constitute it. In other words, the 'I' of one can be defined only in relation to the 'I' of another, who is also a 'You'.

Relational cohesiveness of this type is the very 'glue' of theatre practice, besides being indispensible for that especially pronounced mode of social interaction known as 'ensemble theatre'. The ensemble, as invented by Konstantin Stanislavski and Vladimir Nemirovich-Danchenko for the Moscow Art Theatre, subsequently found numerous variations. These go from the repertory theatres of the 20th century to the core-group model of a Peter Brook in France and, in England, to the temporary, quasi-project-based 'ensemble' cultivated by Declan Donnellan for Cheek by Jowl in the 2000s, and, differently, to the 'ensemble' pursued by Katie Mitchell through the continuity not so much of her actors (difficult to achieve in Britain) as of her production team. They stretch, going sideways (since no development moves in a straight line), to the small-scale ensembles that focus on the actor's presence rather than characterization, where cohesiveness is fostered by constant psychophysical proximity in play. Take, for instance, the Odin Teatret in Denmark, Song of the Goat Theatre and Teatr ZAR in Poland, and Double Edge Theatre in the US, within a myriad of examples of such groups currently working worldwide, the initial inspiration of those cited coming, even when indirectly, from Jerzy Grotowski's practice with the performers who became the Laboratory Theatre.

The sketch offered here is an international one, but it suggests, by its signposts, that one company's relation to another, in terms of connections and differences, defines its uniqueness, as does, at the same time, its relational position in its own social context: thus, as a case in point, Teatr ZAR in the social conditions and idiosyncrasies of Poland today. Questions to do with relation are not about historical lineage (this gave rise to this, which gave rise to this) or aesthetic genealogy (this practitioner – or company – influenced X who influenced Y to follow style Z). They concern place and placing in a bigger picture that assembles, however loosely, the theatres in all their diversity within a particular society and – when taking a broader picture still – the variety of theatres within an international perspective covering the same period of time. One such question might ask whether a company was fully or partly established in its society, or carving out its niche, or struggling to claim a space at all. Another might be concerned with how a company's local position was affected by its international exposure, impact and reputation. Questions such as these are very much about relational attributes, and it is precisely theatre's relational capacity within the dynamics of societies that gives the second principle identifying theatre as a social practice.

Group practice (which need not be ensemble driven), as distinct from solo practice, may well require different analytical approaches. Be this as it may, group- and solo-made works are quite different in their textures, which is inevitable since the former come from multiple contributions occurring simultaneously, while solo constructions depend for their layering on one input. Even so, soloists may draw upon the advice or even direct intervention of others (the case of ORLAN's surgery, for example), and they certainly must draw on infrastructural support, not least that of gallery managers or owners, who hire out their spaces to performers. Nor can the importance of infrastructural support for group work be ignored, since the operations of frameworks, all mobilized by agents who have their respective tasks, are integral to the institutions – organizational systems, buildings, performance venues – through which theatre practice of all kinds is channelled. Its institutional dimension is the third principle that defines the theatre as a social practice.

There should be no misunderstanding. The institutions of the theatre are not confined to bricks and mortar, any more than they are to the enterprise of financiers and producers, on the one hand, and the activities of administrators, on the other. They encompass, as well, the non-material aspects of social life, which anthropologists generally describe as 'symbolic' and which Pierre Bourdieu has specified as being, above all else, the realm of status and prestige.[3] The characteristic of institutions is that they embody values, prejudices and learned and perpetuated evaluations as to what is 'good', 'bad' or 'indifferent', what is to be done or not (usually according to 'accepted' practice), and what is to be kept or discarded for the institutions' endurance, whether in the shorter or longer term. The Moscow Art Theatre (MAT), from its founding in 1897, quickly became an institution that embodied the values of ensemble work, respect for the work of the actor as creative *work*, respect for the work of colleagues and respect for the profession. Among other major innovations that distinguished this theatre from its predecessors was the idea that theatre was not a matter of posturing, ego-satisfaction, commercialism and market-centred entertainment but of an artistic, ethical and spiritual journey.

Social change brought about embodiment change, but despite its many vicissitudes in the course of historical and political trauma, notably during the 1930s until after Stalin's death in 1953, groups in the MAT who had not been completely crushed aspired to embody what had made it the institution it had been recognized to be in the first place. The stature the MAT had gained in the first two decades of the 20th century, above all from its artistic accomplishments, was instrumental in its status as an *institution*, which indicates just how fundamental theatre practice can be for the definition of an institution and the 'symbolic power' – assuming Bourdieu's terminology – that it wields.

Embodiment does not happen by itself. The social classes and groups who form, rule and run institutions imbue these institutions with their values, to which the people working in them conform, not necessarily because of personal investment, but functionally, impersonally; and these classes and groups imbue their establishments with the symbolic power they have asserted socially – which, Bourdieu argues, is not always allied to economic or political power – down, even, to how the bricks and mortar appear to the gaze – solid or makeshift, elegant or shabby, ostentatious or whatever else the semiotic signal of value may be. In theatre practice, the values of those in charge promote not only familiarity with that practice, but also a taste for it, as did, in the past, the MAT for psychological realism, and as do, in the present, Punchdrunk in London, for instance, for quirky, immersive spectacle in found spaces, and Toneelgroep in Amsterdam for intricate interplay between live actors and multimedia.

Taste is a complex phenomenon, and, in Bourdieu's theory, the classes and class fractions at the top of the social hierarchy promote their version of it in order to impose and maintain their social position. In this way, they use 'cultural capital' to acquire 'distinction' (how one social group or class distinguishes its cultural habits and predispositions, which constitute 'taste', from another). Similarly, they use this capital to 'consecrate', in Bourdieu's words, identified artistic practices and 'legitimate' them for the rest of their society's citizens.[4] As a consequence – to bring this discussion to the theatre (which Bourdieu does not do) – taste for this or that theatre comes from above. However, what is crucially missing from Bourdieu's argument is any sense of how practitioners – in this discussion, theatre practitioners – nurture taste through their very practice, educating, one might say, their audiences, not least their social-elite audiences, to grasp that practice and give it its due.[5] Furthermore, Bourdieu fails to consider how artists (his generic term) help to form audiences that are not part of the social elites; and, while he maintains that elites are multiple and different in kind – intellectual elites are not necessarily economic elites, for example – he underestimates what might be called the 'capacity for discernment' not only of intellectual elites (they are not always subservient to money or political power), but also of the artists – theatre practitioners – themselves. This capacity for discernment is a channel for subjective and something like 'free' assessment – as 'free' as the obligations, strictures and stresses of class and group structures can allow.

Theatre practitioners have their own subgroups – the well-born, wealthy, established and prestigious practitioners, by contrast with their opposite, who struggle on all levels; and then there are many between these extremes. However, the value they accord to exercising their art, craft and imagination powers them, enabling them to believe and evaluate positively what they do, and how and why they do it. The 'Why?' of it is not automatically aligned with a search for cultural and social distinction (or consecration, or legitimation), even though societies secrete inequalities. This 'Why? has to do, in some measure, with commitment to, and conviction in, a designated practice. Then there is the sheer pleasure of doing it. On a symbolic level, pride in this practice is a potent element. Again, Bourdieu is so single-mindedly focused on the mechanisms at play in a given field of practice – galleries/ journals that promote some painters/writers at the expense of others, among many instrumentalist factors – that he casts aside the desire of artists to *further* their art by exploring, inventing and enjoying it.[6]

Where theatre is concerned, practice has immediate effect. Its practitioners exercise their art and craft in relation to spectators, who, if generally members of fractions of the middle classes (unless working-class spectators are especially targeted) are indispensable for the act of theatre to occur.[7] The collective event that is a performance relies, then, on the collectivity of spectators who interact with it. These spectators are as diverse as the social groups from which they come, by age, gender, formal education, occupation, salary and so on, and they all bring their distinctive social standing, experience and outlook with them. At the same time, they bring their exposure and access to previous theatre events, as well as empathetic understanding of them, all this building up their capacity for discernment, that is, distinguishing between a and b, not simply intellectually, but with their nerves and heart. Here, in this interchange and 'buzz' between spectators and performers, lies the fourth principle that makes theatre a social practice.

The fifth principle is social context (referred to already), and it is ubiquitous and all-pervasive, absorbing as well as absorbed by theatre makers, spectators, performances, institutions, governments and anything else that composes a particular society in historical time. However, for all its chrono-topic significance (time-space-place), the *idea* of social context is not obliged to be totally restricted to national-geographic boundaries, to this particular society in this particular location. The idea needs to be flexible because the local–global nexus is of paramount importance in contemporary societies. Few societies in the contemporary world are immune to global interconnec-tivity, not only because of the economic networks that bind them in relations of interdependency, but also because of the sociocultural influences they exert upon each other. The subject of research together with the questions posed by the researcher generally indicate the parameters of 'social context' and how elastic they may be, whether they need to extended to the 'global' or confined to the 'local'. In any case, these terms acquire definition from the aspect(s) of theatre/performance selected for research, and the material shows how far it has to be contextualized to make the greatest sense.

The sixth principle concerns *habitus*, adapting the concept for theatre from Bourdieu. *Habitus*, interpreting Bourdieu, is the position occupied in the structures of society by agents-individuals according to their social group and class. *Habitus* thus embraces the material conditions (which are part of social context) that go with the territory and actively affect these agents. At the same time, *habitus* is of the symbolic order insofar as the indi-viduals who form a defined class/group are likely to have much the same values, perceptions, behaviours, expectations and appreciations ('taste' – including what they like or dislike in the theatre); and this commonality grouping individuals holds, irrespective of their individual life trajectories. The material and the symbolic of *habitus* are interlocked, but are not static: *habitus*, for Bourdieu, is both there and mobile (his 'structured structure' and 'structuring structure').[8] Further, the material and symbolic support and sustain each other, and generate practices that are distinctive of each differ-ent *habitus* – cultivating land, working in factories, making theatre; each practice corresponds with its group/class.

The concept of *habitus*, when used in theatre and performance studies, enriches the notion of social context because it pinpoints this question: Who practises theatre and where do they practise it, and in which material condi-tions sustained by which values and other dimensions of the symbolic order? *Habitus* also sheds light on multiple facets of practice. Take only three of hundreds of examples: Meyerhold's 'biomechanics', which, during the early years of the Russian Revolution, he modelled on factory workers; Brecht's *gestus*, which he designed to show how body language was precisely socially embedded; and Pina Bausch's Tantztheater Wuppertal, which is a specific group practice in a tight and totally distinctive group ethos. The capacity of *habitus* to illuminate is as wide as the theatre practices of societies.

Notes

1 For an examination of the ideas in this paragraph, see my three-part essay 'The Sociology of the Theatre: Problems and Perspectives', 'Theoretical Achievements' and 'Performance', in Shevtsova, Maria, *Sociology of Theatre and Performance*, Verona: QuiEdit, 2009, 21–82. These are edited versions of the original essays published in *New Theatre Quarterly*, 5.17/18/19, 1989, 25–35, 180–94 and 282–30, respectively.

2 Take the recent example of the One-on One Festival at the Battersea Arts Centre in London, 6–18 July 2010, whose publicity vaunts 'individual performances, tailor-made for you … your own private and unique journey of performances'. In anticipation of the 2011 Festival, *Financial Times* critic Sarah Hemming noted that conventional expectations of audiences had disappeared: 'Here you were alone, you were constantly on the move and you had to perform. In fact, you were the star of the show' (18 February, 2011).

3 See Bourdieu, *Distinction: A Social Critique of the Judgement of Taste*, trans. Richard Nice, London: Routledge, 2006 [1979], 291 and 'The Production of Belief: Contribution to an Economy of Symbolic Goods' [1977], in *The Field of Cultural Production: Essays on Art and Literature*, ed. Randal Johnson, Cambridge: Polity Press, 2004, 74–111.

4 The whole of *Distinction* develops Bourdieu's socially rooted notion of taste (although for this discussion, see especially pp. 56–7) in relation to which he speaks of cultural consecration and legitimate and legitimated culture. For the latter, see, particularly, pp. 6–7 and 24–8. See also *The Field of Cultural Production*, pp. 50–2.

5 For a critique of Bourdieu's argument from this perspective, see Shevtsova, Maria, 'Appropriating Pierre Bourdieu's *Champ* and *Habitus* for a Sociology of Stage Productions', in *Sociology of Theatre and Performance*, 83–109 (reprinted from *Contemporary Theatre Review*, 12.3 (2002), 35–66).

6 Bourdieu, *The Rules of Art: Genesis and Structure of the Literary Field*, trans. Susan Emanuel, Cambridge: Polity Press, 2005 [1992] is entirely devoted to this aspect of Bourdieu's theory.

7 The question of who spectators are and how and why they go to which performances is a complex one, and most writings in theatre and performance studies on spectators are based on conjecture, often with theoretical assumptions from reception theory. But this is theory, not founded on empirical evidence. See my reference to the inadequacy of such approaches in 'Minority/Dominant Culture in the Theatre' [1993] in *Sociology of Theatre and Performance*, pp. 278–9. For a summary of then-current (1989) sociological research on audiences, where, however, concrete research on theatre spectators is spectacularly missing, see pp. 28–30 of 'The Sociology of the Theatre: Problems and Perspectives' in *Sociology of Theatre and Performance*, pp. 21–37. The reader may wish to consult pp. 289–330 of this book for examples of my empirical studies of theatre audiences, which include pages on working-class audiences targeted by community multicultural theatre.

8 Bourdieu, *The Logic of Practice*, trans. Richard Nice, Cambridge: Polity Press, 1990 [1980], 53.

34   'City'

Nicolas Whybrow

Not surprisingly perhaps for someone who dedicated a whole book to comparing rural and urban life, Raymond Williams' respected selection for his 'vocabulary of culture and society', *Keywords*, includes 'City' as one of its entries (1976: 46–8). Acknowledging its 13th-century English-language origins, Williams goes on to identify the term's transition to 'more general use' as corresponding to 'the rapid development of urban living during the Industrial Revolution'. By the middle of the 19th century, this rendered England 'the first society in the history of the world in which a majority of the population lived in towns'. The spread of this tendency well beyond England occurred rapidly as the second half of the 19th century progressed. Measured by the kind of visual art produced, so Nicolas Bourriaud argues in *The Radicant* (2009: 92), it is this period in history – when the great artists of the day, such as Manet, Monet and Seurat, were impelled to depict 'the birth of industrial civilisation ... by painting scenes of urban life' – that will serve as the principal point of comparison with the current age. For, when future historians come to study *our* era, they too

> will no doubt be struck by the number of works that depict life in the big cities. They will note the countless images of streets, stores, markets, buildings, vacant lots, crowds, and interiors that were exhibited in galleries in our day. From this they will infer that the artists of these early years of the twenty-first century were fascinated by the transformation of their immediate environment and the 'becoming world' [*devenir-monde*] of their cities. (Bourriaud 2009: 91–2)

The growing significance of the city as reflected in art practices is tied, then, to the preponderance of contemporary urban populations: where Williams' observation on the mid-19th century applied to England alone, Bourriaud's comment on the 21st century aspires to take account of the entire world. It is an oft-cited fact of recent years that 2007 recorded the official moment when the global population pendulum swung irrevocably – if that can ever be said of pendulums – towards the end marked 'urban'. By 2030, moreover, two-thirds of the world's population is expected to be dwelling in cities, whereby it should be said that the veritable migratory 'explosions' are set to occur in 'developing situations' – such as Lagos in Nigeria, or Indonesia's capital Jakarta – rather than the established ones of the 'advanced Western zone'. The latter would include a city of high capital activity such as Tokyo: currently top of the global tree with 35 million inhabitants, it will only have grown by a further 1 million in the same time span. Interestingly, Doug Saunders' (2010) account of 'arrival cities' – those temporary 'holding settlements' for migrants on the fringes of urban conurbations across the globe – points out that this urban growth is in fact finite. The majority of global citizens will still be urban dwellers, but:

> Sometime around 2050, according to the most recent United Nations projections, the population of the world will stop growing. After peaking at nine billion, for the first time in history humans will stop being more numerous each year … This will be a direct product of urbanisation: because of migration, smaller urban families will outnumber large rural ones, and, in turn, the flow of money, knowledge and educated return migrants from the arrival city back to the village will push down birth rates in rural areas. (Saunders 2010: 26)

The question of which global cities are 'open for business' and which have 'locked down' when it comes to migration is a contentious one (but not one I have space to address here). Be that as it may, the future can evidently be said to belong to the city, impinging as it does – for better or ill – on the lives of increasing numbers of human beings worldwide.

Urban art and everyday life

Bourriaud's reference to the contemporary prevalence of 'urban art' echoes the prediction of his compatriot, the seminal urban space theorist Henri Lefebvre (1996: 173), who had already declared some 40 years earlier not merely that the global future was urban, but that the future of *art* was urban and 'not artistic', as he put it. Articulated as part of a general thesis towards establishing citizens' rights to their city, Lefebvre was keen to rescue art from the clutches of privileged institutions and return it to the public space of everyday life and the street where it would operate as the usable property of (the) people. The key for Lefebvre was the public's 'participation in play', as manifest in the form of the 'festival' (*fête*) or 'collective game'. Regrettably, in his view, the notion of play had become subordinated to the 'serious culturalism' of the theatre as an indoor, bourgeois institution, when its rightful place was 'the street':

> to city people the urban centre is movement, the unpredictable, the possible, and encounters. For them it is either 'spontaneous theatre' or nothing. ... leaving aside representation, ornamentation and decoration, art can become *praxis* and *poiesis* on a social scale. (Lefebvre 1996: 172–3)

Thus, Lefebvre envisaged a role for art that would integrate citizens and creatively produce the city in their interests. Arguably, present-day 'embodied social networking' practices, such as flash mobbing and their several derivatives, have at least the potential to go some way towards enacting a version of Lefebvre's vision.

Aspects of Lefebvre's theories were echoed in the practices of the Situationist International (SI), an organization for whom he was an early mentor, until they fell out: 'a sort of unfinished love affair', as he himself put it later (1996: 13). Perhaps a part of that 'unconsummated love' related to Lefebvre being a theorist where the situationists' primary impulse was to 'construct situations'; in other words, to make things happen, not least by seeking to reposition art within practices of everyday urban life. As Greg Ulmer (1989: 199) points out – citing Guy Debord, the SI's leading light – the situationists practised 'a "realisation" (or "overcoming") of art ... that extended into performance or action the "insubordination of words ... Our era no longer has to *write out poetic orders*; it has to carry them out"'. Thus, the subversive but delimited force of art (here evoked through a 'poetics of words') should be harnessed so as to be effective in the form of radical, game-changing events on the streets of cities.[1] As Andrew Hussey (2002: 217) observes, the situationists recognized 'the city as a future battleground for the conflict over the meaning of modernity'. And it was 'this battle for urban space, in a literal and metaphorical sense' that was 'in many ways the defining moment in the development of situationist strategy'. Moreover, as Simon Sadler (1998) elucidates in *The Situationist City*, the radicalism of the movement's practice – effected via the 'constructed situation', with its related psychogeographical strategies of *détournement* and *dérive* – is, in fact:

> best thought of as a sort of *Gesamtkunstwerk* (total work of art). Each constructed situation would provide a decor and ambiance of such power that it would stimulate new sorts of behaviour, a glimpse into an improved future social life based upon human encounter and play. (Sadler 1998: 105)

As we have seen, one person who has embraced the perception of the city's increasing importance and, indeed, significantly theorized the evolution of this occurrence, is the curator and critic Nicolas Bourriaud. His earlier book, *Relational Aesthetics* (2002), sets out the terms by which artworks are seen as a network of practices 'which take as their theoretical and practical point of departure the whole of human relations and their social context, rather than an independent private space'. Thus, artworks are to be judged 'on the basis of the inter-human relations which they represent, produce or prompt' (2002: 112–13). Aspiring to a 'radical upheaval' in contemporary art, Bourriaud (2002: 14) attributes such a paradigm shift to 'the birth of a world-wide urban culture' in the latter half of the 20th century and to 'the extension of this city model to more or less all cultural phenomena'. Based essentially on a rapid increase in *movement*, that is, in the possibilities of social communication and exchange, as well as individual mobility, Bourriaud (2002: 15) effectively describes the turn from the artwork as object (a 'lordly item in this urban setting') to that of performance event:

> the development of the function of artworks and the way they are shown attests to a growing *urbanisation* of the artistic experiment. What is collapsing before our very eyes is nothing other than this falsely aristocratic conception of the arrangement of works of art ... The city has ushered in and spread the hands-on experience: it is the tangible symbol and historical setting of the state of society, that '*state of encounter imposed on people*'.

So, relational art directs us to practices in which the prompting of active relations between 'parties' and 'phenomena', within given social contexts, is central or, in fact, *constitutes* the artwork.[2] For Bourriaud (2002: 16), art produces 'a specific sociability', wherein 'it remains to be seen what the status of this is in the set of 'states of encounter' proposed by the city'. Importantly, then, the way is paved for performance to be viewed as the facilitator of art's integration into urban life – '"play-generating" yeast in the everyday', as Stephen Johnstone puts it (2008: 14) – and, in turn, for 'urban life' itself, or the various interacting component parts of the city as a whole, to be seen as a performing entity.

Urban research practice

Given this highly compressed summation of 'urban/art futures', I would like to shift attention now – as a form of 'long conclusion' that may, simultaneously, function as a prelude – to future fieldwork in urban research practice as refracted through the optic of the discipline of performance (studies). In particular, I wish to concentrate on the intersection of two planes of consideration: theory/practice on the one hand, city/performance on the other, whereby I should add that the 'tell-tale forward slash' there – *ponctuation concrète*? – is intended in each instance to imply a form of graphic *transitio* or 'tipping over' of one phenomenon into the other, as opposed to a mere conjunctive coupling, as we shall see.

In her illuminating discussion of the state of performance as research in Canada, Laura Levin (2009: 65) describes 'urban intervention' and 'site-specific', as having become 'virtual stand-ins for performance studies', elaborating on the former as follows:

> While research/creation focuses on the university as performance lab [and] is designed to advance knowledge in the fine arts, urban intervention takes its cue from a much broader range of disciplines, including environmental studies, cultural studies, and sociology. Here, the experience of urban life is the central object of study, with a particular focus on the ways in which bodies shape and are shaped by the environments they inhabit.

Levin's statement is suggestive, then, of the way that the acceptance of performance practices as viable forms of scholarly research – theory flipping into practice, practice being recognized as a form of theory – has been bound up, in its emergence, with interrogations of everyday urban life and space. While this development may, for all I know, be particularly marked in the Canada (or even Toronto) of which she speaks, performance-based urban research is also occurring elsewhere in the world, not least in the UK, as I can testify (though doubtless not to the same exclusively urban/site-based extent). My own take on 'urban intervention' would endeavour to temper the intervention aspect of the term, because it can resonate too easily, and therefore misleadingly, in the reductive realms of 'agitation' and/or 'spectacle'. The work I am more inclined to value is, more often than not, reflective, responsive and integrative – indeed, 'quiet' – even where, or perhaps *because*, it is setting out to effect a 'critical unworking' from within. Moreover, the interrogative tactics of urban performance often come down as much to how the city intervenes in you, the citizen-dweller or visitor. Thus, an embodied reciprocity is at least in evidence, if not the objective of any given exercise undertaken. To be fair to Levin (2009: 65), her subsequent elaboration on 'urban intervention' suggests dimensions more akin to the subtleties of which I speak and she does stress ways in which bodies *are shaped* by (as opposed to shaping) their urban environments.

Performative writing

Leaving aside the implementation of in situ performance itself as urban fieldwork, one question arising for a critical research practice based on interrogating the city is how to find a way of mapping or writing that is true to – or performative of – the implicit movement and morphology of cities, that is, to the way cities themselves variously perform in practice. The city is an intersection, a nexus, a hub, a network and so on. It is made up of infinite and contingent component parts, many invisible or temporary, to the extent that it is always more accurate perhaps to speak of multipli-cities. This captures the degree to which urban space is subject to ongoing change, not least on account of the continuous, random movement of bodies through it. Thus, as has been implied, embodied practices can be said to produce and define urban space as much as, say, the mise-en-scène of the built environment. But, by the same reciprocal token, cities inhabit and produce bodies, too. Cities are constantly 'shifting ground', constantly on the move, constantly dealing with 'arrivals and departures' and the effects of impromptu 'states of encounter'. And this form of 'time-based physicality' – which is inflected, of course, by various 'behaviours and rhythms' – is one of the reasons why we might talk of 'performing cities', quite apart from performance in or about cities.

Given the diversity, complexity and ephemeralness of urban life, the question of how to approach writing the city poses an intriguing challenge. In fact, it is an ongoing debate with a long history, though one that has been conducted primarily outside the discipline of performance. In attempting to establish possible approaches to writing the contemporary *performing* city, I would like to identify one particular voice from that past as potentially providing a way forward for a writing that succeeds in rising to a challenge articulated by Bourriaud in *The Radicant*, namely 'to capture the city [by] following its movement' (2009: 97). I am referring to the rich, diverse and, indeed, frequently opaque theories and practices of Walter Benjamin.

At least three writing methods relating to the city are proposed by his oeuvre, all of which are underpinned by the notion of city and text as spaces of encounter and contestation: as momentary, fractured intersections or dynamic assemblages that have the potential to produce impromptu, thought-provoking conjunctions as well as disjunctions. Benjamin's several city essays (one form of urban writing) – designated 'thought sketches' (*Denkbilder*) – often propose a form of dialectical thinking or 'conceptual intervention' (*plumpes Denken*), to use a Brechtian term (in Fredric Jameson's translation),[3] in their presentation of urban scenes. Most striking in this regard is the portrayal of a chance encounter on a street corner with which the 'Naples' essay (co-written with Asja Lacis) opens. In one impromptu moment on the street – perhaps a 'gestic' one, again in a Brechtian sense – the author demonstrates how an ingrained but comical form of knee-jerk deference exists in relation to the 'God-fearing Catholicism' that pervades the city: a disgraced priest, being paraded through the streets by a mob, bumps into a wedding procession and promptly resumes authority over his mocking flock as he offers his blessings to the newlyweds. Ultimately, it would seem, the church always appears to hold the trump card but only by virtue of its somewhat farcical iterative 'ritual gestures'. Benjamin (1997: 167) goes on to demonstrate how the 'rich barbarism' of social justice is performed in the city via the symbiotic relationship between God-fearing Catholicism and the lawless Camorra clan that implicitly controls Naples: 'Confession alone, not the police, is a match for the self-administration of the criminal world'. In other words, the church is content for a gang of outlaws to act as regulator of criminal and civic life in the city as long as the former can be perceived to be exercising overall, spiritual power. Any crime, so one may infer, is justifiable as long as it admits to its sinfulness before God. Guilt may always be purged, thus extending full licence to the Camorra to go about its 'dirty work' with impunity.

A second form of writing relates to Benjamin's *One-Way Street*, described by Susan Sontag – as Pile and Thrift (2000: 306) point out in *City A-Z* – as a 'mosaic of aphoristic paragraphs, captioned by placards of urban scenery'. In their highly perceptive commentary on Benjamin's montage methodology at work in this 'enigmatic analysis of the intersection of modernity and the city', Pile and Thrift show how seemingly unconnected phenomena are pulled together under a certain heading (or 'urban placard'). Any meaning, they argue, is not stated but merely proposed by the form and, therefore, materializes via an 'active reading' or, again, a conceptual intervention:

> These juxtapositions are a montage of urban images. But these images are meant to be read side by side, and in moving between them they are meant to reveal something of the present, if only a glimpse. … Benjamin hoped to set in motion a train of thoughts that would keep moving. But he was not intent on destroying what was already there; far from it, he was attempting to recuperate the ruins and dust of the modern city and to reassemble them into something that was genuinely new, genuinely unimaginable. (Pile and Thrift 2000: 307)

To give a brief example of the writing in question, one that not only conflates space and text but also proves itself to be startlingly modern in the 21st century, the placard 'This Space for Rent' (Benjamin 1997: 89–90) clearly samples one of the many signs of street-level advertising. Within its first few sentences, the piece sounds the death knell of a disappearing discursive world of 'criticism' and 'paid critics', in which 'perspectives and prospects counted and where it was still possible to take a standpoint'. Now, in the fast-moving urban world, 'things press too closely on human society'. There is no standing outside; instead, we are all implicated, for the privileged space 'where contemplation moved' has gone and it is advertising, that 'most real, mercantile gaze into the heart of things' that has understood best how to exploit this. It would seem, then, that the liminal 'space for rent' itself – as opposed to the sign advertising it – is one of obsolescence on the one hand and an opportunity to write the new on the other.

For Benjamin, *collecting* – or 'catching at the fragments of civilisation' – was an obsession. It could manifest itself, for example, in thoughts while unpacking his vast personal library of books,[4] or in a preoccupation with the itinerant figures of the *flâneur* and urban rag-picker as cultural historians-cum-archivists operating at very different levels of the social scale. One of the so-called 'convolutes' of his *Arcades Project* – the third of Benjamin's 'urban writing' forms I wish to bring into play – is itself entitled 'The Collector' (convolute 'H'), but the monumental work as a whole is an unfinished collection in its own right. Effectively, it is a vast archive of reflections and quotations or, as Gilloch (1997: 19) puts it, 'diverse incongruent elements … rudely dragged from their intellectual moorings'. Where *One-Way Street* condenses montage into well-turned, often cryptic, meditations, *The Arcades Project* (2002) appears at times – and this is not meant disparagingly – to resort to 'throwing the raw materials' at its reader. Again, it is a text that is required to be 'performed into action', an encounter with fragments in discursive space. At the same time, it is a text effectively organized as the replication of a key architectural feature of the 19th-century European city – the arcade. With its apparent order and promises of the fulfilment of urban dwellers' desires, Benjamin was characteristically more interested in the implications of the arcade's *demise*, seeing it as the epitome of the transiency and inherent 'will to decay' of 'phantasmagorical capitalism'. (Quite feasibly, in fact, another instance of 'space for rent'.) In *The Arcades Project* there is an evident attempt not only to examine the intersection of modernity and the city but also – as there is in the Naples street corner and the 'constellation of aphorisms as a street' (Frisby 1994: 101) that make up *One-Way Street* – the intersection of urban and textual space. In other words, Benjamin seeks to write the city performatively, as an active replication of its movement in time, thereby endeavouring to bridge the gap, as Buck-Morss (1989: 3) has suggested, between the practical space of everyday experience and that of conventional scholarly discourse.

Notes

1 While it may be the practices of *art* in the everyday that are at issue, after such radical, widespread street protests across the globe in recent years, and for differing reasons – from the 'Arab Spring' in Cairo, to 'riots' in London, to 'Occupy Wall Street' in New York City – it would seem remiss not to propose an analogy with the principal sentiment being articulated here relating to urban space as a 'primary place of popular expression'.
2 In a protracted debate, Bourriaud has been taken to task over the theory and practice of relational aesthetics for failing to pose more searching questions about the actual nature and outcome of the dialogical relations sought in the encounter between spectator, site and artwork. The notion of relationality has also been variously accused of subscribing rather too easily to neoliberal ideologies.
3 See Jameson, 1998.
4 See Benjamin's essay 'Unpacking my Library: a Talk about Book Collecting' in Benjamin, 1999.

Works cited

Benjamin, Walter. *One-Way Street*, trans. Edmund Jephcott and Kingsley Shorter, intro. Susan Sontag. London: Verso, 1997.

Benjamin, Walter. *Illuminations,* trans. Harry Zorn, intro. Hannah Arendt. London: Pimlico, 1999.

Benjamin, Walter. *The Arcades Project*, ed. Rolf Tiedemann, trans. Howard Eiland and Kevin McLaughlin. Cambridge, MA: Belknap Press, 2002.

Bourriaud, Nicolas. *Relational Aesthetics*, trans. Simon Pleasance and Fiona Woods with Mathieu Copeland. Dijon: les presses du reel, 2002.

Bourriaud, Nicolas. *The Radicant*, trans. James Gussen and Lily Porten. New York: Lukas and Sternberg, 2009.

Buck-Morss, Susan. *The Dialectics of Seeing: Walter Benjamin and the Arcades Project*. Cambridge, MA: MIT Press, 1989.

Frisby, David. 'The Flâneur in Society.' In Keith Tester, ed., *The Flâneur*. New York: Routledge, 1994, 81–110.

Gilloch, Graeme. *Myth and Metropolis: Walter Benjamin and the City*. Cambridge: Polity Press, 1997.

Hussey, Andrew. '"The Map is Not the Territory": The Unfinished Journey of the Situationist International.' In Steven Speir, ed., *Urban Visions: Experiencing and Envisioning the City*. Liverpool: University Press and Tate Publishing, 2002, 215–28.

Jameson, Fredric. *Brecht and Method*. London: Verso, 1998.

Johnstone, Stephen, ed. *The Everyday*. London: Whitechapel Gallery; Cambridge, MA: MIT Press, 2008.

Lefebvre, Henri. *Writings on Cities*, ed., trans. and intro. Eleonore Kofman and Elizabeth Lebas. Oxford: Blackwell, 1996.

Levin, Laura. 'Locating the Artist/researcher: Shifting Sites of Performance Research (PAR) in Canada.' In Shannon Rose Riley and Lynette Hunter, eds, *Mapping Land-*

scapes for Performance as Research: Scholarly Acts and Creative Cartographies. Basingstoke: Palgrave Macmillan, 2009, 62–9.

Pile, Steve and Thrift, Nigel, eds. *City A-Z*. New York: Routledge, 2000.

Sadler, Simon. *The Situationist City*. Cambridge, MA: MIT Press, 1998.

Saunders, Doug. *Arrival City: How the Largest Migration in History is Shaping the World*. London: Heinemann, 2010.

Ulmer, Greg. *Teletheory: Grammatology in the Age of Video*. New York: Routledge, 1989.

Williams, Raymond. *Keywords: A Vocabulary of Culture and Society*. London: Fontana, 1976.

Index

Note: Illustrations/photos are in **bold.** Index items in notes or bibliographies are identified by 'n'.